The Grand Domestic
Revolution

Third Printing, 1985
First MIT Press paperback edition, 1982
© 1981 by
The Massachusetts Institute of Technology

This book was set in Fototronic Baskerville
by The Colonial Cooperative Press, Inc.,
and printed and bound by Halliday Litho-
graph in the United States of America.

Library of Congress Cataloging in Publication Data

Hayden, Dolores.
    The grand domestic revolution.

    Bibliography: p.
    Includes index.
    1. Feminism—United States—Addresses,
essays, lectures. 2. Division of labor—
Addresses, essays, lectures. 3. Housewives—
United States—Addresses, essays, lectures.
4. Home economics—United States—
Addresses, essays, lectures. 5. Women and
socialism—United States—Addresses, essays,
lectures. 6. Architecture, Domestic—United
States—Addresses, essays, lectures. I. Title.
HQ1426.H33   305.4'2   80–18917

ISBN 0–262–08108–3 (hard)
        0–262–58055–1 (paper)

The Grand Domestic Revolution: A History of Feminist Designs for American Homes, Neighborhoods, and Cities

Dolores Hayden

The MIT Press
Cambridge, Massachusetts,
and London, England

Away with your man-visions! Women propose to
reject them all, and begin to dream dreams for
themselves.
—Susan B. Anthony, 1871

Contents

Acknowledgments

The Radcliffe Institute provided the intellectual excitement and exchange which sustained me in 1976 and 1977 as I began to explore the importance of women's history for a full understanding of the politics of housing design. A fellowship from the National Endowment for the Humanities and a Rockefeller Humanities Fellowship provided funds for this research. The Department of Architecture at MIT and the Urban Planning Program at UCLA offered research and secretarial assistance, and funds to acquire photographs.

My thanks go to many individuals, but first of all, to Peter Marris. He read and criticized many drafts of these chapters and often discussed the progress of the book with me. As an urban sociologist, he offered innumerable insights; as my husband, he shared the labor in our home while I researched the kitchenless houses of the past. I would also like to thank my colleagues at UCLA, Kathryn Kish Sklar, whose book on Catharine Beecher stimulated my interest in domestic reform, and Temma Kaplan, whose work on anarchism, socialism, and feminism encouraged me to define my own ideas about ideology. Both of them read the entire manuscript as well as extensive revisions. They made many important critical and theoretical suggestions. So did Jeremy Brecher, whose studies of the many forms of rank and file workers' protest I admire; Alice Kessler Harris, whose broad knowledge of women's history and labor history saved me from many naive assumptions; and Mari Jo Buhle, whose wide knowledge of socialist women and of women's urban reform movements was always most generously offered to supplement mine. Taylor Stoehr read early chapters of the book, and helped with free love issues and utopian thought, as did Madeleine Stern. Gwendolyn Wright, Susana Torre, Sheila de Bretteville, John Coolidge, Sam B. Warner, Jr., Martin Pawley, Gerda Wekerle, Kevin Lynch, and John Habraken discussed many aspects of housing issues with me. Barbara Sicherman offered advice about the careers of settlement workers. I am grateful to them all.

Many scholars offered material I needed. Sylvia Wright Mitarachi shared her detailed, scholar's knowledge of her great-aunt, Melusina Peirce, and lent me the Cambridge Cooperative Housekeeping Society's records; Beth Ganister found the society's last report. Ray Reynolds shared Marie Howland's private correspondence with me; Bob Fogarty reported on a trip to Fairhope, Alabama; Carol Lopate and Helen Slotkin pointed out important material on Ellen Richards; Polly Allen-Robinson and Ann Lane discussed their interest in Gilman with me; June Sochen and Elaine Showalter responded to my queries about the mysterious Henrietta Rodman; Ruth Schwartz Cowan and Susan Strasser taught me a lot about domestic technology; Helen Kenyon shared memories of Ruth Adams; John Nuese showed me Adams's drawings. Annie Chamberlin, Anna Davin, Naomi Goodman, Thomas Hines, Carroll Pursell, Barbara Taylor, David Thompson, Hal Sears, Nancy Stieber, Anne Whiston Spirn, Mary Huth, and Sonya Michel all found, or helped me find, important material, as did many archivists and librarians.

I was most fortunate in having the skilled research assistance of Klaus Roesch for two years. Paul Johnson, Beth Ganister, Ann McNamara, Allen Chung, Penelope Simpson, Maryanne McMillan, and Lina Chatterji also helped with research at various times. I relied on them all. Endless drafts of chapters were deciphered and typed by Ets Otomo; Barbara Haynie, Sylvia Krell, Jeanne Peters, Richard Rainville, Vicki Reiber, and Sara Welch typed parts of the manuscript as well. The MIT Press editors contributed immeasurably through their professional competence and personal interest in the book.

In addition I would like to thank the editors of journals who advised on several articles now incorporated into the book: "Collectivizing the Domestic Workplace," *Lotus: Rivista Internazionale Di Architettura Contemporanea* 12 (Summer 1976); "Catharine Beecher and The Politics of Housework" and "Challenging the American Domestic Ideal," *Women in American Architecture: A Historic and Contemporary Perspective,* ed. Susana Torre, Whitney Library of Design, 1977; "Melusina Fay Peirce and Cooperative Housekeeping," *International Journal of Urban and Regional Research* 2 (1978); "Charlotte Perkins Gilman and the Kitchenless House," *Radical History Review* 21 (Winter 1979–1980); "Two Utopian Feminists and Their Campaigns for Kitchenless Houses," *Signs: A Journal of Women in Culture and Society* 4 (Winter 1978).

I   Introduction

*I demand for the wife who acts as cook, as
nursery-maid, or seamstress, or all three, fair
wages, or her rightful share in the nett income. I
demand that the bearing and rearing of children,
the most exacting of employments, and involving
the most terrible risks, shall be the best paid work
in the world. . . .*
— The Revolution, *1869*

*The private kitchen must go the way of the spin-
ning wheel, of which it is the contemporary.*
— Ladies' Home Journal, *1919*

*The big houses are going to be built. The Baby
World is going to exist. The Grand Domestic
Revolution is going to take place.*
— Woodhull and Claflin's Weekly, *1871*

The Grand Domestic Revolution

A Lost Feminist Tradition

Cooking food, caring for children, and cleaning house, tasks often thought of as "woman's work" to be performed without pay in domestic environments, have always been a major part of the world's necessary labor (1.1). Yet no industrial society has ever solved the problems that a sexual division of this labor creates for women. Nor has any society overcome the problems that the domestic location of this work creates, both for housewives and for employed women who return from factories and offices to a second job at home. This book is about the first feminists[1] in the United States to identify the economic exploitation of women's domestic labor by men as the most basic cause of women's inequality. I call them material feminists because they dared to define a "grand domestic revolution"[2] in women's material conditions. They demanded economic remuneration for women's unpaid household labor. They proposed a complete transformation of the spatial design and material culture of American homes, neighborhoods, and cities. While other feminists campaigned for political or social change with philosophical or moral arguments, the material feminists concentrated on economic and spatial issues as the basis of material life.

Between the end of the Civil War and the beginning of the Great Depression, three generations of material feminists raised fundamental questions about what was called "woman's sphere" and "woman's work." They challenged two characteristics of industrial capitalism: the physical separation of household space from public space, and the economic separation of the domestic economy from the political economy. In order to overcome patterns of urban space and domestic space that isolated women and made their domestic work invisible, they developed new forms of neighborhood organizations, including housewives' cooperatives, as well as new building types, including the kitchenless house, the day care center, the public kitchen, and the community dining club. They also proposed ideal, feminist cities. By redefining housework and the housing needs of women and their families, they pushed architects and urban planners to reconsider the effects of design on family life. For six decades the material feminists expounded one powerful idea: that women must create feminist homes with socialized housework and child care before they could become truly equal members of society.[3]

The utopian and pragmatic sources of material feminism, its broad popular appeal, and the practical experiments it provoked are not well known. Since the 1930s, very few scholars or activists have even suspected that there might be such an intellectual, political, and architectural tradition in the United States. In the early 1960s, when Betty Friedan searched for a way to describe the housewife's "problems that have no name," and settled on the "feminine mystique," Charlotte Perkins Gilman's *Women and Economics* (subtitled

1.1 Housewife making pies while drying laundry by the fire and minding two children, frontispiece, Mrs. L. G. Abell, *The Skillful Housewife's Book: or Complete Guide to Domestic Cookery, Taste, Comfort and Economy*, 1853. Courtesy Henry Francis du Pont Winterthur Museum Library.

The Economic Factor Between Men and Women as a Factor in Social Evolution) had been out of print for decades. Feminists avidly read Gilman's work again, beginning in the late 1960s, but her books reappeared without any rediscovery of the historical context of material feminist thought or political practice that had inspired them. Historians such as Carl Degler and William O'Neill mistakenly characterized Gilman as an extremist.[4] No one recognized that she was but one member of a vital and lively tradition which also included such powerful polemicists and activists as Melusina Fay Peirce, Marie Stevens Howland, Victoria Woodhull, Mary Livermore, Ellen Swallow Richards, Mary Hinman Abel, Mary Kenney O'Sullivan, Henrietta Rodman, and Ethel Puffer Howes, all advocates of the feminist transformation of the home.

The loss of the material feminist tradition has also led scholars to misunderstand feminist ideology as a whole. The overarching theme of the late nineteenth and early twentieth century feminist movement was to overcome the split between domestic life and public life created by industrial capitalism, as it affected women. Every feminist campaign for women's autonomy must be seen in this light. Yet scholars have tended to divide this coherent struggle into separate factions. Typological labels such as suffragist, social feminist, and domestic feminist distinguish too sharply between women who worked on public, or social, issues from those who worked on private, or family, issues.[5] Most feminists wished to increase women's rights in the home and simultaneously bring homelike nurturing into public life. Frances Willard exhorted the members of the Women's Christian Temperance Union to undertake the public work of "municipal housekeeping" and to "bring the home into the world," to "make the whole world homelike." [6] Votes, higher education, jobs, and trade unions for women were demanded in the name of extending and protecting, rather than abolishing, woman's domestic sphere. As Susan B. Anthony stated her aims: "When society is rightly organized, the wife and mother will have time, wish, and will to grow intellectually, and will know the limits of her sphere, the extent of her duties, are prescribed only by the measure of her ability." [7] Whether feminists sought control over property, child custody, divorce, "voluntary motherhood," temperance, prostitution, housing, refuse disposal, water supplies, schools, or workplaces, their aims were those summarized by the historian Aileen Kraditor: "women's sphere must be defined by women." [8]

The material feminists such as Peirce, Gilman, Livermore, and Howes located themselves and their campaigns to socialize domestic work at the ideological center of the feminist movement. They defined women's control over woman's sphere as women's control over the reproduction of society. They held the intellectual ground between the other feminists' campaigns directed at housewives' autonomy in domestic life or at women's autonomy in the urban community. Their insistence that all household labor and child care become so-

cial labor was a demand for homelike, nurturing neighborhoods. By that emphasis, they linked all other aspects of feminist agitation into one continuous economic and spatial struggle undertaken at every scale from the home to the nation. Because their theoretical position represented the logical extension of many ideas about women's autonomy, material feminists exercised influence far beyond their numerical strength. In the half century preceding 1917, about five thousand women and men had participated in feminist experiments to socialize domestic work, while two million were members of the National American Woman's Suffrage Association (NAWSA). [9] Nevertheless, NAWSA's leader, Carrie Chapman Catt considered Gilman the greatest living American feminist; for Harriet Stanton Blatch, suffragist and member of the Socialist Party, Gilman's *Women and Economics* was a "Bible." [10]

By daring to speak of domestic revolution, Peirce, Gilman, and other material feminists developed new definitions of economic life and settlement design that many socialists in the United States and Europe also accepted, although they often relegated these issues to some future time, "after the revolution," just as some suffragists put them off to be dealt with after winning the suffrage. In addition, the material feminists won allies in Europe, such as Alva Myrdal in Sweden and Lily Braun in Germany.

Political activists as diverse as Elizabeth Cady Stanton, Alexandra Kollontai, Ebenezer Howard, and Friedrich Engels acknowledged the socialization of domestic work as a goal they supported. Not only was the material feminist program an essential demand for economic and social justice for one-half of the population. It fired activists' imaginations because it was also a program for workers' control of the reproduction of society, a program as exhilarating as the ideal of workers' control of industrial production.

However, the differences between socialists, feminists, and material feminists on workers' control of the socialization of domestic work was substantial.[11] Socialists such as Engels and Lenin argued that women's equality would result from their involvement in industrial production, which would be made possible by the provision of socialized child care and food preparation. Socialized domestic work was, for them, only a means to this end. They did not consider socialized domestic work to be meaningful work, and they assumed that it would be done by low-status women. On the other hand, some American feminists such as Florence Kelley and Julia Lathrop looked to the capitalist state to provide services to help employed women and did not analyze the indirect benefits to industrial capitalism such services would imply.

Only the material feminists argued that women must assert control over the important work of reproduction which they were already performing, and reorganize it to obtain economic justice for themselves. They demanded both remuneration and honor for woman's traditional sphere of work, while conceding that some women might wish to do other kinds of work. They were not prepared to let men argue that a woman's equality would ultimately rest on her ability to undertake "man's" work in a factory or an office. Nor were they prepared to describe the state as the agency of their liberation. While material feminists did sometimes drift toward these positions (Charlotte Perkins Gilman to the socialist, Ellen Richards to the feminist, for example) usually they stated clearly that women's work must be controlled by women — economically, socially, and environmentally.

Feminism and Socialism

Although the material feminist tradition is today relatively unknown, its emphasis on reorganizing women's labor as the material basis of the reproduction of society is directly relevant to today's political struggles. Material feminism illuminates the historical schism between the two greatest social movements of the late nineteenth century, Marxian socialism and feminism, because it derives directly from a movement, communitarian socialism, which antedated and to some extent generated both. In the early nineteenth century, communitarian socialists such as Robert Owen and Charles Fourier criticized industrial capitalism for its effects on human work and offered programs for economically reorganized communities that always gave equal weight to household labor and industrial labor. Their insights about the importance of domestic work were extended in the material feminist tradition, while Marxian socialists developed the communitarians' critique of industrial work.

Unfortunately, when Marx and Engels caricatured communitarian socialism as utopian and described their own strategy of organizing industrial workers as scientific socialism, they lost sight of the female half of the human race, whose household labor was essential to society and was also shaped by industrial capitalism. Having developed a much more incisive critique of capital and its workings than the communitarians, Marxian socialists talked persuasively to male industrial workers about seizing the means of production and ignored women's work and reproduction. Although Engels conceded that the family was based on "the open or disguised domestic enslavement of the woman," [12] and stated that in the family, the man represented the bourgeois, and the wife, the proletarian, Marxists refused to espouse any tactics aimed at liberating women from this enslavement. Some even opposed suffrage for women. Others used feminism as a derogatory term to criticize political deviation.

Meanwhile feminists, who were organizing both housewives and employed women, questioned the Marxists' so-called class analysis because no woman had the legal rights or economic advantages of a man of her class. Throughout the nineteenth century, employment for women was generally restricted to a narrow range of sex-stereotyped, low-paying jobs; it was difficult or impossible for women to earn enough to support themselves, let alone dependents. As a rule they were excluded from trade unions as well as male trades, while unions campaigned for what they called a family wage for men. Women could not define their own struggles for economic and political autonomy in terms of class struggle organized around their husbands' or fathers' occupations. Instead they worked for equal female rights — suffrage, housing, education, jobs, and trade unions for women.

The split between Marxian socialists and feminists in the second half of the nineteenth century was a disastrous one for both movements. Each had a piece of the truth about class and gender, production and reproduction. The Marxists lost sight of the necessary labor of one half of the population; the feminists lost sight of class structure under capitalism and addressed most of their demands to the state. Only the small group of material feminists led by Peirce, Gilman, Howes, and others carried on campaigns to end the economic exploitation of household labor, holding, ever so precariously, to the belief that women's labor in the household must be the key issue in campaigns for women's autonomy. In order to define their feminist struggle for women's control of their labor, they used economic arguments about women's work similar to the Marxists' arguments about men's work, but they saw gender, rather than class, as the unifying category.

Insofar as material feminists worked in cities and towns, they developed the earlier communitarian socialist tradition of spatial analysis to accompany economic analysis. They argued that the entire physical environment of cities and towns must be redesigned to reflect equality for women. (This was a most significant contribution that corrected some of the earlier communitarians' tendencies to work only in experimental socialist villages.) At the same time the material feminists accepted the communitarians' weakest argument: the belief that after the reorganization of human work and the physical environment, there would be no reproduction of the social relations of capitalist production; therefore, classes in society would no longer sustain themselves. This belief in the peaceful evolution of a classless society left material feminists very vulnerable to fierce attacks from large industrial corporations who had an immediate economic interest in preventing women from socializing domestic work. Through the 1920s this backlash caught them unprepared, because they had no adequate analysis of the power or the workings of capitalism. In this decade, the cooperative movement, which had provided many tactics for the formation of housewives' producers' and consumers' cooperatives used by these feminists, was also often overwhelmed by corporate competition and episodes of Red-baiting.

In part the material feminists' failure to develop a full critique of industrial capitalism was based on their belief in social evolution as an agency of economic and urban transformation. Having read Charles Darwin, Herbert Spencer, and Lester Ward, they were so sure that capitalism would lead to socialism and so convinced that dense industrial cities would become cooperative human communities that they were unprepared for the development of monopoly capitalism and suburban isolation. Here the material feminists shared the optimism of Nationalists, Populists, Socialists, Christian Socialists, Fabian Socialists, and even some liberal reformers of their day, including many architects and urban planners who believed in the industrial city and its liberating potential.

Urban Evolution

The years when material feminists favoring socialized domestic work were most active span the rise and decline of the dense, industrial capitalist city. This era was one of increased concentration of urban population and constant technological innovation, as compared to the subsequent period of monopoly capitalism, which was characterized by decreased residential densities and mass production of earlier technological inventions. The material feminists' campaigns began with first demand for pay for housework in 1868, a campaign contemporary with architects' promotion of collective urban residential space in eastern cities through the design of the earliest apartment houses built for upper-class and middle-class residents and the design of model tenements for the poor. Their campaigns ended in 1931, after more than a decade of Red-baiting of feminists, with the Hoover Commission Report on *Home Building and Home Ownership,* a report advocating single-family home ownership which

1.2 Seven maids, Black River Falls, Wisconsin, about 1905, Charles Van Schaick, photographer. They demonstrate the tasks of sweeping, scrubbing, making pastry, serving, receiving a visitor's card, caring for children, and peeling fruit, but whether they worked for one household or for many is unclear. Courtesy of the State Historical Society of Wisconsin.

eventually led to the development of 50 million low-technology, single-family homes housing three quarters of American families. It was a decisive ideological defeat for feminists and for architects and urban planners interested in housing design.

During this era, material feminists saw that many decisions about the organization of future society were being incorporated into the built environment. Therefore, they identified the spatial transformation of the domestic workplace under women's control as a key issue linking campaigns for social equality, economic justice, and environmental reform. Many architects and urban planners shared the material feminists' hopes, for the feminists' concept of the modern woman provided them with the rationale for housing which would be socially, technologically, and aesthetically more sophisticated than the Victorian bourgeois home. In 1913 one architectural critic rejoiced, somewhat prematurely, because "the ideas of Victorian society about home, the family, and women are as dead as all the other ideals of that time," arguing that modern housing depended on this change.[13]

Far more clearly than their contemporaries today, feminists, designers, and political theorists at the turn of the century saw urban space as a social and economic product. They perceived a single trend to density and technological innovation, as mercantile capitalism gave way to industrial capitalism. The mixed commercial, artisanal, and residential land uses characteristic of port cities under mercantile capitalism (between the eighteenth century and the mid-nineteenth century) had created the typical pedestrian, urban environment that Sam Bass Warner, Jr., has called the walking city, and David Gordon, the commercial city.[14] Then, as industrial capitalism developed, American cities began to explode in size and the industrial city developed. As a national urban population of less then 10 million in 1870 became 54 million by 1920, urban landscapes changed. Factories came to dominate city centers. Alongside them sprawled vast, unsanitary tenement districts housing workers, many of them recent immigrants. While housing was cramped, street life flourished in slum districts. At the same time lavish downtown shopping districts and exclusive hotels and apartments catered to the expanding middle and upper classes. Boulevards and parks provided promenades. Cities increased in area as speculators constructed class-segregated residential suburbs for white-collar workers and managers at the circumference of the city, reached by new mass transit systems and served by new water and utility lines. Public space and urban infrastructure emphasized the new social and economic connectedness of urban life.

When Frederick Law Olmsted, the noted landscape architect and urban planner, analyzed the technologies which were fast changing the quality of life in American cities in 1870, he saw the evolving industrial capitalist city as an instrument for the household's liberation as well as the society's and concluded that more and more women would insist on living in cities, rather than in the country, because of the many advantages to housekeepers offered by new municipal and commercial services. "Consider," he suggested, "what is done . . . by the butcher, baker, fishmonger, grocer, by the provision venders of all sorts, by the iceman, dust-man, scavenger, by the postman, carrier, expressmen, and messengers, all serving you at your house when required; by the sewers, gutters, pavements, crossings, sidewalks, public conveyances, and gas and water works." He went on to muse that "there is every reason to suppose that what we see is but a foretaste of what is yet to come." He cited recent inventions in paving materials and in sewer design. He speculated about the possibility of providing municipal hot-air heat to every home. He proposed that tradesmen exploit the electric telegraph and the pneumatic tube for orders and deliveries. And he suggested that public laundries, bakeries, and kitchens would promote "the economy which comes by systematizing and concentrating, by the application of a large apparatus, of processes which are otherwise conducted in a desultory way, wasteful of human strength." [15]

That Olmsted made no distinction between public sidewalks, public central heating for every home, and public kitchens is extremely revealing. He and other idealists saw the era of industrial capitalism, when public space and urban infrastructure were created, as a time when rural isolation gave way to a life in larger human communities. Rapid urban growth and startling technological discoveries encouraged their belief in the social interdependence represented by new housing and the economic interdependence represented by new urban infrastructure. The poverty, squalor, anomie, strikes, and violence typical of industrial cities did not discourage such optimists. They also overlooked the tendency of municipal infrastructure to reinforce existing economic inequalities. [16] Olmsted believed that industrial capitalism would provide the transition between "barbarism" and municipal socialism. While he adopted this belief as a disciple of the communitarian socialist Fourier, in the 1880s and 1890s many other socialists and feminists, including Edward Bellamy, August Bebel, Charlotte Perkins Gilman, Karl Marx, and Friedrich Engels substituted other theories of human evolution and came to similar conclusions. [17] All these theorists saw industrial capitalism as an economic system which would give way to a completely industrialized, socialist society utilizing collective technology to socialize housework and child care at some future time.

Domestic Evolution

The transformation of transportation technology and urban life in the industrial city encouraged material feminists to contribute their economic and spatial analysis of household work to debates about neighborhood design and housing design. Industrial capitalism had begun to change the economic basis of domestic work; urbanization had begun to change the environmental basis; therefore, some material feminists argued that the role of the housewife and the design of the domestic workplace must evolve in a more collective direction. As Olmsted had noted when describing the evolution of the American city, infrastructure such as water pipes, telegraph lines, and fuel lines contributed to make households more physically dependent upon municipal and commercial services. Materialist feminists concluded that women, rather than men, must control these new services and use them as their base of economic power. From a contemporary vantage point it seems that housework is a paradoxical activity whose form has remained much the same during the last century — the unpaid housewife alone in the home as domestic workplace — while its content has evolved. During the era of industrial capitalism, however, material feminists believed that both the form and the content of housework would undergo drastic change. They believed that domestic evolution would parallel urban evolution rather than contradict it.

In the preindustrial era the majority of women worked alongside their husbands and children on subsistence farms, doing the hard work necessary for the family to survive — spinning wool and flax and making clothes, grinding grain into flour and making bread, cooking in an iron pot over an open fire, making soap and candles, tending kitchen gardens, raising animals. This round of activities contributed to

their families' food, clothing, and shelter, and perhaps produced some surplus to barter with neighbors. With the beginning of industrialization in the United States, women began to be involved in national economies as both consumers of manufactured goods and as wage workers in factories, shops, and offices. Farm women started to purchase textiles, soap, candles, and then canned foods; women, married and single, started to earn wages in textile mills, commercial laundries, and shops, as well as in their traditional female occupation, domestic service (1.2). Because domestic space was as much an economic and social product as public, urban space, the farmhouse, with its capacious storage and work spaces, gave way to urban and suburban dwellings with less space and more areas devoted to the consumption and display of manufactured goods.

These changes in women's work and domestic space were slow, because technological innovation was always much ahead of diffusion. Historians of technology such as Siegfried Giedion have often glossed over the problem of measuring diffusion. However, Ruth Schwartz Cowan, Susan Kleinberg, and Susan May Strasser have studied household technology and shown that most working-class families and many middle-class families lacked various labor-saving devices and appliances long after manufacturers heralded them as liberating housewives.[18] While the diffusion of new inventions was slow, industrialization can be said to have had two major effects on most housewives throughout the nineteenth and early twentieth centuries. Manufactured goods took some part of household labor out of the house. Housewives were still encumbered with cooking, baking, cleaning, sewing, laundry, and child care, but they were newly conscious of their lack of cash in an economy increasingly depending upon cash rather than barter. Industrialization also offered increasing numbers of women paid work in factories (1.3), leaving the housewife without domestic servants, especially in rural areas but also in the cities (1.4, 1.5, 1.6). Married women did not often take paid jobs — fewer than 5 percent were employed outside the home in 1890. The growth of manufacturing meant that while the rest of society appeared to be moving forward to socialized labor, the housewife, encased in woman's sphere, slowly became more isolated from her husband, who now worked away from home; her children, who attended school all day; and the rural social networks of kin and neighbors which were disrupted by migration to the growing urban centers.

Nancy Cott has analyzed the importance of woman's sphere to the United States as a developing industrial, urbanized, capitalist society claiming to be a democracy: "By giving all women the same natural vocation, the canon of domesticity classed them all together. This definition had a dual function in the national culture. Understanding the rupture between home and the world in terms of gender did more than effect reconciliation to the changing organization of work. The demarcation of women's sphere from men's provided a se-cure, primary social classification for a population who refused to admit ascribed statuses, for the most part, but required determinants of social order. . . . Sex, not class, was the basic category. On that basis an order consistent with democratic culture could be maintained." [19] The private home was the spatial boundary of woman's sphere, and the unpaid domestic labor undertaken in that space by the isolated housewife was the economic boundary of woman's sphere. "A woman's place is in the home," and "a woman's work is never done" were the usual, basic definitions of woman's sphere. Above all, woman's sphere was to be remote from the cash economy: "Our men are sufficiently money-making. Let us keep our women and children from the contagion as long as possible," wrote Sarah Josepha Hale in 1832.[20] "My wife doesn't work" became the male boast reflecting housewives' separation from the market economy and the resultant invisibility of their labor.

The frontispiece from a household manual of the 1840s illustrates the material culture of woman's sphere: the housewife is shown performing seven different tasks, always in isolation except for the central medallion, where she is reading to her children (1.7). A household manual of the 1850s comes closer to a true picture by depicting the simultaneity of the housewife's many labors: the woman bakes, dries laundry by the fire, and attempts to amuse her children, including one yanking at her skirt (1.1). This is still an idyllic picture. No advice manual ever illustrated the heavier or

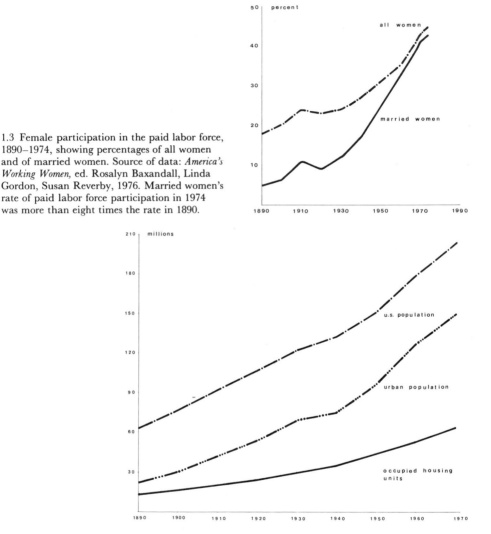

1.3 Female participation in the paid labor force, 1890–1974, showing percentages of all women and of married women. Source of data: *America's Working Women,* ed. Rosalyn Baxandall, Linda Gordon, Susan Reverby, 1976. Married women's rate of paid labor force participation in 1974 was more than eight times the rate in 1890.

1.4 United States total population, urban population, and number of occupied housing units, 1890–1970. Sources of data: U.S. Census of Housing, 1970, and U.S. Bureau of the Census. Household size has decreased from about 5 to about 3 persons. Of the total housing units available in 1970, 69.1 percent were one-family structures. Despite the steadily increasing population in urban areas, only 14.5 percent of all units were in structures including five or more units.

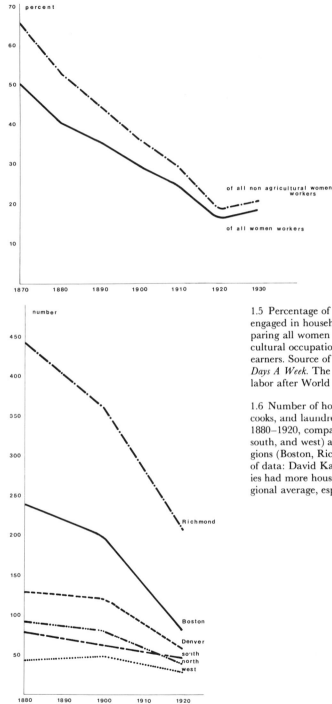

of all non agricultural women workers

of all women workers

1.5 Percentage of women in the paid labor force engaged in household labor, 1870–1930, comparing all women wage earners in nonagricultural occupations and all women wage earners. Source of data: David Katzman, *Seven Days A Week*. The return of women to household labor after World War I is clear.

1.6 Number of household workers (servants, cooks, and laundresses) per 1000 population, 1880–1920, comparing three regions (north, south, and west) and three cities within those regions (Boston, Richmond, and Denver). Source of data: David Katzman, *Seven Days A Week*. Cities had more household workers than the regional average, especially in the south.

more unpleasant domestic work: drawing water from a well, carrying it to the house, chopping wood for fires, sweltering over an iron cookstove, grappling with a heavy block of ice, draining an icebox, or emptying slops. Nor did the manuals picture the tedious sequence of tasks involved in a job such as laundry, for which water had to be heated on a stove, carried, and poured into movable tubs. Then clothes were soaked, scrubbed and rinsed in the tubs, wrung out by hand, hung out to be dried, laboriously pressed with crude flatirons heated on the fire, folded, and put away, drudgery which gave Blue Monday its name.[21]

While the housewife in an eastern city or town seemed to have a far easier lot than her sister on the frontier after the Civil War, even the urban housewife seemed to material feminists to be a curious survival from an earlier, preindustrial era, a worker who dabbled in three, or five, or seven trades at home and badly needed the benefits of industrial technology and the specialization and division of labor. In 1868 Melusina Fay Peirce characterized the housewife as jack-of-all-trades, and Voltairine de Cleyre, the American anarchist lecturer, defined home for an audience in 1898 as "on an infinitesimally small scale a laundry, bakery, lodging-house, and nursery rolled into one." In exasperation Helen Campbell wondered in the 1890s ". . . why, in all this smooth and rushing stream of progress the household wheels still creak so noisily and turn so hard. It is as though some primeval ox-cart were brought in to connect with the

railroad system, or the current of transcontinental travel left its vestibuled trains to ford some river on the way." [22] Charlotte Perkins Gilman criticized domestic backwardness even more sharply in 1903: "By what art, what charm, what miracle, has the twentieth century preserved *alive* the prehistoric squaw!" [23]

Material feminists believed that the solitary housewife doing her ironing or mixing dough (1.7) could never compete with the groups of workers employed in well-equipped commercial laundries or hotel kitchens (1.8, 1.9) beginning in the 1870s. Neither could the isolated home compete with the technological and architectural advantages offered by larger housing complexes introduced about the same time. Since many illustrated newspapers and magazines featured stories about transportation technology, architecture, and domestic technology, material feminists saw these publications as evidence of both urban and domestic evolution. Journalists hailed a pneumatic underground train in New York in 1870; they marveled at the development of electric streetlights and indoor home lighting in New York in 1879; they couldn't say enough about the first electric streetcar in Richmond in 1888 or the first subway in Boston in 1897. This transportation technology encouraged land speculation through multistory residential construction near subway and streetcar stops. Multistory housing also minimized expensive utility lines for gas, water, and electricity. Domestic technology supported increased residential densities as well. Devices such as elevators, improved gas stoves, gas refrigerators, electric suction vacuum cleaners, mechanical dishwashers and steam washing machines which were designed for use in large enterprises such as hotels, restaurants, and commercial laundries, could also be used in large apartment houses.

Because this technology was first developed at the scale suitable for fifty to five hundred people, any group interested in mechanizing domestic work simply had first to socialize it, and plan for collective domestic consumption by organizing households into larger groups inhabiting apartment hotels, apartment houses, model tenements, adjoining row houses, model suburbs, or new towns. What was unique about the material feminists was not their interest in these technological and architectural questions, which also attracted inventors, architects, planners, speculators, and efficiency experts, but their insistence that these economic and spatial changes should take place under women's control.

The material feminists' assertion that women must control the socialization of domestic work and child care attacked traditional conceptions of woman's sphere economically, architecturally, and socially. First came demands for housewives' wages, such as Melusina Fay Peirce articulated: "It is one of the cherished dogmas of the modern lady, that she must not do anything for pay; and this miserable prejudice of senseless conventionality is at this moment the worst obstacle in the way of feminine talent and energy. Let the co-

operative housekeepers demolish it forever, by declaring that it is just as necessary and just as honorable for a wife to earn money as it is for her husband. . . . " [24] Demands for workers' benefits and limitation of hours always accompanied demands for wages to underline the housewife's current status as an exploited worker. For example, Marie Brown in an article for *The Revolution* complained that men could rest at the end of the day while housewives' work was unceasing.[25]

Material feminists' proposals also demanded the transformation of the private domestic workplace, the kitchen, in accordance with theories of domestic evolution: "Shall the private kitchen be abolished? It has a revolutionary sound, just as once upon a time revolution sounded in such propositions as these: Should private wells be abolished? Shall private kerosene lamps be abolished? Shall home spinning, home weaving, home stitching of shirts, home soft-soap making be abolished?" Zona Gale concluded that "the private kitchen must go the way of the spinning wheel, of which it is the contemporary." In the same spirit, Ada May Krecker had written for Emma Goldman's anarchist journal, *Mother Earth,* of the consolidation of home on a large scale: "The same forces that have built trusts to supersede with measureless superiority the myriad petty establishments which they have superseded, will build the big dwelling places and playgrounds and nurseries for tomorrow's children and make them measurelessly better fitted to our socialized ideals of tomorrow than could

1.7 Caroline Howard Gilman, *The Housekeeper's Annual and Lady's Register,* 1844, frontispiece illustrating the round of tasks in "woman's sphere"

1.8 Women workers in a commercial laundry using reversing rotary washers, a centrifugal extractor, steam-heated mangles, and a rotary ironer for collars and shirts, advertisement, 1883. Laundry work was usually hot, wet, and unpleasant, even with these machines, but far easier than the housewife's struggle with tubs and flatirons. From Siegfried Giedion, *Mechanization Takes Command.*

1.9 Workers in hotel kitchen with special preparation areas for vegetables, meats, and pastry, *New York Daily Graphic,* April 3, 1878. Such kitchens were equipped with special stoves, kettles, and other types of cooking apparatus unavailable to housewives.

Selected Proposals for Socialized Domestic Work, 1834–1926, Classified by Economic Organization and Spatial Location

Economic organization and spatial location	Neighborhood or residential complex	Industrial workplace	City	Nation
Producers' cooperative	Bloomer, late 1850s Peirce, 1868 Howes, 1923	Howland, 1874	Appleton, 1848 Howland, 1885 Austin, 1916	Olerich, 1893
Consumers' cooperative	Beecher and Stowe, 1865 Community dining clubs, 1885–1907 Livermore, 1886 Hull-House, 1887 Willard, 1888 Jane Club, 1893 Howes, 1926 United Workers, 1926		Some cooked food delivery services, 1890–1920	
Commercial enterprise	Apartment hotels, 1870–1920 C. P. Gilman, 1898 Some cooked food delivery services, 1884–1921 Rodman, 1914 Hudson View Gardens, 1926		Some cooked food delivery services, 1884–1921	
Nonprofit organization	Household Aid, 1903		Richards, 1890 Addams, 1887	
Nationalized industry		Council of National Defense, St. Louis, 1917	C. H. Gilman, 1834	Bebel, 1883 Engels, 1884 Dodd, 1887 Bellamy, 1888 Lenin, 1919

possibly be the private little homes of today." [26]

The reorganization of American domestic life required more than rhetoric. Pay for housework and the construction of new kinds of domestic workplaces were demands that could be adapted to many types of economic organization. As organizational forms, the producers' cooperative appealed to housewives, and the consumers' cooperative appealed to professional women and political activists. Women industrial workers were more interested in the possibilities of tying services to industrial enterprises as workers' benefits, while women active in urban reform movements often looked for ways to introduce new municipal or national services. Female entrepreneurs chose the small business; domestic economists, the nonprofit organization. Each of these tactics made sense to a constituency desirous of making a particular political point: housewives are workers; employed women are also housewives; production cannot exist without reproduction; the state must help to create good future citizens through services to mothers and their children. Strategists also needed to adopt some clear attitude toward the relocation of the domestic workplace. Should it be in the residential complex (whether a single apartment house or a suburban block), in the neighborhood, in the factory, or in the city or the nation? Successive generations of material feminists developed experiments and proposals aimed at the wide range of possibilities suggested by both economic

structure and spatial location (some of these are shown in the accompanying table).

In the process of mounting their experiments, material feminists had to tackle many issues of class and race as well as gender. While gender determined woman's work, economic class and race affected women's experience of the domestic sphere. The housewife-employer who hired domestic servants differed from the housewife who did all her own work and from the woman who performed domestic work for pay. The paid workers included cooks, maids, and laundresses, most of whom lived in another woman's home. Housewife-entrepreneurs who took in boarders, sewing, or laundry also earned cash. The relative importance of each of these categories (housewife-employer, housewife, housewife-entrepreneur, day worker, and live-in servant) shifted toward the housewife who did her own work during the era of industrial capitalism, as fewer women entered domestic service and more chose industrial work. David Katzman, whose *Seven Days a Week* gives a broad picture of the conditions of domestic service between 1870 and 1930, emphasizes the way in which housewife-employers oppressed live-in servants who were present in one household in ten in 1900. [27]

The larger struggle to gain economic recognition for domestic labor involves the majority of housewives who did all their own work (seven out of ten in 1900) and housewife-entrepreneurs who took in boarders (two out of ten). Their struggles were tied to those of servants. The material feminist reformers who tackled housewives' pay had a terrible knot of prejudices to untangle concerning what was called the servant question. They saw the problems most clearly in terms of gender discrimination. Although they were not always successful, they also tried to deal with class and race. Early material feminist reformers took the stance that because servants were scarce, unreliable, unskilled, and lazy, housewives would have to band together to socialize domestic work and organize both themselves and their former servants in the process. As their movement developed, the leaders came to a more complex understanding of the exploitation servants had endured and of the racism and sexism which prohibited young black women from holding other jobs.[28] Nevertheless, the gap between the servant and the feminist reformer was so great that often reformers did not recognize the role class and race played in their assumptions about how to socialize domestic work. Some of the most dedicated apostles of socialized domestic work were not above titling articles a solution or an answer to the servant question, if they thought that this would increase their audience. However, such titles often distracted from their more basic message about economic independence for all women, and confused their work with that of upper-middle-class women whose only concern was maintaining domestic service in their own homes.

The Suburban Retreat

During the years from 1890 to 1920, while material feminists (and the suffragists, socialists, architects, and urban planners who agreed with them) were planning and creating housing with facilities for socialized domestic work, an antithetical movement was beginning to gather momentum. Between 1920 and 1970, this movement would ultimately reverse urban densities and deemphasize architectural and technological innovation. It was the consolidation of capital through corporate mergers and conquests that resulted in the formation of larger corporate empires typical of advanced (or monopoly) capitalism. This economic transformation affected both urban space and domestic space after 1920. The economist David Gordon has argued that as what he calls the corporate city emerged from the industrial city, corporate management was split from industrial production. Districts of corporate headquarters appeared in some key cities, housed in skyscrapers, alongside banks and international trading facilities. Meanwhile industrial production was relocated at scattered sites in suburban areas. Gordon argues that the relocation of factories was often motivated by desire to end labor unrest, because some corporations believed that they would experience fewer strikes if they moved their workers away from urban tenement districts where the "contagion" of radical trade union activity could spread.[29]

Such moves involved a new concern for workers' housing on the part of previously unconcerned employers. Gordon, Barbara

Ehrenreich and Deirdre English, and Stuart Ewen have observed that corporations began to support suburban home ownership in the late teens for skilled, white, male workers as a way of "fostering a stable and conservative political habit." [30] This tendency was confirmed in Herbert Hoover's National Conference on Home Building and Home Ownership, convened in 1931 to support home ownership for men "of sound character and industrious habits" and provide a long-term program for economic recovery from the Depression. Builders, bankers, and manufacturers agreed that the type of home they wished to promote was the single-family suburban house on its own lot. While its exterior might reflect changing styles, the interior organization of spaces replicated the Victorian homes which had been presented to Americans for almost a century with moral messages about respectability, consumption, and female domesticity. [31]

Campaigns for male home ownership between the 1920s and the 1960s contained the plan (agreed to by both employers and many male trade unionists), that the male would be paid family wages, and that women would be kept out of the paid work force and would be full-time, unpaid housewives and mothers. Stuart Ewen has analyzed this strategy as promoting "the patriarch as wage slave." To dislodge many women from paid jobs in the 1920s and 1930s, conservative advocates of home ownership and family wages attacked all feminists indiscriminately. They were particularly hard on material feminists,

attacking "free-loveism," "unnatural motherhood," and "futurist baby-raising" as consequences of women's economic independence. They used the rhetoric of the 1880s to deplore the "social hot-beds" of apartment hotels and boarding clubs where the family, "an institution of God," was thought to be undermined because women did not do their own housework in these environments. [32]

The development of suburban home ownership as the national housing policy in the United States offered a post–World War I idea to a post–World War II society. Government-sponsored mortgages and tax deductions for home owners in the post–World War II era, defeated feminists but provided a great boon to speculative builders, appliance manufacturers, and automobile manufacturers. As women were ejected from wartime jobs, they moved into suburban married life and the birth rate rose (1.10) along with mass consumption. Builders created millions of single-family houses that did not involve careful site planning, provision of community space, or any design input from architects. These houses were bare boxes to be filled up with mass-produced commodities.

Beginning in the 1920s, appliance manufacturers had miniaturized the large-scale technology developed earlier for hotels and restaurants and used by cooperative housekeeping societies. In their place came small refrigerators and freezers, small vacuum cleaners, small dishwashers, small clothes washers. In the case of labor saving devices which had been architectural, such as

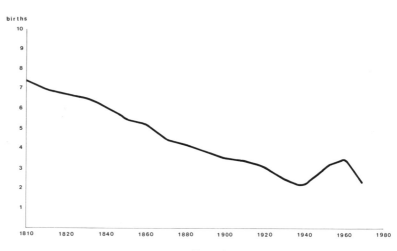

1.10 Total fertility rate for whites, 1810–1970, showing the rising curve of the post–World War II baby boom, coinciding with suburbanization and the rise of the "feminine mystique." Source of data: Daniel Scott Smith, "Family Limitation, Sexual Control, and Domestic Feminism in Victorian America."

built-in compartments with brine-filled pipes for refrigeration or built-in vacuum systems for cleaning, both used in many apartment hotels, the architectural amenities were redeveloped as commodities which could be purchased and plugged in. In this process of the domestication and miniaturization of technology lay the seeds of a future energy crisis, because some appliance manufacturers sold generating equipment to municipalities, a relationship they could parlay into extra profits by designing appliances for maximum energy consumption.[33] Suburban home ownership also increased the demand for private automobiles. Beginning in the 1920s, and continuing in the 1940s and 1950s, advertising became a major American industry, promoting appliances, cars, and all sorts or products in the setting of the suburban "dream house."[34]

By the 1960s, the suburban rings of cities held a greater percentage of the national urban population than the old city centers. By the 1970s, there were fifty million small houses and over one hundred million cars. Seven out of ten households lived in single-family homes. Over three quarters of AFL-CIO members owned their homes on long mortgages.[35] For women, national policies supporting suburban home ownership (and consumer credit) for men meant that women's access to housing had to be through their husbands. Women's access to paid employment was also limited by their suburban location, because women were less likely than men to own cars and had difficulty arranging child care in suburban

tracts with no community facilities. While half of the married women in the United States were in paid employment by the mid-1970s, they continued to have a second job at home. All homemakers, especially the ones without outside employment, experienced what Betty Friedan had called "the feminine mystique" and Peter Filene renamed "the domestic mystique"[36] because men experienced it as well as women, albeit in a different way.

Friedan and Filene considered the feminine mystique to be more of a social than a spatial problem, yet the design of domestic space defied all architectural and technological rationality. By the 1970s, entire urban regions had been transformed into miles and miles of suburban sprawl in defiance of earlier notions of urban evolution and human progress. Yet earlier, at the end of the nineteenth century, advocates of urban evolution had marveled at industrial society's progression "from the simple to the complex." In the 1920s, advanced capitalism turned this progression around, as the technically and spatially complex urban dwelling was replaced by the cruder suburban dwelling with twentieth-century water, gas, and electrical supplies. The hidden costs of this domestic retreat were so high that by the 1970s, increasingly hazardous power sources such as nuclear power plants, liquid natural gas, and attenuated oil pipelines were introduced to meet the steadily rising demand for energy, and the term "dream house" began to have ironic overtones.

Builders and industrialists in the 1970s continued to glorify the Victorian home they had preserved a century beyond its time, the isolated household designed around the ideal of woman as full-time homemaker. They used mass media to glorify this accomplishment as progress and to befuddle the housewife (1.11). Over a century and a half, the content of housework had changed until time spent in the consumption of manufactured products nearly equaled the time spent in cooking, cleaning, and child care. Still the housewife worked alone and her work was never done: time budget studies in the United States and other industrialized countries show that the housewife's hours of work increased rather than decreased after the 1920s, despite labor-saving devices and commercial services.[37] Fast food franchises provided hot meals; television served to keep children quiet at home; housewives had dozens of electric appliances in their kitchens; yet they were less in control of woman's sphere than they had been at the beginning of industrial capitalism. Capitalism had socialized only those aspects of household work that could be replaced by profitable commodities or services, and left the cooking, cleaning, and nurturing for the housewife.

The home was not considered a workplace but a retreat; the housewife's unpaid, isolated labor was still not considered work but consumption.[38] Women who did this lonely work were almost never called workers. As Meredith Tax wrote about the housewife's day in 1970: "I seem to be involved in some mysterious process." [39] As Marilyn French's suburban housewife,

Mira, described her situation in *The Woman's Room,* she was economically and spatially identified with the house her husband owned: "She felt bought and paid for, and it was all of a piece; the house, the furniture, she, all were his, it said so on some piece of paper." [40] For the housewife who rebelled, there was an increasing reliance on psychiatry and on drugs. Doctors prescribed Valium and Librium over 47 million times for United States women in 1978 and drug company advertisements often showed a frowning housewife with apron, broom, and child. One such ad read: "You can't change her environment but you can change her mood." [41]

The Legacy of Material Feminism
Material feminists achieved their greatest influence when strategies for housing Americans in dense urban neighborhoods were popular; their influence waned as efficient consumption was defined, not as the careful use of scarce resources, but as the maximum demand for mass-produced commodities. Although the dense urban environments of industrial capitalism ultimately gave way to an artificial privatism in the United States, and workers' suburban habitations proved that Fourier and Olmsted, Marx and Engels, Bellamy and Gilman had misjudged the pace at which the urban concentration caused by industrial capitalism was hastening socialism and women's liberation, the debates they began have not yet been finished. In the last ten years many of the same questions about women's domestic roles and the

1.11 "Swing through spring cleaning with
Ajax," advertisement, *Good Housekeeping,* April
1965. A surreal vision of the home as workplace,
showing domestic machinery in a garden setting
and suggesting that housework is play, both
themes typical of the domestic mystique of the
post–World War II era.

larger economy that the material feminists raised are once again being asked, but the importance of the design of housing and the organization of neighborhoods for these issues has largely been forgotten.

Most families continue to inhabit single-family housing designed around the ideal of woman as full-time homemaker. As women's participation in the paid labor force continues to rise, women and men come to suspect the conflicts that outdated forms of housing and inadequate community services create for them and their families; yet it is difficult to imagine alternatives. It requires a spatial imagination to understand that urban regions designed for inequality cannot be changed by new roles in the lives of individuals.

The material feminist legacy can stimulate that spatial imagination by providing feminist visions of other ways to live: thousands of women and men who supported socialized domestic work demonstrated their social and technical ingenuity. Material feminists steadily argued for female autonomy among socialists and for women's economic and spatial needs among suffragists. They recognized housewives as a major, potential, political force. Their ability to imagine more satisfying, feminist, domestic landscapes set them apart from the more pragmatic, but less visionary reformers of the era of industrial capitalism. Their debates about where and how to socialize domestic work reverberated with intense emotions.

An egalitarian approach to domestic work requires complex decisions about national standards versus local control, about general adult participation versus efficient specialization, about individual choice versus social responsibility. These same dilemmas, applied to industrial production, have bedeviled all societies since the Industrial Revolution, so all societies can learn from these debates. Any socialist, feminist society of the future will find socializing domestic work at the heart of its concerns, and, along with it, the problem of freedom versus control, for the individual, the family, the community, and the nation.

When material feminists developed their battle plan for the grand domestic revolution, they established their significance not only as visionaries but also as social critics. Material feminists resisted the polite conventions of daily life under industrial capitalism more effectively than any other political group of their era — socialist, anarchist, or suffragist. By mocking domestic pieties and demanding remuneration for housework, they shocked both women and men into analyzing their households and their neighborhoods with a critical consciousness that has not been matched since. When, at their most militant, the material feminists demanded that paid workers perform all household tasks collectively in well-equipped neighborhood kitchens, laundries, and child care centers, they called for architects to develop new types of housing and for planners to create new kinds of community facilities, giving these professions a human importance long since lost by architects working for speculative builders or planners in the zoning bu-

reaucracy. The material feminists argued
for these transformations at every political
level, from the household and the neighborhood to the municipality and the nation, setting an example for others who
might wish to unite such diverse issues as
housework, discrimination against women
in employment, housing policy, and energy
policy.

Material feminists dared to imagine
women's economic independence from men
and to plan for the complete environmental and technological changes such independence implied. Were these utopian
imaginings and extravagant plans? As
Lawrence Goodwyn observes in his history
of the American Populist movement, "If
the population is politically resigned (believing the dogma of 'democracy' on a
superficial public level but not believing it
privately) it becomes quite difficult for
people to grasp the scope of popular hopes
that were alive in an earlier time when
democratic expectations were larger than
those people permit themselves to have today. . . . modern people are culturally
programmed, as it were, to conclude that
American egalitarians such as the Populists
were 'foolish' to have had such large demo-
cractic hopes." [42] It is easy to dismiss the
economic liberation envisioned by material
feminists as foolish, much better to com-
prehend their dreams, study their manifestos and organizations, and attempt to understand those aspects of American culture
that nourished their idealism, their hopes
for feminist homes, neighborhoods, and
cities.

II   Communitarian Socialism and Domestic Feminism

Shaker kitchen, 1873

The extension of the privileges of women is the
fundamental cause of all social progress.
— Charles Fourier, 1808

. . . The isolated household is a source of innu-
merable evils, which Association alone can
remedy. . . .
— Fourierist communard, 1844

Let me tell you, my good friend, that things have
indeed changed with woman. . . . True, we do
not live in the 'phalanx,' but you have noticed
the various houses for eating which accommodate
the city. . . . You would hardly recognize the
process of cooking in one of our large
establishments. . . .
— Jane Sophia Appleton, 1848

The Domestic Critique

The earliest campaigns against traditional domestic life in the United States and Europe were launched by communitarian socialists committed to building model communities as a strategy for achieving social reform. Such reformers believed that the construction of an ideal community would transform the world through the power of its example. They often described the model communal household as a world in miniature, a concept which at once domesticated political economy and politicized domestic economy. Their campaigns against the isolated household were only part of their larger social and economic goals. However, their conviction that the built environment must be transformed to reflect more egalitarian systems of production and consumption persuaded them of the importance of making a full critique of conventional housing and domestic life.

While communitarian socialists conducted hundreds of experiments in the United States during the late eighteenth and nineteenth centuries, the theory behind these experiments was first developed in Europe. Among nonsectarian utopian socialists, both English and French theorists advocated collective housework and child care to support equality between men and women. In England, beginning about 1813, Robert Owen published the first of several plans for ideal communities including collective kitchens, dining rooms, and nurseries. Owen's experiments as manager and then as owner of textile mills at

New Lanark in Scotland between 1800 and 1824 included the Institute for the Formation of Character (2.1), an early attempt at developmental education for the children of working mothers. As Owen described it, "the Institution has been devised to afford the means of receiving your children at an early age, as soon almost as they can walk. By this means, many of you, mothers of families, will be enabled to earn a better maintenance or support for your children; you will have less care and anxiety about them; while the children will be prevented from acquiring any bad habits and gradually prepared to learn the best." [1] Since this institute was intended to support Owen's claim that environment and not heredity shaped character decisively, fashionable visitors in top hats and bonnets came to observe the experiment. In 1825 Owen's architect, Stedman Whitwell, produced a model of an ideal community (2.2) to be built on the land Owen had purchased from a German religious community in New Harmony, Indiana. He called it a "parallelogram," and it is one of the earliest designs for structured, multi-family housing with community facilities to be built in the United States. Although it was never erected, Owen's experiment at New Harmony did include the establishment of community kitchens, a child care center, and an early women's association in the existing buildings there.

Other English radicals in the Owenite movement shared Owen's goals for women and even went beyond them. In 1825 John

2.1 Robert Owen's Institute for the Formation
of Character, New Lanark, Scotland

2.2 Stedman Whitwell, detail from a rendering
of Robert Owen's ideal community, or parallel-
logram, 1825, showing suites of private rooms
under peaked roofs and collective facilities at
corners and in center

Gray offered *A Lecture on Human Happiness* to a cooperative society in London, with an appendix proposing a community with freedom from domestic drudgery for all, stating that household jobs such as cooking, laundry, and building fires to heat rooms should be handled by "scientific principles." [2] In 1826 the Friendly Association for Mutual Interests, a community located at Valley Forge, Pennsylvania, republished his lecture with their constitution. In the same year as Gray's lecture, William Thompson, with the help of Anna Wheeler, made his celebrated *Appeal to one half of the Human Race, Women, against the pretensions of the other Half, Men, to retain them in Civil and Domestic Slavery.* He criticized the home as an "eternal prison house for the wife" and an institution "chiefly for the drillings of a superstition to render her more submissive." He called for economic independence for women, communal upbringing of children, and recognition of the right of women to work outside the home and to receive support during pregnancy.[3] In the next decade Owenite women organized the first women's cooperative association in England around these demands, hoping to raise funds to create "associated homes."

Robert Owen and his followers demanded "a new moral world"; his French contemporary, Charles Fourier, proposed "a new industrial world" and "a new amorous world." The Owenites had a strong feminist theoretical position, but the followers of Charles Fourier were even more adamant. Fourier claimed that "The de-

gree of emancipation of women is the natural measure of general emancipation" and stated that "the extension of the privileges of women is the fundamental cause of all social progress." [4] Therefore he argued that a society which condemned women to domestic drudgery was inferior to one where men and women shared equally in human activities, and women enjoyed economic independence. Fourier identified the private dwelling as one of the greatest obstacles to improving the position of women in civilization; for him, improved housing design was as essential to women's rights as improved settlement design was to the reform of industrial workers' lives. He hoped to introduce structured housing with collective facilities which would make the most elegant conventional private home appear "a place of exile, a residence worthy of fools, who after three thousand years of architectural studies, have not yet learned to build themselves healthy and comfortable lodgings." [5] The phalanstery, or "unitary dwelling," Fourier believed, was an architectural invention to overcome the conflicts between city and country, rich and poor, men and women, by an enlightened arrangement of economic and social resources.

In the United States, Owen inspired about fifteen experiments in model community building beginning in the 1820s; Fourier inspired about thirty Associations, or Phalanxes, based on his ideas, beginning in the 1840s. (A smaller number of experiments of both types were conducted in Europe as well.) The Fourierists or Associationists in America usually preceded their attempts to build the perfect phalanstery with polemics against the isolated household. As one communard explained in a Fourierist journal in 1844, "The isolated household is wasteful in economy, is untrue to the human heart, and is not the design of God, and therefore it must disappear." This author asserted that the phalanstery would increase the residents' privacy as well as their collective advantages:

. . . When we say the isolated household is a source of innumerable evils, which Association alone can remedy, the mind of the hearer sometimes rushes to the conclusion that we mean to destroy the home relations entirely. . . . The privacy of domestic life, Association aims to render more sacred, as well as to extend it to all men. . . .[6]

Another Fourierist communard agreed: instead of sacrificing individuality and independence, the combined household may be so conducted that "the members shall have more privileges and privacy than can be obtained in isolation."

Writing from an experimental community near Cincinnati, Alcander Longley explained: "The combined household is the most glorious feature in a co-operative society, because it frees woman from the household drudgery which is unavoidable in separable households." [7] The goals in the phalanstery were collective child care and employment for women. Marx Edgeworth Lazarus, a prominent intellectual in the movement, stated: "The industrial independence of woman will emancipate her from the necessity of attaching her life and

fortunes to any man." He believed that "Woman will never be free, save in the large home, the varied and attractive industry of the Phalanx, where she has her choice of all the departments of domestic, mechanical, and agricultural labors and arts. . . . There the real charms of maternity will be enjoyed, because there, in the unitary nurseries and miniature workshops, children can be safely and happily provided for, either in the presence or absence of the mother; and the children mutually amuse each other, without requiring, each of them, the continued attention of one or more adults." Associationist women shared Longley's and Lazarus's desire to hasten the disappearance of the isolated household. In 1847 the women of the Trumbull Phalanx in Ohio wrote to the Union of Women for Association, formed in Boston, "Could all the women fitted to engage in Social Reform be located on one domain, one cannot imagine the immense changes that would there ensue. We pray that we, or at least our children, may live to see the day when kindred souls shall be permitted to co-operate in a sphere sufficiently extensive to call forth all our powers." [8]

Although nonsectarian Associationists led this critical response to the isolated household, many reformers involved with sectarian communistic societies also criticized private home life as wasteful and oppressive to women and men. Mary Antoinette Doolittle, a Shaker eldress, claimed that she preferred a collective, celibate life of prayer and work to the destiny of a farm wife whose chief duty would be to "rock the cradle and sing lullabye" in addition to doing housework.[9] John Humphrey Noyes, founder of the Oneida Community, complained of the "gloom and dullness of excessive family isolation," or the "little man-and-wife circle," where one suffered "the discomfort and waste attendant on the domestic economy of our separate households."[10]

In contrast to the private household, which all these reformers denounced as isolated, wasteful, and oppressive, the communitarians hoped to build communal or cooperative facilities for domestic tasks, tangible, architectural demonstrations of the workings of a more egalitarian society. The architectural form of model villages was determined by the economic and social structure of the communities they served, so that the problems of mechanizing and measuring domestic work were solved in a great variety of ingenious ways. At least two types of economic and social organization among communitarian socialists must be distinguished: the community containing nuclear families within it, who retained some degree of private family life, and the community functioning as one large "family" engaged in communal living.

The Community Organization Including Families

Following the manifestos of the Owenites and Associationists, communities which contained nuclear families within them offered collective housekeeping and childcare arrangements, but emphasized the provision of private as well as community

spaces. Usually families occupied private apartments and had access to the shared kitchens, dining rooms, and nurseries. (Even when Fourierist communities called their housing a unitary dwelling, such a structure contained many private spaces.) If a unitary dwelling was impossible, a network of related buildings, including private family houses or apartment houses and various shared housekeeping facilities, might serve the same purpose.

Although the Owenites did not build any major structure in the United States, the Associationists erected many phalansteries. At the North American Phalanx, a community of about one hundred and twenty-five members established in New Jersey in 1843, a communal kitchen, laundry, and bakery were contained in the same building as private apartments (without kitchens) and dormitories, but members were also permitted to build private houses (with kitchens) on the domain.[11] The Brook Farm community in West Roxbury, Massachusetts, also built a large phalanstery, but it was destroyed by fire before the members could occupy it; the Raritan Bay Union in New Jersey erected an elaborate structure of this type as well. As about thirty American Associationist experiments developed between 1840 and 1860, their architecture became a popular topic of discussion, but by far the most impressive buildings were erected for the Familistère or Social Palace, at Guise, France, by the Fourierist Jean-Baptiste-André Godin, beginning in 1859, to provide innovative housing for several hundred iron foundry workers and their families. These apartments included private kitchens, but the Guise complex also contained a large dining hall, cafe, and child-care center (2.3, 2.4, 2.5).

In contrast to the nonsectarian Fourierists' "unitary dwellings," some sectarian groups built villages composed of small, private apartment houses and collective housekeeping facilities. The Harmony Society, a German religious group led by George Rapp, built three towns in the United States between 1805 and 1824. Nine hundred members at Economy, Pennsylvania, lived in such houses and dormitories, each with its own kitchen, but they also had a large communal kitchen and feast hall used on special occasions. The Amana Inspirationists built fifty-two communal kitchen houses, each serving about fifty people, in the seven communal villages which these German and Swiss immigrants established in Iowa beginning in 1855. Residents dwelt in private family apartments (usually four apartments to a house) and in dormitories.[12] Schools, kindergartens, and other workshops were located near the residences and kitchens (2.6, 2.7). Similar arrangements prevail in the Bruderhof and Hutterian communities that are still active in the United States and Canada: small buildings containing several family apartments, some with minimal private kitchens, are served by communal cooking and dining facilities.

The Communal Family

While communities including families most closely resembled the larger society in their housing needs, communities organized as one very large family often produced spectacularly efficient collective domestic services. Almost all of the communities organized as one family were religious groups practicing economic communism. They often wished to abolish the nuclear family in order to promote greater attachment to a shared faith and a shared communal ideology. Total economic communism and a commitment to celibacy or free love (viewed as the sexual counterpart of economic communism) were frequently required by such groups, and they often built large dwellings where members were housed in rooms or dormitories connected to one large kitchen, dining room, and nursery.

Some communal families and their architecture are well known. The Oneida Perfectionists, led by John Humphrey Noyes and Erastus Hamilton, the community's architect, built a very substantial communal home in central New York State for two hundred members, beginning in 1847 (2.8). The masthead of their newspaper, *The American Socialist,* promoted "the enlargement and improvement of home," and in 1862, with the dedication of their Second Mansion House, they claimed that "Communism in our society has built itself a house." [13] Views of Perfectionist communal housekeeping facilities were published in several popular illustrated magazines between 1850 and 1875

(2.11). The Shakers, led by Ann Lee, built nineteen celibate communistic settlements between 1774 and 1826, located from Maine to Kentucky. Their ingenious communal housekeeping arrangements also received wide publicity; usually their "family" dwellings housed thirty to one hundred people (2.9, 2.10).

Socialized Domestic Work

This brief review of housing arrangements designed for communitarian socialists' model villages can only begin to suggest the variety of plans for domestic reform devised in hundreds of sectarian and nonsectarian experiments. It is difficult to assess the effect of such unorthodox domestic architecture on the female and male domestic workers who participated in these innovative projects. Nevertheless, one can examine evidence from various experiments concerning the efficient performance of domestic work and the degree of women's confinement to domestic industries.

Most communitarian socialists hoped to seize economic initiative in three areas: agriculture, industry, and domestic work. By combining the labor of many workers, male and female, they proposed to end the isolation of the individual farmer, industrial worker, and housewife, improving efficiency through some division of labor while keeping all individuals involved with these three areas of work. Improved work environments and equal wages were often advertised to make such communities attractive to both men and women, farmers

and industrial workers. This was the ideal; the reality for female workers often included improved work environments but rarely equal pay, and only occasionally an end to confinement in domestic industries.

From a feminist viewpoint, the major achievement of most communitarian experiments was ending the isolation of the housewife. Domestic work became social labor. Shaker women sang humorous songs about cooking and cleaning while they worked. Workers in the fifty-two kitchen houses which were built by the Amana community claimed that they were the "dynamic centers of the villages." Besides being places for village celebrations, the Amana kitchen houses, with eight or ten women working under a *Kuchenbas,* became centers of news and information. A resident described going to the kitchen house "for the only social life we knew, for snatches of gossip and legitimate news, and just ordinary companionship." [14]

A second achievement was the division and specialization of household labor. Kitchens became shops serving the entire community, like other facilities. Gardening, preserving, cleaning, baking, cooking, ironing, gathering herbs, and caring for children were all skills required within the communal economy which could be learned. Domestic work took its place on organizational charts parallel to agricultural or industrial production. All members, male and female, were required to put in a certain number of hours per day, and all work areas were designed to a certain standard.

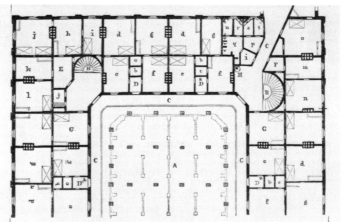

2.3 The Familistère, or Social Palace, Guise,
France, begun in 1859, detail of view showing
housing at left rear; bakery, cafe, schools, theater, restaurant, and butcher shop at left front.
Iron foundry on right not shown. The nursery is
at the rear of the central apartment block. From
Harper's Monthly, April 1872.

2.4 Section and partial plan of an apartment
block at the Familistère, showing collective services such as refuse chutes, piped water, heating
and ventilating systems; the collective spaces,
such as the central courtyard, galleries at each
floor, and water closets on each landing; and the
built-in wardrobes in each lodging room. Dwelling units for families might be made up of one,
two, three, or five adjacent rooms. From *Harper's
Monthly,* April 1872.

2.5 Festival of Labor, held in the glass-roofed
central courtyard of an apartment block at the
Familistère, showing galleries and entrances to
private dwelling units, from *Harper's Monthly,*
April 1872. This is the social space, filled with
people, idealized by every Fourierist group.

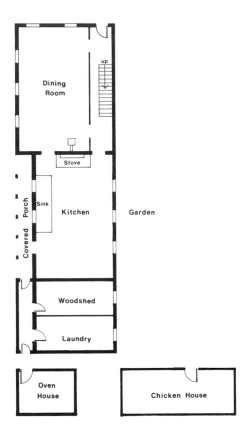

First

2.7 Plan of first floor of kitchen house, Amana, Iowa

First

Second

2.6 Plans of small apartment house, Amana, Iowa, 1855, showing small apartments of parlor and bedroom

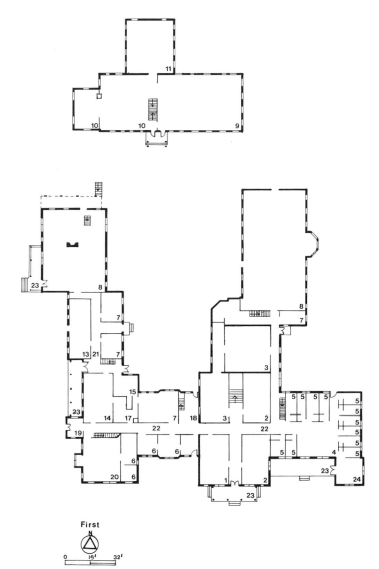

First

0   15'   32'

2.8 Plan of first floor of the communal dwelling built by Oneida Community, Kenwood, New York, 1861–1878: 1, office and cloakroom; 2, reception room; 3, library; 4, lower sitting room; 5, single bedroom; 6, shared bedroom; 7, bathroom; 8, lounge or workshop; 9, workshop; 10, dining room; 11, dining addition; 13, 14, sitting rooms; 15, nursery kitchen; 17, nursery; 18, 21, 22, corridors; 19, vestibule; 23, porch, 24, tower.

2.9 Basement plan, first floor plan, and view of communal dwelling built by Shaker community, Church Family, Hancock, Massachusetts, 1830

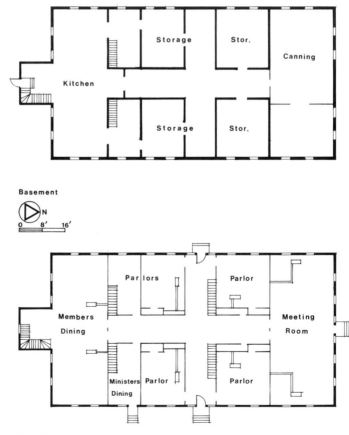

Basement

First Floor

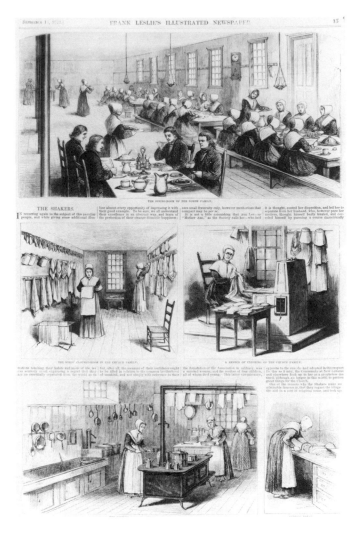

2.10 Collective domestic work in a Shaker community: Shaker women cooking, sewing, mending, and serving food, as shown in *Frank Leslie's Illustrated Newspaper*, September 13, 1873

2.11 Collective child raising at the Oneida Community, the "Children's Hour," and the school, as shown in *Frank Leslie's Illustrated Newspaper,* April 9, 1870. Women are wearing the Bloomer dresses developed by dress reform advocates in the 1840s.

The socialization of domestic labor provided an obvious justification for better design and equipment: fifty private families might need fifty kitchens and fifty stoves, but a communal family, with one large kitchen and one large stove, had the resources to invest in additional, more sophisticated labor-saving devices. Communitarian socialists took pride in providing themselves with the latest in heating, lighting, and sanitation devices, designed to ensure the health of their members and lighten domestic labor. And what they didn't acquire, the women and men of the group might invent.

The Harmony Society devised special insulation and ventilation for its houses. The Oneida Perfectionists installed gas light, steam baths, and steam heat in their communal Mansion House in the 1860s. This last comfort caused almost hysterical excitement: "Good-bye wood sheds, good-bye stoves, good-bye coal scuttles, good-bye pokers, good-bye ash sifters, good-bye stove dust, and good-bye coal gas. Hail to the one fire millennium!" [15] Yet, significantly, the Oneidans retained one wood-burning stove in a small room they called their "Pocket Kitchen." The warmth of a direct heat source in a small space was appreciated as having nurturing qualities which couldn't be improved upon. Here was the community medicine chest and a place for telling one's troubles.

Charles Nordhoff, a traveling journalist who visited many American communes in the 1870s, commented that "a communist's life is full of devices for ease and comfort." [16] Lists of domestic inventions produced by members of various communities are equaled only by the lists of inventions in their other industries. The Shakers have to their credit an improved washing machine; the common clothespin; a double rolling pin for faster pastry making; a conical stove to heat flatirons; the flat broom; removable window sash, for easy washing; a window-sash balance; a round oven for more even cooking; a rotating oven shelf for removing items more easily; a butter worker; a cheese press; a pea sheller; an apple peeler; and an apple parer which quartered and cored the fruit. Members of the Oneida Community produced a lazy-susan dining-table center, an improved mop wringer, an improved washing machine, and an institutional-scale potato peeler. (Their community policy was to rotate jobs every few months, so that skills learned in one community shop might be the source of inventions to speed another sort of task.)

Inventiveness also extended to developing equipment and spaces for child care. For their kindergartens, the Amana Inspirationists built large cradles which could hold as many as six children. Other communes had specially designed furniture at child scale, a novelty not to be found in most nineteenth-century homes. One early twentieth-century commune, the Bruderhof, still supports itself today by manufacturing Community Playthings. Outdoor spaces might be designed with children in mind as well: the Oneida Community had an extensive landscaped playspace; the

Shakers created model farms and gardens for their boys and girls.

Communitarian socialists often found it profitable to manufacture and market their domestic inventions, such as the Shakers' improved washing machines, their window-sash balance, and the Bruderhof's toys, but these inventions were not the only commercial extension of their domestic life. Once "women's" work was officially recognized, timed, and costed it might become a source of revenue to extend domestic services to customers outside the community. Thus a communal sewing room might begin to sell clothes, or a communal kitchen might also function as a restaurant. Among the Shakers, well-equipped facilities for spinning, dyeing, weaving, sewing, and ironing made it possible to fill a demand among outsiders for warm Shaker cloaks. And the Oneidans, by the 1870s, were serving hundreds of meals to visitors every week. Members of the Woman's Commonwealth, a community in Belton, Texas, actually made hotel and laundry management their major source of income, taking over a hotel in their town as both a communal residence and a profit-making venture.

If the first goal of many communitarians was efficiency in domestic industries, the second was ending the confinement of women to domestic work. In most of the experiments described, cooking, cleaning, and child care remained women's work, despite some limited participation by men. But, because of the division and specialization of labor and the introduction of labor-saving devices, women's overall hours of work were limited. Rather than being on call day and night, like the average wife and mother, many communitarian women had leisure to develop their other interests such as reading, writing, participating in musical or theatrical performances, developing friendships, enjoying amorous relationships. This gave them a degree of freedom unimaginable in the larger society, especially if their community provided day care facilities.

Although most experiments managed to limit the hours of work for women, domestic work was not always as highly paid as other communal industries, and women were not always encouraged to enter other areas of work. The celibate Shakers kept all areas of work restricted by sex; men and women never worked together. Other communes, like Oneida and the North American Phalanx, made gestures toward encouraging women to enter administration, factory work, and other nondomestic jobs. Consciousness of the problems of socialization for women's work was high at Oneida, where young girls were told to get rid of their dolls lest they learn to be mothers before they had learned to be persons.[17] Consciousness was not enough, however, for although some Oneida women worked in the community factory, most worked in domestic industries, apparently by choice, and the situation was the same in most other experimental communities, especially those which encouraged women to perfect domestic skills. One old photograph of a sewing class at a

Fourierist community showing only young
women in attendance suggests the kind of
community pressures which countered
some groups' official proclamations on
women's work.

A Lasting Influence

What influence did all these attempts to
develop convincing domestic alternatives
actually exert? Communitarian socialist experiments often produced plans suitable
only for a socialist, feminist society, the like
of which American citizens had not yet
seen. In the most consistent experiments,
there is a sense of unreality: they seem too
perfect, with round ovens, clever tables,
and ingenious cradles. Everyone has been
so busy working out the details of the new
arrangements that they have had no time
to think about the world outside the experiment. Nevertheless, communitarians
developed a domestic architecture on a
collective rather than a private basis, in
workable and complex forms, as well as in
fantastic and unrealistic ones.

This collective domestic world did not,
as some communitarians had hoped,
totally transform the economic and political realities of women's situation within
these communities. It was no more possible
to insert people of both sexes into a phalanstery with a single kitchen, and end role
stereotyping, than it was to insert people of
all classes into such a structure, let "passional attraction" go to work, and watch a
classless society evolve. Nevertheless, the
communitarian socialists' polemics about
design and the new architectural forms

created in experimental socialist communities had a lasting effect on the American
people. They made it very clear that domestic space was a social product.

In particular Fourier's phalanstery
influenced the development of Victorian
buildings for many different social reform
programs — including asylums, peniten-
tiaries, settlement houses, model corporate
towns, and model tenement houses.
Fourier's most important influence, however, was among feminist reformers who
hoped to reorganize the domestic economy.
Nineteenth-century American feminists
who appreciated his ideas were even more
numerous than the twentieth-century Bolsheviks who were fond of quoting Fourier's
feminist aphorisms.[18]

Seneca Falls

Elizabeth Cady Stanton spent two days
with the Associationists at the Brook Farm
community in the 1840s, finding them "a
charming family of intelligent men and
women." [19] As followers of Charles Fourier,
they believed that the isolated household
could never represent the best development
of human sociability, talent, and culture, a
theme that Stanton would repeat throughout her career. A few years later, Stanton
moved to Seneca Falls, New York. There
she was at the heart of upstate New York's
"burned-over" district, a haven for religious revivalists which was also heavily col-
onized by communitarian socialists. In addition to the Oneida Community, founded
in 1847, two Shaker villages had been
founded at Groveland and Sonyea, and no

fewer than eight Fourierist Phalanxes were launched there in the mid-1840s.

In her rousing speech at the Seneca Falls Women's Rights Convention in 1848, Stanton revealed that in addition to her experiences in the Abolitionist movement, her own domestic isolation in a district of communal experiments had sparked her protest on behalf of women. As a housewife, she said, "my duties were too numerous and varied, and none sufficiently exhilarating or intellectual to bring into play my higher faculties. I suffered with mental hunger. . . . I now fully understood the practical difficulties most women had to contend with in the isolated household, and the impossibility of woman's best development if in contact, the chief part of her life, with servants and children. Fourier's phalansterie community life and co-operative households had new significance for me." [20]

Stanton's own political career, while conceived in reaction to the isolated home, dealt with suffrage and legal rights for women, rather than improved housing. At the same time, in her radical paper, *The Revolution,* she and her associate editor, Parker Pillsbury, ran several articles praising experiments in cooperative housekeeping in 1868 and 1869. In 1899 she urged Susan B. Anthony to include cooperative housekeeping on the agenda for the National American Woman's Suffrage Association convention, arguing that "woman's work can never be properly organized in the isolated home." [21]

Stanton's colleague from Seneca Falls, Amelia Bloomer, also campaigned against the isolated home. In the late 1850s, when she had moved from New York to Council Bluffs, Iowa, Bloomer gave an address to a local women's association, "On Housekeeping — Woman's Burdens." She asked "Is there not some way of relief from this drudging, weary work over the cookstove, washtub, and sewing machine; from this load of labor and care?" She believed that one-fifth of all women could, by "some reasonable and just system of cooperation" relieve the other four-fifths of their labors and "give them time for self-improvement and the care and culture of their children." [22] She also advocated a common playroom for children, according to one journalist, who states that husbands objected to the project and refused to finance it. [23]

Bangor

In 1848, the same year that Stanton and Bloomer began to organize for women's rights in Seneca Falls, Jane Sophia Appleton exploited the communitarian socialists' domestic critique to develop a proposal for new forms of urban design. Appleton, a housewife in Bangor, Maine, decided to construct a fictional vision of her city in the year 1978, which included a complete economic and environmental reorganization of domestic work on Fourierist lines. [24] The narrator of Appleton's story explains her ideas to a time traveler from Victorian America: "The household arrangements of this age," her narrator reports, "are some-

what different from yours I imagine. At
this moment you may see an exem-
plification of it, in the gay groups of people
which you notice yonder, just filling the
streets, as they go to their eating houses."

Responds the time traveler, "Eating
houses! Ah! It seems to me that looks a little like Fourierism, but the tall individual
whom I met in the morning, told me that
the community system 'died out' long ago,
and that people lived in families, and
women cooked and scrubbed, baked and
patched, as of old." The narrator cuts in,
"And so people do live in families, and always will, I reckon" but he adds, "Let me
tell you, my good friend, that things have
indeed changed with woman. . . . And
for this progress, we are mainly indebted to
the genius of Charles Fourier, who, by his
profound insight into the evils of society,
induced such changes as gave due compensation to all industry, whether in man,
woman, or child." [25]

True, we do not live in the phalanx, but
you have noticed the various houses for
eating which accommodate the city. Covered passages in some of the streets, the arcade style of building generally adopted in
others, and carriages for the more isolate
and wealthy residences, make this a perfectly convenient custom, even in our cli-
mate, and 'tis so generally adopted by our
people that only now and then a fidgetty
man, or a *peremptory woman*, attempts anything like the system of housekeeping in
your day. . . . You would hardly recognize the process of cooking in one of our
large establishments. Quiet, order, pru-
dence, certainty of success, govern the

process of turning out a ton of bread, or
roasting an ox! — as much as the weaving
of a yard of cloth in one of your factories.
No fuming, no fretting over the cooking
stove, as of old! No "roasted lady" at the
head of the dinner table! Steam machinery, division of labor, economy of material,
make the whole as agreeable as any other
toil, while the expense to pocket is as much
less to man as the wear of patience, time,
bone and muscle to woman. . . .

Ah, you did not *begin to live* in your
benighted nineteenth century! Just think of
the absurdity of one hundred housekeepers,
every Saturday morning, striving to en-
lighten one hundred girls in the process of
making pies for one hundred little ovens!
(Some of these remain to this day, to the
great glee of antiquarians.) What fatigue!
What vexation! Why, ten of our cooks, in
the turning of a few cranks, and an hour or
so of placing materials, produce enough
pies to supply the whole of this city, —
rather more than all your ladies could do
together, I fancy.[26]

Following this description of the large
kitchens and an equally glowing account of
a mechanical laundry on the Penobscot,
the narrator concludes that women workers
in all these domestic industries and others,
"command as high remuneration as
any. . . . In every station, pecuniary independence is her own." [27]

How had this new domestic world come
about? First cooperative stores were established in Bangor, where the poor "combined to purchase their supplies at shops
established expressly for them, that their
small parcels might come to them at
wholesale prices." Second came philanthropic benefactors who built "comfort-

able, cheap dwellings, with the privilege for each tenant of a certain right in a common bakery, school, etc." Third, wise legislation helped the poor and "taxed the *hoarder,* or rich man." [28]

As a result, the author claimed that Bangor society in 1978 offered all the benefits of communitarian socialism with none of the problems of rural isolation or mandatory communal living. Bangor was prosperous, a city of urban arcaded streets and suburban residences, still showing some class distinctions but far more egalitarian than it had been in the nineteenth century. Women received equal pay for woman's work, and the physical space of the city had been shaped to suit this new domestic system.

Appleton wrote her "Sequel to the Vision of Bangor in the Twentieth Century" in 1848 in response to a short utopian sketch by Edward Kent, the Whig Governor of Maine, who had predicted that the women of the twentieth century would be content in their domestic lives without the vote or political power.[29] Provoked by his smug predictions, Appleton took the proposals of Fourier and Owen and her knowledge of a small Maine town, and redesigned her domestic world. The controversy between Appleton and Kent must have entertained Bangor society, since Appleton published both sketches in a volume for the benefit of the Bangor Female Orphan Asylum. Hers was a fictional prophecy which many earnest feminists were to take up in the century to come. Housewives, domestic scientists, and political activists would follow her lead, seeking feminist theory and practice appropriate for households in the cities and towns of the United States, yet equal to the achievements of the earlier communitarian socialists in their imaginative power.

3.1 Catharine Beecher. Courtesy Schlesinger
Library, Radcliffe College.

*It is the aim of this volume . . . to render each
department of woman's true profession as much
desired and respected as are the most honored professions of men.*
— *Catharine Beecher and Harriet Beecher Stowe,*
The American Woman's Home, *1869*

Female Self-Sacrifice and the Home

In 1840, Americans received the first trans-
lations of Charles Fourier's work and saw
the first views of his phalanstery, a neoclassical palace full of mechanical inventions
celebrated by utopian socialists and feminists for the next sixty years. In 1841, in
her *Treatise on Domestic Economy,* Catharine
Beecher published the first of her designs
for Gothic cottages full of mechanical inventions. While Fourier argued for social
services to help women, Beecher argued for
women's self-sacrifice and domestic isolation. Yet there are more similarities than
first appear. Both were interested in increasing women's power; both believed
that new domestic environments were necessary to support women's new roles in an
industrial society. Fourier and his followers
saw women coming together with men in
the phalanstery, while Beecher preferred
the private suburban house where women
derived their power from training their
children and providing shelter for men
from the world of urban work. She became
the ultimate domestic feminist, demanding
women's control over all aspects of domestic life.

Beecher (3.1), the spinster daughter of a
Congregationalist minister, was born in
1800. In 1831 she produced her first book,
*The Elements of Mental and Moral Philosophy,
Founded Upon Experience, Reason, and the Bible,*
which launched her life-long argument for
the moral superiority of women based
upon their highly developed capacity for
self-sacrifice. In 1836, in a long essay cele-

brating the differences between male and
female character, she introduced and elaborated now familiar stereotypes of gender.
She began work in that same year on her
*Treatise on Domestic Economy, For the Use of
Young Ladies at Home and at School,* which incorporated many of these ideas and was
eventually published in 1841. Sklar estimates its effect: Beecher "exaggerated and
heightened gender differences and thereby
altered and romanticized the emphasis
given to women's domestic role." [1] Unlike
her earlier philosophical writings, which
suffered from the stigma of female author-
ship, her *Treatise* was an immediate, popular success, running through yearly editions, adopted as a school text, a classic
succeeded only by her even more popular
work, *The American Woman's Home,*
coauthored with her sister, Harriet Beecher
Stowe, in 1869.

The success of Beecher's *Treatise* and all
of her subsequent domestic publications
centered upon her agile definitions of female dominance in the home. Earlier
American works on domestic economy
assumed that men retained control of the
typical middle-class household, including
women, children, and servants, but as
Sklar has noted, Beecher broke with this
tradition tentatively in the *Treatise* and decisively in the *American Woman's Home.* [2]
While she accepted a conventional
definition of the domestic world as
woman's sphere, she established herself as a
leading advocate of domestic feminism by
claiming that woman's greater capacity for

self-sacrifice entitled her to rule the home.
She argued in favor of the physical and social separation of the population into the
female-dominated sphere of home life,
preferably suburban, and the male-
dominated sphere of work and aggressive
competition, usually urban. Her goals were
breathtakingly political: she hoped to
make gender more important than class, in
order to prevent any disturbance to the
American economic system. Women, she
believed, should not compete with men in
any way, nor should they vote. But her
strategy of domestic feminism was enhanced by two new metaphors of female
authority: woman as "home minister" and
as skilled "professional."

When she harnessed the imagery of religion and business, of power absolute in the
colonial period and power just beginning
to be felt in urbanizing America, these
metaphors of ministerial and professional
activity were supported by a most unusual
economic rationalization. Women were to
do their own housework, without help from
domestic servants. Rather than indicating
a diminution in status, this work was to
provide the opportunity for gaining power
through self-sacrifice (the ministerial role)
and skill (the professional role). Zealous
homemaking was suggested as a route to
self-assertion for women of all classes, con-
ferring purpose on the "aimless vacuity" of
rich women, ennobling the "unrequited
toil" of poor women, and improving the
status of middle-class women.[3]

The ministerial ideal transferred to the
family many of the properties of the Puritan village of seventeenth-century New
England. Beecher planned to recreate its
hierarchy in miniature, describing the
home as a Christian "commonwealth,"
with the housewife as "minister of home."
As the head of the "home church of Jesus
Christ," she could inculcate ten to twelve
offspring with the idea of "work and self-
sacrifice for the public good" and "living
for others more than for self." [4] Beecher
criticized Roman Catholic convents,
boarding schools, and Fourierist phalansteries as attempts to form perfected social and
environmental communities which were
less effective in forming souls than her
own. "The true Protestant system . . . is
the one here suggested, based not on the
conventual, nor on the Fourierite, nor
the boarding-school systems, but on the
Heaven-devised plan of the family state." [5]
Borrowing polemic from the communitarian socialists who were her contemporaries,
as well as from Puritan leaders of covenant
communities, Beecher averred that her
model community — the family commonwealth — would be multiplied *ad infinitum*
across the land.

Beecher supported the metaphor of
traditional religious authority with quasi-
religious rites that utilized the complimentary professional metaphor and its associated technology. Drainpipes and Bible
stands, folding beds and stoves, door
knockers and ventilating equipment became the paraphernalia of the "home
church"; housework its sacred rites. Daily,
weekly, and seasonal chores provided a lit-
urgy best expressed in the proverbs, "a

woman's place is in the home" and "a woman's work is never done." Beecher's famous technological innovations did not shorten the hours of domestic work as much as they raised domestic standards and made them explicit.

Beecher was an advocate of household consumption from the time of the *Treatise,* when she argued that if Americans relinquished superfluous goods, then half the community would be unemployed: "The use of superfluities, therefore, to a certain extent, is as indispensable to promote industry, virtue, and religion as any direct giving of money or time." [6] No longer an economic producer in the crude house of the Puritan covenant community, the Christian woman must become a professional consumer promoting "industry, virtue, and religion."

As an architect, Beecher gained skill over the years. In 1841 her designs were spatially and technically conventional: the houses are boxes with a central core of fireplaces. The interior spaces — a parlor and dining room at the front of the house, backed by a series of small, unrelated spaces including "bedpresses" (tiny bedrooms), closets, and kitchen — do not relate to the exterior elevations and massing. The parlors turn into bedrooms at night, but the designs make few other concessions to flexibility. Beecher suggested a plan for a dumbwaiter, and she mentioned the best method of obtaining hot water for bathing, but these are "back door accommodations," and there is no interior plumbing. The rest of her book was devoted to her

moral philosophy of domesticity and to housekeeping instructions of a more traditional kind, such as recipes for whitewash and advice on what china to choose, how to make a bed, and what upholstery materials wear well.

By 1865, Beecher had broadened her technological knowledge and strengthened her design skills in the service of domestic feminism. "How to Redeem Woman's Profession from Dishonor" presented an elaborate Gothic cottage full of mechanical equipment for the professional housewife, the minister of home. In this design, one can measure the growing correspondence between the woman's role of caring for the family and maintaining the home environment by noting that names have changed for various rooms: the parlor has become the "home room"; the kitchen has become the "workroom"; the dining room has become the "family room." Servants have been dispensed with. Instead of a "dark and comfortless" kitchen, she produces sunlight, air, and a "cooking form" that rationalizes food storage and preparation. The stove is enclosed. The workroom opens into the family room, and Beecher suggests that women may wish to wear their good clothes in all areas. To illustrate the principle of the "close packing of conveniences," almost every household task is described step by step with the architectural arrangements that assist its convenient completion.

In *The American Woman's Home,* of 1869, the adjustment of woman and house is completed. This volume was advertised as "a Book that should find its way into every household in the land" and promoted as "the Cheapest and Most Desirable Book of the Year." The authors, Catharine Beecher and Harriet Beecher Stowe, claimed that they aimed to "elevate both the honor and the remuneration of all the employments that sustain the many difficult and sacred duties of the family state, and thus to render each department of woman's true profession as much desired and respected as are the most honored professions of men." [7]

The plan of the American woman's home recalls nothing so much as the plan of the seventeenth-century Puritan house, with hall, parlor, lean-to kitchen, and central chimney, redesigned with nineteenth-century heating and plumbing. Compared to Beecher's earlier efforts, this plan is fully developed, interior elements are simplified, elevations are refined (3.2). The kitchen has become a streamlined, single-surface workspace, penetrating the center of the house with its mechanical core of water closets and heating and ventilating equipment. Flexibility is maximized with movable decorative screens hiding extra beds and dressing areas, where tropical landscapes and elaborate finials conceal the utilitarian closets. Elsewhere in the house, an aura of religious piety characterizes spaces arranged for the minister of home, as niches with pointed arches make miniature shrines for the display of pictures, busts, and statues.

Inventions proliferate, so that the woman without servants, the minister of home, now has the most advanced technology — for cooking, heating, ventilating, interior plumbing, gaslight — the decade could provide in the private home. It was inferior to the technology available in hotels and restaurants, but far superior to the equipment available in most houses designed by male architects and builders for households with servants. Mechanization is the handmaiden of Beecher's "professional" housewife in her suburban isolation.

The American Woman's Home was the culmination of Catharine Beecher's career as an authority on women's roles, housing design, and household organization. Its publication concluded thirty-eight years of agitation for female dominance in the home with an ultimate architectural resolution. Although the designer was sixty-nine years old, her ability to manipulate space and mechanical equipment had never been greater. In the next half century other domestic experts and designers such as Christine Frederick, Frank Lloyd Wright, and Lillian Gilbreth would only try to live up to her example.

The Model Christian Neighborhood
Both Catharine Beecher and Harriet Beecher Stowe did have a few reservations about the nation ideal of the isolated, single-family suburban house for the Christian wife and mother which they so effectively promulgated. Not every American woman could live in the suburbs or, in the post–Civil War days, could expect to find a husband. So their book included Beecher's plan for a tenement house, to compress the ideal set of family spaces into minimal

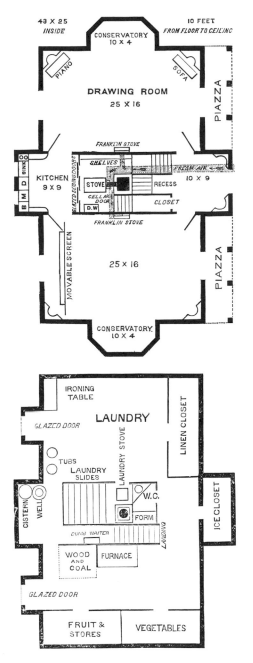

3.2 Catharine Beecher and Harriet Beecher Stowe, *The American Woman's Home,* 1869, plans of basement and first floor, showing careful organization of spaces and mechanical equipment for laundry and cooking

dimensions for the urban poor, as well as a recommendation for settlement houses, nearly two decades before women such as Ellen Richards and Jane Addams were to take up these causes. In addition, Beecher provided a design for a church, schoolhouse, and residence for two female missionary teachers, which she justified by citing conditions in the West and the South, where rural districts lacked both ministers and teachers. Here she anticipated the concern about working women's homes which later reformers such as Mary Kenney and Henrietta Rodman were to pursue.

Finally, there is a brief discussion of a Model Christian Neighborhood, where ten to twelve families might share a common laundry and bakehouse. The authors state that "it should be an object in America to exclude from the labors of the family all that can, with greater advantage, be executed out of it by combined labor. . . . How it would simplify the burdens of the American housekeeper to have washing and ironing day expunged from her calendar. . . . Whoever sets *neighborhood laundries* on foot will do much to solve the American housekeeper's hardest problem." [8] Perhaps the steam washing apparatus, designed by James T. King for commercial laundries in the 1850s, or the gas-heated iron, invented in 1850 by Lithgow, were appealing.[9] Yet it seems that Beecher and Stowe did not expect housewives themselves to furnish the "combined labor," since they call for "one or two good women," probably competent laundresses, to provide the womanpower for a dozen families.[10] While this picture of "combined labor" seems to weaken Beecher's and Stowe's efforts to enshrine individual women as powerful figures in the private home, it suggests that the drudgery of laundry work at home — obtaining water, heating it, boiling, scrubbing, and rinsing clothes, drying them and ironing with a flat iron — exceeded even Beecher's conception of self-sacrifice.

Probably Harriet Beecher Stowe was partly responsible for the "Model Christian Neighborhood." When asked by Elizabeth Cady Stanton to write a piece for her publication *The Revolution* in 1868, Stowe sketched a picture of "A Model Village" in New England with all of the comforts of a town laundry, a town bakery, and a cooked food delivery service:

The future model village of New England, as I see it, shall have for the use of its inhabitants not merely a town lyceum hall and a town library, but a town laundry, fitted up with conveniences such as no private house can afford, and paying a price to the operators which will enable them to command an excellence of work such as private families seldom realize. It will also have a town bakery, where the best of family bread, white, brown, and of all grains, shall be compounded; and lastly a town cook-shop, where soups and meats may be bought, ready for the table.

She was probably familiar with pie shops and cookshops in Europe and the United States which sold hot food and perhaps also knew the English custom of sending one's own roasts or cakes to be baked in the local baker's oven. (3.3). Recalling the experience of living in Europe, Stowe described an ideal cooked food service:

3.3 Neighborhood residents carrying roasts and puddings home after using the local baker's oven, London, 1848

Punctually to the dinner hour every day, our dinner came in on the head of a porter from a neighboring cook-shop. A large chest lined with tin, and kept warm by a tiny charcoal stove in the centre, being deposited in an ante-room, from it came forth, first soup, then fish, then roast of various names and lastly pastry and confections — far more courses than any reasonable Christian needs to keep him in healthy condition; and dinner being over, our box, with its *debris,* went out of the house leaving a clear field.[11]

It was just such a plan that all of the later reformers concerned with operating cooked food delivery services early in the twentieth century tried to create. This proposal by Stowe, as well as the one for a laundry and bakehouse by both authors, points in the direction which younger women such as Melusina Peirce, Marie Howland, and Mary Livermore would decide to take certain ideas about woman's sphere and socialized domestic work in the 1870s and 1880s.

The suggestions about the laundry and bakehouse do seem rather fantasy-like beside the large amount of work that Beecher and Stowe devoted to explaining the practical details in *The American Woman's Home* and to educating women for roles as housewives and mothers. However, all of the educational work, which Beecher intended as a way of ensuring dignity in domestic work through scientific training in nutrition, physiology, architecture, and the like, could also be interpreted as education for a wider sphere than the home. The home economists who later formed elaborate curricula around these subjects often came to espouse collective schemes and public issues as ecologically and economically more advanced than family-centered views. Even Catharine Beecher's own national organization, the Woman's Education Association, became a vehicle for more radical causes in the 1870s, in some of its local chapters. In Boston, Melusina Peirce's proposals for college courses for women and Ellen Richards's plans for a Woman's Laboratory at MIT began in the W.E.A.; in Vineland, New Jersey, which was Marie Howland's territory, the W.E.A. chapter unanimously supported Victoria Woodhull's plans for apartment hotels and child care services, tied to demands for free love.[12]

To "elevate both the honor and the remuneration" of women and "to render each department of woman's true profession as much desired and respected as are the most honored professions of men" were Beecher and Stowe's broadest goals. Many feminists would follow them, including their grand niece, Charlotte Perkins Gilman, who believed that she could reorganize the domestic sphere more effectively than they did, thirty years later. For all their proclamations that women should stay at home and focus on self-sacrifice as a route to domestic power, Beecher and Stowe gave at least a few hints that competence would bring more rewards than passivity, and that women should seek the recognition they deserved, here and now, as well as hereafter. Successive generations of domestic reformers who struggled with the

paradox of trying to gain power in and for
the domestic sphere owed something to
Beecher and Stowe, if only a sense that the
home they envisioned for the American
woman, so admirably designed for aug-
menting woman's domestic power, simply
was not a large enough domain for her executive skills.

If the communitarian socialists provided
the heritage of socialism in model villages,
the domestic feminists provided the legacy
of feminism in one sphere of life. The synthesis, a feminist strategy for domestic reform, would neither be limited to experimental socialist communities nor bounded
by the model private kitchen. It would
transcend women's daydreams, prescriptive
literature, and utopian fiction. Many times
in the next sixty years and more, domestic
reformers would fall back on these forms of
expressing their ideas. But new strategies
were brewing among younger women just
as Beecher and Stowe were putting the
final touches on *The American Woman's
Home,* strategies which would stress not
women's honor, but women's economic remuneration. Most often their proponents
were Yankee women with an interest in
some form of communitarian socialism,
women of strong will and intelligence, who
hoped to transform all American cities and
towns by material feminist strategies designed to promote women's economic
power. The communitarians had taught
them to demand control of the physical environment; the domestic feminists had
taught them to demand control of the
household. They were ready to invent
cooperative housekeeping.

4.1 Melusina Fay Peirce, Berlin, 1876, at about the age of forty. Courtesy Sylvia Wright Miterachi.

Cooperative housekeeping may be wholly practical or wholly visionary. But two things women must do somehow, as the conditions not only of the future happiness, progress, and elevation of their sex, but of its bare respectability and morality. 1st. They must earn their own living. 2nd. They must be organized among themselves.
— Melusina Fay Peirce, 1869

Unnatural Sacrifice

In 1868 Melusina Fay Peirce, an angry housewife, rebelled at what she called the "costly and unnatural sacrifice" of her wider talents to "the dusty drudgery of house ordering." [1] She proposed that women unite to take control over their lives and work, and suggested that totally new approaches to urban design would result. One of the first women to make a detailed economic critique of domestic life in the United States, Melusina Fay Peirce demanded pay for housework and organized the women of her own town to get it. Since she lived in Cambridge, Massachusetts, and her colleagues were the wives and daughters of the literary and intellectual elite, she was assured of publicity. Her campaign against traditional homemaking and traditional housing introduced the term "cooperative housekeeping."

Born in Burlington, Vermont, in 1836, Melusina Fay (4.1) was one of six daughters and three sons of an Episcopal minister, and a descendant of the outspoken Anne Hutchinson. After the death of her mother, whose life, her daughter believed, had been shortened by an endless round of domestic work, she attended the Young Ladies' School of Professor Louis Agassiz in Cambridge. While in Cambridge, she met Charles Sanders Peirce. Peirce was also a student of Agassiz, and perhaps this was his introduction to Melusina Fay. They were married in 1862, and a year later he was invited to lecture in the philosophy of science at Harvard. One biogra-

pher reports that she "joined him in his early scientific work"; another says she was "something of a scientist in her own right." [2] It cannot have been an easy marriage, for the thirteen years it lasted, but she made her protests against male chauvinism in general rather than against Charles in particular.

In 1868, after six years of marriage, thirty-two-year-old Melusina Peirce felt the "costly and unnatural sacrifice" of her wider talents. She wrote of American middle-class men dampening young women's aspirations:

Has a wife an eager desire to energize and perfect some gift of which she is conscious, her husband "will not oppose it," but he is sure that she will fail in her attempt, or is uneasy lest she make herself conspicuous and neglect her housekeeping. Or if a daughter wishes to go out into the world from the narrow duties and stifling air of her father's house, and earn a living there by some talent for which she is remarkable, he "will not forbid her," perhaps, but still he thinks her unnatural, discontented, ambitious, unfeminine; her relatives take their tone from him; nobody gives her a helping hand; so that if she accomplishes anything it is against the pressure — to her gigantic — of all that constitutes her world. If her strength and courage fail under the disapproval, they rejoice at the discomfiture which compels her to become what they call a "sensible woman." [3]

Of course, she never became a "sensible woman."

She identified the cause of women's economic and intellectual oppression as unpaid, unspecialized domestic work. In a series of articles published in the *Atlantic Monthly* in 1868 and 1869, she developed a critique of women's economic position in industrial society. Women, she argued, had made a major economic contribution in colonial times by helping with crops, caring for animals, and making cloth, clothing, soap, candles, and numerous other necessities. Industrialization began to remove these tasks from the home in the early nineteenth century, leaving some women exploited as factory workers and servants, and others idle as lazy, parasitical "ladies" who were forbidden to work at all. Peirce claimed that "for healthy, educated, intelligent adults by the millions to be supported by the extra toil of the rest of the community, as educated women are now, is a state of things entirely contrary to the natural division of labor . . . the most fruitful source of disorder, suffering and demoralization. . . . " [4] For women to regain the importance they had enjoyed in colonial times, she felt, they must be well organized, economically self-sufficient and emotionally independent of men. Agriculture and manufacturing were productive branches of the economy already dominated by men. Distribution and service industries were still developing, and Peirce believed that women could successfully take them over because of their role as consumers. This was the economic basis of her proposal for "cooperative housekeeping."

Cash on Delivery
What was "cooperative housekeeping"? As Peirce defined it, groups of twelve to fifty women would organize cooperative associations to perform all their domestic work collectively and charge their husbands for these services. Through membership fees, such a group could purchase a building to serve as its headquarters, furnish it with appropriate mechanical equipment for cooking, baking, laundry and sewing, and supply a cooperative store with provisions. One or two members would manage the association, and many members would work there, although some women might choose to develop other careers or spend more time with their children. Some workers in the association might be former servants, hired for their particular skills in cooking or sewing. All workers would dress comfortably, abandoning corsets for trousers and short skirts similar to those worn at Oneida. They would be paid wages equivalent to those paid to men for skilled work.

The association would charge retail prices for cooked food, laundry, clothing, and provisions — cash on delivery.[5] Yet because of the economies of scale in this system, achieved through the division and specialization of labor, and through increased mechanization, charges to households would be reasonable. The association would put an end to the private employment of cooks and maids (whom Peirce criticized as often inefficient and lazy) in middle-class households. It would enable many housewives to find time to use their broader talents. It would provide economic rewards for women who were efficient and skilled at domestic work, whether they were former mistresses or former servants. Indeed, Peirce hoped to bring "the whole moneyed and employed class among women into direct and responsible relations with the whole employed or industrial class"; she argued that women experienced at working together would be able to solve the problems of self-determination for women, despite the class barriers dividing them.[6]

Peirce's attitude toward the former servants who were to be involved in her scheme was, at best, ambivalent. On the one hand she insisted that all workers in a cooperative housekeeping society must become shareholders, but she planned to enforce this participation by deducting the cost of shares from wages. "The ultimate working of this rule in assisting the poor to become capitalists in a small way, and therefore in bridging the now ever-widening chasm between the moneyed and the working classes cannot be overestimated," she stated.[7] While her scheme was, in theory, uniting the middle-class sponsors and their former servants in a joint economic venture, she felt that in practice, managerial discipline should be maintained: "rigid superintendence . . . is necessary in order to keep the laundresses from *wasting their time!* This superintendence, or oversight, or 'bossing' — call it what you will — must at first be done, in turn, without compensation, by the members of the laundry committee and their substitutes, just as in charitable associations ladies take turns by the week or the month, in being the 'visitor' of the hospital

or the asylum which they sustain." [8] Thus all cooperative housekeepers were to share in the profits, according to the size of their investment in the venture, but the managers (presumably the larger investors) were to be responsible for output.

Urban Design

The vast changes in domestic organization which Peirce proposed had sweeping implications for neighborhood planning and housing design. She described the physical facilities (4.2) a cooperative housekeeping association would require:

On the first floor should be the counting room, sales room, consulting-room, and fitting room; on the second floor should be the working rooms; and on the third a dining-room (with dumb-waiter), a gymnasium, and a reading room: all of them being so connected that they could be thrown open in one suite when the co-operative housekeepers wished to give their workwomen a ball. The two lower floors should each have a comfortable dressing-room, with lounges, easy-chairs, and toilet conveniences; and not only health, but beauty and cheerfulness, should be consulted in the arrangement of the whole establishment.[9]

Her interest in movable walls and flexible spaces perhaps derived from Catharine Beecher.

When cooperating women had successfully established these industries in a central building, Peirce argued that women architects should design simplified houses without kitchens (4.3, 4.4) for family life:

. . . I am sure women would succeed in planning the loveliest and completest of homes. Houses without any kitchens and

4.2 Diagrammatic plan of headquarters for a
cooperative housekeeping society, drawn by Beth
Ganister from written descriptions by Melusina
Fay Peirce. Note the movable walls, which also
appeared in Catharine Beecher's designs for
dwellings in 1869.

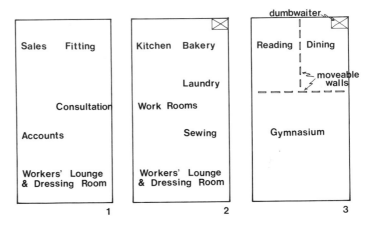

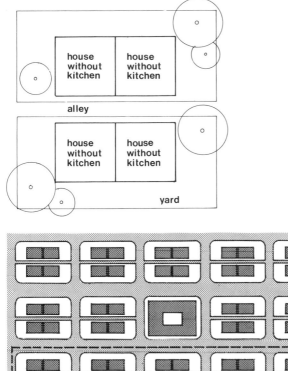

alley

yard

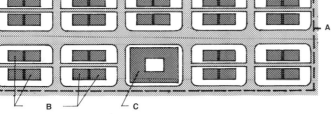

4.3 Diagram of block of four kitchenless houses, by Beth Ganister, based on descriptions by Melusina Fay Peirce

4.4 Diagrammatic plan of cooperative residential neighborhood (*A*), thirty-six kitchenless houses (*B*), and one cooperative housekeeping center (*C*), drawn by Paul Johnson from descriptions by Melusina Fay Peirce

"back-yards" in them! How fascinating! Think how much more beautiful city architecture will be now! The houses, instead of being built around a square, could be set in the middle of it. . . . Every tenth block would contain the kitchen and laundry and clothing house; and for these domestic purposes the Oriental style could be adopted, of interior courtyards with fountains and grass, secluded from the street.[10]

Just why she found the "oriental style" of the harems of the Middle East appropriate is unclear. She predicted that in western towns of intermediate size, where social hierarchies were not too rigidly established and women were used to doing their own housework without servants, cooperative housekeeping would have the best chance to develop. In rural areas, she argued, cooperative farming and cooperative housekeeping could work together, ending the exhaustion and even insanity caused by the isolation of some farm women. In big cities, many cooperative housekeeping societies might exist, and sort themselves out socially, but residents of a single apartment house could form groups to utilize the possibilities of this new housing type (just being introduced for the middle classes) most fully.

Her mention of the apartment house,[11] as well as kitchenless houses, indicated her interest in contemporary developments in urban housing. Before the Civil War most middle-class and upper-class families considered the detached house or the row house the only socially respectable habitations. Workers lived in crowded tenements, with several families to a floor, but one historian notes that before 1860 "it would have been unthinkable for a family of even modest social aspirations to live in anything but a private dwelling, however humble such a house might be." [12] After the Civil War, since urban land costs were very high, some new experiments were made. The terms "apartment house" and "French flats" romanticized middle-class multiple-family dwellings and distinguished them from workers' four- or five-story walk-up tenements, although one critic commented on the "sham elegance and general inconvenience" of such buildings on the West Side in New York.[13]

The social acceptance of the apartment house was enhanced by two multiple dwellings for the rich, one in Boston, the other in New York, completed between the mid-1850s and the late 1860s, the time of Peirce's experiment. Arthur Gilman designed the Hotel Pelham in Boston; Richard Morris Hunt created the Stuyvesant Buildings on Eighteenth Street in New York. These buildings had no common spaces, although Peirce argued that they would be appropriate. Within a few years the Haight House in New York introduced a common kitchen, dining room, and laundry. It combined twenty family suites with fifteen bachelor suites, and became "the chosen refuge of artistic and literary people." [14] Cummings & Sears, a firm of Boston architects, built a small apartment house with such services in 1873 in Boston (4.5, 4.6). Henry Hudson Holly, a well-known architect in New York, designed a cooperative "family hotel" in 1874 for a client in Hartford, Connecticut, with two-story units, some with street access, some reached by a third-floor corridor, all served by kitchen, laundry, dining room, and barber shop in the basement (4.7, 4.8). "Elevators, tram ways, and steam tight cars" were to be used for "the quick and cleanly distribution of food to the private dining rooms" included in each dwelling unit. Of great importance to one observer was the fact that the ingenious circulation system, with six private front doors on the street, in addition to the collective entrance, provided "the external appearance of a row of ordinary first class dwellings," while the new organization of domestic service, on the apartment hotel plan, provided more internal conveniences.[15]

In all these projects, the common facilities were economical and convenient, as the residents pointed out, but they did resemble the services of a boardinghouse, at a time when perhaps one American family out of five included boarders.[16] If the social respectability of the apartment house without any common rooms was in doubt, the status of the apartment house with common services was extremely uncertain. To many middle-class people, boarding implied promiscuity and crowding, later attacked by housing reformer Lawrence Veiller as the "lodger evil."

What might be acceptable for "artistic and literary people," or "Bohemians," was not for prosperous, socially ambitious, bourgeois families. Yet the standard New York lot, 25 feet by 100 feet, required row houses too large and expensive for most

young, middle-class families. As the debate between propriety and economy progressed, variations on the apartment house proliferated, as architects and residents attempted to find an acceptable physical, social, and economic form of urban bourgeois living. This conservative task was not made easier by feminists such as Peirce who seized upon the strongest collective interpretations of the apartment house they could formulate.

If several families were to live in one building such as the Hotel Pelham, she argued in 1869, why not provide the economies of a single kitchen and laundry? [17] What was architecturally difficult with a group of isolated, single dwellings was simple with an apartment block. Peirce's argument for cooperative housekeeping in multifamily dwellings was picked up by Associationists and by other communitarian reformers. The precedent for their arguments came from Charles Fourier, who, before his death in 1838, had identified the apartment blocks of Paris as an intermediate form of housing between the isolated dwelling and the phalanstery. He had suggested that apartment houses could introduce "guarantism," the sixth of eight stages leading to "harmony," or the perfected human society.[18] American followers of Fourier thus insisted that the apartment house was a more complex, more highly evolved form of human habitation than the row house. In the 1870s and 1880s Victoria Woodhull, Stephen Pearl Andrews, Marie Howland, and others reiterated Fourier's call for

4.5 Cummings & Sears, architects, Boston, view
of Hotel Kempton, a small apartment hotel,
from *American Architect and Building News,* June
1877. This structure covers its lot and rises five
and a half stories above the surrounding row
houses, showing the results of pressure to use
land more intensively.

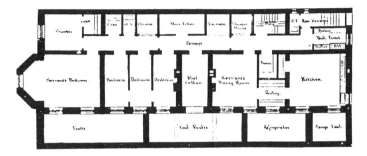

—BASEMENT PLAN.—

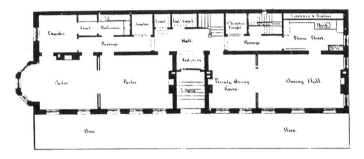
—FIRST FLOOR PLAN.—

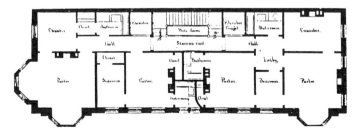

4.6 Cummings & Sears, plans of Hotel Kempton. Servants are housed in the basement, the
residents' dining room is on the first floor, and
nine apartments without kitchens are on floors
one through five.

4.7 Henry Hudson Holly, sketch of a proposed cooperative family hotel for Hartford, Connecticut, 1874. View shows six private entrances to duplex apartments from the street, plus main entrance in the center, from *Scribners Magazine,* May 1874. The architect is attempting to maintain the illusion of private row houses while increasing the density.

4.8 Holly, plans for a family hotel, showing kitchen, laundry, dining facilities, and barber shop in basement. Six private duplexes are entered on the first floor; an elevator beyond the main entrance leads to six more duplexes entered on the third floor, plus common services in basement and staff housing under the roof.

apartment houses with shared facilities, adding a demand for scientific child care.

Peirce's argument was also picked up by reformers interested in housing for the poor. Existing tenements in the 1860s and 1870s provided cramped, minimal workers' housing with little plumbing, which forced tenants to rely on public laundries and public baths. Nathan Meeker, an editor of the *New York Tribune,* suggested that perhaps a reorganization of tenement housing along the lines of apartment hotel design would make life more comfortable for the poor.[19]

All of this theorizing about collective life by utopian socialists, feminists, free love advocates, and sanitary reformers was, of course, contrary to the first intentions of the speculative builders of apartment houses. They wanted to assure prospective tenants that apartments would be just as quiet and private as conventional blocks, where the dwellings were arranged in vertical rows, rather than stacked in horizontal flats. These developers were anxious to promote the social respectability of their new housing, and they abhorred any connection with the forced economies of tenement life, or what they considered the promiscuous social meetings of communal groups. Although Peirce was unable to persuade any developers to try out her ideas for cooperative housekeeping in apartment houses in an American city, in later decades the reformers who succeeded her, such as Howland, Gilman, and Rodman, continued this campaign.

Economic Cooperation

Peirce observed developments in the cooperative movement in the United States as well as trends in the design of urban housing. By arguing that economic cooperation was the route toward women's self-determination, Peirce extended to women an argument familiar to many participants in the labor movements of her day. Beginning in the late 1830s, when a few Farmers and Mechanics Stores had been founded in Vermont and New Hampshire, the idea of consumer cooperatives had spread, largely through the efforts of the Working Men's Protective Union of Boston. By 1860 there were over eight hundred Protective Unions in New York, New England, and the midwest. The Protective Unions offered sickness and old age insurance as well as cooperative grocery stores. The members believed that the profits from Protective Union Stores should be invested in producers' cooperatives, arguing that this was a means of reorganizing society. Some enthisiasts proposed that regional trade between cooperatives producing cotton, flour, cloth, and shoes be established, with products transported on cooperative railroads and ships, as an economic alternative to capitalism. The promoters believed that the Protective Unions could also lead to new forms of housing: "We should proceed from combined shops to combined houses, to joint ownership in God's earth, the foundation that our edifice must stand upon." [20]

For Melusina Fay Peirce to see new kinds of economic power for women resulting from a cooperative store, kitchen, laundry, and bakery, was very much in the spirit of her times. In addition to consumers' cooperatives such as the Protective Unions, many producers' cooperatives had been formed by women after the Civil War. Some were organized by groups of women workers such as the seamstresses in Boston, Philadelphia, and Providence and the laundresses in Troy, New York. Others, such as the Working Women's Association in New York, were promoted by the middle-class feminists, Susan B. Anthony and Elizabeth Cady Stanton.[21] Peirce's proposals combined a consumers' cooperative with a producers' cooperative; she believed that the profits from grocery sales would help the cooks, laundresses, and seamstresses establish a profitable producers' cooperative. Though the mixing of the two types of cooperative enterprise left the roles of the founders ambiguous — they could choose to be customers or to be full-time workers — Peirce encouraged all housewives to work for wages. Thus, she tried to provide for the economic independence of housewives in a way that no consumers' cooperative could have done, despite the various insurance schemes some offered.

Her faith in the evolution of an egalitarian society based on such cooperative enterprises was not less than that of William Sylvis, founder of the National Labor Union, who argued in 1868 that monetary reform to support cooperatives would eventually make labor unions unnecessary, or of Uriah Stevens, founder of the Knights of Labor in 1869, whose program aimed at

the evolution of a cooperative society.[22] What distinguished Peirce's work was her incisive application of the cooperative logic to housewives, whose roles in domestic production and consumption had never before been considered in relation to the popular ideal of cooperative enterprise, outside of experimental socialist communities or informal housewives' arrangements.

Her firm belief in the validity of cooperation did draw on the experience of two earlier generations of women in her family. According to Sylvia Wright, the women of Melusina Peirce's home town, St. Albans, Vermont, organized themselves to do her mother's sewing in order to give her more time to develop her outstanding musical talents.[23] Still earlier, in 1834, Caroline Howard Gilman, Peirce's great-aunt, had suggested that male town officials in New England organize municipal cooked food services, or "grand cooking establishments," to spare housewives toil:

What a desideratum is a cooking establishment, where families can be provided with prepared food, and a still greater to have our meals brought to us, now that the improvements in steam can give them hotter than from our own hearths. They could probably be furnished cheaper than on the present plan. . . . A friend could *drop in* without disconcerting a family, and the lady of the house sit without a thorn. How many more smiles would kindle up around the domestic board, could the wife be assured of her husband's comfort. She has enough to do in the agitating responsibility of her maternal cares; her little ones may be sickly, her own health feeble.

How great a duty is it, then, to study modes of comfort, and preserve the song of cheerfulness in the routine of domestic industry. It is not below the task of legislation, if legislation is a study of the order and happiness of a community, or if legislators would have neat houses, good dinners, and smiling wives.[24]

In addition to her family's experience, Peirce surely knew of the quilting bees, still held in New England in the 1860s, as well as the earlier colonial practices of "change-work" and "the whang," where housewives helped each other with tasks in alternation or gathered in a group to speed a large job such as spring cleaning.[25]

Woman's Sphere and Womanhood Suffrage

Within her discussion of cooperative housekeeping Peirce included a note on "womanhood" suffrage. She argued that just as women could assert more control over their economic lives, so too they could take more control of their political affairs. She advised women not to wait for "manhood" suffrage but to gather in towns and cities, elect their own officers, and set up women's committees to deal with public issues such as education, health, and welfare. In December 1869 she spoke on "United Womanhood" at a meeting in New York called by Jane Cunningham Croly to form a Woman's Parliament. While some conservatives read this as a modest, "womanly" rejection of the "male" franchise, Peirce was a consistent advocate of separate spheres of work for women and men. She and Croly were actually proposing an early version of the "municipal housekeeping" strategy later accepted by many suffrage campaigners who used women's role in the home to justify their concerns about urban life.

For Peirce, womanhood suffrage did not mean deferring to male authority. Peirce advocated direct, voluntary action by women, whether taking up political responsibilities or organizing collective housework: "For women to ask for the right of regulating their own affairs [is] . . . simply ridiculous, they possess it already." [26] Her lack of respect for male power was both the most appealing aspect of her work and the most difficult to carry through in practice. Although she believed that "womanhood suffrage" could develop without men's approval, she conceded that cooperative housekeeping societies might require the approval of "councils of Gentlemen" in their financial organization. Here Peirce made a serious ideological compromise, and one that did not pass unnoticed. Stanton and Anthony's paper, *The Revolution*, praised Peirce's scheme but labelled the Council of Gentlemen as "licking of the male boot." [27]

The House on Bow Street

Between November 1868 and March 1869, Zina Peirce's articles reached a broad audience through the *Atlantic Monthly*, with her cries of protest about women's situation and her proposed solution, to develop domestic work on a sound financial basis through the organized buying power of cooperative housekeeping. Her social circle in Cambridge was a wide one, where she was liked and respected; intellectual support

led to practical support. On the evening of
May 6, 1869, the Cambridge Cooperative
Housekeeping Society had its first meeting,
at the Quincy Street house of Melusina
Peirce's in-laws, Professor and Mrs. Benjamin Peirce. She attracted many Harvard
professors and their wives and daughters,
as well as literary figures and activists. The
group included men and women of all
ages, from their mid-twenties to late sixties.
More than half of the men were Harvard
faculty members, including the Director of
the Harvard College Observatory, the
Dean of Students, the Dean of the Divinity
School, and the curator of the Zoological
Museum. Another had been the Democratic candidate for governor of Massachusetts, and several were influential editors. It
was, in other words, the university establishment, but connections to radical movements were not lacking, especially connections to antebellum communitarian
experiments of the Fourierist persuasion.
Those who attended the first meeting included Mary Peabody Mann, whose
brother-in-law, Nathaniel Hawthorne, was
a former member of Brook Farm, and William Dean Howells, novelist and editor,
whose wife, Elinor Mead Howells, was a
niece of John Humphrey Noyes, the leader
of the Oneida Community. Howells himself later wrote two utopian novels entitled
The Altrurian Romances, as well as journalistic articles about the Shakers. Although
some of Peirce's supporters had family connections to communitarian experiments,
their aim was not communal living but a
businesslike collective arrangement.

At subsequent gatherings a statement
was drafted, calling for a public meeting:

The undersigned, citizens of Cambridge,
invite those who may feel interested, to
meet, at some time and place to be appointed, to consider the subject of *Cooperative Housekeeping.* They desire to learn, by
actual experiment, whether it is possible to
apply to the Manufactures of the Household — namely, Cooking, Laundry-work,
and the making of Garments — the
methods which are found indispensable in
every other department of modern industry
— the combination of Capital, and the
Division and Organization of Labor.[28]

Zina Peirce was ready to begin an experiment as soon as suitable headquarters
could be established and new members
recruited.

Seventy-five to one hundred women
filled the "room back of the Post Office" in
Cambridge on June 10, 1869, to hear Zina
Peirce describe her experiment. This gathering was reported in newspapers in Boston, New York, and London.[29] On July 6,
1869, a constitution was approved, and
committees to seek building lots were appointed.[30] On October 5, 1869, a prospectus, signed by thirty-three women subscribers and two bachelors, Gordon McKay
and Thomas Sergeant Perry, was printed
and circulated to encourage additional
subscriptions. It stated that women in
nine towns were ready to begin similar
ventures.[31]

In the next few months many women
and men were active on the society's committees. Some discussion of purchasing an
old armory came up in November 1869,
but the group eventually voted to rent the

old Meacham House on Bow Street for its headquarters. By December 1869 a board of managers was established.[32] On April 20, 1870, the first regular meeting at the new Bow Street headquarters took place and Mrs. G. W. C. Noble was elected as the new president. Mrs. E. M. Richardson was running the laundry; Mrs. Mann, the bakery. By July 1870 the laundry was directed by Peirce, who managed to break even financially. A committee of men was called in to help drum up business for the store and kitchen, which had not yet opened.[33] Still, many families were away for the summer, and not much happened. By October 1870, when business had not picked up, Peirce understood that a good number of her acquaintances had joined the society without intending to see it through.

Other more committed women were struggling with their husbands' animosity, according to Peirce.[34] "What!" said one man she described as a distinguished Cambridge abolitionist, "*my* wife 'cooperate' to make other men comfortable? No indeed!" Another husband complained that the directors came too often to his wife's house for meetings, and on one occasion, he was furious because he had to wait for the end of a meeting before his wife would sew on a button for him. A third husband permitted his wife to pay her subscription on the condition that she promise never to attend any meetings. A fourth husband would not let his wife become president because if the society failed he felt it might "injure *his* position." Another

hostile man convinced his widowed mother that the society was mismanaged. She had time to spare and became a "thorn in the side" of the managers.

The managers themselves were at first chagrined at the men's opposition and the members' lack of patronage for the society. Then some of them avoided the society's rooms, and only one or two women really worked to make the enterprise succeed. Peirce's husband kept imploring her to give it all up and join him in Europe on a scientific expedition, and for several months in the winter of 1870, she did.[35] In light of the harassment the women received, it is significant, perhaps, that Charles Peirce, Howells, Fisk, Perry, and others among the members' husbands launched an elite Cambridge dinner group, "The Club," which met for all-male dinners on the second Tuesday of every month in the members' homes in 1870. Although scholars have assumed that these eminent men met to discuss intellectual matters, probably their wives' plans to alter their subordinate status and become self-supporting came in for a great deal of ridicule and sabotage, since the men's private behavior was often patronizing.[36]

By April 1871, the Bow Street house was closed. Only twelve of forty member households had given their patronage to the laundry and store. The kitchen had never opened. The society dissolved with the unanimous vote of the Council of Gentlemen, who were true to the middle-class model Peirce had once described. Most of them never forbade their wives to undertake the project, but merely thought them "unnatural, discontented, ambitious, unfeminine." Peirce judged that "a few men sustained the attempt most loyally, but most of the husbands laughed good-naturedly at the whole thing, prophesied its failure, and put their wives out of heart and out of conceit with it from the beginning." [37] She reserved her special rage for "HUSBAND-POWER which is very apt to shut down like an invisible bell-glass over every woman as soon as she is married," and she excoriated the husband of one subscriber, who attended the final meeting on the question of continuance, "determined that the attempt should end then and there," despite the fact that his wife was not an active member.[38] He prevailed. At the time of dissolution, other husbands described themselves as wanting to "prevent misconception on the subject of feasibility of cooperation in this community." [39]

Falling Back on Polemic
Although Melusina Fay Peirce found her practical experience of cooperation in Cambridge frustrating, she was more and more acclaimed as a theoretician of cooperative endeavor. Her articles were discussed in the frontier homes of Greeley, Colorado, and the drawing rooms of London.[40] Her influence in England was at least as great as it was in the United States. In June 1869, a British journal, *The Cooperator,* reprinted extracts from her articles, and they were issued as a book in London and Edinburgh in 1870. The book was subtitled *Romance in Domestic Economy,* and the frontis-

piece showed a couple in a sailboat with the woman at the helm. Following the publication of Peirce's work, a spate of articles and building designs celebrated this new advance in social theory, for England had its full share of Fourierists actively proselytizing for "associated homes" and "social palaces," as well as passionate "cooperators" following the example of the Rochdale weavers, and canny real estate developers initiating the apartment hotel. A long and favorable article on Peirce, published in 1873 and written by Mrs. E. M. King, an active feminist, was followed by a second article and plans for an elaborate "cooperative home" by the well-known British architect, E. W. Godwin, published in *The Building News* in 1874.[41] His drawings showed spaces for cooperative child care (4.9). Three years later Roswell Fisher argued "The Practical Side of Cooperative Housekeeping," on behalf of Queen Anne's Mansions, a residential hotel, "no socialist utopia, but merely the application of modern economical principles and mechanical appliances." [42]

In the mid 1870s, after the Cambridge experiment was finished, Peirce herself traveled in Europe in search of new insights. On a trip to London, she met Thomas Hughes and E. O. Greening, leaders of the British cooperative movement. She visited the Union cooperative stores in London, and in August 1875, in Berlin, met Frau Lina Morgenstern, the organizer of the Housekeepers' Union, a cooperative store with four thousand members, and the founder of public kitchens

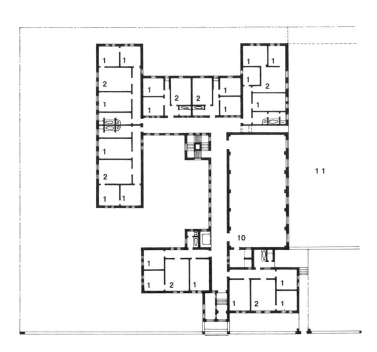

GROUND

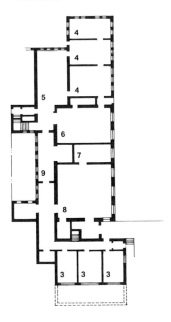

BASEMENT

4.9 E. W. Godwin, plans for a cooperative home, with kitchenless apartments, general dining room and lounge, children's dining room, nursery school, and playroom, *The Building News* (London), April 24, 1874. Basement and first floor: 1, bedroom; 2, sitting room; 3, storage; 4, servant's room; 5, children's dining room; 6, children's playroom; 7, scullery; 8, kitchen; 9, servants' hall; 10, general dining room; 11, children's playground.

(8.6) serving the poor. Upon her return, she addressed the Fourth Woman's Congress in Philadelphia, October 4, 1876, about the success of cooperation in England and the prospects for it in the United States among women.[43] Appended to her address was a new set of rules for experiments in cooperative housekeeping. She was then forty years old and had been separated from her husband for about a year.

In the fall of 1880 Peirce was invited to address the Illinois Social Science Association, and she developed the text of her talk into a book, *Cooperative Housekeeping: How Not To Do It and How To Do It, A Study in Sociology.* Her feminist rhetoric was sharper than ever, especially in trenchant asides to the main argument:

No despotism of man over man that was ever recorded was at once so absolute as the despotism — the dominion of men over women. It covers not only the political area. It owns not only the bodies of its subjects. Its hand lies heavily on their innermost personality, and its power is so tremendous that whatever they are, it is because these absolute lords have willed it.[44]

Criticizing a historian "of the English people," who "hardly alludes to the existence of one-half of that people, its women, from one end of his work to the other," Peirce noted that "the absolute obliviousness of women by men is most extraordinary. . . . In view of all its incalculable consequences, it is the most colossal fact in history." [45] Warning women of "HUSBAND-POWER," exhorting them to take control of their lives, reiterating her criticisms of

middle-class women's idleness and lack of economic power, she once again asserted that cooperative housekeeping was the solution to women's problems. Yet another set of rules for an experiment was attached, and a plea for women to elect an all-female "Woman's House," through "womanhood" suffrage. She predicted that it would take the place of the U.S. Senate,[46] when women became economically more powerful through developing cooperative housekeeping.

The effects of her book were wide-ranging. A suffragist in the *Woman's Journal* scorned her strategy: "Try again, Mrs. Peirce, when we have placed in your hands and in those of your fellow-workers that wonderful little lever entitled the ballot. Depend upon it, you will then be better treated!" [47] Male reviewers were both intrigued and fearful. The *New York Times* congratulated her for "telling women many harsh truths about themselves," but warned the author about making equally strong criticisms of men. "This peppery element does her cause no good. . . . Let her concentrate her fire on woman and paint her blacker than she deserves, if by so doing she may be goaded into the change which is to turn the domestic inferno into a cooperative paradise." [48] The *New York Daily Tribune* called her "somewhat extravagant in her conclusions, wild in many of her statements, and often hysterical in manner," while commending "sensible suggestions" likely to become "at no distant day the basis of a domestic reform." The reviewer suggested that some energetic young ladies "give the plan a fair, persevering trial." [49]

Although quite a few women took this advice and launched experiments on Peirce's plan, later reformers often received more credit for the idea of cooperative housekeeping than Peirce herself. During the years after 1871, when the Cambridge experiment ended, Peirce lived in Cambridge, New York, and Chicago, and was active in many other groups dealing with women's education and culture, promoting such causes as the founding of Radcliffe College, the Boston Woman's Education Association, and the establishment of a women's orchestra. She helped her sister Amy in her musical career and worked as a music critic in Boston and Chicago. She campaigned for better street cleaning and historic preservation. She completed *New York, A Symphonic Study,* a long novel about the difficulties of family life and isolated housekeeping in 1892. In 1903, at age sixty-seven, she restated her lifelong interest in improved housing design when she patented a design for duplex apartments with gallery access. The building would have suited cooperative housekeeping admirably but Peirce confined herself to pointing out many varied activities which could be included on its roof story (4.10).

As she grew older, Peirce became less inventive and more conservative. Anti-immigration propaganda was included in the same volume with her novel when it appeared in 1918, and all her exhortations took on a fanatical fervor, urging the participation of "world-brothers" and

"world-sisters" in two universal industries, "national farming," and "national housekeeping," through which she argued, poverty and immorality could be eliminated. At age eighty-two she was crotchety as well as moralistic, complaining that Edward Bellamy and Charlotte Perkins Gilman had stolen her ideas.[50] Certainly she anticipated almost everything both of them had to say on the subject of domestic industry in the future. Later writers on domestic life, such as Mary Livermore, Ellen S. Richards, Mary Hinman Abel, Helen Campbell, Lucy Salmon, and Arthur Calhoun noted Peirce's work, but for the most part others adopted and altered her programs without adequate acknowledgment.[51] Her version of cooperative housekeeping was an extraordinary synthesis of popular and unorthodox political sentiments: her work attracted and repelled capitalists and socialists, antifeminists and feminists. Later theorists tried to be less controversial.

In her praise of industrial methods, Peirce sounds like many American capitalists of her times, viewing a profitable new field of endeavor. Her rhapsodies over the specialization and division of labor, her contempt for unskilled workers, her plans for training skilled domestic workers, appeal to the entrepreneurial capitalist. Her arrangements for workers, such as lounges, a gymnasium, an eight-hour day, dress reform, and pay for women at male wage levels, would put her among the most benevolent capitalists. Yet when she offered to bring the moneyed class of women into

4.10 Melusina Fay Peirce, patent for apartment
house, Chicago, 1903

responsible relations with the servant class, in aid of women's greater self-reliance, and admitted that this was not a profit-making scheme but a cooperative economic strategy aimed at women's power, she alienated the very businessmen who might have found her techniques appealing.

In her faith in the power of voluntary "association" or "cooperation," and in her belief that one successful cooperative housekeeping society would serve as a model for others across the country, Peirce accepted the strategy of the Rochdale co-operators, as well as that of the American communitarian socialists, whose successful experiments at New Lebanon, Amana, and Oneida were in the public eye. Thus she borrowed the argument of leaders who urged idealists to secede from capitalist society and form more egalitarian cooperative communities. But when she urged women to secede from the existing domestic world, and form more egalitarian, cooperative housekeeping centers in American cities and towns, she pushed "cooperation" to a new extreme. Many men of the cooperative movement felt very threatened by female separatism, especially if they, as husbands, were suddenly to be asked to pay for household work performed by "lady-co-operators."

In her belief in separate spheres of economic and political activity for women and men, and in her desire to develop women's traditional skills in domestic work, Peirce echoed the views of very conventional women. Yet women like Catharine Beecher, who believed in the sacredness of women's sphere and in women's commitment to domestic life, must have been shocked by Peirce's insistence that women begin to charge money for domestic work. As a feminist separatist who wished to control the domestic economy, Peirce outraged the same women who were at first drawn to her proposals because of the high value she placed on domestic skills.

In her desire to improve society through women's associations, Peirce attracted many of the more politically minded women of her times. During the Civil War many American women had developed their skills as administrators and public speakers on behalf of abolition or war relief. Peirce was part of a postwar spirit of sisterly association, soon to become the basis of a national network of women's clubs and the suffrage, temperance, and municipal housekeeping movements. Yet her ideas were not often acceptable to middle-class women who saw women's networks as a way to do good for others, rather than for themselves. This response was exemplified in the New England Women's Club.

The New England Women's Club was founded in 1868 "to organize the social force of the women of New England, now working in small circles and solitary ways." [52] Members included many of the most distinguished women in New England: Elizabeth Peabody and Mary Peabody Mann, Louisa May Alcott, Julia Ward Howe, Caroline Severance, Kate Field, Ednah Cheney, Abby May, Dr. Harriot Hunt. Following the publication of Peirce's articles, they launched an extensive discussion in 1869 of the establishment of public kitchens, laundries, nurseries, sewing exchanges, and industrial schools.[53] Their goal was to help women factory workers and domestic servants support themselves and their children through skilled work. While Mary Peabody Mann was a member of Peirce's experiment, most of the other feminists in this group were not interested in participating as workers in cooperative housekeeping because they were professionals and political activists. So, their plans for the Boston Women's Educational and Industrial Union included both a professional placement service for middle-class women and an exchange for domestic servants, as well as a public kitchen.

Peirce demanded that middle-class women confront the pressing contradictions in their own lives (economic dependence on men and economic exploitation of their domestic servants) before they attacked the larger issues of economic deprivation or political representation. In her pragmatic insistence that justice and charity begin at home, and in her stubborn assertion that middle-class women should use their energies to change their own domestic condition, Peirce pushed many middle-class suffragists and clubwomen of her own era far closer to modern "consciousness raising" than many of them were prepared to go. Thus she often offended the suffragists and socialists who believed that winning political representation or developing strategies to aid workers were more important than having women take economic

control of domestic life and deal with conflicts of both gender and class on this basis.

A woman of extraordinary talent and energy, Peirce displayed great agility in exploiting the weak points of industrial capitalism or consumer cooperation, traditional conceptions of the home or bourgeois feminism. She merged radical ideas of industrial cooperation and conservative approaches to the separateness of women's work because she was seeking a practical economic basis for women's economic self-determination. Cooperative housekeeping was for her a strategy of attack reflecting more fundamental aims:

Cooperative housekeeping may be wholly practical or wholly visionary. But two things women must do somehow, as the conditions not only of the future happiness, progress, and elevation of their sex, but of its bare respectability and morality.
1st. They *must* earn their own living.
2nd. They *must* be organized among themselves.[54]

Whatever the fate of Melusina Fay Peirce's practical attempts to organize her friends and neighbors, her imaginative proposals for new domestic settings, as well as her critique of traditional domestic ideology, spurred others to invention. Some, like Edward Bellamy, minimized the idea of women's economic power through proposals for nationalized domestic industry, while others, like Charlotte Perkins Gilman, avoided the idea of decentralized socialism through proposals for large-scale domestic industry on a capitalist basis, without neighborhood cooperation. Yet the original vision of "cooperative housekeeping" is Melusina Fay Peirce's, with its insights about the design of housing and the organization of neighborhoods.

Peirce took several incompatible popular ideas of her time — technological development, consumer cooperation, female separatism, and women's clubs — and forced each to its logical conclusion. Capitalists could not accept her ideal of nonprofit cooperation. Cooperators could not understand her feminist separatism. Conservative advocates of "women's sphere" found her emphasis on women's economic power distasteful, while advocates of women's legal rights were frustrated by her insistence that women deal first with the issues raised in their domestic lives. In sum, she had a genius for making everyone uncomfortable, because she attacked the interlocked oppression of gender and class in a new way.

5.1 Marie Stevens Howland, 1886, at the age of fifty

Sexual freedom, then, means the abolition of pros-
titution, both in and out of marriage. . . .
Ultimately, it means more than this even, it means
the establishment of cooperative homes. . . .
— *Victoria Woodhull,* Tried As By Fire, or
The True and the False, Socially, 1874

Have the most perfect isolated family possible, it
cannot supply the conditions for integral growth to
the young, nor can it afford sufficient leisure and
freedom from care to the adults. . . .
— *Marie Howland,* 1880

Free Lovers,
Individual Sovereigns,
and Integral Cooperators

Recruitment of a Radical

Melusina Fay Peirce lobbied for cooperative housekeeping, but an extremely conventional sense of Victorian propriety lay behind her insistence that women's "pure and elevating feminine influence" should prevail in a world threatened by "desire" and "lust." Marie Stevens Howland (5.1), Peirce's exact contemporary and an equally powerful critic of the isolated household, took an opposite view of traditional sexual morality, calling "the loss of respectability as defined by hypocrites and prudes," a woman's first step toward "broad sympathies for humanity." [1] While Peirce moved among the literary and intellectual luminaries of Cambridge and Boston, Howland associated with cultural radicals, trade unionists, sex reformers, and socialists in France, the United States, and Mexico. She lived in many experimental communities, and in between campaigns for cooperative housekeeping, she painted quotations from Fourier on her doors.

Despite her unconventional lifestyle, Howland knew what it meant to earn her living. Like Peirce, she believed in economic independence for women. Her first proposal for cooperative housekeeping involved an ideal factory, making the workplace rather than the residential neighborhood the focus of these activities. For her economic independence required not only cooperative housekeeping services for employed women, but also scientific child care. In the 1880s Howland collabo-

rated on the first plan for a city of kitchenless houses and apartment hotels with extensive child care facilities, developing some of the urban implications of these new forms of domestic organization.

Born in 1836 in Lebanon, New Hampshire, Marie Stevens became a radical when she moved to Lowell, Massachusetts, in her early teens, finding work to support her two younger sisters after her father's death.[2] Lowell, founded in 1821, was "the city of spindles," admired by many European visitors. The owners of this industrial town recruited Yankee farm women, boasted about the operatives' contentment, and hailed the opportunities for self-improvement available to them through literary circles and lending libraries. Women operatives were housed in substantial brick boardinghouses, whose sober and well-proportioned facades hid crowded accommodations (5.2). Boardinghouse keepers enforced a strict work regimen, promptness at meals, and weekly religious observance.

As Thomas Dublin has noted, "The central institution in the female community was the corporation boarding house," and "the boarding house, with an average of twenty-five female boarders sleeping four to six in a bedroom, was above all a collective living situation." The boardinghouse residents developed unusual social and political cohesion, which supported their involvement in the strikes of the 1830s and 1840s. The boardinghouses, as "focal points of female labor protest," according

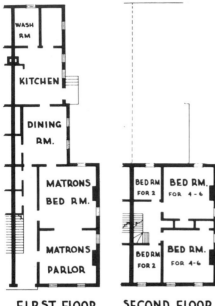

WASH RM

KITCHEN

DINING RM.

MATRONS BED RM.

MATRONS PARLOR

FIRST FLOOR

BED RM FOR 2 | BED RM. FOR 4-6

BEDRM FOR 2 | BED RM. FOR 4-6

SECOND FLOOR

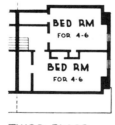

BED RM FOR 4-6

BED RM FOR 4-6

THIRD FLOOR

5.2 Boardinghouse, Lowell, plans from John Coolidge, *Mill and Mansion* (Columbia University Press)

to Dublin, "provided both the participants in and the organizational structure of the labor movement in Lowell in these years." [3] One Lowell operative, Lucy Larcom, recorded the support that "stranger girls" in Lowell gave each other, which changed their consciousness of social and economic life: "Home-life, when one always stays at home, is necessarily narrowing. . . . We have hardly begun to live until we can take in the idea of the whole human family . . . it was an incalculable help to find myself among so many working-girls, all of us thrown upon our own resources, but thrown much more upon each other's sympathies. . . ." [4]

Through the 1830s and 1840s, as the operatives, harassed by wage cuts and speedups, became militant, they published the *Voice of Industry,* which criticized "capitalists and politicians." They also organized campaigns for the ten-hour day and testified in state hearings on worsening industrial conditions. Eliza Hemingway, a Lowell worker, complained in 1845 of the long working hours (5:00 a.m. to 7:00 p.m., with half-hour breaks for breakfast and dinner) and the foul air, filled with lint from the looms and smoke from kerosene lamps. [5] Marie Stevens, after working for years under similar conditions, was in charge of four looms in the factory where she was employed. She acquired an independent industrial worker's contempt for idle, middle-class women who throught of themselves as virtuous "ladies" and looked down upon women who earned their own living. After her stint in Lowell she found

other ways of supporting herself, becoming
a student of phonography (an early form
of shorthand), and then working as a
teacher in the Five Points slum district in
New York in the 1850s. She attended normal school at night, and by 1857, at age
21, she was appointed principal of Primary
School Number 11 in New York. That
same year she married Lyman W. Case, a
radical lawyer from Winsted, Connecticut.
She would continue to think of employed
women, including those with children, as a
constituency for reform in domestic life,
despite changes in her profession and her
milieu.

Marie Stevens met Case at The Club,
where New Yorkers with a taste for cultural radicalism gathered around the flamboyant Stephen Pearl Andrews. (His group
is not to be confused with the Cambridge,
Massachusetts men's group of the same
name.) Andrews was an anarchist philosopher, a pioneer sociologist, and an important writer on sexual morality. In the 1850s
and 1860s he organized various salons for
free-loving "individual sovereigns." The
first was the League Union of the Men of
Progress, which met in a small hall on
Bond Street beginning in 1855. The departments of the League were called Grand
Orders, and Andrews' biographer relates
that "to students of society he offered a
Grand Order of the Social Relations which
aimed at an equally 'grand Domestic Revolution.' " [6] As part of this revolution he
advocated development of "the baby
world," defined as nurseries for fifty to one
hundred children, under the direction of

"scientific and professional nurses, matrons,
and physiologists," who would provide sex
education for their charges as well as child
care. The younger generation would be
prepared for free love while the older generation practiced it, since the scheme
would allow the mothers of young children
greater freedom to participate in free love,
one aspect of the "passional attraction"
Andrews thought of as "the highest law
governing individual conduct." [7]

New Yorkers responded enthusiastically
to Andrews and his Fourierist vocabulary.
A theory of passional attraction, had, after
all, been introduced in the pages of the
New York *Tribune* by Horace Greeley and
Albert Brisbane in the 1840s. Believers in
passional attraction flocked to the League
Union, and then to The Club, or the
Grand Order of Recreation, which Andrews established above Taylor's Saloon at
555 Broadway.

One could find feminists, anarchists, and
radical chic hangers-on at The Club: a
journalist reported "bloomerites in panta-
loons and round hats, partisans of individual liberty late of Modern Times, atheists,
infidels and philosophers" side by side with
"perfumed exquisites from Gotham." [8] Yet
many serious-minded women were part of
this group. Howland identified Jane Cunningham Croly as the "mistress of ceremo-
nies" there, with a "handsome badge of
office." Croly, a successful journalist, the
first American woman to become a syndi-
cated columnist, was the founder, in 1869,
of Sorosis, one of the earliest women's clubs
in the United States, and the organizer of

the Woman's Parliament presided over by Melusina Peirce that same year. According to one scholar, she was also the anonymous author of *The Truth about Love,* a book admired by advocates of free love for its statements that conventional sexual institutions, such as monogamous marriage, were "organized lies." [9]

While readers of the popular press in the 1850s were outraged at revelations of free love at The Club, the discussions which were held there seem quite conservative by twentieth-century standards. The issue was defined in terms of free unions versus legal marriage. As an advocate of "individual sovereignty," Andrews and his disciples claimed that "Man and Woman who do love can live together in Purity without any mummery at all." [10] Mary Gove Nichols and Thomas Low Nichols, associates of Andrews and residents of Modern Times, an anarchist community located on Long Island, developed, in the mid-1850s, a motto which stressed rather stricter conditions for sexual intercourse: "Freedom, fraternity, chastity." [11] Freedom meant the absence of religious or state coercion; fraternity expressed the presence of "passional attraction" or intense spiritual affinity; and chastity implied that intercourse must be for the purpose of procreation.

In a period when moralists prescribed conventional marriage and motherhood as the ideal for all women, it is not surprising that some independent women were ready to listen to discussions of child care and "passional attraction," which promised them more autonomy. Thus "free love" for

the Nicholses and many other sex reformers meant the freedom to reject as well as to accept any sexual advances, including the advances of a legal husband. Hal Sears, in *The Sex Radicals,* shows how free love could become a feminist demand, and also, at the end of the century, a demand that could be linked to Women's Christian Temperance Union campaigns for social purity, if free lovers belonged to the faction arguing that sexual intercourse was only an occasion for procreation. Within the free love movement he locates the exclusivist and varietist factions: "Although both factions generally held that, for sexual purposes, true love created true marriage, the exclusivists argued that such love could exist only between two people; whereas the varietists held that love, like lust, was general rather than specific in its objects, and therefore it naturally sought plurality and variety in its arrangments." [12] Even among the varietists, female autonomy prevailed over license. As Angela Heywood explained, "One is not a Free Lover because she cohabits with one or more men, or with none at all, but rather by the import and tone of Association." [13]

In the atmosphere of The Club, Marie Stevens, at age nineteen, began to hear some of the free lovers' arguments which she would develop herself in later life. Lyman Case, her mentor and first husband, played Henry Higgins to her Eliza Doolittle. She remembered that he "was always coaching me in speech, manners, movements, etc., etc." [14] He taught her languages, including Latin, and he persuaded

her to come to live with him in Stephen
Pearl Andrews's next experiment, the
"Unitary Household" in New York. Although The Club was raided by the police
on October 18, 1855, producing journalistic coverage which, according to one historian, was "only equalled by the fall of
Sebastopol and the arrival from Artic regions of Dr. Kane," [15] neither police inves-
tigations nor hostile publicity restrained
Andrews's entrepreneurial spirit. Fourierist
Albert Brisbane and others went to jail,
briefly; Andrews attempted to organize the
Unitary Household, a new urban community, which incorporated some of his ideas
for a "grand domestic revolution."

The Unitary Household was a large
boardinghouse run on a cooperative basis,
in some ways an urban version of a
Fourierist phalanstery. Established in May
1858 in a house on Stuyvesant Street, it
was moved in February 1859 to a group of
row houses located at 106 East Fourteenth
Street. Individuals and families, twenty residents in all, lived in private suites and
shared common parlors and dining rooms.
The domestic responsibilities were not
shared by the residents, however, but were
managed by one individual, Edward Underhill, and his staff. Underhill had previously worked as a factory operative,
actor, stenographer, and journalist. He was
a strong advocate of free love but claimed
that his only goal for the Unitary Household was

. . . to test the practicability of a cooperative household succeeding under individual
membership, as contrasted with the major-

ity rule of a joint stock association . . . if
people could trust their persons in a public
car, and their children in a public school,
without fear of defilement, I could not see
why they could not with equal safety trust
themselves within a common parlor, par-
take of meals in a common dining-room,
and permit their children to use a common
play-room.[16]

Underhill's and Andrews's insistence on
private space as a requirement for "individual sovereignty" and their choice of an
urban location distinguished this experiment from other communitarian settlements and made it a forerunner of the
many urban apartment hotels built in the
last quarter of the nineteenth century.

The *New York Times* approvingly described the Stuyvesant Street household
under the headline, "Practical Socialism in
New York":

On the first floor, there are two handsome
parlors, lighted by gas, furnished with
taste, adorned with pictures, and provided
with such musical instruments as a harp,
piano, and guitar. In the rear of the parlors
is an extension, in which is the general
dining-room. One table is set for all the inhabitants of four floors. Except at table,
each family retains its own privacy. The
necessary number of servants is provided. . . .[17]

The manager gave each resident a bill
once a week, and the *Times* agreed that the
scheme "proves that aggregation insures
economy." The reporter explained that

The Free-Lovers . . . have invented a
large programme, and . . . some of them,
at least, have begun to do what Mr.
Charles Fourier, and the philosophers of
Brook Farm after him, vainly attempted to

accomplish — unite different families, under a single system of regulations, live cheaply, and what is more curious than all the rest, introduce into the heart of New York, without noise or bluster, a successful enterprise based on Practical Socialism.[18]

With the move to the large space on Fourteenth Street, the community, now numbering about a hundred residents, gained such status as an urban social innovation that it was visited by John Humphrey Noyes from the Oneida Community and Elder Frederick Evans of the Shaker community at New Lebanon, New York.[19] Included among the permanent residents were Underhill; Andrews and his wife; Marie Stevens and her husband, Lyman Case; the poet Edmund Clarence Stedman; and a young journalist, Edward Howland, who was to become Marie Stevens's second husband, with Lyman Case's approval.

The excellent public relations which the Free Lovers' Unitary Household first established with the local press did not last. When the Unitary Household broke up in 1860, the *Times* assailed it as "a positive triumph of lust," in an "Expose" discouraging readers who might have been intrigued by the earlier review. This new article pronounced that "if the morals of the house were bad, the physical discomfort was worse. In no way was the "Unitary Household" a success, and in no way did it approach to economy or decency." [20] The Civil War hastened the Unitary Household's dissolution, and during the early 1860s Marie Stevens Case and

Edward Howland left the group and traveled to Guise, France, to see the new Familistère, which was then being built under the direction of Jean-Baptiste-André Godin, Fourier's leading disciple in Europe.

The Social Palace
The Familistère, begun in 1859, represented the ultimate Fourierist attempt to finance and develop an experimental cooperative industrial community. It offered a far more elaborate set of household and day care arrangements than the Unitary Household of New York. It rested on a far more substantial economic base (a flourishing ironworks making stoves of Godin's design) than any American Fourierist experiment, such as the North American Phalanx or Brook Farm, had been able to develop. Approximately three hundred and fifty workers and their families lived in the buildings of the Familistère, or "Social Palace," at Guise (2.3, 2.4, 2.5). They bought their supplies from cooperative shops, used the restaurant, cafe, theater, nursery, and educational facilities, and enjoyed profit sharing, as well as sickness and old age insurance.

Marie Stevens Case and Edward Howland developed detailed analyses of the domestic arrangements of the Familistère for the popular press in the United States. Readers admired the centrally heated apartments and large interior courtyards, but they regarded the child care facilities with absolute amazement, since the Familistère offered developmental

child care in spaces designed especially for
children. At the Familistère, children were
cared for in a nursery from birth to
twenty-six months, then in a *pouponnat* up
to four years, and in a *bambinat* to six years,
until they entered primary school (5.3). In
the nursery, great care was spent in designing the perfect individual cradle, which
was filled with bran, to eliminate dust.
Moisture caused the bran to form pellets,
which could easily be removed without the
need to bathe the child or change linen.
The nursery also included a special device
for teaching young children to walk, a circular structure of supports surrounding a
center filled with toys and games. The idea
of the kindergarten movement that learning should be fun influenced these arrangements. Full development of children's
abilities was emphasized, rather than rigid
order. The hours of care were matched to
the needs of employed mothers, in much
the same way that Robert Owen had envisioned, but Guise was without all the neoclassical trappings of his Institute for the
Formation of Character at New Lanark.

In American cities in the 1850s, 1860s
and 1870s, care for the children of employed mothers was only occasionally
available; often such children were sent to
orphanages or placed in foster homes. If
they lived with employed mothers, during
the workday they might be tied to a bed-
post or left to wander in the streets. The
New York Hospital's Nursery for the Children of Poor Women (5.4) was an attempt
at care, in 1854, along hygenic lines — children from six weeks to six years were first

washed and then dressed in hospital
clothes before admission for the day. In-
fants were provided with wet nurses.[21] In
France, the crèche system for children, run
by nuns, was a bit less tied to sanitary
precautions, but still extremely discipline-
oriented (5.5). In Germany, Froebel introduced the kindergarten and the ideal of
developmental care which would educate
children. Elizabeth Peabody opened the
first American kindergarten in Boston in
1860, but kindergartens were not available
for children of families of limited means
until Susan Blow opened the first public
kindergarten in St. Louis in 1873.

Marie Stevens Case found the combination of workers' housing and child care at
Familistère an inspiration which she spent
the next two decades trying to recreate in
the United States and Mexico. Returning
to the United States in the late 1860s as
Edward Howland's wife, she settled on a
small farm in Hammonton, New Jersey,
"Casa Tonti," where she began a translation of Godin's work and a novel. For the
next two decades, the Howlands promoted
Godin's ideas and took part in many political groups. Edward Howland described the
Social Palace at Guise in 1872 as "the best
practical solution of the relations of capital
and labor." He saw it as part of the "birth
of a new social and political order,"
whereby France would "lead in the inau-
guration of the increasing happiness of a
social system based upon liberty and sympathetic human love." [22] Marie Howland's
translation of Godin's important book
about the Familistère, *Social Solutions,*

5.3 Child care at the Social Palace, Guise,
France, as shown in *Harper's Monthly,* April 1872.
Many types of play are encouraged in a skylit
environment designed especially for children.

5.4 A day care center for the children of working mothers, New York, Sixth Avenue and Fifteenth Street, from *Frank Leslie's Illustrated Newspaper,* April 5, 1856. Although there are cradles and beds, no toys or special play equipment are available.

5.5 A day care center founded by M. Marbeau and named for Sainte Eugénie, rue Crimée, Paris, for the children of employed women, as shown in *Frank Leslie's Illustrated Newspaper,* May 14, 1870. Three well-dressed women at the rear left are probably philanthropic visitors. The space has been designed for children's activities, but order is the rule more than play.

appeared in 1873 and was widely read. The next year she published a humorous, feminist novel satirizing traditional morality and envisioning the establishment of a Social Palace in a New England town, complete with all of the facilities for child care and cooperative housekeeping available in Guise. A few residents of Vineland, New Jersey, began work organizing the First Guise Association of America using the Howlands' publications, calling for "perfect equality of the sexes," extensive child care, individual sovereignty, common property, friendly criticism, and free love, but this was not a successful venture.[23] It would take Edward Bellamy to build a political movement, Nationalism, on the basis of a more conservative utopian novel, *Looking Backward*, in 1888.

In her novel, *The Familistère* (first called *Papa's Own Girl*), Marie Howland recreates the Social Palace in New England, as a brick building, with slate-colored trim and with three words emblazoned on its front: "Liberty, Equality, Fraternity." Thanks to a benevolent capitalist, the inhabitants of the fictional Social Palace own a brickyard and a silk weaving factory. In contrast to the cramped quarters of the "mill girls" in the Lowell boardinghouses of Howland's youth, the inhabitants are provided with extensive collective spaces for their activities and festivals. The grounds of the Social Palace include flower beds, orchards, hothouses, greenhouses, and "a beautiful grove with shady walks and carriage roads extending to and around the lake . . . the grand resort of the children for picnics,

boat-rides, fishing, and for skating in the winter." [24]

In this community a conventional division of labor still prevails between men and women. They sit on separate councils of directors, where men "manage the industrial and financial matters, the buying of supplies," while women "attend to the working of the domestic machinery, the nursery and the schools, report on the quality of the supplies, call general meetings of the women, and discuss all matters." [25] (This is not unlike the sexual division of labor in Melusina Peirce's program for womanhood suffrage.) The children in the Social Palace follow their elders' example, electing leaders and working in groups of ten to twenty boys and girls in the garden for an hour each day. The facilities for their care are not segregated by sex, however. The *pouponnat*, or child care room, contains bouquets of flowers, busts, pictures, "toys of every kind, and little swings and various furniture for light gymnastic exercises." [26] The children are organized into age groups just as in the Familistère at Guise, with babies up to two and a half years old in the nursery, *poupons* (up to four or five) in the *pouponnat*, and *bambins* doing Froebel exercises, slate exercises, and reading. The children, under the influence of their peers, do not cry very often, and they have all learned to sing themselves to sleep!

Most women living in the fictional Social Palace do their own domestic work; others have servants. Most cooking is done by chefs in the main kitchen. A resident explains: "Many a woman here used her cook-stove at first, but as the palace is all heated by the furnaces in winter, and the kitchen-stove fire not needed, they soon gave it up. Now, even the very poorest go or send their children to the *cuisine* for whatever they want. After dinner I will show you our wine-cellars. They are well-stocked, and the very poorest may drink [from] them." [27] With men and women working separately, and rich and poor existing side by side, Howland's vision is faithful to the Fourierist plans which inspired it: "passional attraction" was to erase class divisions in time, but not immediately; economic independence for women was to change their lives, but not necessarily end the sexual division of domestic labor.

In her own life, Howland was more assertive about women's equality. Both she and her husband worked with the New Jersey Patrons of Husbandry, or the Grange. At the first national meeting of the Grange in 1874 she demanded, and won, the inclusion of an equal number of female and male representatives, and she surprised members by sitting at the same tables as the men rather than on a separate set of benches for women at the side of the room.[28] In her attitudes toward money, sex, and marriage she also remained very unconventional. In her novel a feminist male character declared: "I see very few really happy women; and they can never be happy, until they are pecuniarily independent." [29] Financial independence for women, she believed, would bring sexual

independence. Howland also included many straightforward attacks on self-righteous married women who accepted a double standard of morality for men and for women. Her novel was translated into French and praised by many Fourierists, but the public reaction in the United States was mixed.[30] Her cast of characters included an unwed mother, a divorcée, and a country woman saved from prostitution, all of whom praised women's rights and scorned small town standards of respectability and morality. This made it difficult for Howland to form alliances with many trade unionists, suffragists, and socialists active in eastern cities in the 1870s.

Section 12

The one group in the suffrage movement that tolerated free love doctrines on the grounds of feminists' right to free speech was formed around Elizabeth Cady Stanton and Susan B. Anthony's paper, *The Revolution.* Even though Anthony dismissed varietist free love as a "man-vision," the dynamic, zany entrepreneur and free lover, Victoria Woodhull, became associated with their cause.[31] They backed her attempts to argue, before the United States Senate Judiciary Committee in 1871, that women were already enfranchised under the Fourteenth Amendment.

In the early 1870s, Woodhull, who with her sister Tennessee Claflin edited a lively political paper entitled *Woodhull and Claflin's Weekly,* also began collaborating with Stephen Pearl Andrews, Esther Andrews, William West, the Howlands, and other free lovers from the circle Andrews had gathered in the years of The Club and the Unitary Household. *Woodhull and Claflin's Weekly* advocated free love with a frankness that kept the censors busy trying to shut down their publication for obscenity. In 1870 and 1871 the paper also carried articles describing urban residential hotels with cooperative nursery facilities, Andrews's earlier solution to the child care problems. Woodhull promoted these schemes actively and claimed that they would free all women from housework.

In an editorial, "Sixteenth Amendment, Independence vs. Dependence: Which?" Woodhull stated that

. . . the preparatory steps to cooperative housekeeping are being taken. Thousands live at one place and eat at another . . . dining salons are increasing more rapidly than any other branch of business. . . . The residence portions of our cities will be converted into vast hotels. . . . A thousand people can live in one hotel under one general system of superintendence, at much less expense than two hundred and fifty families of four members each, can in as many houses and under as many systems.

In a speech published a few years later, *Tried as by Fire, or The True and the False, Socially,* Woodhull linked sexual and economic freedom for women with new housing arrangements:

Sexual freedom, then, means the abolition of prostitution both in and out of marriage; means the emancipation of women from sexual slavery and her coming in to ownership and control of her own body;

means the end of her pecuniary dependence upon man. . . . Ultimately it means more than this even, it means the establishment of cooperative homes, in which thousands who now suffer in every sense shall enjoy all the comforts and luxuries of life, in the place of the isolated households which have no care for the misery and destitution of their neighbors. It means for our cities, the conversion of innumerable huts into immense hotels, as residences. . . .[32]

In her paper, in 1871, Woodhull also published Steven Pearl Andrews's insistence that "Fourierism is not dead, merely sleeping." In his tract, *The Baby World,* originally issued at The Club by the League Union of the Men of Progress in 1855, and reprinted by Woodhull, he described "the big house," a cooperative residential apartment hotel for two hundred residents with scientific day care: "There is wealth enough now to house the whole people in palaces if they rightly knew the use of it. The big houses are going to be built. The Baby World is going to exist. The grand Domestic Revolution is going to take place."[33] At the same time that these polemics were appearing in *Woodhull and Claflin's Weekly,* Andrews's and Woodhull's New York free love group became Section 12 of the International Workingmen's Association (IWA).

Section 12 was part of the American IWA, a branch of the First International headed by F. A. Sorge, a German immigrant and strict Marxist. Andrews, Woodhull, and their followers offered their services to make *Woodhull and Claflin's Weekly* the official newspaper of the IWA,

and it was read by many friends and supporters of the International. Here the *Communist Manifesto* was first published in English in 1870. It appeared along with *The
Baby World* and other articles discussing
woman suffrage, housing reform, child
care, sexual freedom, linguistic reform, and
"universal" social science.

No doubt the members of Section 12
had unrealizable goals. No doubt some of
the individual members could behave in
exasperating and egocentric ways, but
what most irritated Sorge and Marx was
their feminism. In a slightly persecuted
tone Sorge complained to the General
Council in London: "The intention of politicians and others is now pretty clear — to
identify the I.W.A. in this country with the
woman's suffrage, free love, and other
movements, and we will have to struggle
hard for clearing ourselves from these im-
putations." [34] That he failed to distinguish
between suffrage and free love as feminist
causes suggests his male supremacism,
compared to other leaders such as William
Sylvis of the National Labor Union who
supported female suffrage without confus-
ing this with free love.

The members of Section 12 marched
(5.6) in two major demonstrations of the
IWA in New York, in support of the eight-
hour day, and in protest against the execu-
tion of members of the Paris Commune.
The banner they marched under demanded "complete political and social
equality for both sexes," a demand that
many of the Commune women would have
recognized. Nevertheless, their ideological

position on day care, housing, and sex reform was never considered acceptable by
the Europeans. Criticizing Section 12 as
infiltrated by intellectual reformers "in-
truding themselves into the ranks of labor
either for intellectual purposes or for advancing some hobbies of their own by the
aid of the working people," Sorge managed
to have Section 12 expelled in London and
to have this decision approved in July 1872
by some other American IWA sections. [35]

This was the context in which Howland
tried to extend her influence. Her chances
of persuading either American suffragists
or trade union leaders to adopt a program
involving child care and free love were
negligible. But she moved on to find a
communitarian socialist milieu where these
were not unmentionable goals. Her novel,
The Familistère, brought Howland into contact with Albert Kimsey Owen, a maverick
engineer, entrepreneur of Pacific City, an
experimental community in Topolobampo,
Mexico. Howland would spend the next
twenty years working with Owen, trying to
realize the advantages of the Social Palace
she had lived in at Guise and described in
her fiction.

Topolobampo
As a civil engineer, from Chester, Pennsylvania, who identified himself as a founder
of the Greenback Party and a member of
the Sovereigns of Industry and the Knights
of Labor, Owen criticized both the sanitary
and social arrangements of capitalist urban
centers: "The cities of Europe and America
are but miserable attempts toward such

5.6 Demonstration organized by International
Association of Workingmen of the United States,
New York City, December 18, 1871. Members of
Section Twelve are shown at center, with Ten-
nessee Claflin carrying banner, Steven Pearl An-
drews at her left, and William West in the line
of march, detail, from *Frank Leslie's Illustrated
Newspaper,* January 6, 1872.

purposes. . . . The way out of these
difficulties is the same which will solve, one
day, all difficulties from which mankind is
suffering. *Purpose, thought, integral cooperation.*" [36] Owen argued that public
corporations should own urban land in
perpetuity to block speculative profits.
Concerned with analyzing consumption as
well as production, Owen called for economic planning by elected urban officials
as the basis of urban design, and he hoped
that many consumers' and producers' cooperatives would thrive in his model city.

Perhaps, as a member of the Knights of
Labor, Owen knew of various cooperative
projects launched by the Knights in northern states. Beginning in 1869, they supported the proliferation of cooperative
enterprises as part of a strategy to achieve
a workers' democracy, including the development of cooperative laundries, bakeries,
grocery stores and even child care centers.
A day nursery established by the Knights
for the children of working women in the
mills of Olneyville, Rhode Island, between
1885 and 1887, received coverage in the
Knights' paper, *People.* [37] In the mid-1870s,
however, Owen's views on domestic space
and services do not seem to have developed
beyond an interest in providing some cooperative services for residents of private
houses in Pacific City, until Marie
Howland persuaded him to consider the
collective facilities of the Social Palace.

She wrote to him in 1875, "Why not —
since so much more money must be raised
to built isolated homes — try for the Social
Palace? No 2000 or 3000 people could be

so conveniently, comfortably, luxuriantly
housed by any other method." Since the
Social Palace would include child care, she
advocated "the training of the little ones.
That is so supremely important . . . the
freeing of woman from the household
treadmill must be effected before she can
cultivate the powers so vitally needed in
the regeneration of the race. . . ." [38] Owen
agreed with many of her suggestions but
hesitated to build anything besides private
dining rooms. Their correspondence went
on for many years, with Howland adamant: "Now Albert, depend upon it, we
must allow people who wish to do so to
form groups and dine together. Let the
cook prepare and all who wish, let them
eat at the general table. . . . I would
rather have a clam and some raw meal
and eat it with you, E. H., and any who
would like to join us *for the pleasure of reunion.*" In the "most perfect isolated family
possible," she argued, adults would not
have "sufficient leisure and freedom from
care," and children would lack the social
stimulation for "integral growth," [39] a
phrase often used by anarchists to suggest
the development of the whole person.

Eventually, Marie Howland became involved in the colony's publications and
then lived in the colony between 1888 and
1893. As she worked with Owen and John
J. Deery, a rather conventional Philadelphia architect employed to draw the plans
for Topolobampo, Howland introduced cooperative domestic services and child care
into every aspect of the colony's design.

Organized on a grid plan overlaid with diagonal streets, Topolobampo was to include three types of dwellings: apartment hotels, row houses with patios, and picturesque freestanding cottages with adjoining cooperative housekeeping facilities. The city plan shows dozens of apartment hotels and row houses, and hundreds of private homes (5.7). Thus, Topolobampo makes the transition from early nineteenth-century concepts of a single phalanstery housing an entire community to late nineteenth-century notions of mass housing consisting of complementary urban and suburban building types bordering endless similar streets. Yet the plan is still an aggregation of earlier building types, and the site is decorated with lakes and flower gardens, cooperative stores and factories, homes for the sick, libraries, and concert halls, all suggestive of an endless supply of communal and private resources, and leisure to enjoy them. There is, as yet, no ideal of urban infrastructure for cooperative housekeeping, which appears only in the 1890s.

Like the provision for public facilities, the space allotted to both private dwellings and collective housekeeping facilities was generous, even inflated. All dwellings were to be built of local stone in the Moorish style (Peirce had advocated the "Oriental" style), and decorated with tiles. The apartment hotels (or resident hotels) recalled various phalansteries built in the United States before 1860, as well as the arrangements of the Unitary Household in New York and the Familistère at Guise. The

plan provided for large suites as well as for single rooms, since Topolobampo's planners, in the Fourierist tradition, did not insist upon the immediate abolition of social classes. In these apartment hotels several hundred people could be accommodated.

As the promoters explained it,

The resident hotel . . . is designed to take the place of the "club house," "flats" and the "apartment house," being an improved and enlarged combination of all. . . . Each house will be a distinct home, showing the individuality of its owner within and on the piazza fronting its private entrance, but there will be a restaurant, dining-room, parlor, library, reading room, lecture hall, nursery, and play area, laundry, bath, and barber room common to all. From the restaurant, meals may be served in the homes *à la carte* at any hour and in the manner ordered by telephone, or the families may go to the *table d'hôte* served at regular hours in the dining-room.

Indeed, the duplex apartments, fronting on a central courtyard, offered all the luxuries of "home life in the city with country freshness." The benefits for women were mentioned:

The woman will be relieved from the drudgery of kitchen and market; the nursery will be a safe place for children when parents wish to go out or away; the "servant question" will be measurably settled.

And the financial benefits of a cooperative organization were celebrated:

. . . our resident hotel is hotel life on a grand and perfected scale, where the guest becomes the host, lives in a house in lieu of a room, owns his own fireside, a *pro rata* interest in that property which is common to

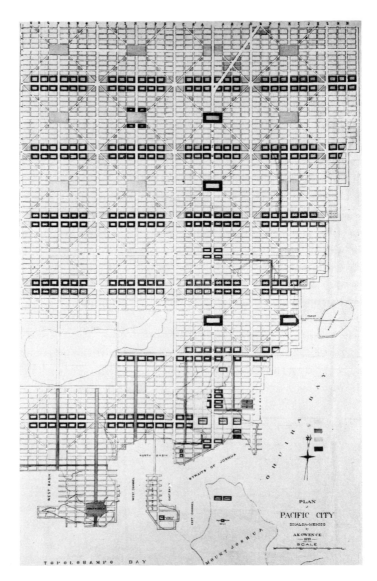

5.7 Plan of Pacific City, Topolobampo, Mexico,
1889, by Albert Kimsey Owen, showing apartment hotels and row house blocks as dark rectangles and freestanding suburban cottages with
cooperative housekeeping facilities as typical
housing in light blocks

his home, and manages and polices the associated interests of the block by a board of directors. . . .[40]

These apartment hotel plans also resemble those developed in New York in the 1880s by the architect Philip G. Hubert, who combined duplex units and hotel facilities and was able to achieve cooperative ownership by the residents in a joint stock scheme. His projects were called Hubert Home Clubs, and at least eight of them flourished in New York. Like Howland, Hubert had strong ties to the communitarian socialist tradition of Charles Fourier, since his father, Charles Antoine Colomb Gengembre, had been resident architect at the Fourierist phalanstery of Condé-sur-Vesgres in France in 1832, before coming to the United States.[41]

The *New York Times* offered an approving response to Hubert's innovation of cooperative apartment house ownership in 1881. Explaining that New York rents were the highest in the world and approving the formation of clubs of families to raise the capital for new apartment houses, the editors enthused: "There has never been anything in the building line which afforded so much hope and encouragement to New York and New Yorkers as the present cooperative scheme. It threatens to effect a great and most desirable revolution in keeping house and securing homes." [42] *The American Architect and Building News* republished this recommendation. Hubert's successful projects included the Hawthorne, the Hubert, the Rembrandt, the Milano, the Chelsea, the Mount

Morris, 80 Madison Avenue, and 125 Madison Avenue. In some of these buildings the cooperative apartments consisted of only a few rooms, but the typical units discussed by the *Times* included twelve rooms and over 2200 square feet to house bourgeois families and their servants. Philip Hubert also experimented with central refrigeration as well as central heating, and held several patents for labor-saving devices. Like the earlier work of Arthur Gilman, E. W. Godwin, and Henry Hudson Holly (4.7, 4.8, 4.9), Hubert's work inspired many feminists, utopian socialists, and futurist novelists to continue to eulogize the social, physical, and economic potential of the cooperatively owned apartment hotel in the 1880s and 1890s. Yet these reformers still tended to ignore the fact that only well-to-do individuals actually lived in such structures and enjoyed their economies of scale. They were just as sure as Fourier had been that the progress of the apartment hotel was an inevitable aspect of human evolution. As the promoters of Topolobampo averred, the apartment hotel allowed living to be "reduced to the minimum cost," and "perfected to the highest possible excellence." [43]

Perhaps the most unusual facility to be offered in Topolobampo was the nursery, "under the charge of trained nurses, in which the mother can place her infant child, even when a few days old, have it watched, and cared for, both by day and night, and as it advances in years, educated until fitted for the public school." One promoter explained that all the child

care arrangements were to be as elaborate
as those devised by Godin at the Familistère, and repeated Howland's assertion in
her novel that in well-designed surround-
ings, the beneficent influence of their peers
would keep most children from crying.[44]

The lavish dimensions of the apartment
hotels were only slightly more grand than
those allotted to the patio house blocks,
where between twelve and forty-eight patio
houses overlooked a central garden and
shared parlor, library, kitchen, dining
room, and laundry, to be staffed by "skillful people" (5.8, 5.9). "Trained persons"
were also to visit each house daily to do
housekeeping chores.

For those who might prefer freestanding
homes, in the suburban blocks (5.10) four
large picturesque kitchenless cottages, each
slightly different from its neighbors, shared
access to a cooperative facility. This central
building included kitchen, laundry, bakery,
and dormitories for the servants who were
to staff the facility.[45] This was the first actual architectural design of a kitchenless
house; Peirce had only described one in
words. Privacy for each family was preserved by the inclusion of private dining
rooms in the houses.

Although none of these extravagant
building plans resembled the small structures actually erected by the colonists,
many of whom were urban, working class
people, the plans were published in 1885 in
a treatise, *Integral Co-operation*, and discussed in various colony publications edited by Howland. Ray Reynolds's lively

history of the community, *Cat's Paw Utopia,*
reveals the financial speculation and administrative chaos which prevented any of
this ideal housing from being constructed.
Indeed, some called the colony a "gigantic
swindle," [46] while others saw it as a tragic
utopian socialist failure. Howland's feminism was not shared by many of the other
members of the community: her views on
free love, her insistence on riding astride on
horseback, and one incident of swimming
naked, were enough for some colonists to
label her a "loose woman." [47] She lived in
Topolobampo between 1888 and 1893 but
ultimately sensed the failure of this experiment in "integral cooperation," and eventually moved to Alabama, where she lived
quietly and worked as librarian at the
Fairhope Single Tax Colony until her
death in 1921 at age eighty-five.

Although the plans for Topolobampo's
housing were unrealized, they were
influential in both the United States and
England, where they were studied by
Ebenezer Howard, a leader of the next
generation of enthusiasts for cooperative
housekeeping. In the plans for Topolobampo where Howland's goals are expressed in physical design, the ambiance is
as suburban as Howard's Letchworth. The
old form of the phalanstery has become
mass housing; it looks forward to the cooperative quadrangles of Homesgarth and
Guessens Court.

Marie Stevens Howland, a charismatic,
enthusiastic supporter of radical causes,
never saw the construction of spacious resident hotels, kitchenless houses or well

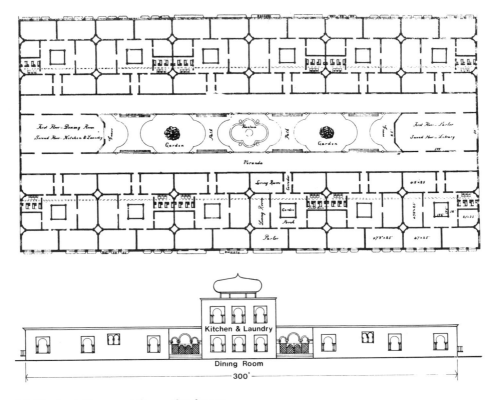

5.8 Howland, Deery, and Owen, plan for one-story courtyard houses with common kitchen, dining room, laundry, parlor, and library, 1885

5.9 Elevation of courtyard house block showing collective facilities, with Moorish arches and dome, a style previously recommended by Melusina Peirce

5.10 Howland, Deery and Owen, plan for block of eight individual freestanding cottages, with cooperative housekeeping building shared by four families, 1885

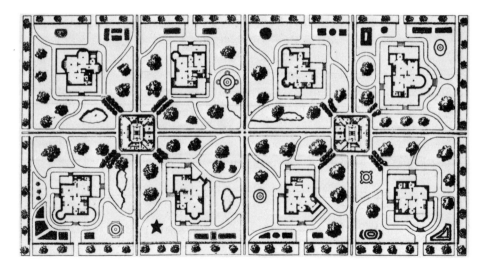

staffed nurseries on her ambitious plans.
But she helped to translate the idealism of
rural Fourierist communities into several
transitional projects — the Unitary Household, the Familistère, and Topolobampo —
which, by their urban location, industrial
economic base, or metropolitan scale,
reflected some new aspect of urban life in
the last half of the nineteenth century. Her
concern for professional child care and for
women's sexual liberation caused her and
her allies to be regarded as eccentric and
even immoral, but she was one of the first
American women in active political life to
challenge the nuclear family, sexual mo-
nogamy, and private child care. This took
her a long way from the New Hampshire
farm where she was born and the Lowell
boardinghouse where she spent her early
teens. For her an expanded, luxurious
boardinghouse became a social goal,
whether it offered the free love atmosphere
of the Unitary Household, or the plush facilities and tropical gardens of Topolobampo.

Howland not only spent time in four unusual communities; she associated with
three of the most flamboyant reformers of
the nineteenth century — Stephen Pearl
Andrews, anarchist and free lover; J. A. B.
Godin, industrialist and philanthropist; Albert Kimsey Owen, civil engineer and promoter of railroad lines and residential
hotels. She was an indomitable writer and
organizer whose skills served all these communities and half a dozen more causes.
Some colleagues thought her so dedicated
to her beliefs, so noble and transparent,
that she used no tact. Others admired her
zeal and the way she rejected in her own
life any idea of a separate "sphere" of work
for women, by attending meetings and
working with men as a journalist and
editor.

Throughout her life she maintained a
large circle of friends, acquaintants, and
correspondents, including Albert Brisbane,
Henry Clapp, and Edmund Clarence Stedman. A friend at Fairhope, Laurie B.
Allen, remembered that "she was like a
college education to me," but Howland
had a very modest view of her own
achievements.[48] "Do you not know," she
wrote a friend from the Unitary Household, "that I have always been a simple,
plain, hard-working woman with not much
in my record to deserve remembrance. The
best thing I have done is the translation of
Godin's work. . . ."[49]

Yet her own work was important. In advocating the development of a community
with paid employment for women and collective domestic services, she was pursuing
goals for woman's sphere articulated earlier
by Jane Sophia Appleton and Melusina
Peirce. But when Howland suggested that
professional child care and freedom for
women to choose their sexual partners be
part of this program, she moved beyond
the wildest imaginations of most feminist
women of the 1870s. She might have been
just one more notorious free lover, yet
Howland's patient work on Topolobampo
helped produce a set of visionary plans and
took her beyond the polemical, scandal-
filled world of other free love advocates

such as Victoria Woodhull and Stephen
Pearl Andrews.

Howland preferred the idealistic ferment
of intentional communities to the cynical
jostling of New York radical circles because
builders of such communities better accommodated her concerns for housing and
child care. In cooperative communities, she
represented the interests of the employed
woman who must balance home and community. Her feminist predecessors were
housewives who were very interested in the
details of cooperative household management, while Howland passed over domestic
work (perhaps too quickly) as a job for
"trained people." Because of her teaching
experience, her own expertise was in child
care, which she considered in great detail.
Her interest in social groups and social
spaces was also far more developed than
her predecessors. As an adult, self-
supporting woman in the free love movement, she voiced the domestic concerns of
the employed woman with children, rather
than the full-time housewife, and explored
their urban implications. This stance made
her unique among American feminist reformers of her day.

6.1 Mary Livermore

The housekeeping of the future is to be co-operative. Women are rapidly learning to organize and work together. In their temperance unions, their clubs, congresses and charitable organizations, in church, missionary, and society work, they are learning what can be accomplished by a union of plans and action.
— Mary Livermore, 1886

Suffragists,
Philanthropists, and
Temperance Workers

Forging a Chain of Vegetables

Mary Livermore, a leader of the American woman suffrage and temperance movements, was a strait-laced woman who most likely would have deplored Melusina Peirce's divorce and cut Marie Howland dead if she had met this free love advocate in the street, though she came to share their enthusiasm for the "associated life" of cooperative housekeeping. With her advocacy in the 1880s, cooperative housekeeping became a familiar term among prominent suffragists, philanthropists, and temperance workers, such as Lucy Stone, Pauline Agassiz Shaw, and Frances Willard. Livermore saw cooperative housekeeping as a challenge to women's powers of organization and hoped to demonstrate that women could reorganize and modernize domestic work effectively, within capitalist society, before "the business organizations of men, which have taken so many industrial employments from the home," seized the remainder.[1] Efficiency and industrial training were her bywords, rather than cooperation or sexual freedom, yet she agreed with her predecessors that economic independence for women was the goal. She asserted that urban evolution would incorporate the socialization of domestic work and took the concepts of managerial and technical skills for women farther than Peirce and Howland. At the end of her career she worked among Nationalists and Christian Socialists to interest them in cooperative housekeeping.

Born in 1820 in Boston, Livermore (6.1) was the daughter of a Welsh laborer, but her mother came from a Yankee sea captain's family.[2] After some years of work as a governess and a schoolteacher, at age twenty-four she married Daniel Livermore, a Universalist preacher with liberal opinions on the subject of women's rights. During her early married life in Chicago, she contributed sketches and poetry to various religious periodicals and became active in temperance organizing. In 1858 she became associate editor of her husband's paper, the *New Covenant,* continuing philanthropic work as well.

The Civil War called forth all her latent executive abilities. Engaging a housekeeper and a governess to care for her husband and two daughters, aged ten and thirteen, and arranging for a laundress to do the wash one day a week, she went to work for the United States Sanitary Commission in 1861. The next year Livermore had to supplement these private domestic arrangements, when dozens of Chicago washerwomen left the city to take the places of farmhands who had joined the Union Army. She and fifty other women borrowed secondhand machinery, rolled up their sleeves, and established a cooperative laundry to do their own wash. She wrote to a friend, "Whenever women are dead in earnest about it and *want* a cooperative laundry, then they can organize one. Not four or five — but half a hundred, to give good backing, make public opinion for it.

They must be women of pluck, of persistence, of *consecrated common sense,* who know how to compel success." [3] This was her first venture in domestic cooperation and one she often referred to in her work for domestic reform over twenty years later. The experience she gained in the laundry venture was, however, very small when compared to the scope of her work providing food for the battle kitchens and military hospitals of the Union Army.

As the Civil War progressed, Livermore and her close friend, Jane C. Hoge, took over the Chicago branch of the Sanitary Commission. Livermore made fund-raising and inspection tours of military hospitals. She helped establish over three thousand local aid societies in the parts of Illinois, Iowa, Wisconsin, Michigan, and Indiana which constituted her district, to such effect that this territory provided over two-thirds of the supplies contributed to General Grant's army. Their efforts grew more prodigious as the problems increased. When Grant's army faced scurvy in 1863, Mary Livermore and her colleague commandeered "18,000 bushels of vegetables, 3,000 cans of fruit, and 61,000 pounds of dried fruit, which were shipped southward at the rate of a thousand barrels a week until 'a line of vegetables connected Chicago and Vicksburg.' " [4] Needing to oversee not only collection but distribution of the supplies she provided, in the same year Livermore visited every military hospital between Cairo, Illinois, and the Union headquarters opposite Vicksburg, Mississippi. This was not all: "Possessing boundless stamina, she also frequently utilized the night hours to write vivid reports on her activities for the *New Covenant* and other periodicals, besides turning out the commission's monthly bulletin and other circulars to the local aid societies." [5] In the same year, 1863, she and Hoge conceived, planned, and directed the Women's Sanitary Fair of Chicago, which raised a large amount of money for the Sanitary Commission and was imitated in other cities.

Suffrage Work
After the War, Livermore turned her magnificent administrative abilities to the suffrage cause, organizing the first woman suffrage convention in Illinois, becoming president of the Illinois Woman Suffrage Association in 1868, and founding a suffrage paper, the *Agitator,* in 1869. During 1869 she emerged as a national leader, as two factions developed within the suffrage movement, the National Women's Suffrage Association headed by Elizabeth Cady Stanton and Susan B. Anthony, and the American Woman Suffrage Association, led by Lucy Stone, Julia Ward Howe, Henry B. Blackwell, Colonel Thomas W. Higginson, and Livermore. Some historians have viewed the American as a "conservative" group[6] compared to the National, because Stanton and Anthony associated themselves with Victoria Woodhull and her group of free love advocates, who were also campaigning for sex reform, child care, and housing reform along with suffrage, while Livermore and her associates deplored free love.

Organizational style — strictness versus
spontaneity — accounted for some of the
schism, but free love sympathizers did
infuriate Livermore even more than her
colleagues. She believed in the reform of
conventional marriage, but had once attempted to persuade a suffrage group to
pass a resolution, "we abhorrently repudi-
ate 'free loveism' as horrible and mischie-
vous to society, and disown any sympathy
with it." [7] (This statement had caused
much consternation, since many suffragists felt they would do their public image
more harm than good by protesting this
connection.)

In 1870 Livermore became editor of the
new, influential *Woman's Journal,* started in
Boston, the official organ of the American
Woman Suffrage Association. The *Journal*
regularly reported on cooperative housekeeping for the next forty-odd years, as
part of a broad campaign aimed at
women's economic independence and
women's control of their own housing.
They covered these struggles at every scale
from women's shared apartments to a town
built by a woman, Preston, California.[8] In
July 1870, early in Livermore's tenure as
editor, an article entitled "Modern Housekeeping" declared: "Domestic work is the
only department of industry in which the
division of work has not been applied, and
labor-saving devices come into general use.
While men have reduced their labor to a
system, and compelled the forces of nature
to toil for them, women still drudge in
their kitchens, washing, ironing, and cooking, with very little improvement on the

methods of their great, great grandmothers." The paper asked, "Where is
Mrs. Peirce's 'Cooperative Housekeeping'
which was so big a star of hope in the hori-
zon of distressed housekeepers a year or
more ago? . . . We still have faith in the
plan and believe it practicable." [9]

At the same time that the *Woman's Journal* supported cooperative housekeeping,
under the editorship of Livermore and her
successors, Lucy Stone, Henry Blackwell,
and Alice Stone Blackwell, it also ran articles supporting male involvement in housework and child care. (These appeared as
well in *The Woman's Column,* its associated
newsletter, after 1888.) They were often
sharp but humorous, detailing extended
debates between men and women about
spheres of work.[10] In one typical example,
heated discussion results in a dawning consciousness on the man's part that it is just
as illogical to assume that all females
should do housework, as it is to assume
that all males should be farmers.[11]

Much of the interest in reorganizing
housework came from the practical demands of running a suffrage journal or
traveling the suffrage lecture circuit. Lucy
Stone wrote to a colleague in 1874:

I am so tired to-day, body and soul, it
seems as though I should never feel fresh
again. I have been trying to get advertisements for the *Woman's Journal* to eke out its
expenses. Yesterday I walked miles; to picture stores, crockery stores, to "special
sales," going up flight after flight of stairs
only to find the men out, or not ready to
advertise. And for all my day's toil I did
not get a cent; and when I came home at

night, it was to find the house cold, the fire nearly out in the furnace, and none on the hearth . . . if only the housekeeping would go on without so much looking after! [12]

In later years Stone often reiterated her conviction that ". . . it is certain that a co-operative kitchen, bakery, and laundry are among the good things which are to come for the relief of women." [13]

Queen of the Platform

Although Mary Livermore was part of the *Woman's Journal* circle, which showed great interest in cooperative housekeeping, she eventually took this message to a much broader audience. In 1872 she resigned her editorial job in favor of organizational administration and lecturing. In 1873 she was president of the Association for the Advancement of Women; in 1875–1878, president of the American Woman Suffrage Association, and from 1875–1885, president of the Massachusetts Woman's Christian Temperance Union. Her public presence commanded attention as much as her outstanding journalistic and administrative work: described as "tall and matronly, with auburn hair," and a "deep rich voice, redolent of integrity and authority," [14] she was the perfect organization president and public speaker. Working the lecture circuit for promoter James Redpath, she delivered an average of 150 lectures per year between 1872 and 1895, earning thousands of dollars and the nickname, "Queen of the Platform," in the United States and Europe.

Livermore's prominence as a suffragist guaranteed a broad audience among church organizations, suffrage groups, temperance groups, and women's clubs. As one historian has described the effect of visiting speakers on early women's clubs, they set an example for timid women who were afraid to speak in public, and they delivered feminist messages. "Prominent feminists in America — Julia Ward Howe, Mary Livermore, and Antoinette Brown Blackwell, for example — continually stirred club women to consider the possibilities of dress reform, cooperative housekeeping, women as architects and ministers and photographers, women as guardians of the public health, and the merits of women as educators." [15]

Although Livermore's associates at the *Woman's Journal* and in the American Woman Suffrage Association supported cooperative housekeeping, and she became known for her advocacy of the idea on the lecture circuit, there was a period in her career when she argued against making cooperative domestic life a priority for the woman's movement and quite vigorously debated its adherents. In 1870, when she arrived in Boston, Mary Livermore began to work with many members of the New England Women's Club. This group had heard Mary Peabody Mann's paper on public kitchens and had discussed Melusina Fay Peirce's plans for a cooperative housekeeping society in 1869, as well as Peirce's scheme for a women's congress elected by "womanhood" suffrage. As Vice-President of the American Woman's

Suffrage Association, fully committed to winning the "male" ballot for women by then, Livermore must have been quite skeptical of Peirce, who was sixteen years younger. In later years Livermore judged Peirce's cooperative housekeeping experiment as "a pre-destined failure," believing that "there was really no practical cooperation in the scheme," although she conceded that the laundry (managed by Peirce herself) was made successful.[16] Since Livermore enjoyed the support of her husband, who had moved to Boston to help her in her work, she may well have doubted the wisdom of "cooperation" with some of the rather uncooperative husbands of Peirce's group.

Within the New England Women's Club and other local groups, Livermore took a critical stance on cooperative schemes she considered utopian. In 1879 she participated in a three-way debate on the subject of cooperation organized by the New England Women's Club. As the *Woman's Journal* reported the event, Mrs. M. F. Walling traced the history of cooperation "from its earliest beginnings down to its latest operations in business, until we felt sure that in Utopia there was but one kind of trading stores." Dr. Mary Jane Safford, a surgeon and feminist who was an old friend of Livermore from Civil War work, then developed a plan for domestic cooperation rather like that advocated by Peirce, with "spacious family homes, built around one common central square, and the common baker and meat cook and laundress and nursery maid and seamstress united to place us all in reform dresses at wholesome

tables . . . all envy and jealousy died away."[17] Mary Livermore took the opposite position and defended existing forms of domestic organization.

Given her extensive experience administering military provisions and hospital supplies on a regional scale, it is not surprising she spoke against a utopia without envy or jealousy, where cooperative stores filled every need. In October of the same year, Livermore made a similar speech defending domestic life to the New England Women's Suffrage Association. Charles Codman, a former Associationist with ties to Brook Farm, offered the rebuttal, advocating cooperative kitchens and suggesting that this would allow the elimination of servants.[18] Her audience being a suffrage group, it is even more understandable why Livermore struggled to persuade members to focus on suffrage as the most significant feminist issue of the time.

"The Happiness of This Associated Life"
Within seven years Livermore changed her position, for in 1886 she declared that "isolated housekeeping must be merged into a cooperative housekeeping," with a long, cogently argued article in *The Chautauquan* to support her assertion.[19] By this time cooperative housekeeping was receiving attention in the national press, following the publication of Peirce's *Cooperative Housekeeping* in 1884 and of Marie Howland's and Albert Kimsey Owen's *Integral Co-operation* in 1885. However, Livermore did not simply climb on the bandwagon. As she had traveled around the country lecturing, she

had, as she said, visited and studied cooperative laundries, kitchens, and dining clubs and had analyzed them from the standpoint of practical management for over two decades. She had come to the conclusion that cooperative housekeeping was inevitable.

To support her assertion, Livermore advanced her first example of a brilliantly managed experiment that had been successful for twenty-five years: the Familistère in Guise, France, which had been so praised by Howland a decade earlier. "Who can estimate the happiness of this associated life, where every family enjoys complete family retiracy, and yet has a common industrial life, founded on justice, that secures abundance and guards against poverty!" [20] Reading this homage to the Familistère, one might assume the author was a committed communitarian socialist. She could not overpraise its virtues, believing that family privacy was protected, while family options were enlarged with the chance to cook at home, to order cooked food and dine at home, or to dine at the public table. As the founder of a cooperative laundry she especially appreciated the laundry at Guise, with unusual tubs designed to expel water by centrifugal force. She commented as well on bathtubs with adjustable bottoms designed to fit children or adults, and superb heating, lighting, and ventilation. (Possibly, since her encomiums are so detailed, she had visited the Social Palace on a European lecture tour.)

In the United States, Livermore claimed that she knew of two successful cooperative laundries, founded in the 1860s and 1870s, including one that served thirty-eight families. She reported the fairy-tale prosperity of the three cooperative owners: "They maintained a handsome account in the bank, bought a house, adopted an orphan girl-baby, and reared and educated her as if she were a daughter or sister." [21] All this, she believed, was due to their "executive ability" and firmness with their customers.

Although Livermore's laundries and the Familistère were producers' cooperatives, she was most interested in consumers' groups, such as several dining clubs she visited. Student cooperative clubs in Ann Arbor, Michigan, and Berea, Ohio, provided students with abundant meals, "excellent in quality," for six to nine cents per meal, or $1.40 to $1.90 per week. She had also been a guest of family dining clubs catering to more affluent members in Ann Arbor and in Evansville, Wisconsin. At Ann Arbor, a steward and a superintendent, elected by the cooperating families from their own group, ran the club for weekly stipends, sending meals to members' houses or serving them in a dining club, which replicated a Victorian home:

There were carpets on the club dining room floors, lace curtains draping the windows, pictures on the walls, birds singing in cages, flowers growing in pots. The table waiters were deft-handed, well-trained girls, the table linen spotless, the silver, glass, and china clear and shining, the cooking excellent. There were five courses at dinner, and the breakfasts and suppers were all that could be desired.[22]

In Evansville the club she visited had gone
through much the same process of organization: a group formed a company, elected
a superintendent, a steward, and a treasurer, bought and fitted up a house as the
club premises, and paid a five percent divi-
dend to its stockholders in the first year.
Both the Evansville and Ann Arbor experiments charged more than the student
clubs, about $2.50 to $2.70 per week per
person.

In New York Livermore observed another approach to the problem, requiring
more capital and even less cooperation, an
early cooked food delivery service, incorporated in September 1885, which delivered
food in double-walled copper boxes insulated with boiling water. Inside were silver-
plated dishes with tight covers. A horse
wagon carried ten boxes inserted into a
tank where steam enveloped them until
they reached their destination. The cold
parts of the meal, bread, butter, salad, and
ice cream, were packed in cool boxes or refrigerators built into the wagon. The project was run by an entrepreneur, not a
consumers' cooperative, but its technology
appealed to cooperative housekeepers.

The New York company's breakfast and
dinner menus reflect the eating habits of
people of means in the Victorian era: "The
breakfast consists of fruit in season; oatmeal, wheaten grits, or some other dish to
be eaten with milk; fish, steak, or chops; a
side-dish such as stewed kidneys, sausage,
liver or bacon; eggs; coffee, tea or chocolate; milk, sugar, bread and butter." Anyone still ambulatory after beginning the

day with this feast could tackle dinner
from a copper box: "Soup, fish, an *entree,* a
roast, potatoes and two other vegetables,
some kind of sauce, or preserves, a dessert,
bread and butter, tea, coffee, etc., all of the
best quality." Livermore, a thrifty veteran
of the Sanitary Commission, accustomed to
provisioning military hospitals, observed in
matter-of-fact fashion, "what is furnished
for two is sufficient for three." She calculated that while the New York company
charged a top rate of $12.00 per person per
week, five people could eat well on their
deliveries for three people, bringing the actual cost down to $4.75 per person. She ob-
served that this was still for the elite: $4.75
was approximately a full week's wages for
a skilled male worker.[23] The affluent would
continue to experiment with such services
for the next forty years.

It is significant that Livermore chose *The
Chautauquan* as the place for her article to
appear. Cooperative housekeeping arrangements of a sort had developed at many
Methodist summer camp meeting grounds,
and at Chautauqua itself, and she and her
readers were certainly familiar with them
as yet another precedent for domestic cooperation for people of moderate means. In
the post–Civil War period thousands of
Americans spent their summer holidays in
tents or small frame cottages covered with
jigsaw ornament, grouped in picturesque
clusters at camp meeting sites such as Oak
Bluffs, Massachusetts, or Ocean Grove,
New Jersey (6.2, 6.3). Revivalist preaching
alternated with lectures and holiday
events, and many families took their

6.2 Camp meeting, Oak Bluffs, Massachusetts,
1851. Society tents are grouped around speaker's
platform, eating tents at left.

6.3 Kitchenless cottage, camp meeting ground,
Oak Bluffs, Massachusetts, c. 1870–1890

meals at the eating tents run for the community.[24]

At Chautauqua, New York, educational activities were emphasized even more than piety. Lectures on intellectual, social, and ethical questions flourished; elaborate resort hotels supplemented private tents and cottages, and both hotel dining rooms and less formal eating tents provided cuisine as well as private kitchens. In 1904, Charlotte Perkins Gilman cited Chautauqua as an excellent starting point for professional approaches to domestic life.[25] Emma P. Ewing, a teacher of cookery and nutrition at Chautauqua for many years, ultimately founded a dinner delivery service in Pittsburgh; Alice Peloubet Norton, head of the school of cookery at Chautauqua, founded the cooked food service in Northampton, Massachusetts.

Management and Labor

Livermore, veteran organizer, always praised good domestic management, whether at Guise, Ann Arbor, or New York. When she argued that women should make greater use of their managerial talents by starting new cooperative housekeeping ventures, this implied for her a reorganization of domestic labor. In her article she reiterated the complaints of housewives that there were not enough trained domestic servants available. In New York, nine out of ten housewives were "as isolated as prairie farmers' wives," she claimed. The cooperators in Ann Arbor "wished to rid themselves of the servant-girl nuisance"; in Evansville, they wanted

"to save money, time, labor, and the waste and annoyance of servants"; in New York they desired to "rid the house of cooks and their waste and disorder." To the pleasures of replacing servants with a trained staff she adds the financial savings of buying food and fuel collectively, and improving working conditions with better stoves and utensils. She criticized the typical private kitchen as "a purgatory" with a crude stove which gave "the cook an experience like that of 'Shadrach, Meshach, and Abednego,' in the fiery furnace — only she does *not* come out without 'so much as the smell of fire' upon her." [26] Jane Sophia Appleton's plea for community kitchens to abolish the "roasted lady" was still appealing.

In comparison to her predecessors, Howland and Peirce, Livermore gave serious thought to the training of the workers in a cooperative kitchen. "Industrial training has, at last, captured the heart of American people," she argued. "How far may girls and young women be included in this preparation for modern industrial pursuits?" Howland had assigned space for skilled domestic workers in Topolobampo and Peirce had proposed specialized work, promised high wages, dress reform, and exercise for the workwomen of her cooperative housekeeping center. Livermore took this further by stating that industrial schools were essential to train young women in specialized aspects of large-scale housekeeping. She believed that such training for women, in the more highly developed domestic arts, would "furnish em-

ployments to women that shall enlarge and
not dwarf them, and yield them the compensation necessary to honorable self-
support." [27] Thus working women would
not have to toil for a fraction of men's
wages as factory operatives, maids, and
nurses; they would not be tempted into
prostitution; rather, they would be the
skilled professionals and craft workers of
the new cooperative housekeeping services.
Livermore had advocated industrial training for women in one of her well-known
lectures, "What Shall We Do With Our
Daughters?," published in 1883. When this
advocacy was united to her plea of cooperative housekeeping, the synthesis was very
influential.

Her argument, that industrial training
for domestic work must be a starting point
for reform, had been discussed briefly in
the New England Women's Club by Mary
Peabody Mann around the time of Peirce's
experiment. It was to become the dominant view of cooperative housekeeping as
carried on by many domestic scientists and
advocates of industrial schools. This idea
always carried the implication that some
women were to be trained as managers and
others as industrial workers. Because advocates of industrial training assumed that
children were not too young to learn useful
skills, this interest in industrial training
could mesh with some of the goals of the
kindergarten movement led by Mann and
her sister, Elizabeth Peabody, as well as
some of the goals of scientific child care advocates such as Marie Howland. But while
industrial training used teaching tech-

niques developed by the kindergartens and
the utopian socialists, its goals for its pupils
were much more limited.

Emily Huntington, founder of the
Kitchen Garden movement, was one leader
in industrial education for poor girls. After
teaching in a mission school for poor children in Norwich, Connecticut, and in the
Wilson Industrial School for Girls in New
York's East Side tenement district, in 1875
she decided to develop classes in housework
for girls of four and five. She substituted
tiny pots, pans, dishes, and brooms (6.4,
6.5), for the geometric Froebel blocks used
in kindergartens. As she explained in her
work in 1883:

The only point of resemblance between
Kitchen Garden and Kindergarten is the
manner in which the children are taught;
the substance of the teaching is entirely
different. While the kindergarten has for its
object the whole training of the child, the
education and development of all its faculties, the object of the Kitchen Garden
is to train little girls in all branches of
household industry, and to give them as
thorough a knowledge as possible of housekeeping in all its various departments —
knowledge which every girl should possess,
whether she use it simply in her own home
or in the homes of others.[28]

Her ideas spread to many schools throughout the United States. By 1884 Huntington
and Grace Dodge formed the Industrial
Education Association, promoting these
classes in public schools and charitable institutions and training teachers for the
work.

Whatever the children's aptitudes, the
philanthropists and teachers of the Kitchen

Garden separated them by race and family background. In Cincinnati, where the Kitchen Garden Association's newsletter was published, in 1883 there existed a kindergarten for girls who live in "lovely homes," a Kitchen Garden for "poor little girls" in the same building, and a Colored Kitchen Garden.[29] Girls were being trained apart from boys, whites from blacks, affluent from poor, beginning at age five.

The situation was slightly better in Boston, where one of the leaders in establishing day nurseries and in promoting industrial education for children was Pauline Agassiz Shaw, a philanthropist with several female relatives active in two reform groups organized by Melusina Fay Peirce. In the late 1860s and early 1870s, when Peirce was most active as an organizer, Shaw was raising five children, but in the late 1870s, she started to use her husband's large fortune to promote projects helping employed women and their children. By the 1880s she had established thirty-one kindergartens (6.6) in various districts of Boston, as well as a chain of day nurseries in Cambridge and Boston which taught domestic skills to older children and to mothers in the evenings. In 1881 she launched the first of several industrial training schools.[30] Working with Shaw was Mary Hemenway, who provided the money for sewing classes in the Boston Public Schools in 1865, and then for cooking classes.[31] (According to one historian, boys learned cooking in these classes as well as girls.[32]) In 1887 Hemenway established the Boston Normal School of

Cookery to train cooking teachers. She was also the financial support of a Kitchen Garden program in Shaw's North End Industrial Home, a community center which eventually became one of Boston's first settlement houses. Among its activities in the mid-1880s were a day nursery, a kindergarten and a Kitchen Garden, a sewing room, a laundry, a cooking school, an industrial cafe, a library, an amusement room, a boys' workshop, and a printing shop.[33] Although a distinction seems to have been made here between girls' and boys' activities, all of the programs were open to all residents of the area, and there was no distinction in admissions between the developmental activities of the kindergarten and the vocational activities of the Kitchen Garden.

Livermore and other advocates of industrial training for girls in the 1880s often compared industrial education for girls with industrial education for boys in carpentry or mechanics, when they spoke about equality. Yet the girls' training was not industrial in its nature. Cooking on domestic stoves and hand sewing were craft skills, and since few classes used restaurant equipment or sewing machines, the girls' skills were less marketable than the boys'. Indeed, the teachers often found that many parents refused to send girls to Kitchen Garden classes if they saw these as classes aimed at training for employment as domestic servants. They only supported classes in homemaking which had no relation to paid employment. While this parental attitude was understandable, it frustrated those teachers and philanthro-

pists whose goal was to enhance the pres-
tige of skills such as cooking and sewing
and thus increase the wages such skills
could command.

At the same time that she promoted industrial training for girls, Livermore advocated that women use their power as consumers, much the way that Peirce had, and
she suggested consumers' cooperatives of
twenty-five families as the unit of organization. She warned women that "the business
organizations of men, which have taken so
many industrial employments from the
home, wait to seize those remaining. . . ."
She argued that if housekeepers did not organize themselves, they would have to pay
their housekeeping money to male capitalists. Livermore believed that women had
shown the organizational talent to keep
men from taking over housekeeping, since
"the country is covered with a network of
women's organizations. . . ." [34]

For those women whose bent was not
managerial but familial, there would be
great rewards gained by moving housework
out of the house. Women would be better
mothers, having more time to spend with
their children. They would be better wives,
creating "charming social centers" to keep
their husbands from "billiard rooms, clubhouses, saloons, hotel parlors, and political
headquarters, where so many men forget
their duties to wives and children, and contract habits which rob them of manhood." [35] One hears the militant tone of
the Women's Christian Temperance Union
in this last phrase, and Livermore was one

of the WCTU's key speakers. A close friend
of Frances Willard, head of the WCTU,
Livermore campaigned for the ballot as
"home protection" against the ravages of
strong drink. Both of them supported the
evolutionary socialists in the Nationalist
movement after 1890, joining the followers
of Edward Bellamy, who envisioned the
home of the future as an apartment hotel
served by cooperative housekeeping facilities. As early as 1888, Willard was lecturing in favor of cooperative housekeeping.[36] This blending of temperance, evolutionary socialism, and cooperative housekeeping illustrates the extent to which
WCTU women who idealized the role of
the housewife could still support socialized
domestic work, and see it as a source of
greater power for the home-loving woman.

By the late 1880s, Livermore's vision of
modernized, cooperative housekeeping,
with trained women workers and expert
women managers, had become a rational-
ized version of the more passionate enthu-
siasms of Peirce and Howland. While
Peirce's constituency had been housewives,
and Howland's employed women with
children, Livermore had taken the issue of
socialized domestic work to suffragists,
philanthropists, and temperance workers.
Although she had no special plea to make
on behalf of science, in her emphasis on
the professional nature of housekeeping,
she anticipated many domestic scientists
who would follow her. She was far more
incisive than one historian estimates, who
judges that her lectures offered "little more

6.4, 6.5 Girls about five years old learning to set
the table and do the wash with miniature dishes
and household equipment designed by the
Kitchen Garden Association, 1883

6.6 Kindergarten class in Boston. The American
flag hangs over the heads of immigrant children.
Rigid organization of space makes this environment as unappealing as the classes in laundry
work for five-year-olds.

than a reaffirmation of moral and religious standards of an earlier and simpler day." [37]

Livermore was a keen observer of her own times with a good grasp of the economic and social complexities of domestic life. Above all, she tried to synthesize earlier material feminists' plans for change with the existing structure of industrial capitalist society. If her predecessors were somewhat utopian, she was supremely practical, looking for the "union of plans and action" necessary to reach a goal. Had she been willing to take command of an actual cooperative housekeeping experiment, her "consecrated common sense" might have "compelled success" for her claims for a new domestic world, for she was a leader who could not tolerate failure. Her generation had tested its competence in Civil War work, which prepared many for public careers. She passed on her love of good organization, a considerable legacy, to the next generation of cooperative housekeepers, who would become more and more involved in the ideals of managerial and technical expertise, as they attempted to organize domestic life for mass society. Yet she did not pass on a practical plan.

While Peirce, Howland, and Livermore had all supported women's economic independence, stressed the economic importance of women's domestic work, and demanded that women socialize household tasks, effective tactics for feminists committed to these demands were still unclear. Should cooperative housekeeping be attempted by producers' cooperatives, model industrial communities, or consumers' cooperatives? A basic economic problem underlay these tactical issues. How could wives charge husbands for their work, or join servants to form producers' cooperatives, and still make these forms of socialized domestic work appear to cost less than those generated by industrial capitalism? A commercial laundry which exploited female and black labor was sure to be cheaper to patronize than a housewives' producers' cooperative, unless the housewives' labor was counted as free. It would also be cheaper than a consumers' cooperative, unless the consumer members drove their own workers as hard as the capitalist's. The larger cooperative movement was enmeshed in these dilemmas, and housewives who believed in the cooperative household had to face them too.

New strains of idealism would be added to keep the ideal of cooperative housekeeping viable after the late 1880s. One possibility was government support for cooperatives, seen as part of municipal or national socialism. Another was regular paid employment outside the home for women that would provide them with the cash to pay for new housekeeping services. Both of these had been implicit in the work of Peirce, Howland, and Livermore but never central to their arguments. Between 1868, when Melusina Peirce had published her first manifesto in the *Atlantic Monthly,* and the late 1880s, when Mary Livermore began extensive propagandizing for the idea, the urban population of the United States had more than doubled, to account for a

third of the total. As a result the next generation of domestic reformers gave urban
issues much closer attention, moving from
the ideal of the housewives' cooperative in
a small community to the goal of full female participation in an urbanized, industrialized society. Material feminism, born
with the demand for cooperative housekeeping, would become a much broader
strategy for women's equality in the widen-
ing circles of reform activity during the
Progressive Era.

*When the last pie was made into the first pellet,
woman's true freedom began.*
*— New York Socialistic City, in the year 2050,
described by Anna Bowman Dodd, 1887*

*"Who does your housework, then?" I asked.
"There is none to do," said Mrs. Leete, to whom
I had addressed this question.
— Socialist Boston, in the year 2000, described by
Edward Bellamy, 1888*

*All the public, domestic work is performed by spe-
cialists, both women and men.
— Mars, a feminist planet, described by Henry
Olerich, 1893*

Domestic Space
in Fictional
Socialist Cities

An Unlikely Coalition

At the Merchants' Exchange in the center of Boston's financial district there met, in the winter of 1888, as unlikely a political caucus as had ever formed in that politically minded city. Its feminist contingent included Mary Livermore and Frances Willard of the Women's Christian Temperance Union; Lucy Stone, the suffragist who succeeded Livermore as editor of the *Woman's Journal*; Abby Morton Diaz, novelist and witty critic of traditional housework; and Helen Campbell, home economist and journalist. The literary world was represented by William Dean Howells, celebrated novelist and editor and a former member of the Cambridge Cooperative Housekeeping Society, and Edward Everett Hale, popular author, Unitarian minister, housing reformer, and uncle of Charlotte Perkins Gilman. Sylvester Baxter, a crusading journalist active in promoting Boston parks, was present. Among the well-known social reformers were Solomon Schindler, a radical rabbi; Colonel Thomas Wentworth Higginson, suffragist, abolitionist, son of members of the Cambridge Cooperative Housekeeping Society; and Lawrence Gronlund, cooperative theorist. A group of retired military officers, all of them members of Colonel Higginson's club, arrived and were welcomed, taking over several positions in the new organization which was forming.[1] What cause could have commanded these diverse political loyalties? Edward Bellamy's Nationalism, a program of evolutionary socialism.

The Boston Nationalist Club's inspiration was Edward Bellamy's best-selling novel, *Looking Backward 2000–1887*, published in 1888. Its popular appeal lay in its fictional solution to the crises of an industrialized United States, a solution blending conventional Beaux-Arts city planning and unconventional uses of futuristic technology. The novel conveyed, through long, didactic "conversations," an image of militaristic industrial discipline regulated by time clocks and a vision of cooperative housekeeping aided by scientific expertise. To his thousands of readers, concerned about the nature of work and home under industrial capitalism, Bellamy presented a reassuring picture of a familiar American city improved by a century of peaceful evolutionary socialism.

The hero of *Looking Backward,* Julian West, falls asleep in 1887 and wakes up in Boston in the year 2000. After his awakening, West relentlessly cross-examines his hosts, Mr. and Mrs. Leete, and their daughter, Edith, about all aspects of life in the socialist city of Boston:

"Who does your house-work, then?" I asked.

"There is none to do," said Mrs. Leete, to whom I had addressed this question. "Our washing is all done at public laundries at excessively cheap rates, and our cooking at public shops. Electricity, of course, takes the place of all fires and lighting. We choose houses no larger than we need, and furnish them so as to involve the minimum of trouble to keep them in order. We have no use for domestic servants."

"What a paradise for womankind the world must be now!" I exclaimed.[2]

In Bellamy's socialist Boston, society is as well organized, according to the author, as an efficient textile factory. Every adult belongs to the Industrial Army in its male or female divisions. Specialists in the Industrial Army cook and serve all food. The State owns all means of production; worker's compensation is in the form of labor credits based on a percentage of overall national productivity. Families or individuals wanting food, housing, or help with special household work like spring cleaning request these services from a state office and have them charged against their labor credits.

Julian West narrates his visit to the "general dining-house":

Going up a grand staircase we walked some distance along a broad corridor with many doors opening upon it. At one of these, which bore my host's name, we turned in, and I found myself in an elegant dining-room containing a table for four. Windows opened on a courtyard where a fountain played to a great height and music made the air electric.

"You seem at home here," I said, as we seated ourselves at the table, and Dr. Leete touched an annunciator.

"This is, in fact, a part of our house, slightly detached from the rest," he replied. "Every family in the ward has a room set apart in this great building for its permanent and exclusive use for a small annual rental. For transient guests and individuals there is accommodation on another floor. If we expect to dine here, we put in our orders the night before, selecting anything in market, according to the daily reports in the papers. The meal is as expensive or as simple as we please, though of course everything is vastly cheaper as well as bet-ter than it would be if prepared at home. There is actually nothing which our people take more interest in than the perfection of the catering and cooking done for them. . . ." [3]

The scene ends with praise for both the fine cuisine and the magnificent architecture of the dining house, which is also "a great pleasure-house and social rendezvous of the quarter."

Looking Backward (and a sequel, *Equality*) enjoyed enormous popular success, were translated into many languages, and were used by many socialist groups as proselytizing handbooks.[4] Bellamy's novels were not especially well written and certainly not original in plot, but their popularity reflects the pervasive popular concern with domestic reform as well as industrial reform that characterized the late 1880s and the desire for some positive image of domestic life in mass society. Forty years earlier Jane Sophia Appleton's "Sequel to the Vision of Bangor" had looked ahead to 1978 to describe an egalitarian society in Bangor, Maine, served by community kitchens. It had not achieved a wide readership. Marie Howland's novel, *The Familistère*, which told of a model community in New England, had a wider circulation on its appearance in 1874 and may have influenced Bellamy in its view of work for women: "Independence, honest self-support, by honest, productive industry, is the thing for women as well as men." [5] Howland's long descriptions of a luxurious community dining room and her provisions for gracious food service at home in the Social Palace were very close

to Bellamy's, as were her 1885 designs for
private family dining rooms in Pacific
City.

Two other utopian novels written by
women in the 1880s addressed the issue of
domestic reorganization as well and may
have been known to Bellamy, although
their tone was satirical. Mary E. Bradley
Lane's *Mizora: A Prophecy,* first published in
a Cincinnati newspaper in 1880–1881, prophesied a nation of Amazonian women
who lived on synthetic foods.[6] Anna Bowman Dodd's *The Republic of the Future, or Socialism A Reality,* published in New York in
1887, contained letters purportedly written
from New York Socialistic City in 2050
A.D., where "all family life had died out"
and "the word 'home' has entirely dropped
out of the language." [7] The author la-
ments: "Husband and wife are in reality
two men having equal rights, with the
same range of occupation, the same duties
as citizens to perform, the same haunts and
the same dreary leisure." [8] These "equal"
rights are based on women's doing all domestic work by machinery, in less than two
hours a day. Children are reared in state-
run day care centers. Food for the entire
United Community arrives in New York
Socialistic City from Chicago through electric "culinary conduits." An inhabitant explains: "When the last pie was made into
the first pellet, woman's true freedom
began." [9]

Although Bellamy and his predecessors
described the socialist city of the future in
words, they made it clear that new approaches to organizing space, especially do-

mestic space, were essential to their visions.
The extraordinary financial success of
Bellamy's book inspired a vast number of
utopian novels with a similar emphasis on
reorganizing physical environments for
production and consumption in mass society in the twentieth century. As the turn
of the century approached, such works proliferated. William Dean Howells's *A Traveler
from Altruria,* which appeared serially in *The
Cosmopolitan* in 1892 and 1893, told of a
land where Christian socialism had been
voted in by the citizens, servants had been
abolished, and housekeeping was cooperative.[10] Eugene Richter's *Pictures of the Socialistic Future,* published in 1893, and translated into English in 1894, discussed new
arrangements of space in socialistic Berlin
in rather more sarcastic terms, portraying a
couple reduced to one room per person for
domestic life, assigned by a lottery. State
institutions cared for the elderly and for all
children. One thousand state cookshops in
the city served meals, of "a simple character," to workers who ate under the eyes of
policemen holding stopwatches. Comments
Richter: ". . . those people who had imagined that it would be like the *table d'hôte*
of the great hotels of the past days, where
a pampered upper class continually rev-
elled in every refinement of culinary art —
such persons, I say, must have felt some little disappointment." [11] While the debate
about urban life in a socialistic society continued between those who believed in
progress and those who foresaw only pain,
a few authors hired architects and illustra-
tors, or dabbled in architecture themselves,

hoping to make their visions of future cities more convincing.

The World a Department Store

Bradford Peck followed Bellamy most closely in his ideas of urban design.[12] A self-made businessman, by age twenty-seven he owned a department store in Lewiston, Maine. Despite his financial success, Peck sought greater meaning in life, believing that as a successful entrepreneur he possessed "the ability and the experience to regenerate America along more efficient and more altruistic lines." [13] He published *The World A Department Store* at his own expense in 1900 as a plan for a future society based on cooperation.

Apart from its wonderful title, Peck's novel included Harry C. Wilkinson's rather convincing renderings of buildings such as a municipal restaurant, similar to the neo-classical city halls of the time (7.1). A "restaurant" flag flew beside the Stars and Stripes. He also included views and plans (7.2, 7.3) for apartments of bedroom, parlor, and bath, grouped four to a floor in two-story buildings. Except for his early use of a complete bathroom, these plans recall the small communal apartment houses (2.6), actually built in the Amana Community in Iowa beginning in 1855 and still in use at that time. The rest of Wilkinson's city plan was taken up with cooperative stores, carrying out the metaphor of Peck's title.

Peck was not content to predict the future; he organized the Co-operative Association of America in Lewiston, Maine, in 1899 to carry out his ideas. He established a reading room and cooperative restaurant, and opened a cooperative grocery store, turning over his own department store to the Association to finance these projects.[14] By 1912, the Association was closed, but Peck continued to agitate for cooperative reform until his death at age eighty-two in 1935, a rare, eccentric entrepreneur like J. A. B. Godin of Guise, France, who attempted to practice what he preached.

A Skyscraper Metropolis

High-rise construction provided much of the environmental drama in King Camp Gillette's futuristic Metropolis of sixty million people (7.4), housed in twenty-five story towers (7.5) in a single conurbation so dense that it freed the rest of the North American continent for park land. Gillette wrote *The Human Drift* in 1894 before making his fortune by the invention of the safety razor.[15] He was born in Fond du Lac, Wisconsin, in 1855. His father was an inventor; his mother wrote cookbooks and perhaps interested her son in the subject of food service.

In his plans for a gigantic cooperative city near Niagara Falls, called Metropolis, Gillette provided a three-level underground infrastructure to promote efficient cooperative dining (7.6). The city was based on a hexagonal grid, two-thirds of it covered with high-rise apartment buildings, the remainder divided between educational facilities, amusement buildings, and facilities for the preparation and storage of food. A typical apartment (7.7), to be shared by a

family of four to eight persons, included
four large sitting rooms, four huge baths,
four windowless bedrooms, a shared library, parlor, music room, and veranda.
(Other units would be sized for individuals
or larger families.) The complex was circular, with interior balconies looking onto a
domed interior courtyard. (Its form was
very similar to Hyatt Regency Hotels designed in the 1960s by John Portman.) Gillette specified a steel frame with brick
infill, complemented by glass block and por-
celain tile for interior walls. In a domed
central dining area residents would enjoy
their meals amid fountains and "exquisite
paintings." Although Gillette devoted
much of his time and money to the United
People's Party and included membership
certificates in the party in every copy of
The Human Drift, his utopia was never constructed. The millionaire socialist's book,
with its futuristic drawings, is all that remains of his vision of an urban world with
collective domestic work.

Gender in Utopia

Many utopian novelists, like Gillette, preferred long discussions of architecture and
technology to careful examination of human relationships. Others, like Howland,
Bellamy, and Peck, gave attention to relationships but lacked the insight or commitment to change women's social roles as
completely as their economic roles.
Bellamy's Edith Leete displayed the flirta-
tious, coy manners of a marriageable Victorian maiden, as did Alice Furbush and
Mabel Clay, Peck's female heroines. Men

and women labored separately in the Industrial Army in Bellamy's socialist Boston
and in the work groups of Howland's Social Palace, maintaining a sexual division
of labor after the socialization of domestic
work. Only one or two novelists who were
part of the free love movement in the
1890s had the imagination and the courage
to attempt to attack all or most gender distinctions in their pictures of future societies. In 1893, with the publication of
Lois Waisbrooker's *A Sex Revolution* and
Henry Olerich's *A Cityless and Countryless
World: An Outline of Practical Cooperative Individualism*, the outlines of utopian societies
without gender distinctions appear. For the
first time since the Owenite manifestos of
the 1830s and the trenchant fiction of *The
Woman's Journal* in the 1870s, men are discussed as domestic workers.

Lois Waisbrooker brought to fiction the
experiences of a lifelong commitment to
feminist, spiritualist, and free love causes.
Born Adeline Eliza Nichols in 1826, she
had little formal education and had labored as a domestic servant: "I have
worked in people's kitchens year in and
year out when I never knew what it was to
be rested." [16] When she was able to meet
the requirements for country schoolteaching she left domestic work for teaching and
became active politically. In the 1870s she
lived in Boston and helped to organize the
Boston Social Freedom Convention along
with Moses Hull, Mattie Sawyer, Angela
Heywood, and Ezra Heywood. She wrote
for all the major free love journals, including *Woodhull and Claflin's Weekly, Hull's*

7.1 View of a public restaurant, by H. C.
Wilkinson, from Bradford Peck, *The World A Department Store,* 1900. It resembles the neoclassical
city halls of this era.

7.2 View of apartment houses with kitchenless
apartments, from Peck, *The World A Department
Store.* Conventional Dutch gables adorn the
buildings; a futuristic motorcar rolls by.

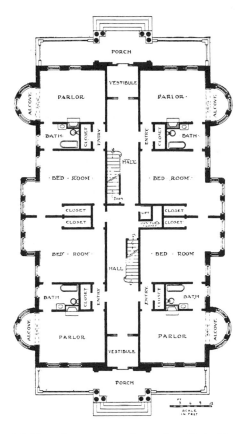

7.3 Plan of an apartment house, from Peck, *The World A Department Store*. There are four apartments without kitchens on each floor. Each has two rooms and a bath, which Charlotte Perkins Gilman defined as the minimum necessary for one adult. Connecting doors suggest the possibility of couples inhabiting adjacent apartments.

7.4 King Camp Gillette, partial plan for Metropolis, from *The Human Drift,* 1894. Included are educational facilities (*A*), amusement buildings (*B*), and facilities for storage and preparation of food (*C*); other buildings are housing. Triangles cover underground conservatories.

7.5 King Camp Gillette, view of apartment buildings in Metropolis. Each is twenty-five stories plus an observatory atop the domed roof.

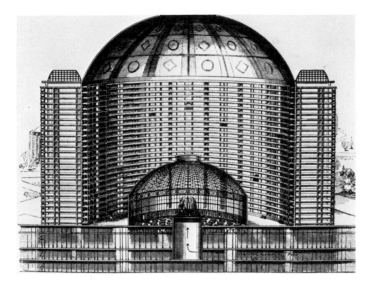

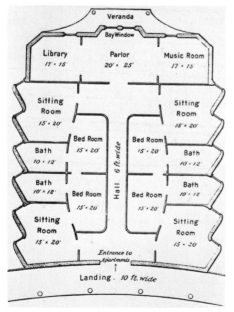

7.7 King Camp Gillette, plan of a kitchenless apartment for a family of four to eight persons. Dark bedrooms and magnificent baths.

7.6 King Camp Gillette, section of steel-framed apartment building showing domed central dining room, with fountain, galleries leading to private apartments, exposed elevators, and underground infrastructure: sewage, utilities (*A*); transportation (*B*); pedestrian arcade lit by triangular skylights (*C*). The resemblance to John Portman's hotels of the 1960s and 1970s is marked. The central space has lost the social intimacy of the courtyard in Godin's Social Palace and become overwhelming in scale.

Crucible, The Word, and *Lucifer.* By the 1880s she was editing her own paper, *Foundation Principles,* dedicated to feminism, spiritualism, and the abolition of rent and profit. She published it in Topeka, Kansas; Clinton, Iowa; and Antioch, California. She also traveled widely as a lecturer and published poetry, suffrage tracts, and fiction. Waisbrooker's novel, *A Sex Revolution,* described a society where women threaten to take up arms against men in order to end all wars. In this crisis men agree to change roles with women, allowing them to rule for fifty years as a social experiment and doing the nurturing and the domestic work necessary to society during that time.[17]

Mars, a Feminist Planet

Henry Olerich, perhaps the most sympathetic of all the futurist novelists of his era, went even farther than Waisbrooker in his portrayal of a nonsexist society. He seems to have worked in isolation and enjoyed limited readership, although he advertised his book as "Bellamy's 'Looking Backward' eclipsed!"[18] Free love journals, such as *The Lucifer,* were the most enthusiastic promoters of his work. An autodidact, with personal whimseys suggestive of Charles Fourier, Olerich was born in 1851 in Hazel Green, a Wisconsin mining town. He farmed with his parents in Wisconsin and Iowa, then after 1874 took up schoolteaching, hotelkeeping, designing tractors, and digging wells, and, in 1894, passed the bar. He also served as mayor of a small town but ultimately went back to being a school

administrator and a hand drill press operator in Omaha, Nebraska. When he was not using his many practical talents, Olerich dreamed of a "cityless and countryless" world which was also a genderless world of equality for men and women.

In Olerich's fictional world of "big-houses," private space for all individuals was complemented by collective kitchens, dining rooms, day care, and recreational facilities. Its organization resembled the urban program for "big-houses" first advocated by Steven Pearl Andrews in 1855 and republished by Woodhull and Claflin in 1871, but its rural setting revealed a different economic and ecological context. Farms, gardens, and orchards enabled residents to grow their own food. Public transportation regularly sped by. The big-houses were located not in the United States in some future time but on the feminist planet, Mars. A "Marsian" visitor, Mr. Midith, tells residents of earth about the wonders of his society:

It may, at first sight, and in your mundane age, seem strange to you to have no family-home like yours; but it is nevertheless a fact. You see society on Mars . . . has had a longer time to evolve than it has had on earth.

You want to bear in mind that we have a family; but that the family consists of a thousand or more men, women, and children, instead of consisting like your family of from one to six or more. . . . Years ago we had cities and towns, and a country similar to yours at the present time; but experience gradually taught us that it is not healthful to live in a crowded, smoky city and town. . . . We also found that a family of husband and wife and their children, living alone in a country home, are largely wasting their lives socially and economically.[19]

His critique of traditional marriage and conventional cities was followed by an account of Mars's evolution.

Olerich provided many site plans and diagrams (7.8, 7.9, 7.10) of his cityless and countryless world, enabling the reader to visualize a typical Marsian's private studio apartment, with a folding bed and four hundred square feet of space (including closets and washroom), handsomely furnished with carpets, paintings, and books. A big-house included six residential wings, of six stories each; big-houses of a thousand people surrounded hollow rectangles of one hundred and twenty big-houses, plus fourteen factories and warehouses, defined by electric tram lines and connected to larger grids of railroads.

Each big-house enjoyed a vegetarian dining room, an indoor child care center, a gymnasium, a library, a scientific laboratory, and many parlors, large and small, richly furnished and decorated with mirrors to reflect the Marsians' "happy faces." All space outside one's private suite was defined as public space, and men as well as women specialists did the "public, domestic work" of cooking and cleaning. All adults shared child care. "Every able-bodied man, woman and youth believes in, and practices independence and self-maintenance. We all detest assistance and protection from others." [20] The amount of required work, under "practical co-

operative individualism," was two hours per day. And Midith chided his listeners: "A lady's day's work is worth just as much to us as a gentleman's, and so it is to you; the only difference is we pay for all it is worth and you do not." [21]

On Mars, when a woman resident of a big-house wished to have a child, she chose any man she liked as her sexual partner. Procreation provided the only occasion for sexual intercourse, in the strictest free love tradition. Olerich explained:

[We] have fathers, but no husbands; mothers, but no wives. No woman gives herself away to a man for any definite length of time; and no man gives himself to any woman for a definite length of time. Consequently, we have no marriages for life, as you have. . . . We believe that a woman, in order to live the purest life, must be free; must enjoy the full privilege of soliciting the love of *any* man, or of *none,* if she so desires. She must be free and independent, socially, industrially, and sexually.[22]

His Marsians followed the Nichols's motto of the 1850s, "freedom, fraternity, chastity."

Children were raised in special quarters in the "big-house" which were designed for their needs: "Several nursery apartments for children and babies are abundantly supplied with toys. The floors of these apartments are composed of a smooth, hard composition, scrubbed or flooded several times a day. The seats, which are along the walls, are all stationary, and hundreds of children, even if left all by themselves in these departments, could do

7.8 Henry Olerich, partial plan of Mars, site of *A Cityless and Countryless World,* 1893. A rectangular grid of electric trolley lines, eight miles wide and twenty miles long, covers the land. Along these lines are located "big houses," or apartment houses, at half-mile intervals, and warehouses and factories at four-mile intervals.

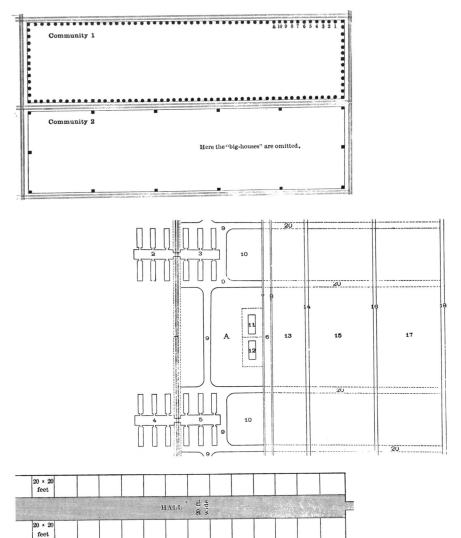

7.9 Henry Olerich, diagram showing trolley line (1); four "big-houses" (2, 3, 4, 5); outdoor nurseries for children (10); swimming pools (11, 12); greenhouses, gardens, orchards, and fields (13, 15, 17, 19); various footpaths (7, 8, 9, 14, 16, 18, 20) and a boulevard (6)

7.10 Henry Olerich, diagram of the residential wing in a "big-house," accommodating thirty people in private suites of four hundred square feet. Note the twenty-foot-wide corridor that suggests a Fourierist gallery of association.

no damage to the buildings and furniture." [23] There were also outdoor nurseries and playgrounds. At puberty, individuals moved into adult apartments.

By 1914 Olerich proposed adapting Marsian ways to the United States. In *Modern Paradise* and *The Story of The World A Thousand Years Hence: A Portrayal of Ideal Life* he redefined the ideal community to permit families and individuals to coexist in a "modern paradise," or cooperative mansion, housing five hundred residents. [24] Cooperative housekeeping and nursery facilities were to be available. Yet for all these detailed plans of ideal societies, Olerich never ventured to experiment in cooperation himself. His narrator had expressed the difficulties succinctly:

The difficult point is this: to devise or outline a social and industrial system in which a large number of individuals co-operate harmoniously, and yet have every individual free to do what he believes to be right, provided he infringes not upon the equal rights of any other person. No man here on earth thus far has been able to outline such a system. [25]

Olerich himself knew that absolute personal freedom and absolute equality between men and women were radical propositions.

In his farseeing abolition of gender distinctions, Olerich remains unique in his time. His fictional visions of nurturing men, who cooked and cared for babies alongside the women of his utopias, are heartening. Other male novelists enjoyed the freedom fiction gave them to theorize about women's liberation from domestic work without asking men to bear any of the organizational or economic burdens this liberation would entail. Many men credited themselves, as theorists, with having provided wise, guiding insights to free their wives and daughters from drudgery, without understanding how patronizing this was. Alone among the many male utopian novelists of his era, Olerich never asked for women's thanks, and he looked forward to the time when all men would do their share.

Fictional Cities and Practical Reform
By 1900, Edward Bellamy, and, to a lesser extent, other literary utopians, had developed a strong following among architects and urban planners. In 1890 Pickering Putnam, a Boston architect, argued for the further development of apartment hotels with food service, and in *Architecture under Nationalism* he began to popularize this building type. Around the same time Ebenezer Howard, still a young civil servant, offered to arrange for the publication of Bellamy's book in England and began to develop the Garden Cities program, which would make him the most influential town planner in twentieth-century Britain and lead to the proliferation of plans for "cooperative quadrangles."

In addition Bellamy made many converts among housewives and feminist activists. His influence on domestic issues seems to have grown rapidly because many other works of utopian fiction and experiments in community dining had prepared the way for a fictional view of "scientific" housekeeping in the year 2000. There was much disagreement about Bellamy's economic and industrial strategies, but not about his domestic proposals. The membership of many prominent feminists, such as Helen Campbell, Mary Livermore, and Frances Willard, in the Boston Nationalist Club reveals their support for him. Bellamy wrote for both *Good Housekeeping* and the *Ladies' Home Journal* to reach a still wider female audience.[26]

When, in 1890, Bellamy exhorted women to organize cooperative laundries and kitchens to gain for themselves the immediate benefits of household reform, providing their former servants with well-paid "professional" employment, "like that of mechanics called into a house to do specific work," his words had swift effect.[27] Fanny Fuller launched "The Roby," a cooperative boarding club in Decatur, Illinois. A Bellamy Club in Junction City, Kansas, and another in Utica, New York, were among the cooperative family dining clubs launched in that year. Nationalist publications reported these activities, as well as women's journals.[28] In that same year, Frances Willard began to raise money for a training school for domestic work,[29] and Ellen Richards, Instructor in Sanitary Chemistry at MIT, with Mary Hinman Abel, a domestic scientist, launched the New England Kitchen, a laboratory kitchen designed to provide nutritious food at low cost through experiments with a variety of equipment, including the Aladdin oven and cooker, invented by Edward Atkinson. Richards commented to the in-

ventor, ". . . the mission of the Oven and Cooker is in the ideal life of the twentieth century, as shown by Bellamy. . . . I believe the idea is destined to give a much-needed relief to multitudes of overworked women. . . ."[30]

While Fuller, Livermore, Willard, Campbell, Richards, and Abel were important converts to Nationalist thinking around 1890, perhaps the most important of all was the young Charlotte Perkins Stetson, who read Bellamy in California and then visited a Nationalist Club. When she published some of her feminist poetry in *The Nationalist* in 1890, at age thirty, she represented the next generation of material feminists who would eventually call for domestic reform and envision new kinds of cities as "paradise for womankind." Meanwhile, professional women were looking for the financially secure employment promised to women by Bellamy, Peck, Olerich, and all the other utopian writers who accepted the idea of women's work outside the home and envisioned new services which would make that employment possible. In such a future society, the career women who were experts in nutrition, settlement house leaders, and trade union organizers could find their places. After the late 1880s their voices for domestic reform joined those of the housewives, free lovers, and suffragists who favored cooperative housekeeping; as much as anything else, utopian fiction had formed their middle class constituency, because the utopian novelists succeeded in encouraging millions of readers to imagine the possibilities of an

egalitarian, industrialized, mass society,
without all the evils of capitalism.

In their domestic schemes novelists often
relied on national or municipal socialism
to provide the food, laundry, and child
care services they devised, a great leap in
scale from the neighborhood producers'
and consumers' cooperatives proposed by
earlier reformers, or the benevolent factory
owners occasionally invoked by earlier
communitarians. Municipal services looked
very inviting to liberals as well as radicals;
even traditional philanthropists could support transferring activities such as soup
kitchens and industrial training courses to
the city budget. A broad audience became
sympathetic to socialized domestic work for
entire urban populations, an audience
which had not existed before Bellamy, and
material feminists were quick to take advantage of it, although their ideological
task increased as their audience became
more diverse.

To go beyond the utopian novelists, they
needed practical skills. To go beyond the
cooperative housekeepers, they needed to
use these skills on behalf of a broader
group than unpaid housewives and low-
paid servants. Women industrial workers
and women professionals were increasing
in numbers, and their particular economic
needs demanded a more complex statement of the nature of material feminism.
How did industrial and professional employment for women affect the creation of
feminist homes, neighborhoods, and cities?

8.1 Ellen Swallow Richards

*We have worked out during our years of residence
a plan of living which may be called cooperative. . . .
— Jane Addams, describing Hull-House, 1910*

*. . . back of cooperative action must be agree-
ment, agreement upon standards, and back of
standards, must be knowledge and understanding.
— Caroline Hunt, addressing the Lake Placid
Conference on Home Economics, 1907*

Public Kitchens, Social Settlements, and the Cooperative Ideal

Professional Approaches to Domesticity

Visitors who thronged the World's Columbian Exposition in Chicago in 1893 found their fantasies about home life in the twentieth century stimulated. Technology accomplished marvels in utopian fiction, but it was at least as persuasive to see the Rumford Kitchen feeding ten thousand people at the fair as to read Edward Bellamy on socialist Boston. It was much more convincing to leave one's children at the model kindergarten in the Children's Building than to study Marie Howland's fictional child care arrangements for a Social Palace. It was far more thrilling to stroll under the electric lights illuminating the fairgrounds in Chicago, ride the electric tramcars, and inspect the electric kitchen, than to decipher the diagrams of Henry Olerich's fictional, electrified settlements on Mars.

The scientist whose work caught the attention of many domestic reformers and housewives at the exposition was Ellen Swallow Richards (8.1), whose Rumford Kitchen was part of the Massachusetts exhibit. The public kitchen, designed as a small, white clapboard house, with a peaked roof and a broad, inviting front porch, promised to fit perfectly into any conventional neighborhood of modest single-family homes. Inside, however, was all the equipment of a scientific laboratory designed to extract the maximum amount of nutrition from food substances and the maximum heat from fuel. The public kitchen appealed to visitors' wit, with mottos and humorous quotations about food by famous authors hung on the walls; it appealed to their palates, with Boston baked beans and brown bread, among other specialties; it appealed to their pocketbooks, with low prices and complimentary analyses of the proteins, fats, carbohydrates, and calories in each portion. This exhibit excited housewives, organizers of social settlements, and faculty from universities where home economics was part of the curriculum. The members of the new National Household Economics Association, founded in Chicago at the exposition, made public kitchens in poor districts part of their platform; Jane Addams of Hull-House ordered the equipment for a public kitchen for her settlement house; Marion Talbot, Dean of Women at the University of Chicago, carried off the exhibit's equipment for her students when the fair was over. A new approach to collective domestic life seemed to be emerging, under the leadership of a small group of highly educated women trained to use the latest technological inventions.

The excitement about public kitchens centered on two new professional fields dominated by women, home economics and social work, which came into being between 1887 and 1910. Together these two fields channeled the energies of many newly educated American women into the reform projects of the Progressive Era, and had a profound influence on American homes and families, especially working-class and immigrant families. These women pioneered the use of applied natural science and social science to analyze the problems of urban life; their subject matter ranged over chemistry, medicine, law, architecture, sociology, and economics, specializations in which many of them were originally trained. They stressed women's collective attempts to improve the public environment and the domestic lives of ordinary people, and cooperative housekeeping was a familiar concept to them.

"We all became acquainted with the ideal picture in the once famous 'Looking Backward' of Edward Bellamy," recalled Mary Hinman Abel, a noted home economist: ". . . instead of fifty incompetent buyers at retail, one efficient buyer at wholesale; a chef . . . master of his art, and also of the new knowledge in nutrition now available; one kitchen fire instead of fifty; . . . the peripatetic housemaid and all other workers responsible to a bureau; the house heated from a central station, where a competent engineer shall extract from each pound of coal all the heat it should yield." [1] During the two decades after Bellamy's novel appeared in 1888, the new generation of professional women like Abel who were engaged in home economics and social settlement work broadened the definition of cooperative housekeeping created by earlier material feminists and utopian novelists. As specialists in nutrition, sanitation, and social welfare, they were the embodiment of an earlier generation's call for experts to deal with domestic life, yet when they examined the domestic world in terms of their new spe-

cialties, they eventually redefined "cooperative housekeeping" in favor of "social housekeeping" and altered the feminist and socialist thrust of earlier theories.

Democracy and scientific standards for the whole society became their slogans, as opposed to Melusina Fay Peirce's call for economic and psychological self-determination for women, or Edward Bellamy's prophecy of evolutionary socialism. The choice of constituencies, the design of experiments, and the arguments in favor of collective domesticity all shifted to reflect a serious concern for poor urban immigrants. The new professionals shared the earlier reformers' commitment to the private home, but they wished to create municipal facilities and services, rather than neighbors' cooperatives, to complement the home. They believed that such services were compatible with a democratic, capitalist society. They saw domestic issues as public issues and domestic skills as public skills: thus was born the concept of "women's public work for the home," undertaken by determined women reformers in corrupt, filthy American industrial cities.

The women whose work most reflected this new approach to domestic life were Ellen Swallow Richards, Instructor in Sanitary Chemistry at MIT, and Jane Addams, head of Hull-House in Chicago. As leaders in home economics and social settlement work, they engaged in organizing activities far broader than Peirce's attempts to organize her neighbors and their servants or Howland's communitarian ventures. Rich-

ards and Addams were concerned with
building coalitions of philanthropists, civil
servants, academics, and professionals to
deal with the vast physical and social problems of the urban slums. They had a much
keener and more realistic sense of class interests than any of the reformers who preceded them, and this knowledge ultimately
showed itself in mistrust of voluntary cooperation. These women tended to prefer
forms of organization that emphasized the
partnership of the state and the skilled professional, the latter usually an idealistic,
university-trained woman who saw herself
as an advocate for the needs of poor
women and children, especially the single
women and married women in the paid labor force who were concentrated in city
slums. In addition to their own professional
recruits, Richards and Addams drew educated women volunteers from groups such
as the Association of Collegiate Alumnae,
the General Federation of Women's Clubs,
and the Women's Christian Temperance
Union. Many of these volunteers have
been called "social feminists," women who
believed in women's rights but were most
active in campaigns for broad social reforms[2] in the areas of sanitation, housing,
health, temperance, and social purity,
areas in which they attempted to obey
Frances Willard's command to "make the
whole world homelike."

In the 1880s and 1890s, the earliest years
of home economics and social settlement
work, professionals and their helpers spent
a good part of their time devising collective
or cooperative services. For every apartment hotel built for the affluent in this era
with collective kitchens, laundries, and
other facilities, there were fifty tenements
crowded with immigrant workers living in
kitchenless apartments from need rather
than from choice (8.2). In Chicago's tenement districts, surveyed by Robert Hunter
in 1900, dwelling units averaged under 300
square feet, divided into small, often
unventilated rooms, occupied by large
families and their boarders, so that an individual had on the average 28 to 32 square
feet of space. At 457 people per acre, these
areas were said to be the most densely pop-
ulated in the world.[3] In these dwellings,
cooking was done in the main room, which
was provided with a stove, also used for
heating. This room might have a sink, but
often shared sinks (or simply pumps) were
in the halls or the back yard. Stinking
basement privies were shared by an average of eight people; as many as half were
illegal privies without proper sewer connections. Ninety-seven percent of the Chicago
tenement units were without bathtubs, despite the fact that many of their almost
one million residents were employed in
slaughterhouse work.[4]

Under such circumstances, cooperative
housekeeping strategies took on a new
significance. Although residents of tenement districts needed more kitchens, baths,
laundries, and kindergartens, it was not
clear that simply reorganizing existing resources could provide them. The elite of
Cambridge, Massachusetts, could afford to
buy $50 shares in a cooperative kitchen,
but the neediest residents of the Nine-

8.2 Tenement house residents: photograph by
Jacob Riis showing a family of seven crowded
into a room with stove and dishes at left, unventilated bedroom with interior window at rear

teenth Ward in Chicago had no capital to
invest in cooperatives. In this context, cooperative housekeeping often became a
philanthropists' slogan, suggestive of the
most efficient ways of giving money for facilities in slum districts, rather than a slogan of the tenement dwellers themselves.
Although housewives in the Knights of Labor did organize cooperative housekeeping
as residents of one New York tenement in
the 1880s, such projects were more likely to
be initiated by reformers with outside
funds.[5] As one reformer, Elisabeth Bisland,
explained it in 1889, cooperative housekeeping schemes could complement philanthropic model tenement projects. Public
kitchens countered "the numberless ills resulting from improperly nurtured bodies";
public baths promoted bathing, as an aid
to "mental, moral, and physical sanity";
public laundries (8.3) promoted cleanli-
ness; and public kindergartens (6.6, 8.4)
lightened the burden of the employed
mother.

Since these facilities were usually organized for the poor, not by the poor, they
reflected the philanthropists', home economists', and settlement workers' ideas of
proper organization. Gone were some
affluent women's visions of cooperative
kitchens delivering elegant, seven-course
dinners and cooperative laundries present-
ing rows of snowy ruffles on dress shirts,
perfectly ironed. A sufficient supply of hot
soup and enough coal to last the week were
more to the point. Expertise first developed
in total institutions such as the kitchens
and laundries of hospitals, poorhouses, and

military camps had to be translated into
attractive, non-profit services which poor
people would voluntarily patronize in
urban districts. To reconcile these new
services with democratic goals, home economists and settlement workers overlaid the
rhetoric and technology of earlier philanthropic reforms with the rhetoric of cooperative housekeeping and the techniques of
new physical and social sciences.

Public Kitchens
As developed by Ellen Swallow Richards
and Mary Hinman Abel, the public
kitchen took the form of a scientific laboratory. The services it offered were advanced
in the name of the employed mother, who
had no time to prepare cooked food for her
family, and the employed father, lured to
saloons for food and drink. By offering inexpensive, nutritious, cooked food to take
home, founders of the public kitchens
promised to combat malnutrition, the un-
economical use of fuel, and the exhaustion
of women workers. Most of all, they promised to replace gin with good dinners. In
an era of urban pollution and adulterated
foods, the kitchens were to be spotlessly
clean spaces for scientific demonstrations of
methods of right living.

"It is a part of the New Philanthropy to
recognize that the social question is largely
a question of the stomach . . . ," contended Mary Hinman Abel in a leaflet
published in 1893, part of a series of publications promoting the establishment of
public kitchens in American cities.[6] The
first public kitchen, The New England

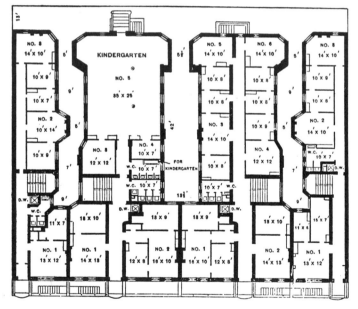

8.3 Reformer's "before" and "after" sketches: tenement wash day versus a cooperative laundry in a model tenement project, *Cosmopolitan*, November 1889

8.4 Model tenement house with kindergarten, 338–344 Cherry Street, New York, Tenement House Building Company, 1887. Dwelling units include two or three rooms. Water closets are shared. Dumbwaiters lift coal from the basement. The kindergarten is for the care of children of employed mothers.

Kitchen designed by Abel and Richards in
1890, improved upon the charitable soup
kitchens (8.5), which were often opened
during times of economic depression and
the saloons which sold food only to customers who bought alcohol as well. The
kitchen was intended to complement a
neighborhood of tenement houses and inexpensive apartment houses, and to educate both poor people and the slightly
more affluent about nutrition.

The philanthropist who supported the
New England Kitchen, Pauline Agassiz
Shaw, had given money earlier for numerous day nurseries and kindergartens in
Boston and eventually supported several
settlement houses.[7] The recipient of Shaw's
gift, Ellen Swallow Richards, was well
known as a scientist concerned with standards of purity in water, air, and food.[8]
Born in Dunstable, Massachusetts, in 1842,
she was the daughter of a farmer and
storekeeper. As a young woman she had
occasionally "hired out" to local families to
make some extra money and had taught
school, but she demonstrated a persistent
desire for more education. In 1873, she became the first woman to receive a B.S. degree from MIT, and was also the first
woman appointed to the MIT faculty,
heading a special "Women's Laboratory"
in 1875, funded by the Boston Women's
Education Association. A deceptively frail-
looking woman with sparkling eyes and
great stamina, she turned her home in the
Jamaica Plain neighborhood of Boston into
an experiment station for new domestic
technologies.

Richards's broad scientific and social interests which won her the nickname
"Ellencyclopedia," made her a key figure
in a network of public-spirited, university-
trained women active in education, settlement work, and government. Her early
publications included the results of work
on copper and vanadium; on the chemistry
of cooking and cleaning; on the testing of
water supplies; and on the detection of
adulterated foods. In 1890, when MIT established the first program in sanitary
engineering in the United States, Richards
taught the analysis of water, air, and sewage.[9] In 1892 she chose the term "oekol-
ogy" to introduce "the science of normal
family life" or "the science which teaches
the principles on which to found healthy
and happy homes." [10] In later years she
was to call this same interdisciplinary field
"home economics" (the economics of consumption) and "euthenics," (the science of
controllable environment).[11]

To assist her in founding an experimental, scientific public kitchen, Ellen Richards recruited Mary Hinman Abel, who
had a good knowledge of philanthropic
kitchens in Europe, such as the *cucini popu-
lari* in Modena and the *Volksküchen* in
Vienna, Leipzig, and Berlin (8.6). Abel was
also an expert in nutrition. On January 24,
1890, the New England Kitchen, at 142
Pleasant Street in Boston, began selling
plain, inexpensive, nutritious, Yankee food:
beef broth; beef stew; vegetable, tomato,
and pea soup; boiled corn and oatmeal
mush; boiled hominy; cracked wheat; fish
chowder; Indian and rice pudding.[12] The

8.5 Soup kitchen, 110 Centre Street, New York, one of eight founded by Commodore James Gordon Bennett, proprietor of the *New York Herald,* to feed the poor after the Panic of 1873. It opened in February 1874, offering soup prepared by the fashionable chef of Delmonico's Restaurant, Mr. Charles Ranhoffer, and served 2,000 people in one day with quart-size tin mugs of soup. According to *Frank Leslie's Illustrated Newspaper,* March 7, 1874, "Experienced philanthropists declared the soup the best they had ever tasted in an institution of the kind," and reporters attributed this to the chef and the fact that "the kettles are cleaned each day, and the rooms are as neat as a New England kitchen."

8.6 Berlin, soup kitchen for the poor, founded by Lina Morgenstern, 1866, shown in *Frank Leslie's Illustrated Newspaper,* May 14, 1870, along with the report that in an eighteen-day period, the kitchen, established by order of the Commissioners of Charities and Corrections, had sold 111,385 quarts of soup to the poor.

kitchen (8.7) looked like a scientific laboratory and was equipped with a new invention, the slow-cooking Aladdin Oven, designed by Edward Atkinson, as well as a
steam plant, a gas table, and various other
experimental equipment. Richards was a
consultant for Atkinson's company and an
enthusiastic advocate of his oven, which,
she believed, would bring about "the ideal
life of the twentieth century, as shown by
Bellamy." [13]

Using the Aladdin Oven, the kitchen
aimed to take "cheaper cuts of meat and
simpler vegetables," and by slow and thorough cooking, make them attractive and
secure "their nutritive value . . . for the
people who sadly needed more nutritious
food." [14] Frequent chemical analyses of the
food, under the direction of Richards and
Dr. Thomas M. Drown of MIT, supported
guarantees of its nutritious value. It fired
the enthusiasm of many philanthropists as
well as experts in nutrition and domestic
technology. In the next four years two
similar enterprises were launched in
Boston's West End and North End, and
others in Olneyville, Rhode Island; at 341
Hudson Street, New York (8.8); and at
Hull-House in Chicago. [15]

Richards and Abel achieved their
greatest publicity from the Rumford
Kitchen (8.9) exhibited at the World's Columbian Exposition in 1893. The kitchen
was named after Benjamin Thompson,
Count Rumford, whom Richards and Abel
admired for his experiments in the design
of stoves and his attempts in 1790 to feed
the poor in Munich "scientifically." In
their leaflets, distributed at the fair, they
quoted Rumford's comments on wasting
energy: "The common kitchen range seems
to have been calculated for the express
purpose of devouring fuel"; "it is a common habit to boil a dish of tea with fuel
sufficient to cook a dinner for fifty men." [16]
Where they differed with Rumford was on
the question of compulsory feeding. Rumford was an authoritarian inventor who
had moved the destitute of Munich into a
House of Industry to begin his experiments
in feeding them, whereas Richards and
Abel hoped to persuade women and men
to patronize their facilities by choice. Although the scientific kitchen was a big success at the Chicago exposition, where ten
thousand visitors passed through in two
months, the urban, philanthropic kitchens
feeding workers every day had serious
problems with popular tastes. [17] Immigrants preferred their national dishes and
spices to the plain, institutional menu
which domestic science dictated. As Richards ruefully admitted, a man from Southern Europe pointed to an Indian pudding,
complaining, "You needn't try to make a
Yankee out of me by making me eat
that." [18]

The advocates of public kitchens were
undaunted by immigrants' preferences for
their own cuisines. They modified their
menus. They attempted to find and educate a younger audience through preparing
lunches available to children in public
schools (taking this business away from
school janitors and their wives). They
brought lunch to women workers in

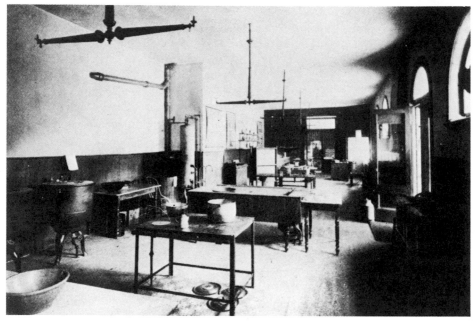

8.7 New England Kitchen, main office, foundec by Ellen Swallow Richards and Mary Hinman Abel, 142 Pleasant Street, Boston, 1890. Equipment included weights to measure food, insulated containers for customers to carry it home, and glassware and gas jets suggesting the scientific laboratories at MIT after which the kitchen was patterned.

8.8 New England Kitchen, branch at 341 Hudson Street, New York, founded December 1891, showing the bare spaces of a laboratorylike area equipped with apparatus for cooking by steam and gas

8.9 The Rumford Kitchen, an exhibit set up by Ellen Swallow Richards and Mary Hinman Abel for the World's Columbian Exposition, 1893, on the exterior a small, single-family clapboard house with a broad front porch

factories, who were often the worst nourished workers because of low salaries paid to women and because of traditional practices in homes and cafes of giving men more and better food.[19] They offered special broths to hospitals and to invalids. They provided food as well to the growing numbers of middle-class professionals residing in settlement houses. They began to give cooking lessons to schoolchildren, housewives, domestic servants, and dieticians.

Although the home economists managed to get by financially and to keep some of their public kitchens running, they were never able to raise the funds to build the new facilities they dreamed of. One English architectural design (8.10) for a public kitchen from the mid-1880s suggests the type of building both European and American experts in nutrition desired to erect. Captain M. P. Wolff, formerly a German military officer, became interested in feeding the poor in England, after learning of various "penny kitchens" and other philanthropic schemes in Scotland and England. With some advice from an English architect, William White, he designed a public kitchen and dining room.[20] It included a waiting hall adjoining the street, where customers could buy cooked food to take home, filling their carrying vessels with hot water as insulation. In the same space, cashiers sold tickets for food. Customers who wished to eat on the premises would proceed to the dining room, passing the lavatories on the way. The dining room was supplied with straight rows of benches

and tables; at the rear was an exit to simplify circulation. The heart of the scheme was a kitchen fitted with roasters, steam kettles, meat cutting areas, and all the specialized equipment of a hotel kitchen. Here was the focus of Wolff's calculations in his pamphlet, *Food for the Million.*

This was also the ideal of Richards and Abel, who hoped that their laboratory kitchens would be found in every town and city. Although the National Household Economics Association, formed in 1893, made public kitchens part of its national program, only in the twentieth century have mass production food chains succeeded commercially. Wolff's ideas about "food for the million" were thought to be a bit ambitious and authoritarian in 1884, but "the Colonel's face is all over the place," in the Kentucky Fried Chicken campaigns of today, and McDonald's boasts of having sold twenty-five billion burgers.

Social Settlements

While public kitchens remained demonstration projects in the 1890s, social settlement houses represented the great success of urban cooperative housekeeping in the late nineteenth and early twentieth centuries. Here advocates of day care centers, public kitchens, and cooperative housing for industrial workers, servants, and professionals, gathered to build innovative residential communities.

Preeminent among social settlement organizers was Jane Addams, the daughter of a banker and politician from Cedarville, Illinois, born in 1860 and described as

8.10 M. P. Wolff, plan for a public kitchen,
1884. Patrons may buy food to take away, in the
waiting hall, or they may eat in the dining hall.
Taps in the waiting hall are to fill double-walled
tin carrying vessels with hot water to insulate
hot food. Dotted lines show circulation paths.

"Saint Jane" and "an American abbess."
The reforms undertaken by her settlement
house illustrate some of the broader trends
in social work and illuminate the ties between the residents of settlement houses,
who developed many community outreach
programs, and home economists, who were
involved in research, teaching, and demonstration work in nutrition, child rearing,
housing, and sanitation.[21]

Beginning in 1889 Jane Addams and
two associates "settled" in an immigrant
neighborhood in Chicago, creating Hull-
House, a secular community of dedicated
reformers, who lived and worked among
the immigrants of the Nineteenth Ward,
attempting to gain firsthand knowledge of
the poverty, disease, and exploitation they
suffered. In 1890 Chicago had a population
of one million, three-quarters of whom
were immigrants, mostly living in crowded
tenements with inadequate light, air, and
sanitation and working in squalid factories
and sweatshops. Addams recruited idealistic doctors, lawyers, academics, and government officials to the immigrants' cause.
Such outstanding reformers as Florence
Kelley, Julia Lathrop, and Dr. Alice Hamilton worked at her side, attacking callous
factory owners and boodling political
bosses. Yet, as Gerda Lerner has noted,
"Jane Addams' enormous contribution in
creating a supporting female network and
new structures for living" has often been
ignored by historians, who have concentrated on her role as a Progressive reformer, or as a representative of a "group

of frustrated college-trained women with
no place to go." [22]

Many reforms first initiated at Hull-
House were aimed at working women
(both factory workers and professionals)
and their domestic needs of child care,
food, and housing. They were backed up
by evening classes of all kinds, musical and
literary events, trade-union organizing (especially for poorly-paid women workers),
social clubs, a public bathhouse, and a
consumers' cooperative for the purchase of
coal. *Hull-House Maps and Papers* (1895), a
pioneer work in urban sociology, reflected
the residents' efforts to analyze the problems of the Nineteenth Ward. Because of
their understanding of urban life and politics, Hull-House residents did manage to
influence social legislation as well as the
emerging field of urban sociology. Through
the 1890s they lobbied effectively for industrial health and safety, the limitation of
child labor, and the legal recognition of
trade unions.

By the mid-1890s, twenty women were
in residence, and forty activities drew 2,000
people per week to the settlement. Addams
chose Allan B. Pond to design a physical
complex around these programs. The result
was aesthetically dreary and socially innovative, heavy red brick buildings of an institutional mien surrounding an urban
block, lightened by the first public playground in Chicago.[23] Meeting rooms at
Hull-House were complemented by apartments, as many of the social workers, reformers, and scholars who came to visit
stayed to live and work at the settlement,

dining together every night while exchanging news and information about reform subjects. By 1911 there were over four hundred settlement houses in the United States, and Addams was president of the national association they formed.[24] A distinctive building type to house the settlements' collective living and community services had emerged as well, emphasizing a combination of residential and social spaces (8.11).

Among Hull-House's many successes, Jane Addams's earliest domestic reform programs are most significant for this study. When Addams arrived in Chicago in 1889, she, along with her friend, Ellen Gates Starr, and their housekeeper, Mary Keyser, "early learned to know the children of hard-driven mothers who went out to work all day, sometimes leaving the little things in the casual care of a neighbor, but often locking them into their tenement rooms," [25] In 1891, with the help of Jenny Dow, she organized a day nursery for these children.

The kindergarten and day nursery movement was already well established, through the efforts of Elizabeth Peabody, Mary Peabody Mann, Mary Hemenway, Emily Huntington, and others. At Hull-House, Jane Addams hung the kindergarten walls with reproductions of Italian madonnas and cherubs, adding culture to child care. The other furniture and equipment were rather casually assembled, however, and she sought none of the carefully designed play equipment available in either Froebel kindergartens or progressive utopian communities. By 1907 the Mary Crane Creche was added to the Hull-House complex, providing more extensive play space and rest areas. Along with the nursery in this new building came demonstration rooms for domestic science activities.

After the day nursery proved successful, in 1893 Addams and Starr undertook the establishment of a public kitchen. "An investigation of the sweatshops had disclosed the fact, that sewing women during the busy season paid little attention to the feeding of their families, for it was only by working steadily through the long day that the scanty pay of five, seven, or nine cents for finishing a dozen pairs of trousers could be made into a day's wage; and they bought from the nearest grocery the canned goods that could be most quickly heated, or gave a few pennies to the children with which they might secure a lunch from a neighboring candy shop." [26] The residents of Hull-House carefully researched the dietary deficiencies immigrants suffered from. One resident, Julia Lathrop, then went to Boston to learn scientific food preparation at the innovative New England Kitchen from Abel and Richards. The Public Kitchen at Hull-House was launched after her return in 1894.

At Hull-House, Addams found that immigrant working women might buy the scientifically cooked food when it was taken around and sold in neighborhood factories at lunchtime or at the end of the day, and that a few households would buy from the kitchen itself, marked with a large

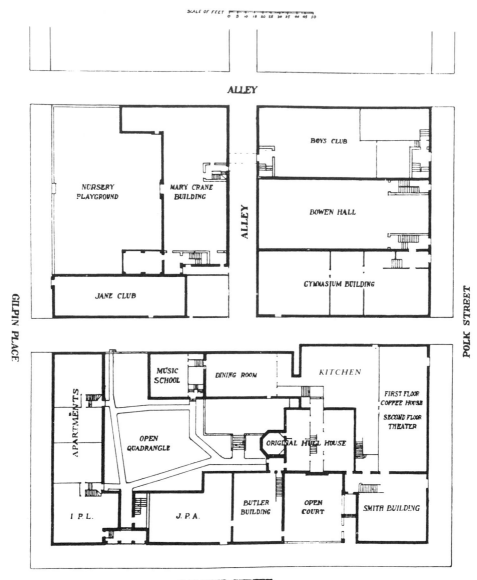

ALLEY

BOYS CLUB

NURSERY
PLAYGROUND

MARY CRANE
BUILDING

ALLEY

BOWEN HALL

GILPIN PLACE

POLK STREET

GYMNASIUM BUILDING

JANE CLUB

MUSIC
SCHOOL

DINING ROOM

KITCHEN

FIRST FLOOR
COFFEE HOUSE

SECOND FLOOR
THEATER

APARTMENTS

OPEN
QUADRANGLE

ORIGINAL HULL HOUSE

I.P.L.

J.P.A.

BUTLER
BUILDING

OPEN
COURT

SMITH BUILDING

HALSTED STREET

8.11 Hull-House, Chicago, plans by Pond and
Pond, Architects, 1889–1916. The original private house on Halsted Street has been surrounded by a public kitchen, residents' dining
room, coffee house, and apartments for residents.
The Jane Club, the Phalanx Club, the gym, the
Creche and playground, and Bowen Hall are located on Polk Street and Gilpin Place.

sign, "Public Restaurant and Bakery . . . Soups, Stews . . . All Ready Cooked to Take Home." [27] Many more immigrant families were disinclined to use the public restaurant or buy the cooked food, because it did not conform to the male workers' tastes. Addams eventually replaced the public restaurant with a coffeehouse, as an alternative to the local saloons, and the scientific kitchen served both this coffeehouse and residents' dining room, where nutritious Yankee food was quite acceptable. Even if immigrant families did not patronize scientific cooking, professional women working in the immigrant districts wanted to simplify their own housekeeping.

Cooperative Living and the Unionization of Women Factory Workers

In addition to feeding women workers, the Hull-House settlement workers tried to help them organize trade unions and develop adequate housing. When Mary Kenney, a young Irish woman working in the bookbinding trade in Chicago, first met Jane Addams, she decided that Addams and her associates were "all rich and not friends of the workers." [28] Yet Addams offered to help Kenney with organizing a union, and the two became friends. Kenney, born in Hannibal, Missouri, in 1864, was four years younger than Addams, but already cynical about working girls' clubs, which offered only outings or charity. Later in her career she was an organizer for the American Federation of Labor and a founder of the National Women's Trade Union League, but even in 1891 she was committed to militant demands for higher wages. Together with Addams, she began to advocate her version of workers' cooperative housekeeping as a tool to help win strikes, a significant new use of the concept directed at a new constituency, single women workers.   This strategy emerged when Kenney began to hold union meetings at Hull-House for women in the bookbinding and shoe trades. As Addams recalled: "At a meeting of working girls held at Hull-House during a strike in a large shoe factory, the discussions made it clear that the strikers who had been easily frightened, and therefore first to capitulate, were naturally those girls who were paying board and were afraid of being put out if they fell too far behind. After a recital of a case of peculiar hardship one of them exclaimed: 'wouldn't it be fine if we had a boarding club of our own, and then we could stand by each other in a time like this?' " [29]

Kenney organized "six members, with a cook and a general worker," who shared one apartment at 253 Ewing Street. Addams supplied furnishings and the first month's rent. On May 1, 1891, the experiment began. As Kenney described it: "We spent one evening each week discussing ways and means and management . . . We had no rules or by-laws. We elected a president, who was also steward, and a treasurer . . . We voted to tax ourselves $3.00 each for weekly dues, which covered expenses for food, quarters, and service." [30] The organization, which called itself the

Jane Club, grew and prospered. By the end of three months the membership had tripled, and they had taken over several apartments. Even in lighthearted moments the labor struggle was not forgotten: Kenney reported that when women members of the boarding club went to dances together, they first checked their escorts' hatbands and cigarbands for the union label. By 1893, the club impressed the skeptical head of the U.S. Department of Labor, who claimed before his visit there that he had never before seen women cooperate successfully.[31] By 1894, thirty members occupied all six apartments of the original building on Ewing Street.[32]

The Jane Club's cooperative housekeeping filled the needs of young, single, female factory workers living on very meager wages, whose only alternatives were to live at home, find a cheap boardinghouse, or perhaps apply to a philanthropic home for women. The Young Women's Christian Association, beginning in the 1860s, had organized some pleasant hostels which supported wage-earning women, but by the end of the century many such homes were overcrowded and run in a manner to make mature inhabitants feel like children. "I don't know which is worse," wrote one working woman, "the cramped, and awful loneliness of a hall bedroom, or the humiliating soul-depressing charity and rules of a Home."[33] Perhaps the strictest limits on space were found by one researcher in 1915 who described a New York women's home as a "hen coop," where the beds were separated by partitions made of chicken wire.[34]

The strictest rules were those of A. T. Stewart, a millionaire dry goods merchant who established a rather nauseatingly genteel "Women's Hotel," "a home for women who support themselves by daily labor," in 1878 on Fourth Avenue in New York (9.7). Stewart's Women's Hotel charged a then extravagant $6.00 per week for room and full board, but the YWCA women called it "a gigantic failure" because "stringent rules made the Hotel not a *home*, but an asylum." They stated: "Women will not relinquish liberty for grandeur. It is too poor an equivalent. . . ." In the end, the rates were too high for it to be a financial success.[35] Since Stewart had made his fortune paying women clerks in his dry goods store low wages, his beneficence stank of hypocrisy. Other employers who paid women low wages might even justify their pay scales by contributions to such charitable homes.

Mary Kenney's Jane Club, managed by the residents, was unique in its relative cheapness, independence from philanthropic assistance, and freedom from fussy rules. When the group reached fifty residents and the Ewing Street building was too small, Jane Addams suggested incorporating the project into Hull-House. She began trying to raise money for a permanent building for the Jane Club and a parallel project for men, the Phalanx Club (a Fourierist name that recalls the communitarian socialist influence on these projects). In 1898 the new building opened, and the Jane Club (8.12) existed as a self-supporting project for several decades,

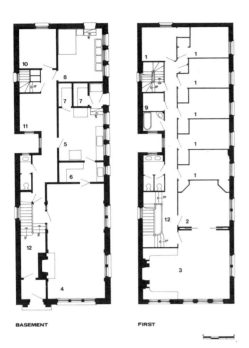

BASEMENT　　　　FIRST

8.12 Jane Club, plans of basement and first
floor by Pond and Pond, 1898: 1, bedroom; 2,
reading room; 3, social room; 4, dining room; 5,
kitchen; 6, scullery; 7, pantry; 8, laundry room;
9, linen closet; 10, trunk room; 11, bicycle storage; 12, entrance hall and stairs. Second and
third floors were all bedrooms.

recreating some of the cohesive atmosphere
of the company boardinghouses in Lowell
for young women without any of the pater-
nalistic atmosphere. Private rooms for most
residents permitted individual privacy.
Again and again the thirty residents emphasized their autonomy, their pride in
managing their own housing as self-
supporting adults.

Women of all classes yearned for the
self-sufficiency of making their own housing arrangements. The success of the Jane
Club spurred wide discussion of cooperative housekeeping arrangements among
small and large groups of single working
women.[36] In the years between 1885 and
1920 any group of women who chose to
rent an apartment or a house together and
share the expenses of cooking, cleaning,
and laundry might call this cooperative
housekeeping.[37] Some were young, some
middle-aged, and some even retired
workers.

Cooperative boarding clubs formed by
employed women and students introduced
many organizing and building projects in
these decades. In 1902 seven art students
formed a successful boarding club in New
York; around the same time Viola Richmond founded the working women's
Turner-Balderston Club for cooperative
boarding in Philadelphia, which occupied
three houses in the city and a vacation
house in the country; the Randolph Club
was another self-supporting women's enterprise in that city.[38] In 1919 the International Ladies' Garment Workers Union established Unity House in New York on a

similar model.[39] The desire of women to control their own housing was expressed again and again.[40] Whether they were factory workers, clerical workers, or even professionals,[41] none of them earned enough to enjoy the independence and security enjoyed by single men of their own social class, unless they formed clubs to "cooperate" toward that end.

Cooperative Living and the Unionization of Domestic Servants

Just as settlement workers concerned themselves with helping factory workers organize cooperative boarding schemes, so they tried to help domestic servants, whose social standing was even lower than the factory workers'. Domestic service was the major occupation for women workers; there were one and a half million servants in the United States in 1900, 95.4 percent of them women, and they were employed by approximately one family in ten. They often worked twelve- and thirteen-hour days, seven days a week, for which they earned an average of $3.16 per week, or less than 4 cents an hour. Over two fifths of the servants were native-born whites, a third were native-born blacks, and about a quarter were immigrants.[42] (Over the next forty years the percentage of white women decreased, and black women increased, as white workers successfully sought other jobs, from which black women were restricted because of race.)[43]

As late as 1940 there were more domestic servants than workers in the railroad, coal, and automotive industries combined,

but one would never know this from the paucity of reports about their conditions by labor economists and statisticians, or the meager efforts of trade unionists to organize them.[44] Although the Knights of Labor included assemblies of housewives and of servants in the 1880s, in general trade unions ignored these workers. The problem of encouraging trade unions among servants employed by many different mistresses, who required them to "live in," was taken up more assiduously by home economists and settlement workers.

In 1885, Florence Kelley, later an activist on labor issues at Hull-House, suggested the creation of servants' boarding clubs as a way to create the social structure necessary to domestic workers' trade unions.[45] She believed that such housing for servants would make it possible to insist upon the eight-hour day and the six-day week and to give servants, half of whom were single women under twenty-five, more "home life." In 1893, Jane Addams, who worked with Kelley, predicted that "the house servant was to pass out of existence just as the family blacksmith had done, and that cooperation would succeed present methods of housekeeping." Ten years later she elaborated this position, arguing that all individuals, even those engaged in service, had a right to experience the "fullness of life" in a democracy. She repeated Kelley's idea of building suburban residences for domestic servants, suggesting that it would help them to feel part of a community of their peers as living in with employers could not.[46]

In the same year, Ellen Richards helped the Association of Collegiate Alumnae and the Woman's Education Association to organize the Household Aid Company, a cooperative residence for twenty servants, rather like the Jane Club, with a training and placement program and a mediation service to deal with employers. Mary Hinman Abel conducted a session of the 1903 Lake Placid Conference, which criticized the "homelessness" of servants who live "in but not of a family of a different social grade." She saw the Household Aid Company's residence project, along with more home economics classes for schoolgirls, as promising lines of change.[47] And who should be found to run the servants' residence but the elderly Emily A. Huntington, founder of the Kitchen Garden movement. After two years, however, it was clear the project was not a financial success, despite the promise that "every effort will be made to excite the ambition of the aid by advancing her position at least once in three months. . . ."[48] Only in the fiction of Charlotte Perkins Gilman, discussed in the next chapter, did a cooperative boarding club for servants, entitled Union House, appear to be a social success and generate a workers' union.

The difference between the voluntary cooperation of the Jane Club, run by its members, and homes for domestic servants that included placement services, run by home economists and social workers, was profound. Even with hourly wages and specialized tasks, the social stigma of being "in service" was great. More to the point were the inexpensive boarding clubs for domestic servants and other workers who were between jobs, such as the Working Woman's Society, run by Alice L. Woodbridge in New York, and the Woman's Lodging House in Chicago, run by Louise Schultz.[49] Yet these were transient homes, so by definition they did not solve servants' housing problems, or help to establish stable trade unions.

Cooperative Living for Settlement Workers

In addition to attempting to alleviate the domestic difficulties of women workers by offering married women day care and cooked food and encouraging single women to organize various types of cooperative boarding clubs, Jane Addams offered a cooperative domestic life to professional women at Hull-House (8.13). In its earliest days, Hull-House consisted of two professional women and their housekeeper, but it developed by 1895 into a residential community of twenty women, and then, by 1911, into a residential community of some fifty-one residents, which included some married couples. In that year thirty-one of the residents were women and twenty, men.[50] As Addams described it, "We have worked out during our years of residence a plan of living which may be called cooperative, for the families and individuals who rent the Hull-House apartments have the use of the central kitchen and dining room so far as they care for them. . . ."[51] As an

8.13 Residents' dining room, Hull-House, with
Jane Addams at right end of center table.
Women professionals predominate among the
residents.

8.14 Cooking class at Hull-House, 1916: "science" on the Bunsen burners and teaching jobs
for home economists.

8.15 Cooking class at Tuskeegee Institute, training black female students to be domestic servants. By 1920, 40 percent of American servants
were black.

idealistic community living in one complex
of buildings, Hull-House resembled earlier
communitarian experiments that drew
members together into a community mansion, such as the Oneida Community or
the Social Palace at Guise, but in its economic organization Hull-House eventually
was closer to the cooperative boarding arrangements of the Unitary Household in
New York. At Hull-House the majority of
residents supported themselves by business
or professional work in Chicago, paying for
their share of the domestic costs and giving
their remaining time to settlement projects.

At first the settlement workers played
down cooperative living as an aspect of
their enterprise because of the associations
with free love or socialism that it might
provoke. One early Hull-House critic objected to "those unnatural attempts to understand life through cooperative living," [52] but since the earliest residents were
all women, complaints about sexual license
were minimal. By the time men came to
live at Hull-House, the community was far
too distinguished to provoke idle gossip
about free love, and single men and single
women residents occupied separate buildings.[53]

Of the residents at Hull-House in 1910,
a large number had been there for more
than twelve years, and the group included
"the secretary of the City Club, two practicing physicians, several attorneys, newspaper men, business men, teachers,
scientists, artists, musicians, lecturers in the
School of Civics and Philanthropy, officers
in the Juvenile Protective Association and

in The League for the Protection of Immigrants, a visiting nurse, a sanitary inspector
and others." [54] The families and individuals who rented Hull-House apartments
could order food served in their own quarters by the central kitchen but many
residents dined every evening in the Hull-
House dining room, where lively discussions of "the science of society," and
political equality were likely to take place.
Indeed, it is significant that Hull-House's
first resident was an elderly Mrs. Sedge-
wick, who had in her youth lived at the
Fourierist experiment at Brook Farm and
"wished to live once more in an atmosphere where "idealism ran high." [55] Some
fastidious visitors, like the British Fabian
socialists, Beatrice and Sidney Webb, described the dining room as "higgledypig-
gledy" and the service as "rough and
ready." Despite these cavils, the liveliness
and political acumen of residents' dinner
table conversations left many more visitors
and temporary residents impressed, among
them the anarchist Kropotkin; the future
President of General Electric, Gerard
Swope; and the soon-to-be-prominent feminist, Charlotte Perkins Gilman. Addams's
pleasure that "the domestic economy is all
under one skilled management" [56] no
doubt helped shape the thinking of
Gilman, a resident for three months in
1895, as well as the young Pauline
Schindler, resident about 1912, who with
her husband, the architect Rudolph
Schindler, was later to experiment with "a
cooperative dwelling" in Los Angeles.

Hull-House's success influenced other settlement houses' domestic arrangements. The presence of some former communitarian socialists in the settlement movement may have helped to support collective living, but feminist activism was a more significant force behind new domestic arrangements. Many of the professionals at Hull-House were single women, pioneers in their fields, who chose university training for a career at a time when this choice often implied a rejection of marriage and family. Dozens of such single-minded career women, like Addams herself, found that domestic life in a settlement solved the logistical problems of spinsterhood, by providing a respectable, adult home life, autonomous yet collective. It was more independent than living with relatives and far more congenial than living alone.

In one sense settlement houses were the great practical success of cooperative housekeeping in the period between 1890 and 1920, the middle-class reformers' proof that collective cooking, cleaning, laundering, and central heating, supported by a new, socially conscious approach to residential architecture, could really work. Yet settlement house residents rarely praised and publicized the forms of cooperative housekeeping they developed to support their own careers. Why? Were they avoiding gossip about their private lives? Were they too engrossed with the larger issues of low wages, inadequate housing, and unsanitary conditions, which harassed the neighborhoods they lived in? Kathryn Kish Sklar has concluded that it was the cooperative housekeeping of the settlements which enabled reformers such as Addams, Kelley, and Lathrop to exert such influence on American society, but this invention has received very little publicity.[57] We know Jane Addams as a leader in legislative reform and social welfare, a suffragist, and a pacifist. Perhaps her greatest achievement was as the creator of Hull-House, first of all a social and physical framework for female careers, and only second a center of community service.

Idealism and Pragmatism

". . . The ultimate glory of the settlements," wrote the architectural critic, Fiske Kimball, "will be to have rendered settlements unnecessary."[58] The first generation of professional home economists and settlement workers could hardly be expected to find their ultimate glory and rendering themselves unnecessary. Instead, they sought ways to increase the demand for their skills and extend their influence, replacing community services with broad educational programs. If they were not needed to run public kitchens, at least they could teach scientific cooking (8.14, 8.15); if they were not needed to provide emergency child care, they could teach mothers about scientific child care; if they were not needed to organize housing for young women workers or domestic servants, they could run evening classes for them in self-help or skills.

As the professionals shifted from the direct provision of services toward the development of legislative reform, education, and counseling, they became more cautious. Although many home economists and settlement workers had enthusiastically supported all kinds of cooperative ventures (defining "cooperative" very loosely) in the 1880s and early 1890s, by the end of the 1890s they were beginning to support only those projects that were initiated and directed by trained specialists. Furthermore, many professionals were prepared to make use of conventional arguments about 'woman's place' in the home to justify their own careers.

Caroline Hunt, a protégée of Ellen Richards, was an influential home economist who lived at Hull-House before becoming a professor at the University of Wisconsin and then head of the Bureau of Home Economics in the Department of Agriculture. She was an important theoretician for the new professions of home economics and social work. In 1908, in *Home Problems from a New Standpoint,* she justified women's mandate to undertake work outside the home, especially in the areas of "the labor problem," factory legislation, welfare, and local government, by saying that households used manufactured products, depended on town water and garbage systems, and required pure foods. Women, Hunt claimed, were the home's "natural" protectors, and should add "to their work for it in private, public work demanded by its changed position." [59] Citing changes in the housewife's role, from producer to consumer, she envisioned an extremely militant woman who understood that ". . . household commodities which had in the past represented her

loving and willing service now represented the broken lives of others." In helping workers to fight for better conditions, women would need a "spirit of cooperation and mutual aid," "the spirit of the best and most helpful family life." [60]

She was justifying women's activism by their traditional roles in the home, explaining political work as "municipal housekeeping," or social housekeeping. Many suffragists were then making similar arguments for women's suffrage. Frances Willard of the Woman's Christian Temperance Union complained to Susan B. Anthony in 1898: "Men have made a dead failure of municipal government, just as they would of housekeeping on the broadest scale." [61] Jane Addams wrote in favor of woman suffrage in 1907, developing this metaphor: "May we not say that city housekeeping has failed partly because women, the traditional housekeepers, have not been consulted as to its mutliform activities?" [62]

This argument for suffrage, based on women's ability to make municipal government and urban life "clean" again, proved to be extremely successful in gaining both male and female support for women's right to vote. In the same way, advocacy of woman's "public work for the home" helped make careers for women in social work and home economics acceptable. But in both cases, those suffragists and specialists who chose to argue on the basis of expediency rather than on the basis of justice found that the domestic stereotypes they used to support votes or careers for women remained to erode many of the gains they made.

As specialists doing "women's work" in professional form, social workers and home economists remained relatively low-paid. In an attempt to highlight the advantages of scientific child care, cooking, and house-keeping, some of these professionals began to try to distinguish their contributions from the unpaid labor rendered by the or-dinary housewife, or the collective efforts of groups engaging in "cooperative house-keeping" in a spontaneous, nonscientific way. Therefore some home economists and settlement workers not only moved away from their early enthusiasm for cooperative housekeeping; they also began to attack untrained women's cooperative ap-proaches. Hunt proposed "women's public work for the home," or municipal house-keeping, as "an ethical substitute" for co-operative housekeeping among neighbors in 1909. Thus cooperative housekeeping was merged with the goals of women's con-sumer organizations, a strategy consistent only with cooperative housekeeping seen as consumers' cooperatives, not producers' co-operatives. The problem was that families were not ready for cooperation, hinted Hunt: "At present human beings are un-able to overcome the difficulties attendant upon the voluntary association of family groups for housekeeping purposes. They lack both the goodness and the wisdom." [63] (She forgot to mention how well Hull-House itself worked, perhaps because of the residents' wisdom.)

She was reiterating conclusions reached at a session of the Lake Placid Conference on Home Economics in 1907, which had decided that many women found it difficult to cooperate because of house-wives' lack of uniform standards, their physical isolation, and their lack of educa-tion.[64] Mary Hinman Abel had come to similar conclusions a few years earlier: "The experienced see an element of danger in the intimacy of the relation between the cooperators, and the persistent call on such qualities as justice, generosity, and unflagging interest in a principle." [65] Abel claimed that cooperative housekeeping would never succeed until women had bet-ter business training and more responsibil-ity in keeping a contract,[66] qualities which, perhaps, home economics courses could teach them.

In 1903 Jane Addams criticized the ig-norance of housewives participating in a cooperative experiment in an Iowa town: "The lack of intelligent consumption and the consequent variety of demand has had much to do with the failure of various at-tempts to adjust housekeeping on collective lines. . . . The experiment really failed because there was no common standard of food values among the women." To sup-port this she quoted an earlier report spon-sored by Ellen Richards: "When 'standards of food' have been recognized by many persons . . . it will be possible for cooper-ative experiments in the purchase and preparation of food to succeed as they can-not without common agreement and stand-ards." [67] In an unusual and especially re-

vealing fit of pique Adams went on in the
same article to lambaste the satisfied members of a successful cooperative dining club
in an Illinois town, young women who
gave their time to art and music, but were
not interested in scientific principles of nutrition. Successful cooperative domestic life
without scientific standards grieved professionals even more than failed cooperative
experiments.

These critiques were discussed at some
length, since many women within both
professions were still fascinated by the
challenge of collective domestic organization. Ellen Richards's *New England Kitchen
Magazine* ran many articles on cooperative
housekeeping in the 1890s.[68] Mary Hinman Abel remained a keen advocate of
public kitchens all her life, and Alice Peloubet Norton, a well-known educator who
followed Abel as editor of the *Journal of
Home Economics,* spent the last years of her
life running a community kitchen for Ethel
Puffer Howes. Debates on cooperative
housekeeping at conferences were well attended, but the National Household Economics Association, between 1893 and
1903, was more supportive than Ellen
Richards's Lake Placid conferences, between 1899 and 1908, or her American
Home Economics Association, which she
formed in 1909.[69] Although Mrs. Melvil
Dewey, who had organized the Lake
Placid Conferences on Home Economics
with Richards, sponsored a special meeting
on Group Living in 1920,[70] and Caroline
Hunt herself wrote confidently of the experiments in housekeeping and cooked

food delivery which represented the hope
of the future,[71] the professionals could not
risk being associated with unconventional
experiments, which were technical or
financial failures, or with unconventional
people who might show sympathy for socialism or challenge conventional sexual
morality. Charlotte Perkins Gilman, a
divorced woman and a Fabian socialist,
might have become a real problem for the
domestic professionals when she championed collective domesticity in *Women and
Economics* in 1898, but she was very careful
to support only professional approaches to
housekeeping, as "good business."

All of the professionals had a ready remedy for untrained housewives' attempts at
cooperation: education in home economics.
If ordinary housewives were too ignorant
to succeed in cooperative endeavors, they
must be educated by the professionals to
understand scientific standards. In the
meantime, the professionals would command the large-scale institutional kitchens,
bakeries, and laundries that were evolving
in connection with colleges, hospitals, asylums, prisons, and hotels. To this end professionals held conferences, made activity
schedules, swapped institutional recipes.
That these projects would not be owned
cooperatively nor exclusively controlled by
women gave home economists and settlement workers very little anxiety, as long as
they did not fall into the hands of the most
mercenary and dishonest capitalists. While
the professionals stressed "the gentle art of
mutual aid," what they lost in socialist ideology, they hoped to pick up in efficiency;

what they lost in sisterhood, they hoped to gain in professional status.

Directing their services to the working class was an important but never fully analyzed part of this stance. When developing domestic services and domestic models, Addams, Richards, and their disciples inevitably asked for modest improvements for modest incomes. Often there was an element of condescension, as they tried to raise minimum standards for the deserving poor; first by providing services and then by educating poor women to make the most of a minimum income as good consumers.[72] They criticized deprivation but they did not usually explicitly challenge the existence of economic inequality or attempt to identify its causes. They presented a higher standard of living to the poor as both a right (in terms of new government services) and a duty (in terms of self-help projects). They did not, however, speak of domestic revolution.

Thus the development of a group of professional women concerned with domestic life resulted in, first, explicit consideration of the domestic needs of immigrants, workers, and domestic servants, and second, an attempt to reconcile those needs with the economic structure of industrial capitalist society. Home economics was the "economics of consumption," according to Richards. For Abel, home economics meant seeking answers to these questions: ". . . what are the material conditions that afford the proper setting for ideal home life, where the adult worker is rested and refreshed, where the child is prepared

for effective citizenship, and where hospitality may exert its cheering and refining influence?"[73] The "economics of consumption," with its concern for effective workers and good citizenship, thus anticipates the slogan of a later era, "Good Homes Make Contented Workers." It was far less militant than Melusina Fay Peirce's demand that women use their latent power as consumers to gain economic independence from men. Peirce had envisioned a female elite running "woman's sphere" for the benefit of all women. The professionals developed a female elite eager to collaborate with men on philanthropic, municipal, corporate, and university activities promoting "democracy." Peirce's effort had ended in defeat at the hands of a Council of Gentlemen who were expected to approve her group's financial dealings, but many of the new professionals were far too tactful and pragmatic to provoke such confrontations with powerful men in government, business, and universities. Reforming "woman's sphere" for them was a means, not an end. Reform of the larger society became their aim rather than control of woman's sphere.

Thus, "women's public work for the home" became a civic-minded extension of private housekeeping activities, with muted feminist implications. That "public work" ultimately implied female suffrage, economic independence for women, and collective housekeeping was clear to many of its advocates, but these were arguments they chose to underplay. Although they never completely forgot the vision of cooperative housekeeping, they consigned it to

the distant future, when goodness and wisdom characterized every housewife in the
land. When Ellen Richards, creator of the
first public kitchen in 1890, described an
ideal single family suburban house in *The
Cost of Shelter* in 1905, and when Jane Addams, who created cooperative living at
Hull-House in 1887, built model rooms for
a single-family house inside the settlement
as a "demonstration center" for lessons in
housework technology in 1907, these ac-
tions presaged just how far American
housing policy for workers' families would
ultimately diverge from cooperative housekeeping.[74] But meanwhile, the early enthusiasm of the home economists and
settlement workers for cooperation was
percolating through other groups, including suffragists, social feminists, women's
club members, and architects, under the
charismatic influence of a former settlement worker and member of the National
Household Economics Association, Charlotte Perkins Gilman. Gilman would give
material feminism greater ideological force
by demanding new forms of domestic
organization in the name of improved
motherhood.

V   **Charlotte Perkins Gilman
and Her Influence**

9.1 Charlotte Perkins Gilman in 1898, at about age thirty-eight

If there should be built and opened in any of our large cities to-day a commodious and well-served apartment house for professional women with families, it would be filled at once.
— *Charlotte Perkins Gilman, 1898*

The apartment hotel is the boarding house at its best and worst. It is the most dangerous enemy American domesticity has yet had to encounter.
— *Editorial,* Architectural Record, *1903*

A slender, dark-haired woman, with a light, penetrating voice and great powers as a speaker, Charlotte Perkins Gilman (9.1) charmed audiences in the last decade of the century in New York and in Topeka, in Kansas City and in London. Her most popular lectures discussed women, men, and the home. Although her eyes flashed with anger or indignation when she spoke of women's oppression, she could quickly change pace, joking, prodding, ridiculing traditionalists who romanticized the Victorian home and woman's place within it: "It is not that women are really smaller-minded, weaker-minded, more timid and vacillating; but that whosoever, man or woman, lives always in a small, dark place, is always guarded, protected, directed and restrained, will become inevitably narrowed and weakened by it. The woman is narrowed by the home and the man is narrowed by the woman." [1]

Gilman was by turns practical and fanciful. She might discourse on economics, illustrating her points with anecdotes based on her days as a boardinghouse keeper in Oakland, California, or her struggles as a settlement house worker in Chicago. Or she might picture for her audience an imaginary society, with an ideal set of economic relationships, a place first created in her utopian fiction, such as the California town, Orchardina, where women did no private housework, or the Amazonian country, Herland, where women had governed for centuries, without men, and socialized domestic work was the rule.

Gilman stood out among all of the feminists and the futurists of her time as the charismatic person who synthesized the thinking of suffragists, home economists, and utopian novelists on the question of the home, and produced a program for collective domesticity which made her a leading figure in feminist circles in the United States and Europe. In her first book, *Women and Economics,* published in 1898, and in many subsequent books and articles, she prophesied a world where women enjoyed the economic independence of work outside the home for wages and savored the social benefits of life with their families in private kitchenless houses or apartments connected to central kitchens, dining rooms, and day care centers.

On the basis of her economic, social, and architectural arguments for collective domestic life, she has been judged the most original feminist the United States has ever produced, and she has been described by various scholars as representing "the full elaboration of the feminist impulse" and as putting forward "radical" proposals based on "socialist" premises. [2] Yet her audience included middle-class women and men who were not socialists, as well as Socialist Party women. In many ways her program was a somewhat conservative synthesis of earlier material feminist ideas with popular theories of social evolution. She was witty, lucid, a wonderfully successful popularizer. She used evolutionary theory to support feminism the way an itinerant preacher might use the Bible. She often ignored issues of economic class, but she commanded attention when she attacked the conventional home and conventional motherhood in favor of the feminist home and feminist motherhood.

In the 1880s and 1890s, both home economists and authors of futurist fiction tended to argue that human evolution would gradually bring about a society where technology lightened all labor and encouraged the socialization of domestic work. They wrote about the late twentieth century or the year 2000; they prophesied cooperative housekeeping in some future time when human relations were perfected. Gilman took this idea, turned it around, and gave the idea of collective domestic life new urgency. Rather than arguing that evolution would help to free women, she contended that free women could help to speed up evolution. In *Women and Economics* she stated that women were holding back human evolution because of their confinement to household work and motherhood. The evolution of the human race, she believed, would be hastened by removing domestic work and child care from the home, allowing women to undertake both motherhood and paid employment, making it possible for all women to be economically independent of men. Thus, she argued that the development of socialized domestic work and new domestic environments should be seen as promoting the evolution of socialism, rather than following it. This was her original contribution.

A Beecher Heritage

Charlotte Perkins Stetson Gilman, born in 1860, struggled most of her life with the need to earn her own living. Soon after her birth her father deserted her mother, who moved nineteen times in the next eighteen years, seeking financial help from friends and relatives. Despite her father's neglect of her family, Gilman was very proud of his ancestors, for his mother was a Beecher, and she thanked him for "the Beecher urged to social service, the Beecher wit and gift of words. . . ." [3] Catharine Beecher, who was the most important role model among her Beecher aunts, came for a visit when Charlotte was five, and she remembered her great-aunt's "little gray curls." [4] Catharine Beecher had spent her energy heightening gender distinctions and designing an ideal single-family home for the Christian wife and mother, but Gilman ridiculed many gender distinctions, questioned women's exclusive dedication to home life, and proposed alternatives to the traditional domestic workplace. Gilman did not criticize men with the militance of Melusina Fay Peirce, nor did she echo the free love phrases of Marie Howland. She was true to the conservative strain in the Beecher family in her concern for efficiency, spiritual values, and motherhood.

Gilman began her public career working for Edward Bellamy's Nationalist movement, after the end of her first marriage. In 1890 she published a poem about evolution, "Similar Cases," in a journal established by Bellamy's followers, and received a fan letter from William Dean

Howells, then active in the movement. Her first public lecture, "Human Nature," was given for the Nationalist Club in Pasadena, California, that same year.[5] She found a sympathetic mentor in Edward Everett Hale, her uncle, who visited her in Pasadena and coached her on lecturing style. He was from Boston, a Unitarian minister, author of a book entitled *Workingmen's Homes* and of a utopian novel. He was also prominent in the Nationalist cause, a friend of Bellamy's, and a Beecher who was used to eloquent women in the family.[6] With Hale's help Gilman was launched as a popular speaker, lecturing for Nationalist Clubs and other idealistic political groups, taking over the pulpit on Sundays from ministers friendly to her cause and working with numerous women's groups as a volunteer.

She developed her characteristic blend of evolutionary theory, Nationalism, and feminism for these audiences. The sociologist Lester Ward, whom she described some years later as "quite the greatest man I have ever known," was struggling in the 1880s to counter arguments for "social Darwinism," or the justification of industrial capitalism as "survival of the fittest."[7] Ward argued that cooperation rather than competition was the key to successful human evolution and stated that social and economic planning could improve the human situation, especially the situation of women: "A state of society if it be bad for one class is bad for all. Woman is scarcely a greater sufferer from her condition than man is. . . . The freedom of women will

be the ennoblement of man." And he said, "Woman *is* the race, and the race can only be raised up as she is raised up."[8] This became Gilman's evolutionary theme for the next three decades, one that she reiterated in churches and sewing circles as well as in the homes of the urban bourgeoisie. A journalist's report of one of her public appearances, she wore "no diamonds but her eyes," conveys the charismatic power of her presence.[9]

Although she developed a broad acquaintance with many groups of earnest reformers, Gilman's closest friend and associate in the 1890s was the Nationalist Helen Campbell, a journalist and home economist, who drew her into home economics circles. Gilman found in Campbell an "adopted mother" who influenced her in many ways.[10] Campbell, twenty-one years older than Gilman, was the author of a study of the economic conditions of working women entitled *Prisoners of Poverty*, a novel about women's economic position, and many children's stories as well. With Mary Livermore and Lucy Stone, Campbell had been among the feminist members of the Boston Nationalist Club in 1890. In 1894 Campbell and Gilman decided to live together in San Francisco and edit a weekly newspaper for which Campbell wrote the "Household Affairs" section. In 1895 and 1896 they worked together again in Chicago, living in the Unity, or "Little Hell," Settlement. At that time Campbell published her popular text, *Household Economics*, which she dedicated to Gilman. In her text there are many arguments which Gilman was later to repeat.

Campbell projected intense fervor for domestic reform: "Living, as we get it in our isolated, individual system, is organized waste and destruction, and women who oppose or refuse to even listen to calm and rational discussion as to better possibilities, what are they but organized obstruction?" [11] She wrote persuasively of planning and furnishing houses to show more concern for children's needs. She spoke of the need for family privacy, which could not be met by conventional domestic architecture: "We are not private or separate in any decent sense at present." In the future she envisioned domestic industries "subservient and reduced to order" as part of a structured community of housing and services, "a whole great building expressing the thought of human living at its best." [12] Campbell probably introduced Gilman to the work of Melusina Fay Peirce, which she cited in the final chapter in her book on "Organized Living." She developed a critique of Peirce's "cooperative housekeeping" proposals which was repeated by many home economists: "It is not in my opinion co-operation that is required since families are intended to live their own lives . . . but *combination* in a business sense and with business methods could reconstruct the housekeeping of a community." [13]

In order to organize women to deal with household issues, Campbell and Gilman founded the Chicago Household Economic Society, a branch of the National House-hold Economics Association which had been established in 1893 during the Women's Congress at the World's Columbian Exposition. The NHEA worked primarily through women's clubs before merging with the General Federation of Women's Clubs in 1903. Ellen Richards and Mary Abel both served among its national directors. The organization included advocates of both neighborly cooperation and businesslike combination, with committees on cooperative laundries, cooperative bakeries, and public kindergartens, as well as on principles of nutrition and training for servants. A committee on housekeepers' clubs was "to formulate plans to simplify housework in village communities, to suggest plans for cooperation in laundries, poultry and egg raising on a small scale, and to furnish information on all topics connected with housework." [14] This committee was chaired by Mary Coleman Stuckert of Chicago, who had exhibited architectural drawings (9.2) and a model of a new community of forty-four row houses with cooperative housekeeping facilities at the Columbian Exposition in the Woman's Building.[15]

The NHEA's explicit goals pertained to the "servant problem" as much as to the larger issues of collective domesticity. The NHEA desired "Bureaus of Information where there can be an exchange of wants and needs between employer and employed." [16] The Chicago branch, with its prospectus and constitution drafted by Campbell and Gilman, proposed to establish training classes for household servants, housekeepers' alliances to engage the grad-

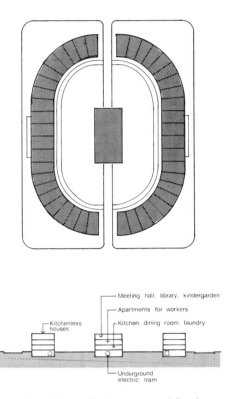

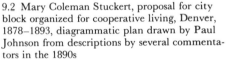

9.2 Mary Coleman Stuckert, proposal for city
block organized for cooperative living, Denver,
1878–1893, diagrammatic plan drawn by Paul
Johnson from descriptions by several commenta-
tors in the 1890s

uates, and central offices to register employees, employers, speakers, and teachers.
It also advocated establishing people's
kitchen buildings in "every poor quarter of
the city" similar to the New England
Kitchen and the Rumford Kitchen.[17]

Despite her ties to the Nationalists,
Gilman remained aloof from other American socialists in the 1890s, preferring to
work with feminists and "sharply disagree-
ing with both theory and method as advanced by the followers of Marx."[18] She
said:

My Socialism was of the early humanitarian kind, based on the first exponents,
French and English, with the American enthusiasm of Bellamy. The narrow and rigid
"economic determinism" of Marx, with its
"class consciousness" and "class struggle" I
never accepted, nor the political methods
pursued by the Marxians. My main interest then was in the position of women, and
the need for more scientific care for young
children. As to women, the basic need of
economic independence seemed to me of
far more importance than the ballot. . . .[19]

As a "humanitarian socialist" who followed the early English and French
thinkers Owen and Fourier, and rejected
Marxist analysis, Gilman could have
moved into the popular cooperative movement of the 1890s, where many of the Nationalists felt comfortable. This she refused
to do because of an unhappy experience in
her girlhood, during the period when her
mother was moving constantly from place
to place. One stay in a crowded cooperative household of ten people in Providence,
Rhode Island, when she was fourteen was

particularly agonizing. The eccentricities of the Swedenborgians and spiritualists in the group, the inefficient distribution of domestic chores, and the lack of personal privacy led her to develop a lifelong hatred for cooperative communities and enterprises.[20] She not only rejected cooperative living, cooperative stores, and cooperative communities, but denounced Peirce's version of cooperative housekeeping as a total failure. She believed in "industrial training" and "good business" in much the same way as Mary Livermore and Helen Campbell, but she wanted a more comprehensive theory of social change. This the Fabian Socialists provided.

In England in 1896, Gilman met Beatrice and Sidney Webb and George Bernard Shaw. She thought them both clever and witty. Their Fabian socialist group had begun as a splinter from the Nationalist movement in England, so she shared with them a common admiration for Bellamy and found their strategy of working slowly within the existing political system toward the nationalization of industries an acceptable one. Fabian socialism deplored violent confrontation between capital and labor and relied on the efforts of skilled civil servants and politicians, enlightened capitalists, and leading intellectuals. As a poet and author of fiction, as well as a political polemicist, she found their ideal exciting. They, in turn, were stimulated by her militant cultural feminism and encouraged her to put her ideas into the book which made her famous, *Women and Economics.* In this work she intro

duced the feminist apartment hotel as an element of urban evolution.

Feminist Motherhood in a Feminist Housing Complex

In *Women and Economics,* Gilman criticized society for confining women to the house and to motherhood: "Woman has been checked, starved, aborted in human growth; and the swelling forces of race-development have been driven back in each generation to work in her through sex-functions alone." [21] For her "sex-functions" meant motherhood. She wrote: "The more absolutely woman is segregated to sex-functions only, cut off from all economic use and made wholly dependent on the sex-relation as a means of livelihood, the more pathological does her motherhood become." [22] In other words, the more women attempted to look pretty and to behave coquettishly in order to find husbands to support them economically as wives and mothers, the more they held back the strength and intelligence of the human race. Yet motherhood was, according to Gilman, "the common duty and the common glory of womanhood." In a world where women were economically independent, she believed that motherhood would be voluntary. Although women might limit the number of their children she felt sure that "women as economic producers will naturally choose those professions which are compatible with motherhood," that is, roles in new, collectively organized household industries.[23]

Coming from a divorced mother who found it difficult to care for her child while earning her living, Gilman's plea for supports for feminist motherhood was particularly poignant. The spatial setting for feminist motherhood, according to Gilman, was the feminist apartment hotel, with private suites without kitchens and complete cooking, dining, and child care facilities for all residents which permitted them to combine jobs and motherhood. She urged entrepreneurs to consider developing such an institution:

If there should be built and opened in any of our large cities today a commodious and well-served apartment house for professional women with families, it would be filled at once. The apartments would be without kitchens; but there would be a kitchen belonging to the house from which meals could be served to the families in their rooms or in a common dining-room, as preferred. It would be a home where the cleaning was done by efficient workers, not hired separately by the families, but engaged by the manager of the establishment; and a roof-garden, day nursery, and kindergarten, under well-trained professional nurses and teachers, would ensure proper care of the children. . . . This must be offered on a business basis to prove a substantial business success; and so it will prove, for it is a growing social need.

She also offered schemes for suburban residences without kitchens:

In suburban homes this purpose could be accomplished much better by a grouping of adjacent houses, each distinct and having its own yard, but all kitchenless, and connected by covered ways with the eating-house. . . . Meals could of course be served in the house as long as desired; but when people become accustomed to pure, clean homes where no steaming industry is carried on, they will gradually prefer to go to their food instead of having it brought to them.

These eating houses were to be both workplaces and neighborhood social centers. Her vision of collective meeting places for "free association among us, on lines of common interest," included "great common libraries and parlors, baths and gymnasia, work-room and play-rooms, to which both sexes have the same access for the same needs. . . ." [24] Just as Gilman believed that the human race was evolving in a more cooperative direction, so, too, she was sure that the physical form of human habitations was subject to evolutionary forces.

Her proposals for feminist apartment hotels echoed much of the architectural determinism of earlier Fourierists and free love advocates as well as the Nationalists led by Bellamy. In 1890, the year Gilman had first joined the Nationalists, several designers had published proposals for the renovation of row house blocks for cooperative housekeeping and the construction of new urban row house blocks and apartment hotels (9.3, 9.4, 9.5) with collective housekeeping facilities. John Pickering Putnam, in 1890, in *Architecture Under Nationalism*, promised that apartment hotels would not only spare women domestic drudgery, but would also reduce poverty by their efficient use of resources. As Putnam asserted, "The selfish and narrowing isolation of the separate dwelling will give way to the

9.3 George Duysters, proposal for adding a co-operative kitchen to a standard row house block, New York, 1890, diagram by Paul Johnson from a description in *The Nationalist*

9.4 Leonard E. Ladd, U.S. Patent No. 430,480, "Improvement in Dwelling Houses," Philadel-phia, 1890, showing block of one-family row houses served by a central kitchen

Street

Private family houses

Street   Covered passageway   Cooperative kitchen   Street

Private family houses

Street

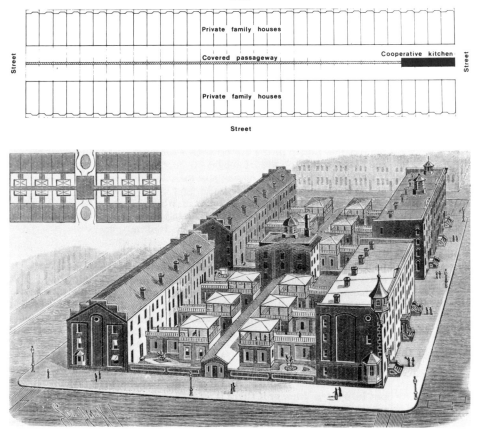

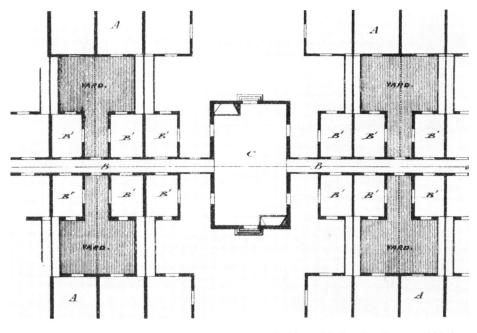

9.5 Ladd, partial plan showing central kitchen
(C), corridor joining kitchen and houses (B), private dining rooms (B'), and houses (A)

cooperative apartment-house as surely as the isolated hut of the savage yield to the cities and villages of advancing civilization." [25]

Putnam was a Nationalist architect in Boston whose practice consisted of apartment houses and hotels. In his claims for the efficacy of the apartment hotel as a tool for social reform, all of the wildest and most improbable assertions made on behalf of the Phalanstery by earlier communitarian socialists were restated. He claimed that his plans for a Nationalist apartment hotel (9.6) offered "the possibility for a greatly enlarged and delightful social intercourse . . . as near an approach to the ideal of a human habitation as has yet been devised." [26] Carried away by his calculations of projected savings, he proposed to cover the country with apartment hotels. Putnam also saw the apartment hotel as an automatic slum-clearance scheme: "Ample space will be saved for verdure around each edifice, and there will be no crowded, insanitary, half-dilapidated firetraps for *the poor*." [27] He believed that apartment hotels would prevail in the country and at the seashore, allowing greater preservation of "the natural beauties of the landscape" than other forms of resort development permitted.

His actual plans emphasized the flexible design of living spaces, with three types of units: private apartments fully equipped with kitchens and dining rooms; apartments without kitchens but with dining rooms served by the public kitchen; and apartments without either kitchens or dining rooms, whose residents used the collec-

tive facilities. Among the shared facilities in his building were a kitchen, laundry, cafe, and small dining rooms, as well as central steam heating, electric light, elevators, and fireproof stairways. True to the Victorian conventions of gender, respected by Edward Bellamy (but not by Gilman), Putnam added a gentlemen's smoking room and a ladies' parlor, where residents of each sex could gather for conversation.

Gilman's advocacy of the apartment hotel echoed Putnam's and opposed conservatives who believed that such places were bad for women. In 1903 the editors of *Architectural Record* examined apartment hotels and found that in addition to businessmen and country residents, "thousands of steady New Yorkers have been moving into them — people who are neither business nor Social Bohemians, and people who pass as much time in the city as do the great majority." The boom in apartment hotel construction did suggest the most rapid urban evolution: in less than two years, plans for ninety apartment hotels had been approved in New York, enough to house fifteen thousand people. The editors felt that ". . . the adoption of apartment hotel life by any considerable section of the permanent population of New York could not but be regarded with grave misgivings by all observers of American morals and manners." The editors conceded that apartment hotel life could be cheap and could reduce trouble to a minimum, but "while the apartment hotel is the consummate flower of domestic co-operation, it is also, unfortunately, the

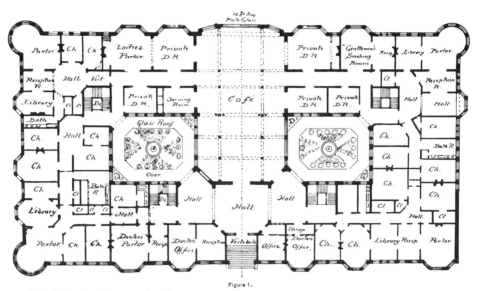

Figure 1.

9.6 John Pickering Putnam, plan for an apartment hotel, *American Architect and Building News,*
1890, "as near an approach to the ideal of a human habitation as has yet been devised"

consummate flower of domestic irresponsibility. It means the sacrifice of everything implied by the word 'home.' No one could apply the word to two rooms and a bath." They called the apartment hotel "a big, bold, twentieth century boarding house," and, they added, "the apartment hotel is the boarding house at its best and worst. It is the most dangerous enemy American domesticity has yet had to encounter." [28]

Noting their concern that American women often chose to live in boarding-houses after marriage and were already all too likely "to consider the care of the household a burden," the editors expressed concern that many women found industrial, charitable, social, or intellectual pursuits more interesting than domestic life. The *Record* editors moaned that "a woman who lives in an apartment hotel has nothing to do. . . . She cannot have food cooked as she likes; she has no control over her servants; she cannot train her children to live in her particular way; she cannot create that atmosphere of manners and things around her own personality, which is the chief source of her effectiveness and power. If she makes anything out of her life at all, she is obliged to do it through outside activities — through her club memberships or charitable work." [29]

While moralists had insisted and continued to insist that the apartment hotel was "no place for a lady," clearly the job of creating "an atmosphere of manners and things around her own personality" in the private home, cited as the chief source of a "lady's" effectiveness and power, was what

Thorstein Veblen called "conspicuous consumption." It is not surprising that many middle-class women found the domestic life of a "lady" stifling rather than stimulating. "If she makes anything of her life at all, she is obliged to do it through outside activities," said the editors. This was exactly Gilman's goal. More and more civic and political activities were open to women as well as paid employment.

Architectural Record lectured women about dignity: the apartment hotel ". . . could not have become as popular as it is now without the acquiescence of large numbers of women; and it is devoutly to be hoped that many more women will not be foolish enough to follow this example, thereby sacrificing the dignity of their own lives and their effective influence over their husbands and children." [30] Gilman repeatedly challenged such pious appeals for married women to avoid apartment hotel life. In 1903, in *The Home,* she criticized private houses as "bloated buildings, filled with a thousand superfluities." In 1904 she wrote about urban evolution and women's liberation: ". . . we hear a cry of complaint and warning about the passing of the American home. Everything else has passed, and without wailing; passed, as must all rising life, 'from the less to the greater, from the simple to the complex.' " She explained that "this very apartment-house, with its inevitable dismissal of the kitchen, with its facility for all skilled specialist labor, has freed the woman from her ancient service. . . ." Calling for feminist apartment hotels equipped with child-gardens, play-rooms, and nurseries, she exhorted, "let us then study, understand, and help to hasten this passing onward to better things of our beloved American Home. Let us not be afraid, but lead the world in larger living." [31]

Professional Domesticity

If Gilman's ideas about physical design derived from the free lovers and Nationalists interested in housing reform, her ideas about economic organization came from the home economists and social settlement workers who were promoting domestic evolution. She believed that it was only a matter of time before cooking and childcare left the private home: "It should always be held in mind that the phrase "domestic industry" does not apply to a special kind of work, but to a certain grade of work, a stage of development through which all kinds pass. All industries were once 'domestic,' that is, were performed at home and in the interests of the family." She admired Marie Howland's work on scientific child care, as developed at the Social Palace in Guise. She echoed Mary Livermore's call for industrial training for workers. In her glorious new domestic world of apartment hotels, kitchenless dwellings and neighborhood social centers, "trained professionals" were doing the work. Gilman railed at men for abandoning to women "the chamberwork and scullery work of the world . . . all that is basest and foulest . . . grease, ashes, dust, foul linen and sooty ironware — among these her days must pass," but she was not prepared to transfer a share of all "woman's" work to men. Instead, she argued for paid jobs for professional domestic workers, stating that what is "basest and foulest" in private housework would be susceptible to the "swift skill of training and experience," wielded by "efficient workers," by "those who like to do such work." [32] She slated middle-class women for jobs as entrepreneurs, managers, and chefs; high school graduates with training in domestic science would assist them as dishwashers, cleaners, maids, and child care aides.

Gilman insisted that all new forms of housing, child care, and domestic service be developed by entrepreneurs, "on a business basis." Here she was defending the directors of vocational training programs. While not all home economists and social settlement workers disparaged the efforts of ordinary housewives to "cooperate" and improve their domestic situation, many did believe that it was a mistake for women to demand remuneration for housework without the extensive discussions of scientific child care, nutrition and sanitation which were the professionals' stock-in-trade. Thus Gilman rejected consumers' and producers' cooperatives organized by housewives, and recommended corporate forms of organization, with paid workers:

This is the true line of advance; making a legitimate human business of housework; having it done by experts instead of by amateurs; making it a particular social industry instead of a general feminine function, and leaving the private family in the private home where it belongs.

This is not cooperation, but it is good business.

It is one of the greatest business opportunities the world has ever known.[33]

To show just what "good business" meant, in her serial novel *What Diantha Did,* published in *The Forerunner* in 1909 and 1910, Gilman invented a female entrepreneur, Diantha Bell, manager of a restaurant, a cooked food delivery service, a maids' hostel and placement service, kitchenless houses, and an apartment hotel in a California town called Orchardina. She endowed Diantha Bell with all of the skills home economists insisted women should acquire. When she cooked, the food was exquisite. When she dusted, a troublesome society matron in white gloves could find no fault. When she did the accounts, the grocery bills plummeted. Although she dealt with the public, she lost no social respectability, for her mother was her chaperone. Most important, she managed her employees in a firm, authoritative manner. Former live-in servants working an eight-hour day as "professional" maids or cooks enjoyed private rooms in a hostel run for them by Diantha Bell. She paid somewhat better wages than their former mistresses and protected them from sexual harassment by male employers. Following the name of the enterprise, Union House, the workers formed a " 'House Workers' Union," but it was a company union, for Gilman was committed to benevolent capitalism, financed by inherited wealth and managed by an entrepreneur with the workers' interest at heart. There were no conflicts between labor and management in Diantha Bell's business.

Gilman created a young, socially prominent, wealthy widow, Viva Weatherstone, to provide Diantha's capital. Viva encouraged Diantha to see domestic reform in terms of profit as well as female emancipation:

"I don't think even you realize the *money* there is in this thing!" she said. "You are interested in establishing the working girls, and saving money and time for the housewives. I am interested in making money out of it — honestly! It would be such a triumph!"

". . . My father was a business man, and his father before him — I *like it.* . . . there's no end to this thing, Diantha! It's one of the biggest businesses on earth, if not *the* biggest!" [34]

Having persuaded Diantha to expand her business, Viva purchased special insulated containers to deliver food and a gasoline motor van for deliveries, then rented these marvels of technology to Diantha at 10 percent interest. As the cooked food delivery business at Union House prospered, Viva made an even bigger investment, and hired an architect, Isobel Porne, to build twenty kitchenless houses and an apartment hotel, the Hotel de las Casas. Isobel had been stuck at home doing housework until Diantha came to town. Resuming her career as an architect, she designed the hotel complex, "a pleasure palace," with swimming pool, billiard rooms, card rooms, reading rooms, lounging rooms, dancing rooms, tennis courts, roof garden, flowers, "rare trees," "winding shaded paths" be-

tween the houses, "great kitchens, clean as
a hospital," and central lighting and heating. "What do you think of my investment?" asks Viva Weatherstone. As the
story closes, Viva congratulates Diantha
and herself: "I have taken money out of
five and seven per cent investments, and
put it into ten per cent ones. . . . I am a
richer woman because of you. . . ." [35]

What Diantha Did left no doubt about
the economic basis Gilman proposed for
domestic reform: benevolent capitalism.
Gilman did not challenge women's responsibility for domestic organization nor the
hierarchy of social and economic class in
Orchardina. In another utopian novel,
Moving the Mountain, she was equally optimistic about the basis for such changes in
American society, asserting her belief in
"no other change than a change of mind,
the mere awakening of people, especially
the women, to existing possibilities." [36]

As the most influential feminist theoretician of her time, Gilman constantly exhorted women to seek the goal of collective
domestic life. A prolific writer and an effective lecturer, she said of herself: ". . . I
was not a reformer but a philosopher. . . .
My business was to find out what ailed society, and how most easily and naturally to
improve it. It might be called the effort of
a social inventor, trying to advance human
happiness by the introduction of better
psychic machinery." [37] She left it to her
disciple, Henrietta Rodman, to attempt to
build a Feminist Apartment Hotel on the
principles of professional domesticity and
good business practices.

The Feminist Paradise Palace

In April 1914, Henrietta Rodman, active
in New York feminist and socialist circles,
founded the Feminist Alliance. Rodman
had been involved in many trade union
struggles in New York, and had won recognition for her drive to organize the public
schoolteachers. Now, wishing to attack
broader issues, she recruited some wealthy
women active in Crystal Eastman's Congressional Union for Woman Suffrage as
well as some middle-class professional
women and their husbands. In addition to
attempting to have women admitted to
law and medical schools, the Feminist Alliance won a campaign for maternity leaves
for teachers (previously New York's Board
of Education had fired teachers who became mothers). They demanded American
women's rights to retain their citizenship if
they married foreigners. In their more sociable moments they held a fancy dress
ball where guests were invited to come in
women's costumes ranging from primitive
to futuristic.[38]

Most ambitious of their projects was the
Feminist Apartment House. Gilman had
described it in detail; Rodman was determined to see it built. Perhaps she saw herself as Diantha Bell, creating another Hotel
de Las Casas in Orchardina. She cast Alva
Vanderbilt Belmont and Fanny Garrison
Villard of the Congressional Union in the
roles of rich, enlightened benefactresses. In
1906, Gilman had written:

We have so arranged life, that a man may
have a home and family, love, companionship, domesticity, and fatherhood, yet

remain an active citizen of age and country. We have so arranged life, on the other hand, that a woman must 'choose'; must either live alone, unloved, uncompanied, uncared for, homeless, childless, with her work in the world for sole consolation; or give up all world-service for the joys of love, motherhood, and domestic service.[39]

The settlement houses inhabited by career women were the great exception to Gilman's generalization. Rodman and the other members of the Feminist Alliance were determined to rearrange home life so that women could combine a career and marriage successfully, by creating women's housing less tied to specific types of work than the settlement houses. They planned to offer an organization similar to the Jane Club run by women workers, but to construct an edifice equal to the apartment hotels built for male residents with varied occupations.

The group hired Max G. Heidelberg, a radical New York architect, to design their building. He had both socialist and feminist interests as an activist on housing issues in the Cooperative League of America and as a member of the Executive Committee of the National Birth Control League.[40] For the Alliance, Heidelberg designed a twelve-story building for a site near Greenwich Village, including kitchenless apartments, collective housekeeping facilities, and a roof-top nursery school. The building of about four hundred rooms, divided into one hundred and seventy one-to-four-room suites, required a capital of half a million dollars.[41] In the ambitious calculations about its size and quality, the project resembled A. T. Stewart's ill-fated Woman's Hotel of 1878 (9.7), but the Alliance's project was to be controlled by its residents and to provide day care for the children of employed women, thus recognizing that family and paid work for women were not incompatible activities.

Rodman believed that Alva Belmont, Fanny Villard, and other wealthy investors would guarantee most of the capital. Villard had worked for decades with the New York Diet Kitchen Association which provided food for the poor, and with various nurseries and kindergartens, the National Household Economic Association, three suffrage groups, and the Women's Peace Party. Her husband was a cofounder of the Edison General Electric Company. Alva Belmont had come to feminism late in her life but was a heavy contributor to suffrage causes, the Women's Trade Union League, and Max Eastman's magazine, *The Masses.* Most important, she had been a flamboyant patron of architecture in her earlier days as a reigning society matron. Richard Morris Hunt had built her a three-million-dollar pseudo-French chateau at Fifth Avenue and Fifty-Second Street in 1881, a two-million dollar "cottage" at Newport in 1892, and another estate at Sands Points, Long Island. To Rodman she appeared a likely supporter for this feminist architectural enterprise.

In addition to $480,000 from wealthy patrons, the organizers hoped to raise one year's rent in advance from the residents, the rather small sum of $20,000. Single women could live in the building, as well

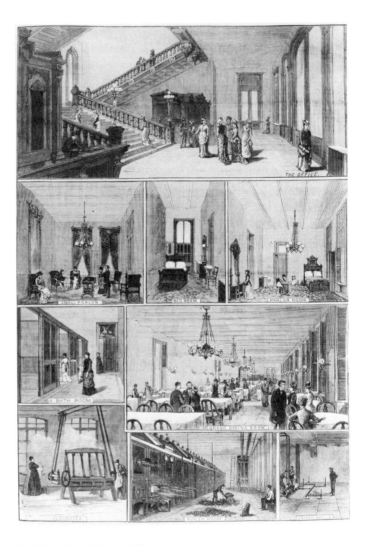

9.7 Views of the Woman's Hotel, an apartment hotel for working women, showing office, parlor, bedrooms, bathrooms, dining room, laundry, boiler room, and driven wells, from *Harper's Weekly,* April 13, 1878

as married women with their children and husbands; all resident parents, male and female, were expected to help with child care. Rodman said: "I maintain that every child has a right to a real father, one who has sufficient leisure to take a real interest in his children." [42] She planned that the building would be staffed by "trained help from the domestic science departments of the high schools," working eight-hour days, in order that the resident career women would be freed from chores. Thus the pressures forcing women to choose between marriage and a career would disappear: "Imagine Dr. Katharine B. Davis chained down to household drudgery. Or imagine Inez Millholland Boissevian becoming a dishwasher for life! Heretofore many such women have had to give up marrying altogether in order to obtain their freedom. We hold that it isn't necessary: that all that is necessary is to make a home with all the household drudgery out of it." [43] The professional women assured themselves that they would make things much easier for the domestic workers, with good wages and limited hours. Yet Rodman conceded that her real interest was not in helping domestic workers but in providing a home for employed, educated women. Having won teachers the right to marry, she was now attempting to provide housing which would support them and other professionals while they struggled with both careers and children.

Heidelberg, who chaired the Feminist Alliance's Committee on the Socialization of the Primitive Industries of Women,

made some attempt to eliminate domestic drudgery through design. There would be no wallpaper and no picture moldings. All corners would be rounded, all bathtubs would be built in, all windows would pivot, all beds would fold into the walls, and all hardware would be dull-finished.[44] Of course, the women with high school training in domestic science would still be cleaning inside the built in bathtubs, if not under them, and washing the pivoting windows.

Rodman wanted to believe that new domestic technology and the professionalization of housework would solve all domestic problems, but her husband, Herman de Frem, was more alert to the economic and social issues involved. As Executive Secretary of the Feminist Alliance, he claimed there was a need for greater democracy in the house and argued that "it should be made cooperative in every sense." [45] Rodman, steeped in Gilman's polemics against cooperation in housekeeping, claimed that cooperators would not actually get as much work done as paid "professionals." While the discussion raged, the project was criticized from outside as a "feminist paradise palace" by Laura Fay-Smith, writing in the *New York Times.*

Fay-Smith sneered at feminism and railed at women who refused the "responsibilities" of motherhood. A militant anti-feminist, she was none other than Melusina Fay Peirce's younger sister, the mother of six (two of whom died very young), who had spent most of her life in St. Albans, Vermont. She argued that if nature had intended women to be feminists, then women of the future would be square-shouldered, flat-chested, and equipped with "large feet on which to stand their ground." They would be born with "money as their only standard of value." Fay-Smith asserted that true women know their place is at home, as mothers, because this was what nature had ordered. She fired a parting complaint: "The feminist wants to hire other women to do what she ought to do herself; she wants to climb high above the harsh labors of the house, on the shoulders of the women whose hard necessity compels them to be paid servants." [46] In her portrayal of conflict between women as employers and employees, Fay-Smith did identify a problem that the feminist organizers could not resolve: how to escape from stereotypes about "women's" work without exploiting women of a lower economic class.

By refusing to shift one half of the domestic burden back on to men, the women of the Feminist Alliance separated themselves from the "professional" domestic workers whom they planned to employ. No one asked how the "professional" domestic workers could also be mothers. Debate centered on whether or not a feminist apartment hotel promoted or destroyed "natural" motherhood for middle-class women. No critic picked up on Rodman's scrutiny of "natural" fatherhood, and asked what "real men" ought to do around the house. No one asked how the professionals who were supporting themselves and their children could survive without

their jobs. In the last rounds of the debate, the editors of the *New York Times* actually agreed with the Feminist Alliance's assertion that removing housework from the house was desirable, but the editors reproved the activists for mixing up this technological and social advance with feminism, "whatever that may be," and thereby "making a difficult problem harder." [47]

The *New York Post* analyzed all of the Feminist Alliance's economic calculations, questioning whether child care could cost only sixty-five cents per day, with a ratio of one nurse to every five babies, and one kindergarten teacher to every ten pupils. They questioned as well whether or not the cost of apartments, with meals, could average ten dollars per week, and concluded: "The only wonder is why, if women teachers, literary workers, and musicians can be fed on 53 cents a day, there should be such a clamor for a minimum wage for shop girls." [48]

Ultimately the alliance between elderly, wealthy women interested in suffrage and philanthropy, and younger women and men who were cultural radicals, socialists, and feminists broke down. "Motherhood" had been the point of public attack, but the unresolved problems of domestic service versus domestic cooperation caused the group's internal disagreements. The struggle to unite socialism and feminism was at a very early stage. Feminists with capital who could afford the new physical environment for collective domestic work never thought of voluntarily sharing that domestic work themselves. Men and women with

socialist sympathies who defended the
Feminist Alliance's project in *The Masses*
had no analysis of the conflicts of either
gender or economic class involved in
reorganizing domestic work.[49] The problems of housewives and servants were still
very little understood, although almost half
a century had passed since Steven Pearl
Andrews and Victoria Woodhull had attempted to promote apartment hotels for
everyone as part of a "grand domestic revolution" in New York City. The closer
such domestic projects got to practical real-
ization, the greater the ideological difficulties seemed to be. Not one feminist woman
nor one socialist man in Rodman's group
(with the possible exception of her husband), wanted to do any domestic work
themselves. Talk as they might about the
dignity of labor, or about creating good
jobs for well-trained workers, no one
wanted to be a well-trained domestic
worker. Everyone wanted to pay someone
else to do this job, but they were never prepared to pay more than they earned themselves as writers, or teachers, or white-collar
workers.

A Social Inventor
The inability of Gilman's followers to build
the Feminist Apartment Hotel did not
affect Gilman's own career very much. She
had already moved from writing political
polemics to utopian fiction, the genre of
the 1890s at which she was particularly
adept. *What Diantha Did* (1909–1910) was
succeeded by *Moving the Mountain* (1911). A
final utopia, *Herland* (1915), depicted eco-

nomically independent, wise, and athletic
women in an egalitarian society with mar-
velous architecture and landscape architecture, a society without men. Since her first
book had been translated into seven languages, many feminists in the United
States, England, France, Sweden, and Germany revered her. *Women and Economics* was
considered a "bible" by college women at
Vassar, and many women's groups around
the country attempted to put some of
Gilman's ideas into practice, with the establishment of community dining clubs
and, especially, cooked food delivery services, rather than more expensive apartment
hotels. Gilman's great achievement was to
broaden the constituencies for domestic reform established by her predecessors. She
reached beyond the small numbers of
women in the cooperative movement, the
free-love movement, the suffrage movement, and the home economics movement,
in order to aim her argument at middle-
class married women and men living in
small towns all over the country as well as
in big cities. She argued for domestic reform because of its benefit to the entire human race, and her logic was difficult to
resist.

Carefully defining a strategy for domestic reform which relied on the professionalization of housework, avoiding claims for
housewives' cooperatives where work was
shared, and rejecting demands for free love
environments where sex might be shared as
well as work, Gilman had produced an ambitious domestic program which she believed was viable in a capitalist society.

Like her many predecessors, including
Melusina Fay Peirce and Marie Stevens
Howland, Gilman had identified economic
independence for women as the real basis
for lasting equality between men and
women. Like them, she had argued that
the physical environment must change if
women were to enjoy this economic independence. But despite basic agreement
among many domestic reformers on these
issues between 1870 and 1900, no single reformer, before Gilman, had been able to
speak to a very broad range of supporters.
Only she was able to make the dream seem
so tangible, so sensible, so extraordinarily
realizable to people of common sense and
good will, that tens of thousands of people
began really to believe in new kinds of
American homes.

Yet her success was not an unqualified
one. She never gave enough credit to the
reformers who had preceded her, and thus
she failed to build upon earlier theory or to
unify the small and somewhat different
constituencies they had created. Peirce was
most concerned about middle-class housewives, both with and without servants;
Howland about married women workers
with children. Richards and Addams
turned their attention to single women
workers and single professional women.
Gilman subordinated all these interests to
those of professional, married women with
children who chose to work outside the
home, demographically the smallest group
of all.

In part this appeal to different consti-
uencies was a sign that times had changed,
but it also reflected Gilman's optimistic
rather than realistic view of women's employment patterns. In 1868 Peirce addressed housewives and servants who represented an overwhelming majority of adult
women. In 1885, when Howland wrote
about employed women, they represented
nearly 20 percent of adult women, but
only 5 percent of married women, creating
a rather limited audience for her proposals
on child care centers located in factories.
Nevertheless, Howland had at least chosen
the right location. Married women workers
did hold more factory jobs than jobs as
servants or as professionals at this time.
This situation remained more or less the
same during the era of home economists'
and social settlement workers' struggles for
public kitchens and for single women's
housing in factory districts. By 1910, 25
percent of all women were employed, and
10 percent of married women. Gilman's
hoped-for constituency of professional
mothers was to be drawn from this 10 percent. But she organized against the odds:
in 1910 only 12 percent of all employed
women were professionals, while 25 percent
were still domestic servants (1.5).[50]

Professionals who were mothers were an
infinitesimal group compared to single professionals, or to domestic servants and factory operatives who were mothers. True,
the professionals were increasing their
numbers dramatically, and the married
ones among them represented the fondest
hopes of a new generation of educated
women who did not wish to sacrifice their
careers for motherhood. However, they

were the exceptional women of their time. The housewife who did not work for wages was still the typical married woman, and the majority of professional women did not marry.[51]

Many of Gilman's theoretical difficulties can be attributed to her desire to reach a new constituency of professional women who were also mothers, a constituency which had not yet reached substantial numbers. If, in the short run, Gilman wanted to appeal to married career women, then she had to reject housewives' cooperatives and turn to either "professional" workers or to men to get the domestic work done. If she wanted to appeal to women for whom careers might not always be considered socially acceptable, then she had to denounce any associations with free love and organize an irreproachable program based on monogamous marriage or celibacy. By making these choices, she insisted that the apartment hotel was an ideal environment for the respectable, monogamous, married couple with children, just as the cooked food service was an ideal business venture for the female capitalist and professional domestic economist. Ironically, Gilman was often perceived as supporting just those groups she disavowed: in the popular press her name was often linked with "cooperative housekeeping," and her status as a divorced woman who shared child care with her ex-husband was considered less than fully respectable.

In particular, her choice of the apartment hotel, with its commercial services, as the setting for feminist motherhood created difficulties for Socialist Party women who found that Gilman's program left them without suitable tactics for a socialist, feminist struggle. Gilman had an exciting but expensive program for changing women's lives. She depended on enlightened feminist capitalists to lead the way. Not only did she reject class conflict between men, which the Socialists knew how to analyze, but she also rejected housewives' economic struggle and argued that housewives did not perform productive labor in the Marxian sense. Here she overlooked Melusina Peirce's insights and those of all of the material feminists of the earlier generation. Although she had the best analysis of feminist motherhood yet developed, she failed to convey to Socialist Party women the full force of the earlier feminist position about the economic value of domestic work.

While Gilman herself believed that feminists should struggle in capitalist society to transform the home, she offered no tactics except her faith in female capitalists to socialists who believed that they should wait until "after the revolution" for "the big, socialized kitchen." Gilman did help Socialist Party women to fight cultural conservatives within the party, such as John Spargo, who argued that housework was a woman's job. Spargo had a particular hatred for feminist proposals for collective living, stating that "A glorified Waldorf Astoria is inferior to a simple cottage with a garden." [52] But Gilman merely helped socialist women to defend a feminist critique of the private home, not to take this fur-

ther into a socialist, feminist plan for action.[53]

In the long run, her failure to appreciate
producers' cooperatives, which allowed
women to control their own domestic work
collectively, led her to a naive argument
favoring "good business." In the same way,
her rejection of free love — the demand
that women control their own sexuality
and reproduction — weakened her rationale for collective services such as day care.
Nevertheless, her contribution to the feminist and socialist movement of her day was
a powerful critique of "the isolated home"
and "the sordid shop," of "a world torn
and dissevered by the selfish production of
one sex and the selfish consumption of the
other." [54] Accompanying this critique was
her remarkably vivid presentation of another, more humane, social and physical
environment, the feminist apartment hotel
suitable for feminist motherhood, and her
assurance that "when the mother of the
race is free, we shall have a better world,
by the easy right of birth, and by the calm,
slow, friendly forces of social evolution." [55]
By linking feminist ideals with improved
motherhood, Gilman achieved national
stature as a social theorist. Small-town
suffragists, metropolitan planners, and specialists in the higher education of women
all tried to put her ideas into practice.

20th Century Food Co., New Haven, 1900

*Now let the cook lady strike; who cares? All I
have to do is to step to the telephone or drop a
post card and order dinner, have it served hot at
the door, well cooked and of excellent variety, for
less money than you could do it yourself, to say
nothing about wear and tear of nerves. It is emancipation, I say, sing the long meter doxology, be
thankful there are those to blaze a trail out of the
wilderness and lead the people into the promised
land of delightful housekeeping.*
*— Clergyman in New Haven, patron of a cooked
food service, 1901*

We're in Missouri, and we're ready for anything.
*— Participant in a neighborhood Cooperative
Kitchen, 1907*

Midsummer in Carthage, Missouri, 1907. The sun beat down on this small town day after day, as women trying to organize a forthcoming suffrage convention met in formal parlors and fanned themselves in the summer heat, without a breeze to lift the curtains. They hurried home to see about the next meal, to face the ordeal of cooking on hot, cast-iron stoves, where they baked bread, muffins, and pies, roasted meats, and cooked vegetables, a never-ending round, from breakfast through lunch and dinner. The same women, keeping up with their laundry and cleaning through the long summer days, idly speculated about the future after suffrage was won, the future without private housework envisioned by Charlotte Perkins Gilman.

A future without housework? An impatient husband, an ex-senator, challenged the ingenuity of the local women's group, by complaining about his wife: "She is always cooking, or has just cooked, or is just going to cook, or is too tired from cooking. If there is a way out of this, with something to eat still in sight, for Heaven's sake, tell us!" [1]

His ultimatum was debated in a long session among women in one of the hot, formal parlors and argued out at a larger meeting of near neighbors, with almost sixty men, women, and children present. A large white clapboard house, with broad verandas on two sides, shaded by tall oaks, was rented. Horses and wagons, loaded with dining room tables and chairs, converged on the rented house and stopped near the broad porch. On the porch, the women drew lots, and one by one, the tables were carried inside. The winners placed their tables next to the tall windows in the library and dining room on the ground floor. The losers put theirs in the centers of these rooms. The women brought tablecloths, napkins, and silverware from home in boxes and hampers. Muslin curtains were hung at every window. As the tables were set, a few women added jars of homemade relishes, pickles, peach and strawberry preserves, mint jellies. The rooms were readied for sixty people to dine.

A manager, two cooks, two waitresses, and a dishwasher were busy in the kitchen, preparing for the evening meal of steak, stuffed baked potatoes, baked beans, brown bread, lettuce salad, blanc-mange with orange sauce, and coffee. The member families, having paid $3.00 per adult per week, for three meals per day (or half that price for children under seven), enjoyed that meal. Said one husband, "Never to hear a word about the servants that have just left, or are here, or are coming to-morrow — perhaps! . . . We're in Missouri and we're ready for anything." [2] Said another husband, at first a skeptic about this "Home for the Help-less," "I'm down as a life-member, let me tell you right now! The meals may be plain but they are balanced. The quality makes up for any amount of frills and trimming." [3]

After a month of successful operation, as autumn drew in, a reading room was furnished. Books, magazines, lamps, and upholstered chairs appeared to make a comfortable indoor sitting area. If the men were satisfied by the Cooperative Kitchen, the women were greatly relieved. Probably some of them took over their old dining rooms at home and turned them into proper office spaces, for handling the massive correspondence an effective suffrage group required. Others spent more time with their children; one learned to drive a car; one did a bit of writing. The two single schoolteachers, who belonged to the Cooperative Kitchen and lived there too, were delighted to be treated as adult women, as social equals, despite their lack of spouses and households of their own. Their rooms cost $7.50 per month, their food, $12.00, but at last they were free from being patronized as somebody's "boarders."

Even the hard-pressed workers in the Cooperative Kitchen were a little better off than before. Rather than living in affluent households where one servant did everything, six of them shared work in the kitchen. Their salaries were higher, although their work was as difficult, and the hours almost as long. The cooks, paid $7.50 per week, plus room and board, worked from before breakfast until after dinner, with two hours off every afternoon and every other Sunday afternoon free. The manager received $35.00 per month and room and board for her family. On her shoulders rested the burden of mediating between the members of the consumers' cooperative, who expected "serv-

ice," and the women workers, who were putting in the long days of hard work. Her "personal charm, business ability, and trained mind" [4] were called upon constantly. She was the sole support of her family and running the Cooperative Kitchen was one of the few executive jobs open to a woman in Carthage, especially one interested in nutrition. The cooks and the waitresses preferred working for her to answering the calls of their former mistresses at all hours of the day. She was well-organized, and they knew what to expect. Only the dishwasher was dissatisfied, but after two dishwashers quit, a much better salary brought a new recruit who stayed.

For four years, the Cooperative Kitchen flourished in Carthage. Its neighborly dinners, sociable birthday celebrations, and dances for the teenage children of members were popular. Then a long drought threatened the town's financial prosperity. Rising food prices brought an end to $3.00 weekly subscriptions. When the weekly price of meals rose to $4.20, many families chose to economize at home. [5]

As the Carthage experiment indicates, while home economists lectured about scientific cooking, novelists fantasized about kitchenless houses, and feminists exposed the weaknesses of the traditional home, many pragmatic middle-class women organized various types of community kitchens to provide food for their families. Two pioneers in the movement for community kitchens explained, "Here is a chance for a woman gifted with com-

mon sense, some business ability, and a fair
knowledge of cookery, not only to release
or relieve other women, but to add to the
family income or even to earn her livelihood." [6] In small towns, suburban communities, and big cities, many housewives
and a few professional cooks and home
economists took up this challenge. They organized cooperative and commercial ventures: chiefly neighborhood dining clubs
and cooked food delivery services. Between
1884 and 1925 many of these experiments
thrived, patronized by relatively affluent
families. Women active in the suffrage
movement and in women's clubs often
spread the word to others about how much
time dining clubs and cooked food services
saved.

Mary Livermore had visited dining clubs
and inquired about cooked food services on
her lecture tours in the 1880s and gave favorable reports on one club in Evansville,
Wisconsin, and another in Ann Arbor,
Michigan, as well as on a delivery service
in New York. Suffragist publications, including The Woman's Journal and The
Woman's Column, carefully covered such
ventures throughout the 1880s, 1890s, and
1900s, as did other women's magazines
such as Ladies' Home Journal, Good Housekeeping, and Woman's Home Companion.
Those clubs which failed did not discourage them. In the Woman's Journal, Lucy
Stone wrote in 1893, ". . . it is certain
that a co-operative kitchen, bakery and
laundry are among the good things which
are to come for the relief of women, but
which will still leave the individual home

intact. The Philadelphia experiment
[which ended after six months] has been
one of the lessons in the preparatory school
for the final result." [7] Bellamy's Nationalist
magazines and leading daily papers in
New York and Boston also followed these
experiments. Home economists corre-
sponded with the organizers, surveying the
results.[8]

From all of these sources, and the menu
cards, constitutions, and sets of rules and
regulations that have survived, a most surprising picture emerges. "Cooperative
housekeeping" became a reality in at least
thirty-three experiments throughout the
United States: thirteen community dining
clubs and twenty cooked-food delivery
services, which lasted between six months
and thirty-three years. (See Appendix for
details.) Sorting out the details of these associations, the claims made for them, their
successes and failures, some patterns appear. The dining clubs averaged over four
and a half years' duration. These were invariably in small towns, where from five to
twenty families enjoyed the social contacts
of a shared dining room. The cooked food
delivery services averaged over five and a
half years' duration. They were more likely
to flourish in large cities and their suburbs,
where efficient service was preferred to
neighborly socializing. Both types drew
middle-class families, especially ones in
which wives engaged in extensive outside
activities, and they attracted many single
men and women as well. The neighborhood dining clubs combined cooperative
purchasing of food with collective prepara-

tion and dining. They emphasized social innovation, while the food delivery services tended to be run by entrepreneurs on a commercial basis and to emphasize technological innovation. The delivery services were often more expensive to patronize.

Certain districts, such as the "burned over district" of upstate New York, the Boston suburbs, parts of New Jersey, and areas of Illinois, Iowa, and Ohio were established as pockets of communitarian socialist culture before 1860. The location of some dining clubs and cooked food services in these same areas suggests that for at least half a century beyond 1860, they continued to welcome innovators who had strong commitments to an ideal of community life. Some experiments tended to cluster, as a successful endeavor inspired imitations (Jacksonville, Decatur, and possibly Springfield, Illinois, in the 1890s; or Evansville, Portage, and Madison, Wisconsin, between 1885 and 1903). Others persisted in a single location or area, suggesting that individuals or even successive generations kept trying again (Cambridge, Boston, and Brookline, Massachusetts; or Montclair, East Orange, Princeton, and "Acadia," New Jersey; or Evanston, Illinois, in 1890 and again in 1918). Even more suggestive is the correlation between the small town experiments and the actual sites of earlier communitarian socialist experiments, such as the Oneida Community (ten miles from Utica); the Trumbull Phalanx (five miles from Warren, Ohio); the Raritan Bay Union and the North American Phalanx

(both twenty-five miles from Princeton, New Jersey); the Integral Phalanx (twenty miles from both Decatur, Illinois, and Springfield, Illinois) or the Brook Farm Community (less than two miles from Brookline and Cambridge, Massachusetts).

Community Dining Clubs

An editor of the *Independent* described numerous dining clubs all over the country in 1902: "Many of these have been run successfully for a number of years; and in some cases community dining halls have been built expressly for the purpose. The cooperative kitchens are very diverse in form. The simplest and most flexible type is where a dozen families club together and hire a cook and one or two assistants, and rent a kitchen and dining rooms, either buying or contributing the kitchen utensils and table ware." [9] A club in Warren, Ohio, stands out as the most positive experience of community dining, since it continued for over two decades. Similar to the Cooperative Kitchen in Carthage, it involved men actively, and included women with important commitments outside family life.

The Mahoning Club, the neighborhood dining club in Warren, was slightly smaller than the Kitchen in Carthage. It began in 1903 when a couple bought an old house too large for them (10.1). What could they do with the extra space? Instead of taking in boarders, they proposed a community dining club, according to Harriet Taylor Upton, who gave a long, favorable account of this club in 1923: "There were women in the neighborhood who had fine homes,

10.1 View of community dining club, The Mahoning Club, Warren, Ohio, established in 1903, from *Woman's Home Companion*, October 1923

but who were weary of directing incompetent servants; there were professional and business women who wanted home cooking but had no time to cook for themselves; there were unmarried men who longed for pies and rolls, 'such as Mother used to make.' " The Mahoning Club was formed with twenty-two members, who rented a large dining room, kitchen, and store room from the couple who had purchased the house.

Next came problems of organization: "At first only the women catered; but it was soon seen that women in business had less leisure than men, since they were usually the employed and not the employers. Therefore the rule was changed, and each member of the club must take his or her turn at managing." [10] Each member managed the menu and budget for a week at a time, but married women often served a week's stint for themselves and another for their husbands. Unmarried men and women did their own catering unless they paid a substitute. The desire to make the setting homelike generated an etiquette of cooperative serving: "The woman who caters sits at one end of the long table, serves the coffee, the vegetables, and looks after the comfort of all as if they were guests in her own home. Her husband carves and serves from the other end of the table. When an unmarried man caters he invites different women members to serve at different meals. An unmarried woman does the same with the men members. There are always some women who are quite willing to serve, and some men who enjoy

carving, and of course these are called upon most often." Three meals were served every day. Holidays were celebrated with special feasts and birthdays with presents. Costs ranged from $3.25 per week (in 1903) to $7.00 (in 1923). "Even with this increase, no family now at the club can live for the same amount at home."

The Warren members, taking their turns at running the club, supervised a staff consisting of a cook, a dishwasher and two waitresses. When the woman most active in the founding of the club died, others took over, and the club continued, for an amazing span of over twenty years, with a waiting list for membership and a remarkable reputation for "common sense, good management, and friendliness." When the number of private cars increased and Warren grew from a town of seven thousand people to an industrial city of thirty thousand, the club changed little. It expanded beyond its original neighborhood base, accepting new members by majority vote. The "atmosphere of home" was still greatly valued; fresh flowers appeared on every table. One member conceded, "To be sure, it would not be possible for twenty or thirty people of differing ages and conditions to admire each other blindly, but as a rule an unusual friendliness exists." [11]

These enterprises and similar community dining clubs founded in Jacksonville, Illinois; Junction City, Kansas; Decatur, Illinois; Sioux City, Iowa; and Longwood, Illinois, to mention a few other towns, seem to confirm Melusina Fay Peirce's prediction, made in 1869, that cooperative housekeeping would enjoy its greatest successes in small, midwestern towns where women were used to doing their own work and class distinctions were not rigidly enforced. Of the thirteen such clubs for which membership figures are available, none included less than five, or more than twenty families, with the average around twelve to fifteen. Many were near neighbors. Only one is known to have been affluent enough to build a community dining hall before establishing its operations; most rented or purchased houses to use for cooking and dining. None charged less than $2.50 per week for all meals for an adult; and no pre–World War I fees exceeded $4.50.

The rules of the Junction City Bellamy Club, in Kansas, which lasted for five years, suggest the friendly common sense necessary to sustain such a neighborly endeavor:

It shall be the duty of members to assist and encourage the officers in the conduct of the club.

1. By remembering to be reasonable in their requirements, bearing in mind that the weekly dues are small and that judgment and economy are necessary to make the receipts equal to the expenditures.

2. By never forgetting that they are not in a boarding house carried on for the purpose of gain, but are members of a mutual cooperative society, whose members give their time and energy to the work without any recompense except that shared by all, viz., the successful working of the club.

3. Members should consider it a duty to make known any shortcomings of servants or fare to the Vice-president, whose business it is to hear and endeavor to redress grievances; and refrain from inflicting them on their fellow members.

4. It shall be the imperative duty of members to speak as well of the club as they would of their own families; failing to do this they should withdraw, as no members are desired who are dissatisfied.[12]

Perhaps the most important point is that the cooperating members, advocates of Bellamy's Nationalism, are instructed to treat each other as they would treat family members, remembering the voluntary character of the association. The members in Junction City maintained strict economy, as did members of a club in Longwood, Illinois, which lasted for two years, and stated that its purpose was "to simplify the labor of daily living, the idea being to have meals no more luxurious than those of families of moderate means."[13] In Sioux City, Iowa, after a six-month trial, five families concluded that a similar experiment ". . . was all we expected it to be, and a success if one cares less for the home life than for the labor it brings. We attempted no cooperation further than the kitchen and dining room, but we think cooperative housekeeping practical if the people engaged in it are congenial."[14]

Almost always the attempt to establish congenial, neighborly cooperation between families of moderate income was accompanied by an assumption that the servants were a group apart. In Carthage, members hoped for a relationship with servants like that between a businessman and a stenographer.[15] But while the tasks might be shared by members and workers — since all clubs required some labor from their female members, and many required male members' participation as well — members and workers never sat down at the same table together. All thirteen clubs hired cooks, waitresses, and dishwashers, who earned between $11.00 and $2.50 per week, plus room and board. Thus there were rigid social and economic distinctions between the members and their employees, and these clubs were not experiments in communitarian socialism. There was, however, more male involvement than early theorists might have predicted, perhaps as a result of women's participation in suffrage activities.

Harriet Taylor Upton, whose account of the Warren experiment was so favorable, was a Warren, Ohio, woman who served as treasurer of the National American Women Suffrage Association for many years, and then became National Vice-Chairman of the Republican Party after suffrage was won. For many years the NAWSA office operated in Warren, Ohio, but neither Upton's autobiography nor the official suffrage histories explain whether or not NAWSA officers and members ran the Mahoning Club. Nevertheless, Upton spoke as a prominent suffragist and a woman holding a high political appointment in a major party, when she argued, in 1923, that the Warren dining club: ". . . is a plan of general cooperation, which works pleasure and profit for each member. Pleasure, in having meals prepared and served, losing nothing of the home atmosphere. Profit, in the fact that

this can be done at less cost than in one's home." [16] Over twenty years of successful community dining backed her assertion. In the Warren experiment and others, a previously male, urban amenity, the club dining room, was translated into a neighborhood facility for participating men and women, an economical approach to a new domestic world.

That the cooks in Warren and in other clubs were still servants, rather than "professionals" with status equal to the members, was an unresolved problem, but the burden that these clubs and their workers lifted from individual housewives cannot be underestimated. For example, a club in Utica, New York, ran from 1890 to 1893, and when former members were questioned ten years later about its success, one man was reported to say that if the club had continued, "his wife would probably be alive now." [17] This comment seems particularly ironic in light of the reason why the club was discontinued, that it "did not pay." Here, in a phrase, is the heart of the economic problem many clubs encountered: if a housewife's labor was never timed or counted, then it was very difficult to persuade husbands, or the community at large, that kitchen workers should receive wages comparable to the wages of a valued "professional" worker, or that experiments which placed a cash value on cooked meals should be continued. On the frontier, in the nineteenth century, wives had often died worn out from the physical strain of childbearing and housekeeping. This tradition would take a long time to overcome.

Cooked Food Delivery Services

In many urban centers and some small
towns, cooked food delivery services were
preferred to community dining clubs. At
first they delivered food by horse and
wagon (10.2), and then automobiles increased the speed of food delivery after
1910 (10.3). Usually slightly more expensive than community dining clubs, they
had regular subscribers. In addition, often
they were patronized on a temporary basis
by families whose domestic arrangements
were dislocated by travel, illness, or lack of
servants. These cooked food delivery services attempted to offer a well-balanced
meal of several courses, which could be
consumed in the privacy of the family dining room. The food service was equal to
that offered by a good residential hotel,
where inhabitants could order meals sent
to their apartments from the kitchen, but
it was far more flexible and without the social stigma of apartment hotel life. These
"meals on wheels" allowed customers to
continue to live in their own homes with
none of the unsettling difficulties that
shopping and cooking, or hiring and super-
vising servants offered. About one quarter
of the cooked food delivery services became
financially successful enough to offer additional services, such as laundry, maid service, child care, catering for special occasions, or school lunches. Only two of the
twenty services were actually run by
cooperating housewives, although nine
were organized as consumers' cooperatives requiring membership, and run by

home economists. Nine were run by
entrepreneurs.

The most participatory of all of these
food delivery experiments was established
by eight housewives, in the town of Palo
Alto, California, for two years during the
mid-1890s. The women shared meal planning and buying of supplies.[18] A Chinese
cook prepared the food; a Stanford student
was hired to deliver it; nursery maids and
housemaids were also hired in common.
This experiment may even have had the
blessing of Leland Stanford, since he was
reported in the *Woman's Journal* in 1887 as
endorsing cooperative housekeeping: "One
of the difficulties in the employment of
women arises from their domestic duties;
but co-operation would provide for a general utilization of their capacities. . . ."[19]
While small experiments with four to eight
families might succeed, just as the neighborhood dining clubs had, larger groups
had more problems. A Philadelphia matron criticized a group delivering food in
one neighborhood: "Would you like to
think that you were eating for your dinner,
the same things that everybody else in the
square was eating?"[20] Although nine
cooperating families living in one square in
Philadelphia had relatively few problems
in transporting cooked food to adjoining
houses, groups which drew their members
from a wider radius had to face great logistical difficulties.

A Well-Financed Failure

During the winter of 1890, in the Chicago
suburb of Evanston, Illinois, the Evanston

10.2 Pittsburg [sic] Dinner Delivery Company,
horse and wagon, boy carrying heat retainer,
1903. Courtesy Western Pennsylvania Historical
Society.

10.3 Views of cooperative kitchen, 1 Mountain-View Place, Montclair, New Jersey, established by Emerson Harris and Matilda Schleier, from *Ladies' Home Journal,* September 1918, showing main building and liveried black waiter delivering cooked food in heat retainer from a truck.

Cooperative Housekeeping Association mounted a spectacular experiment, organizing a cooperative laundry and cooked food delivery service to provide seven hundred meals a day to forty-five member families in their homes. With great fanfare, socially prominent families raised $5,000 in capital. They equipped a kitchen and laundry of hotel standard in the center of town. They purchased three specially fitted delivery wagons, each with space for sixteen huge "Norwegian kitchens," double-walled galvanized tin boxes, 24 inches by 36 inches by 5 inches, insulated with boiling water, stacked around a stove to keep the food hot in transit.

On December 8, 1890, luncheon was delivered to over two hundred people all over Evanston. According to a New York newspaper, "soups, roasts, steaks, vegetables, puddings, etc., were delivered, so the subscribers said, in as palatable condition as though they had just come from their own kitchens." [21] The charge was $4.00 per person per week, for three meals per day, but this did not cover the full costs of the elaborate central kitchen and the wagons, pulled by horses throughout the town in biting cold weather. The members had far greater problems than raising their prices could solve.

First was the response of their former servants to the scheme. The forty families of wealth and position who had formed the society intended to fire most of their former cooks and laundresses but keep their maids to clean their houses. A servants' league was formed. In some cases, the maids went on strike when the cooks and laundresses were fired. In others, servants agreed that never again would any of them work for any of the families who had organized this new enterprise. [22] Because the servants believed that cooperative housekeeping meant a "speed-up" for some, and a layoff for others, they reacted as industrial workers would react to the same sorts of changes. The efforts of the Evanston residents to combine forces allowed their servants the possibility of collective action as well. In this case the servants were not able to better their own conditions, but they did help to frustrate their former employers' plans.

The second problem facing the Evanston group was the refusal of Chicago wholesalers to sell it food. The *New York Sun* quoted one such response: "I'm sorry, but we can't take your order. If we sold goods to you, we would be boycotted by every retail grocer in Evanston." [23]

Third came the difficulty of hiring a competent person to manage the endeavor. According to various accounts, the first steward, Harry L. Grau, was either incompetent or dishonest. [24] His replacement collapsed in poor health. Possibly both men underestimated the amount of "woman's" work involved in the feeding of forty-five households.

If their food service had run smoothly, the Evanston cooperators might have held out against the servants and the retail grocers, but the social and economic dislocation their scheme created was too great to withstand without competent manage-

ment. Feeding two hundred and sixty-eight
people three times daily no longer seemed
impossible, but it was difficult. As the
Evanston experiment closed in January
1891, after two months' trial, one of the
leading women insisted, "I know the thing
can be done and I ache to do it." [25] Meanwhile, the women of Evanston applied
their energies to hiring new servants, or
trying without success to persuade their
former servants to return.

A comparison between the Jane Club in
Chicago and the Evanston experiment illustrates the problems of class conflict in
women's struggles to minimize the difficulties of domestic life. The Jane Club had
been formed in 1893 to promote cooperative housekeeping among factory workers
in Chicago. Both the women in the Jane
Club and the women of Evanston wanted
freedom from worry about domestic arrangements. There the resemblance ends.
The Jane Club members needed subsistence — basic food and shelter. The Evanston members wanted not subsistence but
more efficient conspicuous consumption.
Because the Jane Club women were living
at a minimal standard, they were not exploiting other workers. Their cook and
"general worker" earned about as much as
the members did. The members did not
need to oppress other workers in order to
improve their own situation substantially
by mutual aid.

The Evanston cooperators, on the other
hand, belonged to a class which already
enjoyed affluence based on profits produced by other workers. Evanston residents
lived on the income from successful businesses. Both wives and servants filled the
role of assisting the men of Evanston in the
processes of consumption and display. In
principle, cooperative housekeeping promised more efficient, less wasteful use of
food, fuel, and labor, and conservation of
these resources could benefit an entire community, if the community were organized
to redistribute such resources equally. In
Evanston, however, a partial approach to
"cooperation" produced painful results:
servants who lost their jobs were desperate,
while "co-operators," who hoped for more
leisure, couldn't understand why they
faced so much opposition. Perhaps there
were idealists in the Evanston group, who
came to understand class conflict and gender conflict more clearly as a result of their
experiences. Between 1918 and 1951 an organization called the Community Kitchen
flourished in the same town, suggesting
that the ideal was passed on from one generation to another. Some of the economic,
social, and technical problems which had
defeated the cooperators in 1891 were
solved by 1918.

Entrepreneurs and Technological
Wonders

If consumers' cooperatives dealing with
cooked food services had rather mixed results, services organized by entrepreneurs
fared somewhat better. Nine out of twenty
cooked food delivery services were commercial operations, with staying power for an
average of over four years. They delivered
between twenty-five and one hundred hot

meals per day, charging between $.15 and $1.00 per meal. A housewife with a reputation for good cooking, Bertha L. Grimes of Mansfield, Ohio, was in business for at least four years. She launched her enterprise in 1901 to serve five local families, and soon she was delivering about one hundred and seventy-five meals a day at a moderate price ($2.75 per week for two meals a day) to homes within a six-mile radius of her own, where she had established an extra-large kitchen.[26] She enjoyed tinkering with the available containers to perfect the technology, as did Samuel H. Street, a cereal manufacturer who founded a cooked food service in New Haven, Connecticut.[27] Both believed in the future of the cooked food business in the twentieth century.

While community dining clubs usually cultivated a cooperative, homelike atmosphere using existing neighborhood spaces and equipment, the organizers of cooked food services often became technocrats competing for the best food containers and the best vehicles for food transport. Double-walled, light metal containers filled with boiling water had been proposed for public kitchens in London in 1884, and massive copper or tin boxes fitted into special wooden wagons were tried in New York in 1885 and in Evanston in 1890. In England, John Ablett developed the London Distributing Kitchens, using similar flat metal boxes with many compartments (10.4, 10.5, 10.6).[28] Others thought that they could do better. George Chamberlain of Springfield, Massachusetts, resigned

from his position as an editor of *Good Housekeeping* magazine in 1903 in order to manufacture the container he believed would become the standard one for cooked food and thus became an essential part of American domestic life. The contraption he hoped would make him a millionaire, called the Heat Retainer, was a covered, galvanized iron bucket about fifteen inches high, filled with insulation and lined with aluminum (10.7). In this bucket could be fitted a hot soapstone, and then a nest of porcelain-lined, covered dishes containing a complete dinner or lunch. With Chamberlain's Heat Retainer, hot food cooked in community kitchens or cooperative dining clubs could be transported to private houses by horse-drawn wagon. Although Chamberlain's product was heavy and ungainly, it apparently worked. When members of the Toledo branch of Sorosis, a national women's club, asked Bertha Grimes in Mansfield to send them lunch in Heat Retainers in 1905, the food she sent one hundred miles by train arrived piping hot.[29]

A domestic revolution of a technical sort did seem to be at hand. Work at home could be reduced to setting the table, while professional cooks dealt with menus, marketing, food preparation, and dirty dishes. In 1909 and 1910, Charlotte Perkins Gilman's serial novel, *What Diantha Did*, elaborated on the marvels of technology marshaled by the wealthy Viva Weatherstone on behalf of Diantha Bell's cooked food service. In one scene Weatherstone displays a large food container she has ordered in Paris:

They lifted it in amazement — it was so
light.

"Aluminum" she said, proudly. "Silver-
plated — new process! And bamboo at the
corners you see. All lined and interlined
with asbestos, rubber fittings for silverware,
plate racks, food compartments — see?"

She pulled out drawers, opened little
doors, and rapidly laid out a table service
for five. . . .

"What lovely dishes," said Diantha.

"You can't break them, I tell you," said
the cheerful visitor, "and dents can be
smoothed out at any tin shop. . . ."

Mrs. Weatherstone laughed. "I'm not
through yet. . . . I went to several factories," she gleefully explained, "here and
abroad. A Yankee firm built it. It's in my
garage now!"

It was a light gasolene motor wagon, the
body built like those old-fashioned moving
wagons which were also used for excur-
sions. . . .

Mrs. Weatherstone smiled triumphantly.

"Now, Diantha Bell," she said, "here's
something you haven't thought of, I do believe! This estimable vehicle will carry
thirty people inside easily . . . and outside, it carries twenty-four containers. If
you want to send all your twenty-five at
once, one can go here by the driver." [30]

The success of Weatherstone's forays into
European food container design and Yankee automotive engineering is proven when
a family of subscribers to the cooked food
service invites a disbeliever to join them at
dinner. Mrs. Ree, "who hovered fascinated,
over the dangerous topic," was described as
"a staunch adherent of the old Home and
Culture Club," who disapproved of the
cooked food service but was curious about
its workings. On half an hour's notice by

telephone, for an extra fee of twenty-five
cents, her meal was added to her hosts':

Mrs. Ree had a lively sense of paltering
with Satan as she sat down to the Pornes'
dinner table. She had seen the delivery
wagon drive to the door, had heard the
man deposit something heavy on the back
porch, and was now confronted by a
butler's tray at Mrs. Porne's left, whereon
stood a neat square shining object with silvery panels and bamboo trimmings.

Mr. Porne's eyes sought his wife's, and
love and contentment flashed between
them, as she quietly set upon the table
three silvery plates.

"Not silver, surely!" said Mrs. Ree, lift-
ing hers, "Oh, aluminum."

They did keep silent in supreme contentment while the soup lasted. Mrs. Ree laid
down her spoon with the air of one roused
from a lovely dream.

"Why — why — it's like Paris," she said
in an awed tone.

. . . The meat was roast beef, thinly
sliced, hot and juicy . . . Mrs. Ree enjoyed every mouthful of her meal. The
soup was hot. The salad was crisp and the
ice cream hard. There was a sponge cake,
thick, light, with sugar freckles on the dark
crust. The coffee was perfect and almost
burned the tongue.

"I don't understand about the heat and
cold," she said; and they showed her the
asbestos lined compartments and perfectly
fitting places for each dish and plate. . . .

Mrs. Ree experienced peculiarly mixed
feelings. As far as food went, she had never
eaten a better dinner. But her sense of Domestic Aesthetics was jarred. . . .

"I don't see how she does it. All those
cases and dishes and the delivery
wagon!" [31]

Although Gilman's fictional cooked food
service used Parisian plates, and the soup

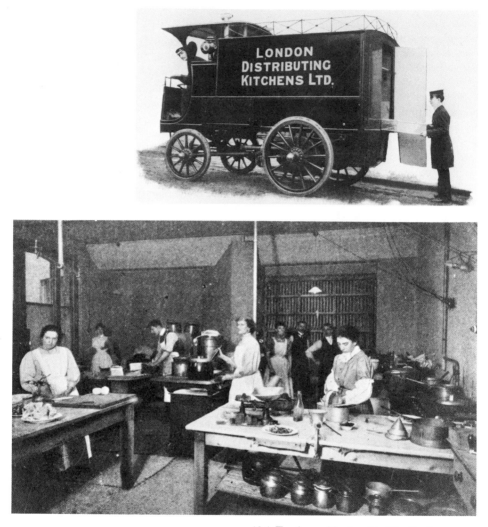

10.4 Trucks used by London Distributing
Kitchens, from *Lady's Realm*, February 1902

10.5 Workroom of London Distributing Kitchens, much less like a laboratory than the New
England Kitchen (8.7)

10.6 Metal container used by London Distributing Kitchens, a flat box which fit into a wagon. Evanston's "Norwegian kitchens" were probably similar.

10.7 Twentieth Century Food Company, offices, New Haven, Connecticut, run by Samuel Street. George Chamberlain, former editor of *Good Housekeeping*, invented the heat retainer: (1) outside of pail; (2) top; (3) padded cover; (4) rack holding heated soapstone; (5) pans for food; (6) pan for coffee or soup, sealed with pasteboard disk. From M. Alice Matthews, "Cooperative Living," 1903.

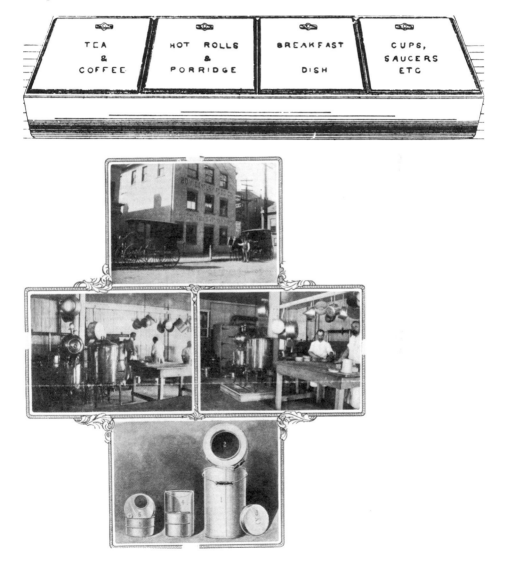

itself tasted "like Paris" to Mrs. Ree, probably Bertha L. Grimes of Mansfield, Ohio, was Gilman's real-life model. Yet even Grimes's operation was technologically complex compared to a community kitchen established by Myrtle Perrigo Fox and Ethel Lendrum. In 1919, the *Ladies' Home Journal* published their far more down-to-earth instructions on how to transport food, using "fruit jars slipped into cases made from cylindrical cereal cartons." For the family on a tight budget, Fox and Lendrum reported that "a one-and-a-half-pound oatmeal carton can be rolled in newspaper cut to fit and slipped into the larger three-pound carton. Asbestos pipe covering may be used for the inner lining, but it costs more." [32] They required that patrons of their community kitchen provide their own containers and an ordinary market basket to pack and transport them (10.8). Their kitchen served twenty-two people, with neighborhood boys and girls earning dimes for delivery on foot; no magical vehicles drove up to the patrons' doors in working class neighborhoods.

Wartime
Whether or not the oatmeal boxes wrapped in newspaper really worked, 1919 was wartime, and a mood of patriotic dedication increased the demands for all cooked food services. Eight of the delivery services either boomed in wartime or first gained their start because of war conditions. Six were located in the suburbs of large eastern cities and patronized by women whose servants were in wartime

factory work, or who were doing war work themselves.

Public kitchens for married women workers were established as well in urban centers. Miriam C. Senseney launched a public kitchen in 1917 in Saint Louis, supported by the Woman's Committee of the Council of National Defense, to meet the needs of immigrant women workers in defense industries. Its location at 1729 South Seventh Street was surrounded by large factories employing women. Four day nurseries were in the area. A cannery and a cooking school were established nearby by a wartime food conservation committee. In the settlement house tradition, a model apartment, an old clothes clinic, and a laundry were set up in the same building as the kitchen; a model poultry unit was installed in the back yard. [33]

The workers' dining room had 60 seats. A large sign hung over the entrance, "This is your kitchen — we do your cooking for you." Wagons carried food to nearby factories, and take-out service was also available for $.10 per meal. The kitchen served 960 persons with a breakfast of cereal; 480 with a lunch of soup and roll; 250 with dinner of meat, starch, and dessert. Women of the neighborhood responded to the kitchen by helping with scrubbing and furnishing the premises as well as buying food, but on Sundays, their only day off, they preferred to stay at home to cook for themselves and their families. [34]

In wartime all of these endeavors had the support of the Woman's Committee of the Council of National Defense. Iva

Starting a Community Kitchen

Just How it Can be Done With Little Outlay

By Myrtle Perrigo Fox and Ethel Lendrum, Home Demonstration Agent

HERE is a chance for a woman gifted with common sense, some business ability, and a fair knowledge of cookery, not only to re- lieve or relieve other women, but to add to the family income or even to earn her livelihood. You can start a community kitchen with three or four families as patrons. Serve two meals a week until you are asked to cook more. A modest beginning will enable you to gain your capital and experience at the same time.

Do not force your meals upon any- one. Make none of your patrons feel that it is their duty to buy from you. Let them all understand clearly that they need patronize you only when it serves their own interests to do so.

You need no extra equipment to begin with and no capital. You can start in your own kitchen with the utensils you use for your own meals. We started a kitchen because we wanted it established ourselves, and it is popular because our neighbors' needs coin- cide with ours. We have served twenty two people at a time—no more only because we were not ready to cook for them.

People who are accustomed to maids, but have been unable to find them, people who cannot afford them, people who do not like to have them about, families with invalid mothers, women who earn their own living—all are glad to buy these ready-to-serve meals.

We have started a kitchen in a public school in a neighborhood where the mothers do not know how to feed their families, and they marvel at the results we produce for twenty- five cents. As a matter of fact, when the school girls do the cooking we can furnish a meal for less. They are planning soon to feed one hun- dred from their kitchen.

It means real economy in the purchase of food, not only because we buy in quantities, but because we buy only what is needed to provide well-balanced meals.

It means better-cooked meals. One skilled cook gives her undivided attention to the work, instead of having it done by many bad cooks.

It means a saving of fuel.

And it means a saving of talent. Many a gifted woman has been spoiled to make a poor housekeeper.

The meals served from a community kitchen will not be beyond the average purse. On a cash-and-carry basis you can serve a good dinner for twenty-five cents. You can add a delivery charge of ten cents if your patrons prefer service. School- boys gladly earn the dimes.

THE problem of cook- ing these meals in one place is simple, but there are many pitfalls between the kitchen and the dinner table. You cannot walk the streets with a platter of meat in one hand and a bowl of soup in the other. They would not stay hot if you could.

When we were con- sidering the question of containers we looked about for something easy to handle, easy to obtain, easy to replace. Fruit jars slipped into cases made from cyl- indrical cereal cartons answered the question. A one-and-a-half-pound oatmeal carton can be rolled in newspaper cut to fit and slipped into the larger three pound carton. Asbestos pipe covering may be used for the inner lining, but it costs more.

To serve a family of four, you need three cases, one quart jar, two pint jars, one pint bottle, one baking powder or cocoa tin and per- haps a bowl or a pan for a meat loaf. These containers will easily fit into an ordinary market basket.

To make the cases, use two three-pound oat- meal or coffee cartons, two smaller oatmeal cartons, which will hold quart jars, and two cartons just large enough for pint jars. Have your patrons own their baskets and containers, and tell them that when they want dinners they must bring their baskets beforehand. Nothing spoils a good dinner more quickly than having no containers to serve it in.

TO MAKE your meal satisfactory to your patrons your food combinations must be carefully chosen. To make your venture profit- able to yourself your food costs must be care- fully considered. To be served, the food must fit into your containers.

If you are serving twenty people with dinners at twenty-five cents each you must not spend more than three dollars and fifty cents for food. If you buy it for less your profit will be so much the greater, but the quality of your food must be maintained.

After you have decided upon your menu and considered containers, you must determine the

The Cooked Dinner on the "Cash-and-Carry" Plan

quantities of the various foods you will buy. So there are four stages in your meal plan:
1. Decide upon your menu.
2. Look it over to see whether it will go into the containers.
3. Determine your quantities.
4. Figure up the costs to see if you can afford to serve the meal.

POTATOES can be served escalloped, creamed, au gratin, mashed or baked, or they can go into a stew.

Roasts, fillet of beef, pork tenderloin frenched, meat loaf and stew are easily packed.

Serve the vegetables and salads that are in season in your own locality. In spring and mid- summer vegetable salads are perhaps most ap- petizing, or strawberries and pineapples can be used. In winter, apples, grapefruit, oranges and bananas furnish good foundations. Coleslaw is in season a large part of the year.

For desserts you can use frosted cup cakes or cookies, steamed pudding with sauce, fruit cus- tard and strawberry shortcake.

There is this to remember: The bigger the variety the smaller portions of each item you need serve. You can thus make the whole cost of the meal less by adding inexpensive items like soup or vegetables and serving smaller por- tions of your expensive meats or fruit salads. Your meal will not only be cheaper, but it will be more satisfying. You will please both your

patrons and yourself. While the so-called one- dish meals will do for suppers or lunches, they do not make satisfactory dinners, partly be- cause they do not look like enough when served.

MEATS and potatoes, vegetables, soups, salads and some desserts can be packed in quart and pint jars. Your meats you can slice and slip into a jar on top of potatoes. Fillet of beef, pork tenderloin frenched, even meat loaf, can be served in the same way. Or, if you wish to, you can bake and serve your meat loaf in agate bowls or in small bread tins.

If you don't need them for steamed pudding your meat can be served in your baking-powder tins. Stew can be served in quart jars. Swiss steak can be put into a pint jar with gravy over it. Cakes and cookies can be wrapped in oil paper.

By taking the inner carton out of a large container you can pack baked potatoes, steamed puddings in their baking powder tins and per- haps pint or half pint jars of gravy or dressing together. In summer it would be well to put the cold things in cartons to keep them chilled.

When you have bought your food, the next thing you do is to make sure you have a basket for every family to be served, plainly marked with the name and number of portions desired and the proper number and kinds of containers.

Begin your cooking early. If you do so you will be able to eat your own dinner in peace. Probably the average person can cook a meal for twenty people in four hours. Your cartons

will enable you to pack your food at least an hour ahead of mealtime.

Make your desserts first, unless the meat calls for long-time cooking. When you have put your meat and vegetables on the fire, and your jars for the hot foods are warming in the oven or on the back of the stove, you can pack your salads and desserts. Place salads and cold desserts in the ice box in summer, or outdoors in cold weather, and hot desserts in the oven.

Pack your hot foods, meat, vege- tables, soups, and so forth, and put them into the oven. The funnel you used in your canning will come in handy. When thoroughly heated, slip jars into the cases, stuffing crumpled paper into any crevices which may be left. Put covers tightly on the cartons and place them in the proper baskets. Before you part with your baskets, check them all up carefully to make sure each patron has all the kinds and the proper quantities of food. Your mind will rest much easier if you can say to yourself: "I know I put meat in every basket."

NOW, let us suppose you have received orders for twenty dinners, not families. Try for your menu the following:

Pork Tenderloin With Gravy
Mashed Potatoes
Strawberry Shortcake

Twenty pieces of pork tenderloin frenched will weigh about two pounds and a quarter. One peck of potatoes will be required. The number of carrots will depend entirely upon their size. Four quarts of berries will do, al- though of course "the berrier the better." Double the shortcake receipt which calls for two cupfuls of flour. Now see if you can afford to buy this meal:

2¼ pounds of pork tenderloin, at 45 cents	$1.02
1 Peck of potatoes	.35
Carrots	.20
¼ Pound of butter	.15
1 Quart of milk	.11
Fat for meat and gravy	.06
1 Pound of flour	.07
2 Ounces of lard, at 20 cents a pound	.03
Baking powder and salt	.01
Strawberries, at 15 cents a quart	.60
Sugar, at 10 cents a pound	.10
	$2.73

You see you are well under your three-dollar- and-fifty-cent limit; and if you feel that your patrons will not be sat- isfied with this meal you can increase the quan- tity of meat or add an- other vegetable or a salad.

Now, let us pack up this meal for a family of four. The meat and potatoes will go into the quart jar. A pint jar will do for the carrots, another for the straw- berries, the half-pint bottle for the gravy. The potatoes will go into the quart case; the carrots into the pint case; take the inner carton out of the other large case and put in the bottle of gravy, with the paper- wrapped biscuits on top. The jar of strawberries can be slipped into the extra inner carton.

SUPPOSE you take another menu. Try the following this time:

Asparagus Soup
Meat Loaf With Escalloped Potatoes
Pineapple-and-Strawberry Salad
Chocolate Cup Cakes

This calls for one large bunch of asparagus, five pounds of chopped meat, one loaf of bread and one egg, a little seasoning, three pineapples, one quart of strawberries and three heads of lettuce.

A recipe using a cupful and a half of flour will make the cup cakes, with the addition of one square of chocolate and one cupful of sugar for the frosting.

The soup will take a pint jar, the potatoes a quart jar and the gravy a half-pint bottle; the salad, a pint, and the meat loaf can be put into the baking-powder tin, the chocolate cup cakes wrapped in paper. This meal will cost:

1 Bunch of asparagus	$ .15
2 Quarts of milk	.26
4 Pounds of beef, at 25 cents a pound	1.00
¾ Peck of potatoes, at 35 cents a peck	.24
1 Quart of strawberries	.15
3 Pineapples, at 15 cents each	.45
3 Heads of lettuce	.15
Cup cakes	.23
Bread for the loaf	.08
1 Egg	.04
Seasonings	.05
	$2.80

You will notice that so far these menus do not include bread and butter, coffee, tea or milk, but our patrons have been willing to add these items for themselves.

The Community Kitchen Dinner Served at Home

10.8 Advice on "Starting a Community Kitchen," from the *Ladies' Home Journal*, June 1919

Lowther Peters, an anthropologist, published a report for this group in 1919 stating:

The accelerated absorbtion of women into the war industries merely intensified a condition to which economists and sociologists had been calling attention for half a century, a condition which was already apparent to thinkers at the beginning of the nineteenth century, but whose amelioration was to wait for slower processes of adjustment than those advocated by Fourier and Owen.[35]

Peters had the backing of many noted home economists on her committee, for there was a general belief that the social and technological advances developed during wartime would become the basis of civilian progress in peacetime: "The impression is prevalent that mass feeding of some kind, such as cooperative housekeeping, communal kitchens, or some modified form which will result from experimentation on a large scale, will be retained as a permanent institution after the war."[36] Citing war kitchens in Europe as a precedent, especially the one thousand National Kitchens established in English cities, the traveling kitchens established in trams in Halifax, England, and the mobile kitchens used in devastated areas in France, she argued that conservation of scarce food resources, better nutrition, and economic redistribution could all be aided by permanent government-supported programs for community kitchens. Ellen Richards had made similar arguments in 1890, but without the urgency wartime added.

The *Ladies' Home Journal* was only one of several popular women's magazines to elaborate this theme enthusiastically in 1918 and 1919, with articles about new ways of living involving community kitchens, laundries, and day care centers, as well as kitchenless houses. Zona Gale, a playwright and well-known feminist, produced the most polemical of the pieces in the *Journal*'s series on community kitchens. Gale believed that taking into account the diets of the poor as well as the diets of the rich. "the centralized cooked food supply and distribution must be evolved and made economically available," in order to raise the standard of nourishment in the United States as well as to minimize waste. Citing wartime progress in the food conservation movement, and listing the successes of apartment hotels, cooked food shops, and community kitchens, she concluded: "The private kitchen must go the way of the spinning wheel, of which it is the contemporary."[37]

The logic of Gale's argument had never seemed clearer than during World War I. Yet the problem of cost still remained. If community dining clubs and cooked food services performed work for pay, then cash was redistributed from husbands to wives, or former housewives to former servants. While the private kitchen might be old-fashioned, the new services seemed expensive to husbands who had been paying no wages at all to their wives. Wartime brought inflation, which increased costs. After wartime, women of all classes lost their jobs to returning veterans. Some were

forced to return to domestic service from
factory work. For the first time in half a
century the percentage of women seeking
jobs in domestic service rose. At the same
time inflation caused the costs of cooked
food clubs and services to rise, and some
experiments were discontinued. As Mary
Hinman Abel explained, the nub of the
problem was the economic value of a
housewife's or servant's day: "the value of
the housewife's labor in buying and cooking the food for the family" had to be
rightly estimated.[38] If not, even the neighborhood dining club which saved a
woman's health could be closed because it
"did not pay."

Kitchenless house, 1922

The Feminist flat is revolutionary, strikes at the root of the economic system, may involve vast readjustments of land-tenure, communal building and taxation. But we are not afraid of revolution, for we are the pioneers of a sex-revolution.
— W. L. George, 1913

. . . The home will no longer be a Procrustean bed . . . which each feminine personality must be made to conform to by whatever maiming or fatal, spiritual or intellectual oppression. . . .
— Alice Constance Austin, 1917

Charlotte Perkins Gilman popularized the ideal of efficient, collective kitchens, laundries, and child care centers which removed women's traditional tasks from the private home. The organizers of dining clubs and cooked food delivery services, who attempted to carry these ideas out in practice represent one group of reformers who came under Gilman's broad influence. Architects and urban planners are another.

Like the organizers of dining clubs and cooked food services, the architects and urban planners who became interested in socializing domestic work had to deal with economic, social, and physical reorganization. What economic arrangements were necessary to build housing designed for greater sharing of domestic tasks? Could new household services be provided within a landlord-tenant relationship, on a commercial basis? Or was it necessary for residents to control the ownership of their own housing collectively in order for them to control the reorganization and cost of domestic work? Another set of related questions concerned the design of the housing itself. On what scale should designers attempt to organize housing units for socialized domestic work? A few families? Or a few dozen families? Or a few hundred? Or a few thousand?

The architects and planners who chose to grapple with these issues between 1900 and 1930 were not usually doubtful or cautious by nature. They tended to see themselves as creating, for the first time, truly modern housing, in response to the needs of twentieth century women and their families. But these professionals, who represented the avant-garde in their fields (in social terms if not in aesthetic terms), reached relatively little agreement about what this modern housing should be, in comparison to the designers active between 1870 and 1900 who had almost all agreed that the apartment house or apartment hotel was the building type for household liberation.

Urban and suburban development had contributed to this disarray. Earlier reformers had been able to make bold comparisons between the isolated single-family house in the country or city and the adjacent dwelling units gathered in one large urban apartment house, concluding that the evolution of human habitations was inevitably linked to the apartment house as the larger and more complex building type. By the early decades of the twentieth century, this argument had lost its edge. Apartment houses with extensive collective services were inhabited only by a few affluent families, and the technology of central heating and electric light which had been pioneered in these buildings was more readily available to all types of middle-class homes. Although some reformers, such as Lewis Mumford, maintained in 1914 that "the cooking community will be a product of the city" and argued that "the apartment house stands there, waiting for the metamorphosis," [1] other reformers had turned their attention to suburban areas as the most promising sites for change.

In suburban areas land cost less, and its relative cheapness permitted lower densities than the urban apartment house, with greater privacy. New residential building types were being developed that could accommodate social experiments such as the garden apartment and the bungalow court. They were the creations of designers interested in working at the neighborhood scale and replicating some of the structure of the neighborhood dining clubs. Suburban areas also promised designers the possibility of creating entire new communities of several thousand people. Some of the most imaginative professionals saw the suburban new town as an opportunity to design infrastructure in order to supply collective services to private suburban dwellings on a scale that apartment house designers had never even imagined. Thus they turned the arguments for urban evolution around to favor new towns.

Three geographical centers of excitement about socialized domestic work and new forms of housing developed, where experiments were made which ranged in size from two families to several hundred, and in style from neo-Tudor half-timbering to International Style concrete and glass. In the urban regions around London, England, from about 1898 to 1922; Los Angeles, California, from 1910 to 1922; and New York City, from 1917 to 1930, debates on these issues thrived among designers associated with the Arts and Crafts Movement, the Garden Cities Movement, the trade union cooperative housing movement, and the Regional Planning Association of America. This period of architectural innovation reveals a great proliferation of experimental housing prototypes, some projects demonstrating subtle social planning, and others great technological ingenuity.

London

The leading advocate of cooperative housekeeping in England, Ebenezer Howard, admired American reformers such as Edward Bellamy and Marie Howland.[2] He developed a new building type to support their ideas — garden apartments, with a central dining room and kitchen — and helped to imbue a new generation of American designers with enthusiasm for cooperative housekeeping. A shy, balding man with a bushy mustache and rimless glasses, Howard, a stenographer in London, read Bellamy's *Looking Backward* in 1888 and became infused with messianic energy. In 1889 he helped the British Nationalist Club prepare plans for a utopian experiment in Essex, and his notes for the design of this colony, published in *Nationalization News* in 1893, became, after five years' revision, *Garden Cities of To-Morrow,* a theoretical treatise which made him the most influential English town planner for the next three decades. Howard and his associates Raymond Unwin and Barry Parker developed the Cooperative Quadrangle, where housing and domestic work were shared by cooperating tenants, as the basic residential neighborhood of an ideal Garden City (11.1, 11.2, 11.3). These quadrangles promised to recreate the social and physical coherence of preindustrial villages, so architects sometimes designed them complete with half-timbering and thatched roofs. Financiers who supported Howard, however, wished to begin building a Garden City at Letchworth with fewer cooperative domestic arrangements, so the first few years of construction there were dedicated to conventional dwellings — detached houses, semidetached houses, garden apartments, and row houses with private kitchens.

The novelist, H. G. Wells, taunted Howard until he finally introduced cooperative housekeeping at Letchworth in 1909. Wells complained that it was folly to build conventional houses and ignore the value of cooperative housekeeping, since he argued that "in a few short years all ordinary houses would be out of date and not saleable at any price." [3] Howard told Wells to be patient, since he planned an experiment that would make people "green with envy" rather than "red with laughing" about its success. Howard and Wells belonged to the Fabian intellectual circle in England, in which Gilman had been so well received in 1896 and 1898. In *A Modern Utopia,* Wells had fantasized about kitchenless dwellings in a tone reminiscent of Gilman: "A pleasant boudoir, a private library and study, a private garden plot, are among the commonest of such luxuries. . . . There are sometimes little cooking corners in these flats — as one would call them on earth — but the ordinary Utopian would no more

think of a special private kitchen for his dinners than he would think of a private flour mill or dairy farm." [4]

By 1909 Howard had embarked on the construction of "Homesgarth," thirty-two kitchenless apartments in a Cooperative Quadrangle at Letchworth (11.4, 11.5, 11.6), emphasizing his innovation as a pragmatic response to "the servant question" and "the woman question" when he addressed middle-class clients. In 1913, Howard and his wife moved into Homesgarth, and he congratulated himself on her liberation. He compared himself to James Watt, who had harnessed the power of steam to run an engine, arguing that he, Howard, had managed to "wisely and effectively utilize a little of this vast volume of now wasted woman's ability and woman's energy. . . ." [5] Since Howard's first Cooperative Quadrangle was constructed within a large, successful new town made up of conventional homes, the success of the larger project ensured a world audience for his experimental work. One English critic wrote approvingly of Gilman's theory and Howard's attempt to put it into practice: "The Feminist flat is revolutionary, strikes at the root of the economic system, may involve vast readjustments of land-tenure, communal building and taxation. But we are not afraid of revolution, for we are the pioneers of a sex-revolution." [6]

Eventually, Howard's cooperative housekeeping projects included Homesgarth, Meadow Way Green (11.7) in Letchworth (1915–1924), and Guessens Court (11.8) in

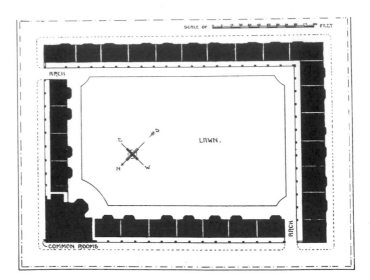

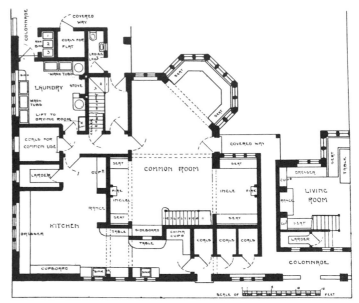

11.1 Raymond Unwin and Barry Parker, site
plan for housing with central kitchen, dining
room, and laundry for Yorkshire workers, from
The Art of Building a Home, 1901

11.2 Unwin and Parker, plan of central kitchen,
dining room, and laundry, Yorkshire workers'
housing.

11.3 Unwin and Parker, plan of five-bedroom
houses.

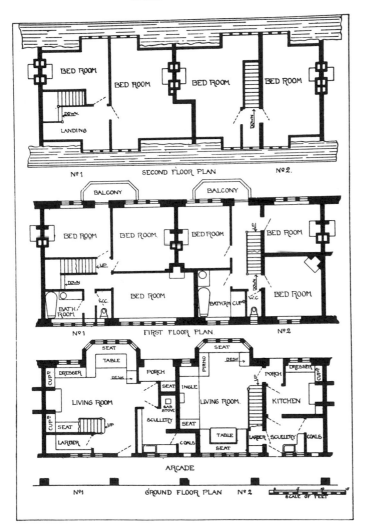

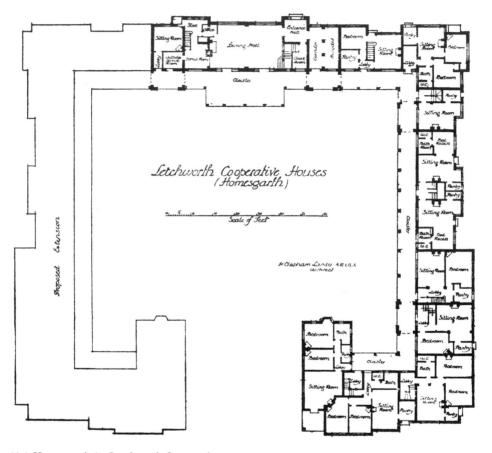

Letchworth Cooperative Houses
(Homesgarth)

Scale of Feet

A Clapham Lander ARIBA
Architect

11.4 Homesgarth (or Letchworth Cooperative
Houses), the first Cooperative Quadrangle, plan
by A. Clapham Lander, 1909–1913, Letchworth
Garden City, England. An arcade connects
kitchenless apartments with the central dining
hall and kitchen.

11.5 Homesgarth (Letchworth Cooperative Houses)

11.6 Tenants' dining room, Homesgarth

11.7 Meadow Way Green, a Cooperative Quadrangle at Letchworth, 1915–1924

11.8 Guessens Court, a Cooperative Quadrangle
at Welwyn Garden City, by A. Clapham Lander, 1922

Welwyn (1922), as well as special projects for single workers and the aged. Howard managed to establish an appropriate scale for community cooking and dining, to arrange sufficient privacy for residents, and to develop adequate financing for housing and services. Homesgarth and Guessens Court stressed kitchenless apartments; Meadow Way Green included a mixture of kitchenless houses and apartments so that families, groups of roommates, and single people could be accommodated. Meals could be taken in the central dining room or in one's private dwelling. In some projects, "lady tenants" were expected to take turns (for two weeks at a time) managing the catering arrangements, helped by a full-time cook and a part-time charwoman; in others all of the service was provided by paid employees.

Various architects undertook these commissions. While Parker and Unwin had influenced Howard in 1900, H. Clapham Lander designed Homesgarth and Guessens Court, one a gabled, eclectic quadrangle with tiled roofs, half-timbering, and arcades; the other a more severe, neoclassical quadrangle. M. H. Baillie Scott built Waterlow Court in the Tudor style in Hampstead Garden Suburb in 1909 (11.9). It offered a common dining room and lovely gardens for the fifty-odd professional women who inhabited its harmonious, cloister-like spaces.

The cooperative housekeeping units in the Garden Cities proved the sensitivity of Howard and the architects who collaborated with him to the housing needs of spe-cial groups including single women, the elderly, widows and widowers, childless couples, and two-worker couples. They recalled the work of Howland, Owen, and Fourier, as well as Oxford and Cambridge residential colleges, but they were very sensible, comfortable, modest places, in contrast to their utopian or institutional prototypes. The quadrangles continue as housing to this day, but they never spurred the mass demand for such facilities which Howard had envisioned.[7] Critics and historians have consistently overlooked them as an integral part of Howard's overall Garden City plans, although this idea influenced many architects throughout the world. Le Corbusier made extensive marginal notes about Cooperative Quadrangles in his copies of Howard's works, and the historian, Robert Fishman, believes that his projects such as the Immeubles Villas in the 1920s and the Unités of the 1950s reflected Howard's ideas as well as the legacy of Fourier.[8] In the United States, architects in Los Angeles and in New York admired Howard's work and attempted to adapt some of his ideas to local housing needs.

Los Angeles

The bungalow court appeared in Los Angeles about 1910 as a new form of low-cost or moderate-cost housing, consisting of a number of small attached houses or separate bungalows grouped around a central garden. Although no one built kitchenless bungalows, the site plan of the bungalow court had much in common with the Cooperative Quadrangles of Letchworth,

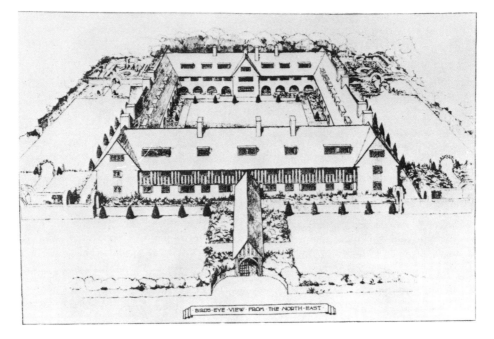

BIRDS·EYE·VIEW·FROM·THE·NORTH·EAST

11.9 M. H. Baillie Scott, Waterlow Court, housing for professional women, Hampstead Garden
Suburb, 1909, view

Welwyn, and Hampstead. Arthur S. Heineman and Alfred Heineman of Pasadena, California, brothers with a successful architectural practice in the town where Gilman had lived in the 1890s, were among the first to promote the bungalow court. Bowen Court (11.10), an early example of their work, was built in 1910.[9] Twenty-two bungalows bordered a curving center garden, with a sewing room and laundry for women tenants, overlooking a play area. The majority of the bungalows included living room, kitchen, and one bedroom (11.11), but a number were double bungalows (11.12), with two units, "planned for two or more persons who may wish to live under the same roof, but desire separate establishments." [10] A heavy sliding door allowed residents to join these twin units, or not, as desired.

The advantages of husband and wife enjoying "separate establishments" with connecting doors had been discussed by Gilman, as well as proposed by the utopian novelist Bradford Peck (7.3).[11] The Heinemans were the first to build such units. In the organization of domestic work at Bowen Court they did not go as far as Ebenezer Howard, because every unit included a private kitchen, but they hoped to encourage collective sewing and laundry by the facility they offered, as well as making child care simpler. The designers assumed that the women of Bowen Court would be doing their own laundry, sewing, and child tending, rather than handing this work over to paid professionals, so this was a very tentative gesture in the direction of socializing domestic work. Around 1913 Alfred S. Heineman also designed an apartment hotel for the affluent, left-wing activists of Pasadena, with the modest name "Parnassus," where he provided for a full paid staff, so the arrangements at Bowen Court were geared to tenants' income rather than the designer's philosophy.[12] In much the same way, Howard had provided paid staff in two of his projects, but left the "lady tenants" to cope in a third one.

The closely placed units of the bungalow court invited tenants' cooperation — as the Heinemans understood and as Charles Alma Byers pointed out in Gustav Stickley's influential journal, The Craftsman, in 1914.[13] However, the pattern of ownership of bungalow courts discouraged residents from organizing collective kitchens, laundries, and child care facilities. These courts were usually rental housing, rather than cooperatively owned housing, so tenants had no security of occupancy. Landlords preferred to keep most bungalow courts without collective facilities and to maximize privacy, just as the developers of apartment houses in the 1870s had been wary of social innovation that would make it difficult to rent their units or manage their properties. Howard had conquered these difficulties in England by organizing residents' groups to own and run the Cooperative Quadrangles, but no California architect was prepared to undertake the organization of tenants on a similar scale. The one California designer who was able to go beyond Howard's provisions for collective domestic work, Alice Constance

11.10 Arthur S. Heineman and Alfred Heineman, Bowen Court, Pasadena, California, 1910,
view showing two-story building with sewing
room above children's play area, from the *Ladies'
Home Journal,* April 1913

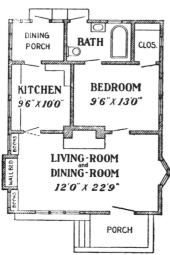

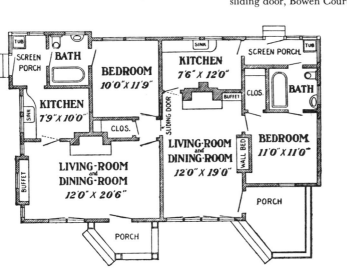

11.11 Plan, single bungalow, Bowen Court

11.12 Plan, double bungalow with connecting sliding door, Bowen Court

Austin, worked for a group committed to residents' cooperative ownership of an entire socialist city.

Llano del Rio

On the first of May 1916, hundreds of men, women, and children marched in a May Day parade at Llano del Rio, California, young girls in white dresses, boys in white shirts and dark knickers, men in their best dark suits and ties, women wearing ribbons and badges across their light summer dresses. Residents of an experimental cooperative colony, they were farmers and urban workers who planned to build a socialist city as an alternative to the capitalist city of Los Angeles. As they marched on May Day they sang familiar socialist songs, but their final destination was a half-finished frame building, where they examined architectural models of the unconventional community they hoped to create, a garden city of kitchenless houses, designed by Alice Constance Austin (11.13). Austin's design for Llano del Rio, California, joined feminist and socialist concerns in a project that developed the urban infrastructure necessary for cooked food delivery and laundry service and carried Howard's proposals for cooperative housekeeping to their ultimate conclusion in terms of urban design.

In her plans for the cooperative colony at Llano, and in her book, *The Next Step,* Austin, a self-educated architect from Santa Barbara, articulated an imaginative vision of life in a feminist, socialist city.[14] She maintained that the traditional home functioned as a Procrustean bed which "each feminine personality must be made to conform to by whatever maiming or fatal, spiritual or intellectual oppression." In her ideal city, labor-saving devices in the home and a central laundry and kitchens would relieve woman "of the thankless and unending drudgery of an inconceivably stupid and inefficient system, by which her labors are confiscated. . . ." [15] The substantial economies achieved in residential construction without kitchens, she believed, would permit the construction of the centralized facilities and the infrastructure to connect them with the housing.

Austin first developed a kitchenless house (11.14), with living room, patio, two bedrooms, and bath on the first floor and sleeping porches above, about 1916. Her client, Job Harriman, the organizer of Llano del Rio, a lawyer and a leader in the Socialist Party in Los Angeles, had called upon his supporters in 1914 to build a cooperative colony in the Antelope Valley after his defeat in the mayoral election of 1911. He presented Austin, as the community's architect, with nine hundred people who wanted a plan for something better than the subdivisions that land speculators were creating in Los Angeles. Criticizing the "suburban residence street where a Moorish palace elbows a pseudo French castle, which frowns upon a Swiss chalet," Austin proposed a city composed of courtyard houses of concrete construction.[16] Built in rows, they would express "the solidarity of the community" and emphasize the equal access to housing supported by the socialist municipal government. Austin allowed for personal preferences in the decoration of her houses by providing renderings of alternative facades. (She thoughtfully set aside some land in her city for future architects' experiments as well as for a few conventional single-family dwellings, which she thought some conservative residents might insist upon having.)

Austin's housing designs emphasized economy of labor, materials, and space. She criticized the waste of time, strength, and money which traditional houses with kitchens required and the "hatefully monotonous" drudgery of preparing 1,095 meals in the year and cleaning up after each one.[17] In her plans, hot meals in special containers would arrive from the central kitchens to be eaten in the dining patio; dirty dishes were then to be returned to the central kitchen for washing by machine. She provided built-in furniture and roll-away beds to eliminate dusting and sweeping in difficult spots, heated tile floors to replace dusty carpets, and windows with decorated frames to do away with what she called that "household scourge," the curtain. Her affinity with the Arts and Crafts movement is apparent in her hope that the production of these window frames would become the basis of a craft industry at Llano, along with simple, locally made furniture.[18]

Each kitchenless house was to be connected to the central kitchen through a complex underground network of tunnels (11.15). Railway cars from the center of the city would bring cooked food, laundry, and other deliveries to connection points, or "hubs," from which small electric cars could be dispatched to the basement of each house. Although this system was obviously going to be expensive, Austin argued the economic and aesthetic advantages to a socialist municipal government of placing all gas, water, electric, and telephone lines underground in the same tunnels as the residential delivery system. Eliminating all business traffic at the center would produce a more restful city — residents had access to the center on foot, public delivery systems handled all their shopping, and goods coming to the city could arrive at a centrally located airfreight landing pad. Private automobiles would be used chiefly for trips outside this city of ten thousand people, perhaps to neighboring towns built on the same plan.

By relying on underground delivery systems for food and laundry, Austin placed herself in a technological tradition which had begun with Henry Hudson Holly and the "steam-tight cars" of his Family Hotel project for Hartford in 1874 (4.7, 4.8). Mary Coleman Stuckert had introduced underground trams in her project for Denver row houses in 1893 (9.2), and John Ablett had proposed a similar food delivery system in 1900 for Chicago.[19] The visionary architect Charles Lamb, produced renderings of such a scheme for New York City apartments in 1908.[20] Most spectacular of all was the work of the inventor Edgar Chambless, of Los Angeles, published in 1910. He included three levels of underground trams below the kitchenless

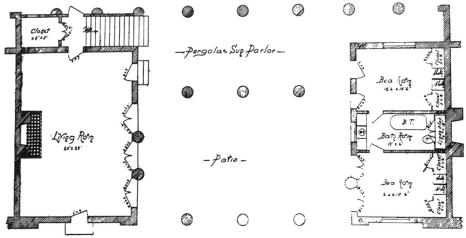

11.13 Alice Constance Austin showing her kitchenless house to clients, 1916

11.14 Austin, first floor plan for a kitchenless
house at Llano del Rio, California, 1916

11.15 Austin, site plan for a sector of Llano, 1916

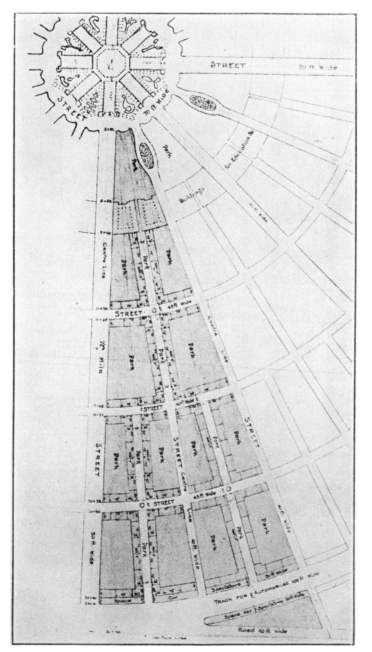

row houses of his endless Roadtown, offering mass transit, private houses, and cooperative housekeeping in a single structure (11.16). Chambless, like Ebenezer Howard, believed that he had solved the servant problem and improved upon the apartment hotel. He saw himself taking "the apartment house and all its conveniences and comforts out among the farms by the aid of wires, pipes, and of rapid and noiseless transportation," thus creating a linear settlement linking city and countryside.[21] Both Charlotte Perkins Gilman's *The Forerunner* and the *Ladies' Home Journal* praised the Roadtown; Austin seems to have known it as well, although her unique contribution transcended the technological inventiveness of such designers as Stuckert and Chambless.[22] While Austin shared Chambless's interest in delivery services, she was committed to the broader social goals of the Arts and Crafts Movement and the community planning idea developed in the Garden Cities movement. Thus she enhanced the mechanical schemes of the many inventors who focused on transportation, by giving equal attention to planning community facilities, designing low-cost workers' housing with handcrafted details, and developing careful landscaping.

A comparison of Ebenezer Howard's diagrammatic plan for a garden city with Austin's diagram for Llano del Rio shows his undeniable influence on her basic layout. In *Garden Cities of To-Morrow* Howard had outlined the economic and social structure of a town of thirty thousand inhabitants housed on a site of one thousand acres surrounded by a "Green Belt" of allotment gardens and farms. His civic buildings were set in parkland, ringed by a "Crystal Palace," which served as a pedestrian shopping arcade and winter garden. A radial street system culminated in a ring railway line. Austin accommodated ten thousand people on six hundred and forty acres, surrounded by a greenbelt of unspecified size. Her civic center recalls Howard's Crystal Palace, with eight "rectangular halls, like factories, with sides almost wholly of glass," leading to a glass-domed assembly hall.[23] The major difference is that while Howard's kitchenless dwellings were built as small enclaves within larger Garden Cities of conventional homes, Austin added infrastructure to make a clear statement about the possible form of a town without private housework.

In retrospect, one can see three stages of the development of this argument about city form. In 1885, Howland, Deery, and Owen had scattered several types of kitchenless dwellings on a plan for a cooperative city without any serious discussion of their relationships. In 1898, Howard had declared that one type of housing, the Cooperative Quadrangle, should become the basis of a cooperative new town, and by 1913, he'd shown exactly how to make such housing work. By 1916, Austin had shown how to provide services for kitchenless dwellings on an urban scale. For the first time, housing for a cooperative city was conceived as something more than the sum of various separate residential complexes.

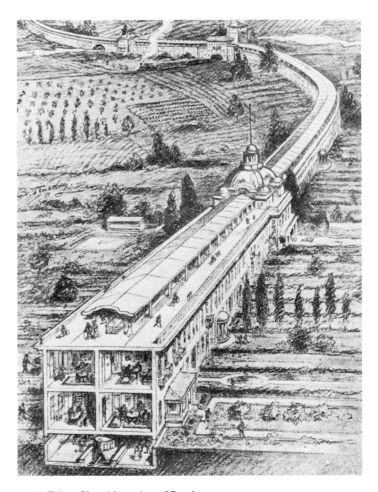

11.16 Edgar Chambless, view of Roadtown, 1910. He called for a soundless monorail below and an open promenade above two levels of dwellings with cooperative housekeeping centers located at intervals. From the *Ladies' Home Journal,* February 1919.

Between 1834, when Caroline Howard Gilman had proposed "grand cooking establishments" run by municipalities, and 1916, when Austin designed her socialist city, no American designer had explored both cooked food service and municipal delivery systems simultaneously. Ellen Richards and Mary Hinman Abel had established public kitchens, without linking them to housing. Anna Bowman Dodd had imagined fictional "culinary conduits" without describing them in any detail. Bertha Grimes, Samuel Street, and others had delivered cooked food without paying any attention to housing or urban infrastructure. Austin's work made an imaginative synthesis of all these possibilities. Although Austin's plans were within the technological limits of the time, the idealistic farmers and workers at Llano lacked the capital to construct her ideal city. She continued to try to interest builders in her ideas. Throughout the 1920s and the 1930s, she was unable to do so. The next experiment in designing for cooperative housekeeping in Los Angeles took place on a much smaller scale.

A Cooperative Dwelling

Six years after Austin displayed her plans for kitchenless houses at Llano, the architect Rudolph Schindler built a "cooperative dwelling" in Hollywood for himself, his wife, Pauline Gibling (a former Hull-House resident), and their friends, Clyde and Marion D. Chase (11.17, 11.18). Schindler, an immigrant from Vienna to Los Angeles, was beginning to establish himself as an important practitioner in the International Style, a figure to be reckoned with in the evolution of modern architecture. In 1922, with his wife and friends, he hoped to establish a prototypical dwelling for modern adult life, which offered several individual workspaces, two shared sleeping spaces for couples, and a shared domestic workplace.

Schindler expounded his ideas in a way which echoed Charlotte Perkins Gilman's interests in evolutionary theory. He claimed that "our house will lose its front-and-back-door aspect. It will cease being a group of dens, some larger ones for social effect, and a few smaller ones (bedrooms) in which to herd the family." [24] He defined the cooperative dwelling: each person would have a private studio space in which to "gain a background for his life." [25] Two outdoor patios were substituted for conventional living rooms. One kitchen was shared by both families, so that, according to Schindler's biographer David Gebhard, the wives would take turns to cook so that the household tasks would not become repetitious for either."

Although the house is considered one of Schindler's finest buildings, and Gebhard has called it "a radical rethinking of the whole man-made environment," the placement of the shared kitchen gives one pause.[26] The women's private studios adjoined the kitchen and connected it with the entrance halls, so that the only indoor circulation through the building was through the women's "private" studio spaces. The house thus incorporates two

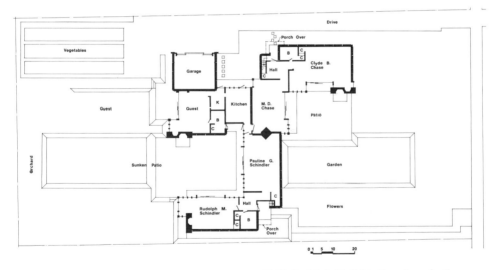

11.17 Rudolph M. Schindler, view of a "cooperative dwelling" for four to six adults (two couples and one or two guests), Kings Road, Hollywood, 1922. This was Schindler's own house.

11.18 Plan of Schindler's "cooperative dwelling"

major inconsistencies in its organization, one physical and one social. On the level of physical design, no major circulation path to a shared facility should ever pass through any space described as a private. This was an error in terms of Schindler's stated program. On the level of social design, no dwelling for "cooperating" adults should distinguish between living spaces for men and living spaces for women. Although the women seem to have agreed to do the domestic work, their private living spaces should have been unaffected by this sexual division of labor.

If Schindler escaped the cave-man "front-and-back-door" domesticity he ridiculed so heavily, he still failed to understand all the problems of domestic cooperation in practice. But for the first time, an architect committed to modern forms had taken hold of the ideal of cooperative housekeeping, and, however awkward the cooperative arrangements were in practice, they were expressed in glass, wood, and concrete, using Schindler's "Slatbuilt" system, without recourse to the eclecticism of Arts and Crafts architects such as Heineman or Austin or the predictable Garden City Tudor. Free of decorative half-timbering, unencumbered by heavy mantles, leaded windows, and inglenooks, Schindler's house was an important aesthetic statement, as well as a social statement.

New York
New York followed Los Angeles as the center of both intellectual and political fer-

ment about new housing during the late teens. In 1919, Charles Harris Whitaker, a New Yorker and editor of the *Journal of the American Institute of Architects,* argued that "architects must restudy the house itself as an industrial establishment, where every unnecessary step and all useless labor are to be eliminated. . . . Freeing men and women for social contact is vitally more important than cloistering them in a home." Whitaker then enumerated the advantages of central heating, cooking, laundry, and kitchen for a group of houses, asking a rhetorical question in conclusion: "Shall we dare to predict, then, that the ideal house of the future will be kitchenless . . . ?" [27]

Under the leadership of Whitaker, the *Journal of the American Institute of Architects* cosponsored a competition with the *Ladies' Home Journal* in 1919, seeking a prototypical solution for post–World War I housing. Two prizes were awarded, both to schemes with provisions for some socialized domestic work: one a zany inventor's fantasy (11.19), the other a stiff, axial Beaux-Arts scheme (11.20). Yet the designers shared a common hope for cooperative housekeeping facilities. One winner, Milo Hastings, stated, "The community kitchen, which has made great strides during the war, requires only a more efficient system of house-delivery to make it a permanent service in the industrial community," since he expected that more and more women would choose to work outside the home. [28] His scheme, which resembled Austin's earlier plans, provided trams to deliver cooked food to every back door. The other winner, Robert A. Pope, noted, "Without the opportunity for association and cooperation, man becomes morbid, melancholy, hateful." As a designer he had a solution, a neighborhood of duplex houses centered on a group of community buildings, to house "the nursery, the kindergarten, and the primary schools . . . with provision for experiment in community laundry, sewing-room, kitchen, and dining-room, also for reading room, small library, and evening school." He believed that these buildings might "develop the nucleus which will make democracy a real and living thing" and hoped that his housing scheme might "repair many of the blind cruelties of an uncontrolled industrial order." [29]

In the postwar years, Whitaker became an influential member of the Regional Planning Association of America and worked with Henry Wright, Clarence Stein, Lewis Mumford, Edith Elmer Wood, and Catharine Bauer among the many reformers in that group. In 1914 Mumford, at the precocious age of nineteen, had written the very first article of his long and distinguished career, boosting cooperative cooking; Wood, one of the judges in the 1919 competition, was to join with Ethel Puffer Howes in 1926 at the Institute for the Coordination of Women's Interests. The RPAA included the most brilliant planners of the period, concerned with creating good housing for wage workers and conserving land for recreation. Wood and Bauer lobbied for federal and state financing for low-cost housing; Wright and

Stein attempted to build model projects derived from the Garden Cities and adapted to an American landscape modified by the automobile.

At Sunnyside, Long Island, and Radburn, New Jersey, Wright and Stein went beyond Ebenezer Howard in finding ways to separate housing and pedestrian spaces from automobile circulation and to insert children's play areas into their site plans.[30] In a later project at Baldwin Hills, in Los Angeles, they created small "tot-lots" for every few dwellings and planned several large day care centers. Yet they had moved quite far from Howard's Cooperative Quadrangles and Whitaker's call for experiment with kitchenless houses. They recognized the implications of child care for site planning more fully than any other American architects before them, but they were less interested in mothers than in their children. Providing for cooked food did not interest them at all, although Edith Elmer Wood and Ethel Puffer Howes saw Sunnyside and Radburn as excellent projects for the further development of community services to aid employed women.

Workers' Cooperative Housing Associations

Workers' cooperative housing groups were also concerned about the special facilities required by families with children; often they cared more about the needs of employed women than the architects of the RPAA. During the late teens, several New York trade union groups were gathering

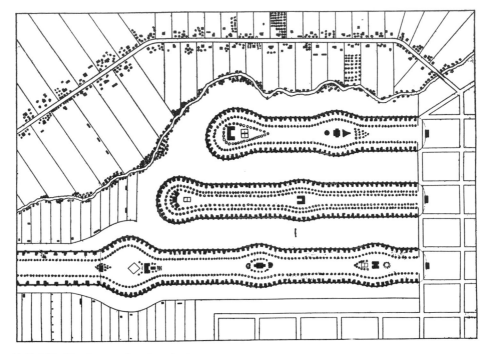

11.19 Milo Hastings, project for suburban
houses linked by an electric tram delivering
goods, one of two first prize winners, competition for post–World War I housing, sponsored
by the *Journal of the American Institute of Architects*
and the *Ladies' Home Journal,* 1919

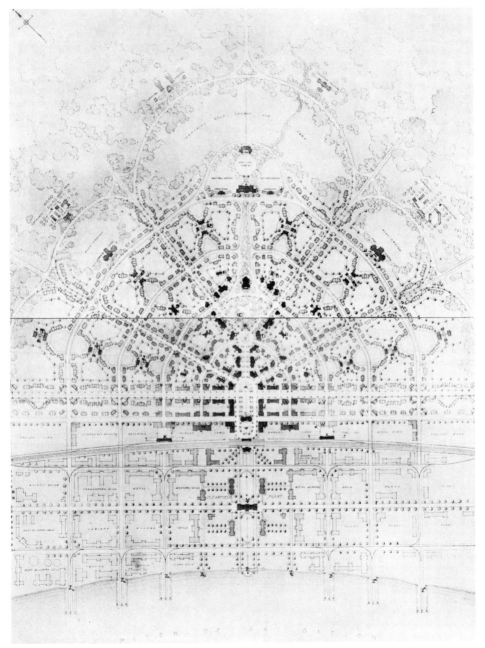

11.20 Robert Anderson Pope, project for a city with suburban duplex residences served by community centers, one of two first prize winners, competition for post–World War I housing.

the funds and resources to build cooperative housing projects. Often they began by organizing boarding clubs, cooperative restaurants, or cooperative ownership of existing apartment houses, developing residents' organizations before they began to build. Workers' desire to control their own housing, demonstrated in the Jane Club and other workers' cooperative boarding clubs of the 1890s, had grown stronger by the teens. Groups were venturing beyond single-sex boarding clubs and were planning for married and single workers of both sexes and their dependents, because families needed housing which they could occupy on a permanent basis.

In New York, Chicago, and other major cities, slums were miserable and unsanitary; neither federal nor state governments offered subsidies for low-cost housing before 1926. Workers with families who did not get a place in one of the very few philanthropic housing developments were at the mercy of rent-gouging slumlords. Any trade union that could help its members defend themselves in the housing market offered powerful assistance to their self-respect.

For many different groups, the ideal became a cooperative apartment house with a nursery and dining room, just what Rodman's Feminist Alliance wanted in 1915. By emphasizing worker's solidarity, rather than feminism and "professional" service, many trade union groups did build such housing in New York City after 1917. Trade unions had the administrative and financial resources the feminist movement

did not, and by directing such resources to housing the unions demonstrated their ability to meet their members' needs in an area where employers, speculators, and municipalities had failed. The best of the trade union projects created not only housing but also lively centers of political culture for their residents. In terms of social programming they were excellent prototypes for workers' housing despite very tight budgets, and the services they offered exceeded many projects built in the 1960s by trade unions with far greater resources.

In the actual construction of cooperative housing projects, Finnish workers' groups were often the leaders, along with Jewish workers' groups. In 1919, James Warbasse visited the first of sixteen cooperative apartment houses the Finnish Homebuilding Association established in New York before 1924. Since these groups also built cooperative restaurants and clubhouses their social facilities were extensive.[31]

While the Finnish workers in Brooklyn were called "free lovers," "unpatriotic," and un-American for their efforts,[32] they set a pace in building cooperative housing and restaurants that many other workers tried to match. Groups of Jewish workers, especially those in the needle trades, were very active in organizing housing cooperatives in the same period. Around 1918 the United Workers Cooperative Association took over an old apartment house on Madison Avenue for its members and established for them a restaurant, library, and music room.[33] By 1923 they had es-

tablished a successful summer camp for
members at Beacon, New York, and by
1925, they broke ground on a large project,
ultimately seven hundred and fifty units,
located near Bronx Park. Known as the
Coops, it included an auditorium, a secular
Jewish school, a library with ten thousand
books, and a combined kindergarten and
nursery, open from 7:00 a.m. to 7:00 p.m.,
for the children of residents. Nearby they
established other cooperatives: a laundry,
butcher shop, tailor shop, produce store,
grocery, newsstand, and cafeteria.

The Workers' Cooperative Colony, or
Coops, were designed by Herman Jessor,
then a young architectural draftsman in
the firm of Springsteen and Goldhammer,
for a fee of $100. They cannot be consid-
ered forward-looking in terms of style
(11.21, 11.22). The collective facilities were
all located in the basement, so there was
no outward expression of their importance
in the massing of the building. The landscaped courtyards, with flowers, trees, and
goldfish ponds, created effective social
space often used for demonstrations and
rallies, but were extremely conventional in
form. Jessor's attempt to duplicate the suburban Tudor facades popularized in the
Garden Cities a decade earlier was bal-
anced by a touch of socialist realism in the
lintels of the stair entrances, where low re-
liefs of factories with smokestacks and of a
hammer and sickle suggested the radical
orientation of the residents, all of whom
were wage workers and many of whom
were Communists.

One innovation in programming did
make it possible for extended families to
live in the complex without sharing an
apartment. Groups of twelve bed-sitting
rooms, with one kitchen shared by twelve
residents, provided economical private
dwelling space in the Coops for single people and the elderly, some of whom had relatives nearby. The arrangements of a cooperative boarding house or a worker's home
were thus united to the family apartments,
many of which were built with kitchenettes
rather than with kitchens, for economy.
While most families dined at home, they
did develop a cooperative restaurant
nearby in 1927, and in 1937 the building
contained a cooperative dining club.

The Coops were a hive of political activity. A resident recalls that May Day parades were special: "There was nothing
that could equal May Day, nothing at all
in my memory as a kid. We had May Days
before we came to the Coops, but the
group feeling wasn't there. Here, *everybody*
was participating, everybody came out,
everybody was dressed up, wearing the red
bandannas and the little overseas caps if
they were in the Young Pioneers. You got
new clothes for May Day, just like you
used to get them in the old country for
Passover, I suppose." [34] Children learned
about political militance early. Three
eleven-year-old residents, taken on a school
trip to Yankee Stadium, refused to go into
the baseball game, because the stadium's
ushers were on strike, and the boys had
been brought up never to cross a picket
line.[35] This political culture led to reason-

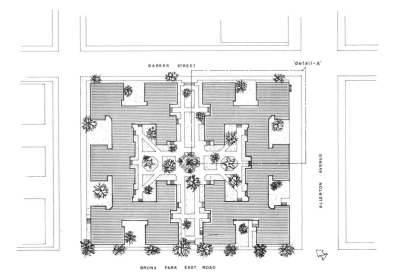

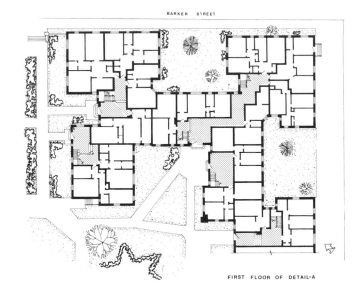

11.21 Herman Jessor, Workers' Cooperative
Colony, 750 units of housing with collective
services, organized by the United Workers Cooperative Association, the Bronx, New York, 1926,
partial site plan showing first part of project.

11.22 Partial floor plan, Workers' Cooperative
Colony, detail *A* of 11.21

able arrangements for the Coops' own
employees.

The maintenance staff in the Coops included porters, plumbers, electricians,
handymen, a gardener, and other workers.
They created a union, one of the first
unions of residential building service workers in the United States. Here Charlotte
Perkins Gilman's and Henrietta Rodman's
hopes for unionized service workers earning
good wages were fulfilled for the first time
since the development of the apartment
hotel in the 1870s, but the workers were
mainly male. In the cooperative shops,
where similar policies prevailed, these arrangements caused financial difficulties.
The neighborhood cooperative stores and
services did not survive because "high overhead expenses made them uncompetitive
with local retail stores and one by one they
were forced out of business." [36] The high
overhead came from paying workers union
wages for an eight-hour day.

The Coops still exist, and some descen-
dants of the founders live there, although
they never solved all their financial
problems. In the Depression, the Coops'
directors refused to evict anyone for non-
payment of rent; instead, they took in
neighbors evicted by Bronx landlords. By
1931 their financial situation was poor, but
a ten-year moratorium on their mortgage
was negotiated. In 1943, a private landlord
took over, after prolonged discussion of
whether or not the members would agree
to a rent increase in order to retain control.
They voted against an increase because of
possible effects on their neighbors. Al-

though they no longer owned their own
buildings, the community retained much
of its social and political cohesion. As the
members got older, they led in the development of services for the elderly in the
Bronx.

Other Workers' Groups
The clothing workers who created the
Amalgamated Houses benefited from the
Coops' experience and from state loans
available to nonprofit groups building
housing after 1926, so that they were able
to build a project almost as large as the
Coops and remain financially independent. [37] Purchasing thirteen acres of land in
the Bronx, southeast of Van Cortlandt
Park, the Amalgamated Clothing Workers
built over five hundred units of cooperative
housing between 1927 and 1929, organized
in five-story walk-ups, for union members
and other workers who could afford a
down payment of $500 per room. Herman
Jessor produced another Tudor-style
project for this group, again placing the
collective facilities in the basement. The
cooperative services at the Amalgamated
included a supervised playground, a cooperative commissary, a kindergarten, tea
room, library, and auditorium. (A second
apartment project on Grand Street included a novelty — a baby carriage garage
for three hundred carriages.) The tenant
owners bought electricity, milk, and ice
wholesale and distributed it themselves;
when Consolidated Edison threatened to
raise their electric rates they switched to
diesel power and cut their costs further.

Opening just at the outset of the Depression, the Amalgamated soon had a high percentage of unemployed (60 to 70 percent) among its residents, but because of union financing and low-interest state loans, the cooperative was able to help its members by offering some rent rebates, while managing to meet its mortgage obligations.[38]

The United Workers and the Amalgamated were the two largest workers' housing cooperatives of the twenties, but many other groups emulated their example. In 1927 the Unity Cooperative Housing Association of young women workers and the Workers' Mutual Aim Association of single men and childless couples joined to develop a cooperative, furnished apartment house for three hundred wage workers. They renovated an existing building on 110th Street overlooking Central Park which opened in 1928. For $125 down and $20 monthly, workers received small apartments with access to the restaurant, library, reception room, and gymnasium.[39] For a slightly more affluent group, Mary E. Arnold, the dynamic entrepreneur of Consumers' Cooperative Services, built sixty-six units in 1930 at 433 West Twenty-first Street, with a dining room on the first floor. The group had begun with a chain called "Our Cooperative Cafeterias" and cooked food shops in 1919, then expanded with a bakery, a laundry, and circulating libraries. Their apartments rented for $25 to $35 per room per month.[40]

Just how much housing policy in the Soviet Union influenced any of these workers'

groups in New York is unclear. In the U.S.S.R. architects such as Moses Ginzburg and the Vesnin brothers were at work on projects for kitchenless apartments with collective kitchens and day care facilities, called "communal" houses, throughout the twenties; architectural competitions for housing projects were held; N. A. Miliutin planned Sotsgorod as a city of communal houses.[41] While some of the trade unionists certainly knew of these developments in housing policy in the Soviet Union, it is not likely they were following Soviet architectural debates closely. The Soviet architects (11.23) experimented with concrete and glass and often favored the two-story apartment layouts developed by Le Corbusier. Nothing could have been more removed, aesthetically, from the mock Tudor style of the Coops and the Amalgamated, inherited from Howard's Garden Cities. In the English and American tradition, attempts to reorganize the social program for housing tended to be wrapped in utterly conventional facades; in Europe and the Soviet Union, architects were determined to break with tradition in terms of form and content simultaneously, often producing far less liveable results, as exemplified by the gray and cold ambiance of Ginzburg's Domnarkomfin housing in Moscow.

Speculators' "Cooperatives"
In addition to the idealistic workers' housing projects promoted by Whitaker and other RPAA members in New York and the numerous apartment blocks created by

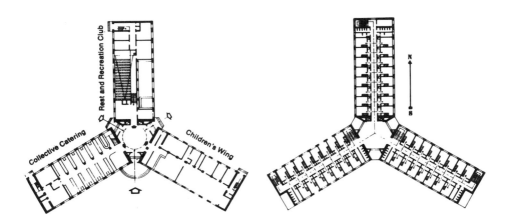

GROUND FLOOR
Collective Facilities

ACCESS FLOOR

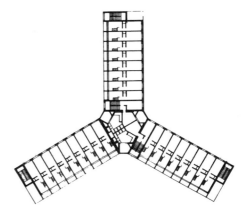

LIVING UNITS
Upper and Lower Levels

11.23 K. Ivanov, F. Terekhin, and P. Smolin,
plan for a communal house with collective catering and day care, U.S.S.R., 1920s. Apartments are two stories and are reached by corridors on every third floor.

trade union groups there in the 1920s, a few projects in that city continued the tradition of apartment hotels or apartment houses with extensive collective services. If residents were permitted to own their units (an arrangement first introduced by Philip G. Hubert in the 1880s), such buildings might be called "cooperative" apartment houses, but these were distinguished from the unions' limited equity cooperatives in that buyers were permitted to speculate by owning more than one unit, subletting units freely, and selling them at market value.[42]

Some of the speculative "cooperative" projects had extensive community facilities, advertised with a rhetoric of "community," such as Dr. Charles V. Paterno's Hudson View Gardens, built in 1924. An extremely successful developer, Paterno had for many years built New York City apartment houses for renters. He lived in a large mock-Tudor castle on the edge of the Hudson River at Washington Heights, and next to his home he erected Hudson View Gardens, a Tudor development of three hundred and fifty-four three- to six-room units, designed by George H. Pelham. Its amenities included central heating and hot water, central refrigeration, a restaurant, a staff of maids available on an hourly basis, a commissary where groceries could be purchased, a Community Steam Laundry, a supervised playground, a "scientifically equipped" nursery with a trained nurse in charge, a beauty shop, barbershop, post office, central telephone service, central radio reception, and private police service.

Any tenant buying an apartment from Paterno owned a share of all of the community services.

While Hudson View Gardens had great potential appeal for professional women who might have liked to see their children cared for and their dinners served for them, Paterno and Pelham disavowed feminist intentions. Use of the restaurant was recommended on an occasional rather than regular basis in the advertising brochure: "Though housekeeping is easy at Hudson View Gardens, there are times when everyone prefers to dine out." The nursery was promoted in similar terms: "Probably every mother has occasionally wished that she could dispose of her children while she went to a party or a matinee or simply collected her own scattered thoughts. . . . The mother who lives at Hudson View Gardens can have a short vacation whenever she wants one. . . . "[43] A section entitled "Perfect Kitchen Equipment" described the labor-saving devices installed within each private kitchen: a hand-operated dishwasher; a patented folding clothes dryer; a central refrigeration compartment with brine-filled pipes; a built-in ironing board; and an incinerator for garbage. With these devices, Paterno believed that middle-class women would find that housework could be "interesting and pleasant."[44] Nevertheless a determined career woman with children who might scorn "scattered thoughts" and have doubts about "interesting" housework could, if her income were high enough, find the essential services here that would enable her

family to manage. Hudson View Gardens
was a respectable apartment community, a
far cry from the apartment hotels which
had seemed so wicked and dangerous
twenty years earlier. It offered both privacy
and community, for a price. Indeed, Paterno offered what Gilman had suggested,
what Henrietta Rodman had been ridiculed as an unnatural mother for demanding ten year earlier, private homes with
professional services of every kind near at
hand. But these services were not intended
to support women's desires to undertake
paid employment. Nor were they presented
as women's right. Paterno saw them only
as a privilege for those whose husbands
could pay.

Summer Cooperative Housekeeping
Indeed, affluent New Yorkers could also
move into kitchenless houses and enjoy
complete environments designed for cooperative housekeeping, in a few summer
communities such as Yelping Hill, built in
West Cornwall, Connecticut, in 1922. In
an article written in 1907, Charlotte
Perkins Gilman had predicted that possibilities for organizing collective domestic
work could be realized in summer resorts
and summer schools, as well as in urban
apartment hotels, perhaps thinking of the
New Jersey community nicknamed "Acadia," referred to in the *Woman's Journal* in
the 1880s, or Candace Wheeler's community at Onteora in the Catskills, built in
the 1890s.[45] The idea of a summer colony
without kitchens caught the imagination of
Henry Seidel Canby, editor of the *Saturday*

Review in New York, Henry Noble
McCracken, president of Vassar College,
their spouses, and their friends. They purchased property in West Cornwall, Connecticut, and began construction of
Yelping Hill, a cooperatively owned community of kitchenless houses with a community living room, child care program,
and dining room. The colony was in operation every summer until World War II.
The group still exists.

The designer and one of the leading
members of the community was Ruth
Maxon Adams. Born in Beloit, Wisconsin,
in 1883, she had studied at Vassar College
and the New York School of Applied Design for Women and then started her own
interior design firm in New York in 1915.[46]
Adams remodeled an old barn (11.24) to
serve as community center, guest quarters,
kitchen, and dining room. She built seven
kitchenless houses for the member families
on the wooded slopes and meadows of the
Connecticut hills. All were elegantly detailed. Her own house (11.25) is perhaps
her best building, a romantic Tudor cottage dramatically sited on the edge of a
cliff. On the first floor, an enclosed porch,
bedroom, and sitting room look over a
lovely valley. The second floor, entered
through a gabled door reached by a picturesque stair, included a sleeping porch and
her design studio. The entire community,
with its eclectic, charming buildings, sensi-
tive landscaping, domestic cooperation,
and literary high-mindedness, would have
cheered Ralph Waldo Emerson, William
Morris, or Charles Ashbee.

11.24 Ruth Adams, barn remodeled to serve as
social center, community kitchen, and dining
room, Yelping Hill, Cornwall, Connecticut, 1922

11.25 Ruth Adams, elevation of one of several
kitchenless houses, Yelping Hill, 1922

Even the college students who came to earn their board by a bit of domestic work must have taken pleasure in a season in this summer utopia, but Yelping Hill did not represent a full commitment to a feminist life style. It operated, for twenty years, in much the same way as the cooperative dining clubs discussed in the previous chapter, but on a grander scale, with seven employees (manager, cook, chambermaid, three waitresses, and gardener, some of them part-time). The cost of service and meals was very high: $10.25 per person per week in 1923,[47] or more than the cost of housing an entire family for the same time in some of the workers' cooperatives.

The summer colony of kitchenless houses at Yelping Hill remained, like the Hudson View Gardens, too expensive for most Americans. Predictably enough, even the Yelping Hill members were not immune from the accusations of free love which bedeviled many who would reorganize their housing. Ruth Adams visited the site many times during the planning stages, appearing on each occasion with a different man — whether client or builder — and arousing endless speculation in the nearby village about her seemingly insatiable sexual appetites.[48]

Prototypical Designs and Feminist Organization

What did this rush of architectural experimentation in the teens and twenties contribute to the material feminist tradition of economic independence for women and socialized domestic work? Many prototypes

for housing were developed which could be exploited by women's groups concerned with these issues. Ebenezer Howard's group introduced the Cooperative Quadrangle as a successful physical and social design (albeit one which required a large, conventional town as its setting) and suggested that the constituency for innovative housing was small but could be identified and organized, just as a market for apartment hotels had been found. The experience of Los Angeles architects represented no advance on London in terms of practice, because the Heineman project was rather tentative. Austin's was never built, and Schindler's was a significantly flawed design. However, Austin raised the issue of urban infrastructure for socialized domestic work, a most significant theoretical advance. Los Angeles designers also advanced the debate about the scale of domestic cooperation, suggesting that it could work for five people, or ten thousand, and not just for Howard's forty or fifty quadrangle residents. Their planning also emphasized organizing producers' cooperatives, rather than forming consumers' cooperatives and hiring household labor, as most of Howard's tenants had done.

The experience gained in New York was on a far larger scale than that of either London or Los Angeles. The avant-garde architects and planners of the RPAA discussed many ideas but limited their innovations to child care facilities when they developed actual projects. The trade-union builders, who organized hundreds of units of cooperatively owned housing, with child-care facilities, commissaries, and restaurants, established the feasibility of workers' limited equity cooperatives and demonstrated their ability to develop community services for large groups. Feminism for these builders was limited to the need to provide for some employed women; the male trade unionists did not stress women's choices or autonomy. Herman Jessor was very limited in his architectural training and financial resources, compared to the RPAA designers, who also had limited financial resources, or to George Pelham and Ruth Adams, who undertook work for the affluent. These last two were not innovators aesthetically, but their budgets enabled them to achieve substantial realizations of the ideal of socialized domestic work, although the social and economic arrangements of their clients were based on hired labor rather than shared responsibilities.

Conflicts of gender abound in all these experiments, among working-class as well as middle-class and upper-middle-class participants. Ebenezer Howard and Rudolph Schindler congratulated themselves on liberating their wives through better design, without any thought of ever doing domestic work themselves, and Schindler continued blithely unaware of any errors in his approach, despite the fact that he and his wife separated after a few years of moving into the "cooperative dwelling." [49] Indeed, almost all of the architects and planners discussed here fell into the trap of patronizing women, of designing for greater efficiency rather than for economic justice.

This was as true of the workers' cooperatives in New York, which ran beauty contests and expected that women would do the cooking, as it was of the middle-class communities of the Heinemans or Stein and Wright, who expected women to sew and mind children. (It was also true of similar projects in the Soviet Union.)

Howard's associate, C. B. Purdom, wrote of the Cooperative Quadrangles, "It is not, as some say, that women are beginning to rebel against the home as their ancient prison. It is simply that the unscientific drudgery of housekeeping and maintaining an out-of-date house is becoming more apparent and intolerable." [50] W. L. George's comment that the feminist flat would strike "the roots of the economic system" were forgotten. Alice Constance Austin spoke of the traditional home as a place which "confiscated" women's labor, but even she mitigated a plea for justice by calling the home "stupid" and "inefficient." Her expectation that women in her socialist city might use their time for child rearing rather than for careers also underlines the extent to which almost all architects failed to recognize Gilman's basic economic arguments, while accepting her social criticism of the home. None of the architects and planners discussed here, with the exception of Edith Elmer Wood and Milo Hastings, argued for women's economic independence or believed, as Gilman and Henrietta Rodman had, that married women might want to work full time and have families. They thought that some working-class women unfortunately might need to work,

or that both working-class and middle-class
women deserved labor-saving domestic arrangements, easier child rearing, and less
isolation. As a result architects and planners who were sincere advocates of cooperative housekeeping as an aspect of modern
housing design were unable to contradict
self-proclaimed "efficiency experts" such as
Lillian Gilbreth or Christine Frederick who
claimed that technology could achieve
these same goals without transforming the
traditional home or the woman's role as
housewife.

By the mid-twenties, architects and
planners had translated some of Gilman's
ideas into schemes for new housing and
new towns, but they could not progress beyond superficial feminism without understanding her basic plea for economic
justice for women. Thus, as feminist organizing continued in the late twenties,
with Ethel Puffer Howes' campaign to
coordinate women's jobs and community
services, housing design seemed to some
feminists to have lost the preeminent place
Gilman, Peirce, and Howland had assigned
it in earlier manifestos. At the same time
architects and planners were unable to
generate a feminist discussion of the projects they had built, in order to try again.
There were not enough feminist architects
and planners to make the theoretical connections, although Edith Elmer Wood,
working with Ethel Puffer Howes, continued to try to provide a feminist critique for
architects and planners and an architectural critique for feminists.

12.1 Ethel Puffer Howes, 1925

*. . . home making as at present conducted is a
sweated industry.*
— *Ethel Puffer Howes, "True and Substantial
Happiness,"* Woman's Home Companion,
1923

*When you start taking drudgery out of the home,
the first step is getting together; the next is finding leaders and training them.*
— *Ethel Puffer Howes, "The Revolt of Mother,"*
Woman's Home Companion, *1923*

A Philosopher Takes Command

In 1868 Melusina Fay Peirce campaigned
for cooperative housekeeping with a series
of articles in the *Atlantic Monthly*. Fifty-four
years later Ethel Puffer Howes (12.1)
launched her proposals for community
kitchens, day care, and women's work outside the home in the same periodical.[1] A
comparison of their careers illustrates how
much the theory and practice of material
feminism had developed in that critical
half century. While Peirce had emphasized
the need for women to reorganize
"woman's sphere," Howes stressed her desire to enlarge the scope of "male" career
possibilities for married women. Peirce had
studied at the Young Ladies' School of
Agassiz and was a pioneer campaigner for
women's undergraduate education before
Harvard admitted women at all; Howes
studied at Harvard and received a Ph.D.
from Radcliffe. Peirce had been frustrated
in her aspirations for a scientific career,
but Howes enjoyed a successful academic
career in philosophy before turning to domestic reform. Although both believed in
cooperation as an economic strategy for
women, for Howes, this was a concrete
term linked with the activities of the Rochdale pioneers, the Finnish and Jewish cooperative homebuilders in New York, and
many successful community kitchens; for
Peirce, cooperation had been a broader,
vaguer, and more elusive ideal. Howes enjoyed years of administrative experience as
Executive Secretary of the National College Equal Suffrage League and as an active member of the American Association
of University Women, while Peirce, despite
her many memberships in women's organizations, was never a really capable administrator. Howes recruited experienced
and committed people, whereas not all of
Peirce's "cooperators" had stood behind
her. In short, Howes was a seasoned general, while Peirce had been a young ideal-
ist. Yet Howes had hardened opposition to
face. Her experiment may be said to be an
emphatic defeat for housewives' cooperatives and feminist motherhood, while
Peirce's was but an early skirmish in the
domestic revolution. Understanding the
strengths of Howes's leadership, as well as
the weaknesses of her strategy, is essential
to any feminist who chooses to take this issue further.

Ethel Puffer was born in Framingham,
Massachusetts, in 1872, the oldest of four
gifted sisters. Considered "one of the most
brilliant students" ever to graduate from
Smith College, she earned her B.A. in
1891, at age nineteen, and accepted an in-
structorship in mathematics there before
traveling to Berlin and Freiburg in 1895
for graduate study. In Germany she began
work on the aesthetics of symmetry, which
she returned to pursue at Harvard, combining work in philosophy and experimental psychology with George Santayana,
William James, and Hugo Munsterberg. In
1898, a larger group of faculty examined
Puffer, finding her "unusually well
qualified" for the doctorate, but Harvard
could not award a woman a Ph.D. at that

date; only in 1902 did Radcliffe finally confer her degree.[2] In 1899 Ethel Puffer was invited to join the Harvard psychology faculty as an "assistant" (the lowest possible rank), a post which she held for nine years, although her name was not listed in the catalog for fear that the presence of a woman faculty member might "create a dangerous precedent."[3] Yet Howes earned the friendship and respect of M. Carey Thomas, President of Bryn Mawr College; her second book, *The Psychology of Beauty*, became a classic college text.

In 1908, at age thirty-six, she married Benjamin Howes, a civil engineer, and in her early forties, she bore two children. She continued to work, holding the position of Associate Professor of Philosophy at Wellesley. When she experienced "a perfect delirium of finishing an important article on aesthetics," her husband shared household work: "Ben has helped me out somewhat — cooked everything one day," she wrote to her mother.[4] Yet becoming a wife and mother provided obstacles to her career, which had already been curbed somewhat by the prejudice of the male academic world which had insisted that her brilliance not be revealed in such improper places as, for example, the Harvard faculty catalog, and restricted her later teaching career to women's colleges such as Simmons, Wellesley, and Smith.

After World War I and the winning of suffrage for women, Ethel Puffer Howes decided to devote the rest of her career to political organizing on domestic issues. At age fifty, she asked herself just what the "woman movement" meant. Suffrage had been won, but this was only removing a legal disability from women. What more did women want? In "The Meaning of Progress in the Woman Movement" she quoted Mary Wollstonecraft, Elizabeth Cady Stanton, John Stuart Mill, Gilman, and Carrie Chapman Catt as feminists who had argued for removing women's legal and political disabilities. Gilman, she believed, went farthest in terms of her anticipation of "practical efforts for the management of women's lives," yet Howes felt these efforts were still directed toward removing women's disabilities: "Progress in the full sense can, then, not be attributed to the woman movement, because no real objective has been set or attained. She concluded, "The 'woman question' has never had an answer."[5]

Howes therefore set out to restate the question and propose an answer. Like Gilman and Rodman, she considered both motherhood and serious careers essential to women's happiness. She raged at the attitudes that forced women to choose between the two. She showed how the expectation that all women would marry placed an insurmountable obstacle in the way of their professional training and early work: "As it is now, every young woman in the full tide of her effort is under sentence of death, professionally."[6] Of the notion that educated women should find all their pleasure and satisfaction in the home, she asked, ". . . would an entomologist find the full expression of his science in keeping the household free from insect pests? . . .

Would an engineer be justified . . . in confining his bridge-building to his own estate?" [7] She admired Ellen Richards and her ideal of professional training in home economics, but she did not think that married women should accept the idea that cooking and laundry were their only "professions." To accommodate both marriage and career, Howes advocated continuous part-time work for women with children and community services run by professionals or by neighbors to handle cooking, cleaning, and child care. She wrote:

A noble task for the women of this generation is to evaluate their own conscious purposes. I believe their ideal will take shape somewhat thus: First: to order their lives for the loving companionship and nurture of children. Second: to find and establish in public esteem the right ways to continue their trained vocations in harmony with home ties. Third: to make all these things practically possible by reducing, through inventions and organization in mutual aid, the present feudal proportions and absurd overstressing of the household mechanism.

She believed that "the next few years ought to see an evolution from the present household-factory into a simpler form, community or group administered." [8]

In another article she spelled out what "trained vocations in harmony with home ties" meant: continuity rather than competition for married women. "Continuity" meant lifelong involvement in one's career, but not at the competitive pace that men demanded of themselves. She believed that women could demand and receive professional respect for part-time work while raising children. It even seemed possible that

such an approach would have far-reaching effects: "Might it not have an epochal effect on the progress of science if one half of the able people in the world should consciously, explicitly, and proudly refuse to compete?" [9]

She saw a domestic revolution as an essential support for the legitimate career goals of women and arranged the most complete campaign yet mounted for achieving such change. She would attack simultaneously with popular articles in mass circulation magazines to reach all housewives and theoretical articles in academic journals to reach professional women. She would deal simultaneously with women and their potential employers; she would draw on the knowledge of women experienced in large-scale domestic management; and she would attempt to convert young women just reaching maturity through college courses designed to improve their "mental hygiene" by raising basic questions about women's roles as paid workers and as mothers.

Woman's Home Companion

Howes turned to the practical tasks of raising money for research, recruiting dedicated, able colleagues, and finding an audience. Working with Gertrude Lane and Myra Reed Richardson, editors of *Woman's Home Companion,* Howes launched a popular campaign for women's cooperative home service clubs in 1923 that outdid all of the *Ladies' Home Journal*'s previous efforts to promote kitchenless houses and community kitchens in 1919 and 1920.[10] Howes first visited cooperatives — the Evanston Community Kitchen; the Chatsfield, Minnesota, Laundry; Mary E. Arnold's Our Cooperative Cafeteria; the People's Kitchen; the Village Cooperative Laundry in New York City; the Finnish coperative bakery in Fitchburg, Massachusetts; and the Mainline Community Kitchen in Wynnewood, Pennsylvania — and she wrote about them for the *Companion*. Then she, Lane, and Richardson encouraged readers to tell them about "everyday problems," resulting in a flood of two thousand letters about housewives' isolation, overwork, and depression, which Howes analyzed: "home-making as at present conducted is a sweated industry. . . . "[11]

Finally, in September 1923, readers were invited to enter a contest to describe "The Most Practical Plan for Cooperative Home Service in Our Town." Offering $100 for the best letters, the editors required that each entry include a pledge signed by at least six women:

1. RESOLVED, that it is the duty of the women of this country to free themselves from irrational drudgery for the sake of their higher duties as wives and mothers, and as individuals.

2. RESOLVED, that, as a means to this end, we will organize here and now some form of cooperative home service.[12]

From Portsmouth, Virginia, came an account of six housewives who shared all cooking, laundry, and child care in a central workplace and had built an enclosed playground for their children. Others wrote of a cooperative preserving club in Massa-

chusetts, a cooperative laundry and sewing room in Iowa, a produce cooperative in South Carolina, and a home specialists' group (for making bread, pies, cakes, candy, and lace curtains, and doing heavy cleaning, and sewing) in Michigan. A servant had been hired only in two cases where laundry was mentioned (a black laundress in Portsmouth who earned $7.50 a week, and a white laundress in Iowa who earned $15.00); otherwise women were doing their own work. Melusina Fay Peirce's vision of women forming producers' cooperatives to reorganize housework was finally being realized.

Throughout these campaigns Howes warned women that commercial labor-saving devices were not a solution to their problems. In a stinging article, "The Revolt of Mother," she argued: ". . . Quite apart from the fact that millions of us are not able to command them, the washing machine won't collect and sort the laundry, or hang out the clothes; the mangle won't iron complicated articles; the dishwasher won't collect, scrape, and stack the dishes; the vacuum cleaner won't mop the floor or 'clean up and put away.' "[13] She identified women's larger need, for "true and substantial happiness," which had been the avowed aim of the Seneca Falls Convention in 1848. She noted that "the franchise was only a means to an end" and reiterated that housewives must organize themselves to earn economic equality and respect for their work.[14]

Smith College

At the same time Howes was organizing housewives, she presented her ideas to the American Association of University Women and in 1923 chaired their committee on "Cooperative Home Service." [15] Next she raised a grant from the Laura Spellman Rockefeller Foundation to develop a research institute to attack a number of theoretical and practical issues. Smith College agreed to sponsor the undertaking, so Howes was able to tie her domestic reform programs to women's higher education — a major conceptual advance in terms of preparing college women for the dilemmas they would face when trying to "order their lives so that their individual powers and interests, developed by education, should not, in the pressure of normal family life, be diffused or dulled." [16]

The Institute for the Coordination of Women's Interests (12.2) became the base camp for Howes's broad campaign in favor of socialized domestic work between 1926 and 1931. Howes marshaled historians to research the experience of managing careers and homes, career guidance specialists to devise new strategies for conquering employers' prejudice against women, a housing expert to study the architectural implications of employed women's needs, and home economists and child care experts to demonstrate the feasibility of services to assist employed mothers.

Alice Peloubet Norton, a pioneer of the home economic movement in the United States, had been an associate of Ellen Richards and Mary Hinman Abel, and had taught cookery and nutrition in the Brookline, Massachusetts, schools, at Chautauqua, and at the University of Chicago. She edited the *Journal of Home Economics* between 1915 and 1921 and in the 1920s represented the small but significant minority in her field who still believed in cooperative services. When she joined the institute, Norton was sixty-five, but she conducted her work with shrewdness and energy. First came research on cooked food. Using Iva Lowther Peters's wartime research as a starting point, Norton studied four community kitchens established during the war (Evanston, Illinois; Montclair, New Jersey; New York City, and Wynnewood, Pennsylvania) and three commercial kitchens (Brookline, Massachusetts; East Orange, New Jersey; and Flushing, New York).[17] Norton also looked at the lifestyles of Smith College alumnae who were employed, particularly the 20 percent who found some food service essential — whether a community kitchen, delicatessen, or cooked food shop.[18] From the results of her survey concerning costs, delivery policies, and menus, she shaped the policies of the community kitchen established by the institute in the fall of 1928, which served over two thousand dinners to Northampton residents during one academic year (12.3). Although Norton died that year, the experiment was successful, and the institute sent a model of a "community house" with a community kitchen to a New York exhibition.

12.2 The Institute for the Coordination of Women's Interests, 58 Kensington Avenue, Northampton, Massachusetts, photograph by Penelope Simpson. The Cooperative Nursery School and the Dinner Kitchen were established here between 1926 and 1931.

12.3 "The New Housekeeping Based on Friendly Cooperation," sketches showing women sharing the use of small electric appliances, *Woman's Home Companion,* June 1927

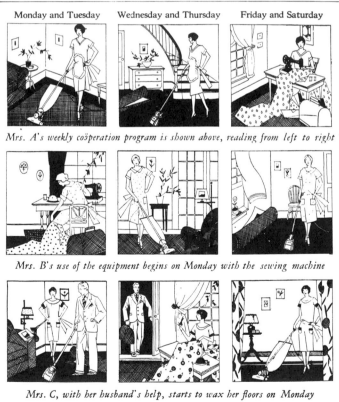

| Monday and Tuesday | Wednesday and Thursday | Friday and Saturday |

Mrs. A's weekly coöperation program is shown above, reading from left to right

Mrs. B's use of the equipment begins on Monday with the sewing machine

Mrs. C, with her husband's help, starts to wax her floors on Monday

Edith Elmer Wood, one of the most energetic housing reformers whom the Progressive Era had bred in many American cities, was an activist campaigning for urban and suburban housing designed for workers, a key member of the Regional Planning Association of America, and a consultant to public bodies and international committees. For the institute, Wood agreed to travel to Europe to research and write a book entitled "Aids to Homemaking in Seven European Countries": England, Holland, Belgium, Norway, Denmark, Sweden, and France. She researched cooked food services, community dining rooms, cooperative laundries, and day nurseries, especially those connected with housing, such as the Cooperative Quadrangles at the Garden Cities of Letchworth, Welwyn, and Hampstead, and the *servicehus* of Otto Fick in Copenhagen.[19] Some of these projects had been in successful operation for fifteen years or more, and she evaluated their promise for the United States, informing Howes and other feminists of the architects' advances in this area.

Dorothea Beach, a graduate of Simmons College who had specialized in kindergarten methods and headed the Temple University Department of Home Economics, was recruited as Demonstration Manager. Her tasks were to oversee the two cooperative ventures, the Nursery School launched in 1926 and the Dinner Kitchen begun in 1928, in order to make these enterprises models which could be copied anywhere in the United States at minimum expense. The Nursery School cared for twenty-five

children (ten of them for the full day), with the institute's staff working with cooperating mothers.[20] Fathers joined in at policy meetings. Within the school the reigning spirit came from Robert Owen's Institute for the Formation of Character, for Howes wrote, "Perhaps the controlling thought of the cooperative nursery may be most simply expressed in the words of Robert Owen, who founded the first infant school in Lanark, Scotland, in 1800 — 'to form their dispositions to mutual kindness.' " [21]

With child care programs, Howes reached out to the kindergarten and nursery school experts of the United States. The secretary of the institute and Howes's right-hand woman was Esther H. Stocks. She was skilled in child care and worked in the cooperative nursery school.[22] Stocks also helped to establish an experiment in training and placing "home assistants" in the homes of employed women.[23] Where previous generations of women had launched schools for servants, the Institute was attempting to eliminate condescension and pay well for this work, stressing the workers' "individual interests" as well as the employers'.

Guiding women into successful part-time careers was also part of the institute's mission. Writing and designing were two specialties that its counselors suggested could be pursued at home.[24] They recommended a minimum of two years of full-time work after graduation before women attempted to work free-lance. The institute also ran conferences for Smith Alumnae and considered establishing a vocational guidance bureau for those who wished to return to work. Howes taught a "consciousness-raising" course for freshmen at Smith as well.[25]

This, then, was the first team of post–World War I feminists interested in domestic reform. Howes had an extensive knowledge of the cooperative movement, and Wood was sympathetic to cooperatives and to Fabian socialism. Both of them, as well as Norton and Beach, were mature feminists and professional women with decades of experience. Uniting theory and practice as no group had ever done before them, the team at the institute struggled for a grand synthesis of the elements of a domestic revolution and a new vocational world for women. As Howes had stated their goals:

. . . the satisfactory organization, in a college project, of a new type of service for homes, of a cooperative nursery group, of a cooked food supply adjusted to moderate incomes, means not so many bits of ground won in home economics, but so many props in the social framework so necessary to any ultimate solution. All our analyses of the professions for their adjustment to women's needs, all our case histories of successful integrations of professional and home interests find herein their meaning and enter as elements into the synthesis.[26]

Most important, each of these services was to be run in the manner most appropriate, whether by entrepreneurs or by cooperating neighbors. This solved the problem many earlier reformers had found difficult. Food in return for cash, from a nonprofit company, and child care in return for personal participation, made sense to many women, in a way that participating in cooking or paying for child care did not.

Yet within six short years, Howes's synthesis had disintegrated. *Woman's Home Companion* stopped supporting cooperation, and the institute that had attempted to unite the strivings of several generations of feminists was closed. What stopped them?

Defeat in the Publishing World

At the end of the 1920s, *Woman's Home Companion* turned from advocating that women form producers' cooperatives and warning them against domestic appliances which did not meet their needs. Its policies like those of other women's magazines, were bending under the impact of its advertisers. Advertising and marketing firms spent one billion dollars to promote private domestic life and mass consumption in 1920; their annual volume had risen over 1,000 percent since 1890, and continued to rise throughout the 1920s.[27] Stuart Ewen has shown how cleverly advertising copywriters interwove the rhetoric of women's liberation with arguments for domestic consumption: vacuum cleaners gave women new life, toasters made them "free." [28] Advertisers' blandishments were complemented by the introduction of consumer credit systems to encourage housewives to buy.

In 1927 a transitional article in the *Companion* suggested that women form cooperative groups to purchase electric appliances they could not afford individually, thus substituting cooperative consumption for cooperative production.[29] In 1928 an editorial, "Housewives, Incorporated," claimed that the main lesson housewives learned in producers' cooperatives was that buying in large quantities is economical. This was followed by the editors' pronouncement that producers' cooperatives were similar to major corporations, because both enjoyed economies of scale. The editorial concluded with a recommendation that housewives buy nationally advertised goods.[30] Producers' cooperatives were never given editorial support again.

Perhaps the greatest mistake Howes made was failing to measure the greed of corporations manufacturing domestic appliances and trying to market them. One day in 1927 Howes even brought, as a visitor to the institute, Lillian Mollner Gilbreth, an industrial engineer who herself had eleven children, a smug superwoman who tried to Taylorize every work process in the home. Corporations paid her to explain how housewives could "efficiently" do all their own work at home, and Ewen argues that she was the embodiment of the commercial pressures of the era. These were the same forces that would remove articles on cooperation from women's magazines and engulf many of the institute's arguments about cooperative kitchens and nurseries in the rhetoric of consumption. But the dangers of Gilbreth's private "efficiencies" were not apparent to Howes. The institute's programs were directed at helping individual women pursue their career aspirations, but its members were not yet ready to attack corporate manipulation of female consumers for economic gain. While World War I had opened up many prospects for services for employed women, it had also stimulated defense industries which, in the postwar years, needed new markets and saw the production of domestic appliances such as refrigerators and washing machines as their most promising field of growth. But women had to be at home, to buy these devices and run them, so advertisers were busy equating consumption and women's "liberation."

In the same mood in which the earlier *Companion* articles on cooperation were contradicted, so Edith Elmer Wood's book on cooperative home services in Europe met a dismal fate. Rejected by Macmillan in 1927, it has disappeared, the only one of her six excellent books that never made it into print. A few handwritten notes and extensive correspondence concerning her final manuscript survive, but the reasons for the book's disappearance are not clear.[31]

Worst of all, Howes was recruited to participate in the defeat of her own ideas. President Hoover organized a national Conference on Home Building and Home Ownership in 1931, dedicated to a campaign to build single-family houses in the private market as a strategy for promoting greater economic growth in the United States and less industrial strife. Howes was invited to serve on the Committee for Household Management, Kitchens, and Other Work Centers. In this forum she got to write a few pages about "substitute services" for the home, reviewing such housing developments as the Amalgamated Clothing Workers project in the Bronx, and Radburn, New Jersey. She discussed the need for child care centers and cooked food services as part of housing complexes.[32] Volumes were prepared to support the other side of the argument in aid of the conventional, isolated home and the purchase of appropriate appliances. The tone of the Hoover Report recalls that of the Muncie, Indiana, Chamber of Commerce, reported in the mid-1920s: "The first responsibility of an American to his country is no longer that of a citizen, but of a consumer. Consumption is a necessity." [33]

Defeat at Smith College

If businessmen wanted to define the housewife as an avid consumer who had plenty to do without a career, academics wanted to define the educated woman as one who had nothing to do with housework at all. Many Smith students and faculty simply did not believe in compromising women's career ambitions. To them, Howes's pragmatism about the difficulties of combining marriage and career seemed defeatist. Some believed that the institute would undermine the career woman's chances of competing in a male world by suggesting that women's real interest in life was marriage and part-time work. Determined to break down the prejudice expressed in the slogan, "career or marriage," Howes did fail to support women who were single-minded about their careers and refused to

marry. She attempted to fit these single women into her system, by claiming that whether they wanted to marry or not, they would be seen by employers as potentially marriageable: the unmarried woman working full-time, she said, ". . . must recognize that she is, as an actual fact, whatever her personal intentions or traits, in a class of extra-hazardous risk for any profession. . . ." She counseled dampered ambition: "Dignity, self-respect, and common sense will be served by her accepting, without apology to an unreasonable feminist ideal, whatever variety of non-competition she individually chooses to espouse." Some angry women never listened to another word, but Howes continued: "It is, perhaps, well that women, in work as in affection, should, by Margaret Fuller's concept, 'not calculate too closely.' " [34]

Howes alienated single career women; in addition she did not phrase her arguments to appeal to guardians of women's education. Since she believed that marriageability effectively made women unequal, she proclaimed: "The serious higher education or professional training of women today is literally founded on self-deception; a solemn farce in which all the actors consent to ignore the fact that the most natural, necessary, and valuable of human relations will in all probability soon ring down the final curtain." [35] Professors (both male and female) were offended by her phrase, "solemn farce." Some of them chafed at the second-rank status accorded to all woman's colleges and were intent on stressing Smith's academic standards. They feared that the idea of not competing would dull women students' interest. They worried that Howes's freshman course in sociology, where she presented the home-versus-career dilemma as a necessary part of "mental hygiene" for women, would lead to the introduction of applied sciences related to home economics in all parts of the curriculum. At Vassar and Connecticut College for Women, some marriage-minded students were demanding courses relevant to their homemaking "careers," [36] and Smith faculty rightly deplored this trend. Ultimately the institute was rejected by the Smith faculty for its "unintellectual and unacademic concerns." [37]

When the institute was threatened, the only constituency it had really won over, the Smith alumnae, were too scattered to support its efforts on behalf of feminist motherhood effectively. So the institute's publications in the Smith Archives survive, detailing the happy children in the child care center, the splendid cooked dinners of beef loaf, Pittsburgh potatoes, summer squash, and butterscotch pies delivered from the community kitchen, and the prospects of creative part-time work in landscape architecture. The functioning cooperative nursery school, with fathers involved, survived, and became part of the education department at the college. In 1969 some male faculty at Smith had what they called "a lively, thoroughly masculine discussion," over all of Howes's programs and hopes for women.[38] Feminists have made more sympathetic pilgrimages to 58 Kensington Avenue, site of all of the institute's efforts, in recent years.

Howes and her colleagues, who told women how to manage their resources rather than how to rebel against prejudiced husbands and employers, conceded too much in their eagerness to treat all aspects of women's domestic dilemmas, but on their integration of feminist theory and practice, history and strategy, they cannot be faulted. The institute constructed a feminist landscape by erecting intricate bridges between the progressive islands of scientific nutrition, developmental child care, and defined career structures for women. Beyond their landscape lay a dismal swamp of chauvinism and capitalism. A look at the broader situation in the 1920s suggests why Howes was so prepared to compromise and conciliate, why she dropped a clear demand for economic independence for women (stated by Peirce, Howland, Livermore, and Gilman) and instead stressed "not calculating too closely," or balancing home and career. The decade of the 1920s began with women's presence in the wartime labor force and the achievement of suffrage. But these feminist victories were contemporary with the infamous Red Scare, which included the worst right-wing attempt to smear the feminist movement in American history, and Howes, the most brilliant of Gilman's gallant disciples, was unable to prevail against this pressure.

VI   Backlash

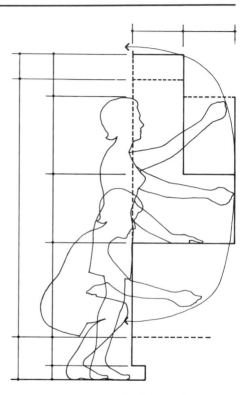

Time and motion analysis of woman in a
kitchen

*Consumptionism . . . the greatest idea that
America has to give to the world; the idea that
workmen and the masses be looked upon not sim-
ply as workers or producers, but as* consumers.
— *Christine Frederick,* Selling Mrs.
Consumer, *1929*

Madame Kollontai
and Mrs. Consumer

The Red Scare and Women

While Ethel Puffer Howes was expert at
building coalitions and counting her
friends, she was never fully able to recognize her enemies and understand that they,
too, were forming alliances. Perceiving that
many groups in society favored domestic
reform, she struggled to make the whole
support system more than the sum of individual specialties such as efficient home
management, improved housing, adequate
child care, or special career counseling for
women. Among the groups she reached out
to, the home economists, housing experts,
child care experts, and career counseling
experts, there was real commitment to
helping working women meet their needs.
But in the United States as a whole,
women's organizations were under heavy
attack beginning with the Red Scare of
1919–1920 and continuing until the end of
the decade.

The infamous spiderweb chart, a list of
feminist activists and organizations circulated as propaganda by the War Department, smeared moderate women's groups
such as the General Federation of Women's
Clubs, the Woman's Christian Temperance
Union, the Young Women's Christian Association, the American Home Economics
Association, the American Association of
University Women, the League of Women
Voters, and other women's civic, religious,
and political organizations. It represented
them as part of a "red web" aimed at de-
stroying America through pacifism and socialism. The Women's Joint Congressional
Committee, an interorganizational
women's lobbying group on Capitol Hill,
was greatly weakened by such attacks,
which denounced its member organizations
as sympathizers with the 1917 Bolshevik
victory in the Soviet Union, and suggested
that the WJCC had been infiltrated by
such "reds." [1] Nonpartisan cooperation between Democratic and Republican women,
led by National Party Vice-Chairmen Harriet Taylor Upton of Warren, Ohio, and
Emily Newell Blair of Carthage, Missouri,
was attacked as a clever attempt to tap
party treasuries in order to break down
party machinery in favor of Soviet
influence.

The *Dearborn Independent,* published by
Henry Ford, ran the spiderweb chart, as
well as hostile articles claiming that American women who were organizing women
workers and demanding maternity benefits
for mothers and children were taking orders from Alexandra Kollontai in Moscow.[2] Alexandra Kollantai, former Com-
misar of Public Welfare and head of
Zhenotdel (the women's section of the Central Committe Secretariat) in the U.S.S.R.,
was an experienced political activist and a
leading Bolshevik feminist. The President
of the National Association of Manufacturers reiterated this fear in a speech delivered
at a Department of Labor conference on
women workers in 1926, claiming that
"one Madame Kollontai, whose headquarters are in Moscow but whose parish is the
world, is exercising a very large if not a
dominating influence" upon some of the

activities of American women's organizations.[3] (He added the slander that Kollontai lived with her eighth husband!) Similar attacks were made by members of the Woman Patriots, an organization active in the Red Scare whose journal, *The Woman Patriot,* was "Dedicated to the Defense of the Family and the State AGAINST Feminism and Socialism."[4]

While the influence of Kollontai in the United States was greatly exaggerated, the avowed intention of leaders in the Soviet Union to develop maternity leave policies and insurance for women workers, to socialize domestic work, and to build one third of the new Soviet housing in the 1920s in the form of kitchenless apartments with nurseries and community kitchens (11.23) aroused real fear among those who believed that a woman's place is in the home.[5] Lenin, in 1919, argued that "owing to her work in the house, the woman is still in a difficult position. To effect her complete emancipation and make her the equal of the man, it is necessary for housework to be socialized and for women to participate in common productive labor. Then women will occupy the same position as men. . . ."[6]

The new institutions developed after the Bolshevik revolution — such as factory kitchens and nurseries — made it possible for Soviet women to enter the paid labor force in increasing numbers, but they ignored the value of women's existing skills and the importance of those skills to the quality of all workers' lives. Lenin believed that "in most cases housework is the most unproductive, the most savage, and the most arduous work a woman can do. It is exceptionally petty and does not include anything that would in any way promote the development of the woman. . . ."[7] While he was prepared to turn women into paid factory workers, he had no intention of giving men responsibility for child care. He declared, "We are setting up model institutions, dining rooms and nurseries, that will emancipate women from housework. And the work of organizing all these institutions will fall mainly to women."[8]

Inflamed by the idea of government support for women in the paid labor force, Red-baiters who attacked American feminists did not see that their movement had few ties to Lenin, Kollontai, and the U.S.S.R. Even the Communist men and women in the Workers' Cooperative Colony in the Bronx were not especially well informed about Soviet housing developments. The American material feminist tradition favoring women's economic independence and socialized domestic work was an indigenous, radical tradition, which drew upon communitarian socialism, anarchism, free love, and feminism. It stressed local, voluntary cooperation and the organization of consumers' and producers' cooperatives. Although a few home economists had proposed municipal services for women workers, centralized national services were never mentioned except in the utopian novels of Anna Bowman Dodd and Edward Bellamy.

Nevertheless, in 1919 and 1920, the Soviet argument that women were to be considered workers first and housewives second struck fear into American industrialists and businessmen, who believed that the acceptance of a large number of women in the paid labor force on a permanent basis would destroy the American economy. They saw women workers and black workers in new wartime jobs (filling in for soldiers); they believed that women would use the ballot to change the economic and political balance of power in America. At the same time, unrest peaked among white male workers. A wave of strikes and demonstrations in the United States in 1919, involving over four million workers, and a number of demonstrations by unemployed veterans in 1919–1920, led many politicians and businessmen to believe that growth and prosperity in the 1920s depended on keeping women out of the labor force and developing homes of a rather different character than either existing tenements or the collective alternatives the Bolsheviks and the American material feminists advocated.

Industrialists began to consider the strategy of offering white male skilled workers small surburban homes, to be purchased on home mortgages, as a way of achieving greater industrial order. The Industrial Housing Associates, the planning firm that published *Good Homes Make Contented Workers* in 1919 (13.1) explained to industrial clients that "Happy workers invariably mean bigger profits, while unhappy workers are never a good investment." They continued, "A wide diffusion of home ownership has long been recognized as fos-

GOOD HOMES MAKE CONTENTED WORKERS

13.1 Title page, *Good Homes Make Contented Workers,* Industrial Housing Associates, 1919

tering a stable and conservative habit.
. . . The man owns his home but in a
sense his home owns him, checking his rash
impulses. . . ." [9] Or, as another official
put it, "Get them to invest their savings in
homes and own them. Then they won't
leave and they won't strike. It ties them
down so they have a stake in our prosperity." [10] All of these statements reflected attitudes expressed by the National Civic
Federation of America, an association dedicated to amicable settlements of conflicts
between capital and labor (13.2).

If it seemed a good idea to employers to
define the male worker as "homeowner,"
women needed an identity too — perhaps
Lillian Gilbreth's "home manager" (very
similar to Catharine Beecher's "professional" housewife or "home minister" of
1869). Woman as "home managers" would
study the best ways to keep the "home-
owners" functioning as stable, conscien-
tious workers, husbands, and fathers. But
Christine Frederick proposed an even better term in the late 1920s. Mr. Homeowner
would marry "Mrs. Consumer." (Here, too,
Catharine Beecher had led the way, suggesting that the use of "superfluities"
would keep the American economy going
in the 1870s.) It was a small step to define
consumption as a "patriotic duty," or
women's patriotic duty.

The Red Scare was a time when conservatives emphasized the political importance of women's roles. The attempt of
Lenin and Kollontai to promote industrial
production as a patriotic act for women

13.2 Political cartoon showing the role of the
National Civic Federation of America in ending
conflict between capital and labor. The happy
worker carries a full dinner pail and, in his
pockets, a deed to a house and a bank book,
while his employer enjoys foreign contracts.

was analogous to the attempt of Henry Ford and Christine Frederick to promote the patriotic duty of consumption. The Soviet "Communal House" and the American suburban house were opposed as the stage sets for these roles. (In terms of technology and housing design the Soviet Union was where the United States had been in the mid-nineteenth century, which perhaps accounted for the oversimplified notion of socialized domestic life Lenin and many Soviet architects advanced.)

In the United States two home economists, Lillian Gilbreth and Christine Frederick, became the key ideologues of the antifeminist, pro-consumption, suburban home. In her book *Household Engineering: Scientific Management in the Home,* published in 1920, Frederick attempted to apply Frederick Taylor's ideas about scientific management to housework.[11] Although this was a logical impossibility, since scientific management required the specialization and division of labor, and the essence of private housework was its isolated, unspecialized character, nevertheless both Frederick and Gilbreth created surrealistic sets of procedures whereby the housewife "managed" her own labors "scientifically," serving as executive and worker simultaneously. Corporations and advertising agencies then hired Frederick and Gilbreth as consultants to promote their products with their pseudoscientific management schemes, and ultimately Frederick became a specialist on selling things to women.

By 1928, in *Selling Mrs. Consumer,* dedicated to Herbert Hoover and addressed to

marketing and advertising executives, Frederick developed advertising techniques aimed at what she called women's suggestibility, passivity, and their "inferiority complexes." [12] She supported the industrial goal of "progressive obsolescence" and proposed the creation of consumer credit and home mortgages for young couples.[13] Housing units did not imply shelter to her but rather endless possibilities for sales: She coyly described the 5,000 "nests" built every day and encouraged advertisers to sell to young brides and grooms.

There is a direct and vital business interest in the subject of young love and marriage. Every business day approximately 5,000 new homes are begun; new "nests" are constructed and new family purchasing units begin operation. . . . The founding and furnishing of new homes is a major industrial circumstance in the United States. . . .[14]

This was the final corruption of home economics, representing not women's interests but businesses' interests in manipulating women, their homes, and their families.

As Frederick put it, "I have never been able to escape, as a *home* economist, a considerable need for understanding *business* economics just as the capital-labor relationship in America has been vastly improved by recognition of unity, so will the consumer-distributor-producer relationship be improved by mutual study." She called "consumptionism" the "greatest idea that America has to give to the world; the idea that workmen and the masses be looked upon not simply as workers or producers, but as *consumers*. Pay them more, sell them more, prosper more is the equation." [15]

The workingman's wife had a new identity as Mrs. Consumer under the Hoover administration. Hoover's Conference on Home Building and Home Ownership in December 1931 put government support behind a national strategy of home ownership for men "of sound character and industrious habits." This project did tap the energies of older campaigners against slums and even some feminists such as Ethel Puffer Howes, who wrote a "minority report" on community services, but its basic support came from manufacturers concerned with selling cars and consumer goods, real estate speculators, and housing developers. Lillian Gilbreth and Mrs. Henry Ford sat with these men on the planning committee. [16]

Fifty Dollars for the Best Answer

Despite a willingness to serve business and government which led them to anti-feminism, Christine Frederick and Lillian Gilbreth were not repudiated by the women's movement. Indeed, Frederick was asked to organize and judge an essay contest on "the future of the American home" by Carrie Chapman Catt in 1923. Catt, a longtime suffragist, had headed the National-American Women Suffrage Association's drive to victory in 1919 and 1920. She converted the organization into the League of Women Voters, and its paper, *The Woman's Journal,* established by Mary Livermore and Lucy Stone in 1870, became *Woman Citizen,* which Catt edited. For half a century *The Woman's Journal* had

covered experiments in cooperative housekeeping of all kinds, from Melusina Peirce's society to the quadrangles of Letchworth Garden City. Its editors had reiterated the importance of reorganizing the home to improve women's work. However, Catt and the league, as a "propaganda organization," were smeared in the Red Scare, and while she was railing at "lies-at-large" spread by the Woman Patriots as late as 1927, she was not able to lessen the damage the smear tactics did to the organized women's movement. Just why she chose Frederick to organize and judge the *Woman Citizen's* contest is not clear. It took place in the same year that Ethel Puffer Howes was running her contest on "Cooperative Home Services," in *Woman's Home Companion,* but conveyed a very different message.

The contest began with an article on "Woman's Oldest Job," on February 10, 1923, which asked:

What is the future of the American home? Must it be revolutionized because of lack of household help? Will the wife and mother of the next generation do all her own housework with the aid of mechanical devices? Is cooperative housekeeping the answer? Or meals served to individual homes from some central kitchen? Or will the tide of labor that has turned from kitchens turn back again? [17]

The editors included a fourteen-point questionnaire, which devoted seven of the fourteen questions to servants — their availability, cost, and working conditions. They then noted present lines of attack on the issue: first, simplification of housework, to "discover how far a woman can go forward solving the problem by herself"; and second, collective solutions, which they called "alleviations. . . . for the city, apartment hotels, with meals served in the dining room; in some communities, a common dining room maintained as a sort of community club; the development of a system of delivering meals, already cooked, to your house." The third tactic, changes in the social and economic status of domestic work, including the introduction of the eight-hour day and special training courses for domestic workers. The tone of Frederick's instructions to contestants was quite biased as to the value of these three strategies. The first was cautiously recommended, the second lightly dismissed, the third, heavily supported.

In the next six months, articles and contest entries chosen by Frederick were published in the *Woman Citizen*. Emphasis was given to good domestic service on a daily rather than live-in basis. "The Eight Hour Day at Home" was accompanied by a supporting editorial, "How Shall We Dignify Housework?" [18] Then followed "Help Wanted — Why" which argued, "preserve the domestic assistant at any cost." [19] "Domestic Labor — Privileged" argued that young women should prefer working in good families as live-in servants to laboring for a "soulless corporation." [20] The entries which received prices were: first, "Business Ideals at Home"; second, "Teamwork on Woman's Oldest Job"; and third, "The House Work Problem Minus Help." The reader would conclude that a well-to-do

housewife could solve her problems through "business ideals," paying domestic help $16 for a forty-eight hour week, allowing servants paid vacations for two weeks per year, providing a medical check-up and sanitized uniforms (laundered on the employee's own time, however). A less well-to-do woman would be thrown back on "teamwork," or "family teamwork with the woman of the house as the leader," or on the "minus help" joys of an efficiently redesigned kitchen in which to perform "varied" tasks. These compromises were completely class bound: if you were wealthy, you paid for your "businesslike" servants; if not, you marshaled daughters and sons, or used technology as the "new servant" to keep you company in the kitchen. [21]

"Help" from Unexpected Sources

In order to make the first goal of obtaining "trained" or "businesslike" servants possible, *Woman Citizen* lobbied for more government funds for home economics training for women, oblivious to the sex role stereotyping involved. They praised "Help for Homemakers, with the Government's Compliments," in 1924, when describing the educational activities of the Home Economics Bureau of the Department of Agriculture. They were especially delighted to report on what they called "Reinforcements on the Housework Problem," from the National Association of Wage Earners in Washington, D.C., where Nannie H. Burroughs established a center for training black women workers as domestic servants.

The *Citizen* editors commented, "Up to this time, as far as we know, there has been no conscious direct effort on the part of colored women to help solve the housework problem. Considering how little there has been on the part of white women, who form the majority of the employers, this sort of organization deserves three cheers." [22] The racism displayed was extraordinary: the editors obviously believed that only white, middle-class women had a "housework problem," which black women could help them solve. The black women's "housework problem" was invisible. They might complain of the worrisome duties of one household, but their employees would have to solve the problems of two, their employers' and their own.

Male Participation?

The *Citizen* did publish three essays of slightly different character, suggesting some additional domestic solutions and compromises. One was a discussion of community nursery schools. Another was Mary Alden Hopkins's "Fifty-Fifty Wives," which described the difficulties of sharing housework with husbands experienced by women who held outside jobs, but concluded that getting men to do domestic work was so difficult that "the self-supporting wife who wants to keep her job and wants to keep her home, must sacrifice even her sense of sacrificing." [23] The author of "Housekeeping — A Man's Job," came to different conclusions, describing her talks with a male domestic science major who argued that more and more

housekeeping would be done as a business outside the home, by men. [24] This was just the solution Melusina Fay Peirce, Mary Livermore, and Charlotte Perkins Gilman had feared would be chosen by male capitalists, once it proved inevitable and profitable. Marie Clotilde Redfern observed some young couples whose male members did seem to share tasks: ". . . the husband and wife start off together in the morning, he to his office, she to government or other work of the kind, and when they return about five p.m., if they have not taken their dinner at some cafeteria on their way home, both pitch in and get the dinner together. But no children! Not one of these young couples has a child." [25] Thus another series of compromises was laid out; women could have careers and homes if they either refused to have children or else did their housework uncomplainingly; women could get men to offer households new goods and services if they allowed male capitalists to control the quality and price.

Tracing the debates about housework and child care through the domestic policies expressed in this journal, one can get some sense of the pressures that material feminists were up against. The alliances that advocates of socialized domestic work had attempted to forge with leaders in the fields of home economics, housing, child care, and domestic technology were steadily undermined. Home economics was shifted toward the education of "trained" servants or "minus-help wives"; child care was left as a private burden for the mother; domestic technology was developed on the private rather than community scale; men were exempt from any chores at all; and the employed mother was counseled to accept two jobs, one at the office or factory and another at home; the career woman was counseled against motherhood. The "winners" of this contest had been selected in such a way as to show that women could not win at all. The material feminist demand for economic independence for women and socialized domestic work, a demand advanced by feminists since the 1840s, was about to disappear from public view.

Frederick's grand schemes and those of the industrialists and marketing experts she worked for had to wait until a decade and a half of depression and war had passed, but the post–World War II domestic retreat was based on just the arguments she had made. What Betty Friedan called the feminine mystique and Peter Filene described more accurately as a "domestic mystique" shrouded the late forties, fifties, and sixties: men thought of themselves as home "owners" and women as home "managers" in tens of millions of suburban tract houses, financed with V.A. mortgages and furnished on easy credit terms. When a new generation of feminists appeared, most of them the children of those families, they had one powerful demand to make, an end to the sexual division of domestic labor. But the new feminists, who tried to share child care and housework with men, did not understand the history behind the domestic environments they inhabited.

They took for granted three-bedroom houses with kitchens full of appliances; they knew nothing of earlier generations of feminists' opposition to the isolated home. They knew nothing about the Red Scare; they had never heard of Alexandra Kollontai, or Melusina Fay Peirce, or even Charlotte Perkins Gilman. But in every newspaper, TV commercial, and women's magazine they confronted Mrs. Consumer.

Housework? he said, Housework? *Oh my god how trivial can you get. A paper on housework.*
— Husband of feminist theoretician, 1970

Is our housekeeping sacred and honorable? Does it raise and inspire us, or does it cripple us?
— Ralph Waldo Emerson

Women versus Men

In the 1960s and 1970s, millions of women in America challenged domestic conventions within their own homes, protesting the sexual division of household labor and demanding that men participate in "woman's work."

"When's dinner?" inquired a hungry man.

"Whenever you fix it," might have been the tart reply.

"Honey, bring some milk for the coffee."

"It's in the refrigerator."

"Sweetheart, don't you think the bathtub needs scrubbing?"

"Here's the cleanser."

"Dear, why is Susie crying?"

"I don't know and I'm late for my meeting. I'll be back about eleven."

Fired by articles like Pat Mainardi's call to action, "The Politics of Housework," and supported by the other members of small consciousness-raising groups, women, especially middle-class women in their twenties and thirties, revolted against traditional domestic roles.[1] Some of them won their lovers and husbands over to the cause. After all, what man wanted to be called a "pig" whose role was to get the house dirty and never clean it up?

Guilty men began doing a share of the shopping, the child care, and the cooking necessary to keep newly "liberated" households running. Sons were trained to do domestic chores, daughters taught to resist them. Parents scrutinized children's literature and television programs for too many illustrations of mothers in aprons, which might refute the new images of shared domesticity. Popular magazines published marriage contracts which specified the distribution of domestic responsibilities between husband and wife and reported the battles for "fifty-fifty" sharing in endless detail.[2] Major newspapers gave "lifestyle" coverage to rural and urban communes where new roles were tried and to couples with unusual household arrangements. Home life was forever changed, some feminists thought. They believed that they had reversed the gender discrimination of centuries by forcing and cajoling men into sharing domestic work with them.

Yet the changes in home life were more complex. Some men began sharing domestic work. Others deserted their families or got divorced. Although the two-worker couple became the predominant family type, the single-parent family became the fastest increasing family type, followed by the adult living alone. Reported incidents of violence against women, including wife-battering and rape, increased. Incest began to be discussed as a common family problem, along with male alcoholism and female dependence on tranquilizers and other drugs. If partriarchal control of home life was breaking down in the 1970s, it was not happening without terrible struggle.

Women versus Women

Then the pie and cake moms began marching, ranks of smiling women carrying homemade pies and cakes, wearing pastel dresses, frilly aprons, and high-heeled shoes, who headed up the steps of state legislatures all over the country. In the spring of 1976 these pie and cake brigades, organized by anti-feminist Phyllis Schlafly, visited male lawmakers to protest the Equal Rights Amendment. Bringing home-cooked foods to these men was part of Schlafly's campaign. The demonstrators were as well organized and as well disciplined as the women of their grandmothers' generation who had joined antisuffrage groups such as the Women Patriots. Like their predecessors, they had financing from powerful corporate interests; like them, they voiced their politics in sentimental slogans about motherhood and the sanctity of home, slogans Catharine Beecher could have written. With their fresh makeup, neat house dresses, and bouffant hairdos ready for the TV cameras, these women were trying to look like the children's book pictures of Mom that the feminists couldn't stand. Their slogans about home rejected the new feminist consciousness and opposed the new male domestic roles. These women saw household work as nurturing work, and young feminists had underestimated their commitment to home life and woman's sphere.

The young feminists' image of the world was very much based on their own experience. They didn't know much about the physically grueling domestic work their great grandmothers had done, and they didn't understand their mothers' concern with well-equipped kitchens. Their childhood and adolescent memories of the feminine mystique, which had enveloped their mothers in suburban domestic isolation, persuaded them that escaping claustrophobic domestic work themselves was the only answer. "Out of the House," the title of an exhibition by feminist artists in 1978, was their slogan.

To some extent demographic and economic history seemed to support them. Women's participation in the paid labor force had been rising for over a century until women comprised 41 percent of paid workers in 1978. Married women's and mothers' participation had climbed even faster. While in 1890 only one married woman in twenty had worked for wages, by the mid 1970s, one out of two did so. Among the mothers of school age children, over half were employed; one third of the mothers of preschoolers were employed. Seven out of ten employed women worked full time.[3]

For most of these working women, the slogan "Out of the House" implied new problems within the house. Those unusual women who were well educated and assertive, who held well-paying but demanding jobs as executives, doctors, lawyers, architects, stockbrokers, and professors, had the greatest number of options for changes in their domestic lives. If they were single, they could forgo marriage, children, and housework and live for their careers, eating restaurant meals and entertaining rarely. If they married, they could perhaps persuade equally career-minded husbands to join them in such choices. "We are both so liberated," explained one husband who didn't like cleaning, "the house is a mess."

The career woman could also try to deal with husband and children, job and house all at once. *Superwoman* was the title of one manual of advice for such women, many of whom suffered mental and physical exhaustion and then began the search for a domestic surrogate.[4] Articles began to tell "Out of the House" women how to find the perfect housekeeper, maid, or nanny. In contrast to their employers, the domestic surrogates were almost always poor women who worked because of financial necessity. Some were recent immigrants, some were minority women, some were students.

Indeed, most women in the labor force were there from necessity rather than choice: secretaries, sales clerks, bookkeepers, elementary school teachers, typists, waitresses, sewers and stitchers, nurses, cashiers, and domestic servants. These were traditionally stereotyped as female jobs, often low paying and repetitious, often involving some form of traditional "woman's work" such as serving food, caring for the sick, or sewing. Women's annual earnings from full-time, year-round work averaged only about three-fifths of men's earnings. In the late 1970s, the earnings gap between men and women was steadily increasing.[5] Many employed women preferred home life to low-paid factory or office work and claimed that their second, unpaid jobs as homemakers meant much more to them than their paid work, which was necessary to meet their bills.

Both low-paid women workers and full-time housewives were exasperated with well-educated feminists who had no idea what an assembly line was like but complained about the drudgery of housework. They were infuriated with government experts who classified the skill levels of thirty thousand jobs in the *Dictionary of Occupational Titles* and rated foster mothers as less skilled than stable grooms; nursery school teachers and child care attendants as equal to parking lot attendants; practical nurses as less skilled than poultry farmhands, and homemakers as less skilled than dog pound attendants.[6] They liked housework; they were proud to stay home and do it. Don't call housework and child care mindless drudgery, call it highly skilled work and reward the worker, they said. This meant roses on Mother's Day, taking charge of a husband's paycheck, and perhaps demonstrating against the ERA.

Women versus the State

One more position evolved, that domestic work deserved not roses but wages, paid by the government.[7] In some ways this was a renewal of earlier campaigns for maternity benefits and welfare rights. Once all wives and mothers were paid wages the stigma attached to being a mother on welfare would end. Even women who thought that paid work and housework were two different worlds, who didn't care about wages while they were married, demanded that state protection be extended to "displaced homemakers," separated or divorced women and widows who technically did

not qualify for their spouses' alimony, Social Security, or pension payments. They
argued that they had earned these payments doing housework.

Contemporary Feminism and Material Feminism

By the late 1970s, the feminist movement
as a whole in the United States had no
clear policy on women's unpaid domestic
work performed in the private home.
There were two conflicting positions on domestic life with feminist activists' support:
male sharing of housework and "wages for
housework." This made it possible for antifeminists mobilized against the ERA, who
were largely housewives and mothers, to
believe that by attacking feminism they
were protecting the home. Yet feminists
and antifeminists had more in common
than they realized. Both feminists and
antifeminists accepted the spatial design of
the isolated home, which required an inor-
dinate amount of human time and energy
to sustain, as an inevitable part of domestic
life. Only a few activists who staffed ref-
uges for battered women and their children
had begun to question traditional housing
design.

The material feminist critique of the
home as an isolated domestic workplace
was so far forgotten that caring for young
children, making two or three meals per
day, doing the laundry, cleaning the rugs,
furniture, curtains, floors, doing the shopping, most feminists (and cooperative husbands) never asked themselves why they
were doing these tasks in isolation. Fifty

14.1 Potholder, 1977

14.2 Aerial view, suburban tract houses, Long
Island, New York, 1967.

million small homes sat on the landscape across the United States (14.2). Most of the time men and women viewed these "modern," appliance-filled houses, with their living rooms, kitchens, dining rooms, bedrooms, and multiple baths, as perfectly natural domestic environments. If feminist women negotiated with men about whose turn it was to do some chore, they negotiated in terms of time. Your task or mine? The issue of household space and its design was almost totally ignored. They would have been taken aback to hear their houses described as perfect symbols of Victorian rather than modern womanhood, requiring a paradoxical combination of self-sacrifice and economic consumption. They would have been surprised to learn that earlier generations of feminists would have described these same houses as enemy outposts in the domestic revolution.

The material feminist tradition had offered two insights into women's oppression: a spatial critique of the home as an isolated domestic workplace, and an economic critique of unpaid household work. Contemporary feminists have lost the first insight, and instead added a social critique of the sexual division of labor, which attacked the concepts of women's sphere and man's world. While this advance is important, it has not brought success, because contemporary feminists have overlooked the private home as a spatial component of their economic oppression in the same way that material feminists overlooked the sexual division of labor as a social component. To attack the exploitation of women's

unpaid household labor successfully, it is essential to remove not only the idea of woman's sphere but its spatial embodiment, the isolated home.

At their most coherent level, earlier agitators for the "grand domestic revolution" offered programs that united housewives and employed women by stressing that both performed socially necessary, skilled work that deserved fair compensation. They established themselves as champions of women and the family through their demands for socialized domestic work and nurturing neighborhoods as improvements of woman's sphere. Many current feminist campaigns tend to divide housewives and employed women; they appear to attack women's sphere, not extend it. Employed women do not encourage each other to think of themselves as housewives, although they usually have a second, unpaid job at home. Housewives sometimes oppose the employment of women as harmful to woman's sphere and social reproduction, although in 1970 the average American woman could expect to spend 22.9 years of her life in the paid labor force. Clearly a more synthetic feminist organizing strategy is needed which will underscore the common concerns of all women, a new strategy which will make it clear that employed women and housewives have an overwhelming mutual interest in the creation of homelike neighborhoods which do not separate home and work as capitalism has done.[8]

Such a strategy would need to incorporate all the insights material feminism and contemporary feminism have offered. The home is a workplace, needing redesign, but it does not have to inspire flight. Housewives are unpaid workers, needing respect and remuneration, but they do not need pity. And men are potential workers in domestic situations who must do their share.

Patriarchy and Woman's Sphere

Would acceptance of men as potential domestic workers and recovery of the spatial critique of the home be a sufficient basis for a renewed campaign to create homelike, feminist neighborhoods? Why did the material feminists' experiments fail so often, if their orientation was sensible?

Material feminism was at once private and public, familial and social, personal and political. Many of the problems material feminists did not solve can be explained by the oppressiveness of women's sphere as a concept defining female and male behavior in terms of private and public life in the late nineteenth and early twentieth centuries. The concept of woman's sphere was a product of both patriarchy and industrial capitalism. As Eli Zaretsky has noted, "Just as capitalist development gave rise to the idea of the family as a separable realm from the economy, so it created a 'separate' sphere of personal life, seemingly divorced from the mode of production." [9] Thus capitalism incorporated the patriarchal home, which antedated it. What Zaretsky calls the separate sphere of personal life was woman's sphere, and it imprisoned even those women who fought against it, because it was extremely

difficult for them to articulate their domestic grievances as part of public, political life. The most powerful, continuous agitation for material feminism consisted of angry conversations in thousands of domestic workplaces — kitchens. Women remembered their mothers and grandmothers, worn out with domestic chores and child raising, warning them not to let men exploit their labor in the same way. Transferring these conversations into a more public setting was impeded by both the economic and political bounds of woman's sphere.

For ordinary housewives the first obstacle to entering public life was the burden of work in woman's sphere. Reformers who perceived the political importance of domestic issues were often the same women whose domestic responsibilities left them little time for outside activities. So women who have published one or two articles promoting socialized domestic work often seem to disappear from public life, apparently discouraged or defeated. Yet one finds their granddaughters, their nieces, their best friends, or their cousins taking up the same crusade. Or perhaps, some years later, in another city, the same woman appears again to make a similar feminist argument. She may have a different, married name, and the intellectual history makes no sense at all, unless one attributes the delays to domestic reasons, caused by caring for husband, children, relatives, or moving to a new place because of a husband's job. Through the breaks in public life, domestic life and domestic rebellion went on.

Woman's sphere also restrained women's political work because it embodied conventions of womanly or morally respectable behavior which restricted women from public, political life. Material feminists always faced insinuations that a commitment to free love or immoral sexual behavior was behind any attempt to alter women's traditional household roles and responsibilities. They were called "loose women" and told that the apartment hotel was "no place for a lady." As a result many believers in material feminism, even prominent political activists as diverse as the Republican Harriet Taylor Upton and the Communist Ella Reeve Bloor, did not debate domestic issues in public, although they debated votes or trade unions.[10] Instead many suffragists and socialist women held forth on domestic reform in private to their daughters, nieces, granddaughters, and grand-nieces. When they wrote on domestic issues, they preferred to write for the woman's page of socialist journals or for women's periodicals, where they expected to find a sympathetic, all-female audience.

Even in these publications, there was much concern for propriety. Since a certain notoriety was attached to these ideas, and to women whose names appeared in print, some reformers wrote anonymously or used pseudonyms. Others simply avoided names altogether in public speeches and articles, by referring to earlier reformers as "a lady-cooperator," or "an enterprising woman from Ohio," without using the leader's name.

Patriarchal definitions of woman's sphere thus inhibited women's open political work on domestic issues before mixed audiences, as well as the continuity of their political work. The ideology of woman's sphere also limited their own self-conscious political activity. Material feminists working on domestic issues lacked a high degree of political self-awareness about their own roles as political organizers and those of their colleagues. They often failed to build political support for their ideas beyond woman's sphere because they did not always treat each other as political workers. Often they perceived themselves or other feminists as housewives concerned with improving the home. Charlotte Perkins Gilman was especially careless in this respect, reserving her rare footnotes or acknowledgments for men in the academic world of sociology rather than for other feminist women whose subject of research was the home. Except for Ethel Puffer Howes, who also enjoyed a successful academic career as a philosopher, no advocate of socialized domestic work adequately acknowledged her intellectual and political debts to her predecessors or her contemporaries.

There were some benefits from the close, female relationships characteristic of woman's sphere, which were fostered to some extent by women's isolation from men and from public life, and transferred to this political tradition. Older women were generous mentors for younger ones. Mary Peabody Mann worked with Melusina Peirce at the start of her career and brought her knowledge of many reform circles; Helen Campbell, an experienced journalist and home economist, worked with young Charlotte Perkins Gilman; Alice Peloubet Norton, a cooking teacher and home economist, a former protégée of Ellen Richards, worked with Ethel Puffer Howes, to make sure her experiment included a successful demonstration kitchen. So there was support, as older women became political advisors to the younger ones, but it was often confused with mothering, especially when the support that women involved in domestic reform were able to give each other went beyond a mentor relationship into shared housekeeping.

Susan B. Anthony went to stay with Elizabeth Cady Stanton's family when Stanton said, "Come here and I will do what I can to help you with your address, if you will hold the baby and make the pudding." [11] Helen Campbell kept house for Gilman and her family when Gilman was writing. Ellen Richards showed the settlement workers at Hull-House how a public kitchen could change their own domestic lives, as well as their clients'. In many cases it was easier for young women reformers to acknowledge domestic assistance than to acknowledge intellectual and political assistance. Gilman saw Campbell as "my adopted mother," rather than her political mentor, and this reflects the complex political character of the domestic sphere as much as the individuals' personalities. Domestic support was political support, but this was not always obvious, even to political leaders.

Material feminists identified each other as housekeepers and mothers reforming woman's sphere together. This contributed to their tendency to overlook or reject men as potential domestic workers. One comes across the occasional heretic, such as Lillie D. White, who wrote in *The Lucifer* in 1893: "Why is it necessarily any more a woman's place to wash dishes, scrub floors, make beds, etc., than it is a man's? Why not teach our boys to do all these things as well as our girls?" [12] Yet among all the vehement nineteenth century feminists only a handful ever suggested that men do housework, or that boys and girls be trained equally in domestic skills. This is the ultimate proof of the power of woman's sphere as a concept shaping political consciousness. Except for occasional participation by men in financial matters such as buying provisions wholesale, doing accounts, drawing up menus, or, possibly, discussing the care of children, most material feminist experiments were designed and run by women.

The exclusion of men from responsibility for domestic work — in either private or socialized forms — ensured that male displeasure was the reason most cooperative housekeeping experiments faltered after a few months or years. Men compared private domestic service with socialized work and found that private, unpaid labor was cheaper and more deferential. Housewives tended to complain that men did not stand for their wives' cooperating because they were no longer able to have their personal preferences catered to in terms of foods and meal schedules. Indeed, some men objected not to the product but to the process, if household work was no longer done by their wives with their own hands. Said one husband: "What! *My* wife 'cooperate' to make other men comfortable. No indeed!" Although some home economists believed that housewives lacked the skills and the "goodness" for cooperative ventures, the editors of the *New England Kitchen Magazine* refuted this argument in 1895: "Woman's conservatism forsooth! It is man's selfishness rather, that hinders cooperative housekeeping." [13]

Those men who did not demand personal service from their wives' own hands demanded a scientific or economic efficiency incompatible with a full transformation of woman's sphere. Robert Ellis Thompson, author of *The History of the Dwelling-House and Its Future,* stated in 1914 that "the cooking of food must be taken from the house, and conducted in large cooperative kitchens, by men and not by women." Thompson regretted that the burden of cooking had been imposed on women, as a sex, because he considered food preparation "a scientific problem," and he claimed that "women have not the scientific mind." Discussing experiments in cooperative cooking, he conceded, "There is indeed, a record of failures, each of them due to the fact that the experiment was left in the hands of women." [14] Even more taxing than Thompson's assumption that women could not be scientific was other

men's demand that women create economically "efficient" or inexpensive alternatives to private housework. In a capitalist society, this could only be achieved by exploiting low-paid workers to offer the cheapest cooking, laundry, and sewing. Even then, no paid worker was cheaper than an unpaid wife.

The Market Economy and Women's Sphere

Material feminists had to deal with incompatible, simultaneous demands for womanly behavior and capitalist efficiency, neither of which they could accept if they were to create feminist, egalitarian organizations. Women can never gain their own liberation from stereotypes of gender at the expense of other women of a lower economic class or another race whom they exploit by paying them low wages to do sex-stereotyped work. Black women and white women, Yankee women and immigrant women, housewives and servants, had to break out of woman's sphere together, or else not at all. Any exceptional woman who escaped unpaid or low paid domestic work could always be sent back to woman's sphere again by men, unless the grand domestic revolution touched all women and all domestic work.

The material feminists only half understood this, not because they were "bourgeois feminists," but because patriarchy left them few choices. Reformers such as Peirce, Howland, Livermore, Richards, and Gilman grew up in households marked by real financial need. In particular, Peirce and Gilman grew up watching their mothers suffer from attempting to get by economically, and failing in health and spirits. Most of them also undertook some kind of domestic work for pay at some time in their lives. Peirce and Gilman took in boarders after their divorces; Richards occasionally "hired out" as a servant as a young woman; Livermore spent time as a governess. These reformers never forgot what it meant to be a woman who needed money, but they were unable to defy male privilege and the market economy simultaneously when they mounted their experiments. They needed workers as well as managers. They had excluded men as potential domestic workers, so this left only other women, of a lower class.

The full impact of class and gender issues showed up in Melusina Peirce's experiment in the late 1860s. When Peirce spoke of middle-class women "bossing" the laundry workers in her producers' cooperative, the conflict between women appeared in all its complexity. Peirce believed that middle-class women's economic efforts would allow the "poor, wronged workwoman throughout the world to raise her drooping head," [15] but, while she insisted on shared ownership of the cooperative, she trusted only middle-class housewives to manage it to earn the Council of Gentlemen's approval. To succeed socially Peirce had to win support from middle-class husbands. To succeed economically, she had to undersell every bakery, laundry, grocery, and restaurant in her neighborhood. Therefore her goal of implementing equal-

ity between women through the device of a producers' cooperative was compromised before she began.

Peirce might have been able to save the experiment if she had taken one of two bold courses. She might have compromised with male authority completely and satisfied the Council of Gentlemen if she had been willing to exploit the female workers as ruthlessly as contemporary capitalists. Or she could have defied the Council of Gentlemen altogether if she had been able to develop an organization whose members — former mistresses and the former servants — had agreed to go on strike together to withhold all cooked food and laundry until they forced male capitulation to their demand for pay. But the strike was not in the arsenal of Peirce or her successors, because the bonds between women of different classes were not yet firm enough to permit them to use this weapon.

Only by overcoming the class and race divisions between women can feminists ever become powerful enough to end the exploitation of women's unpaid labor. However, the material feminists who followed Peirce did not draw this conclusion from her experiment. Instead of working for more cohesive producers' cooperatives, Marie Howland and Mary Livermore advocated consumers' cooperatives, which made women's common interests less clear, although they did introduce new types of socialized work, including child care. In another tactic, Ellen Richards attempted to use the power of municipal or federal government to affect women's lives. She found that working-class men exerted more authority than municipal home economists when they discouraged their wives from patronizing her public kitchens. Then Charlotte Perkins Gilman attempted to develop the power of female capitalists to defy patriarchal conventions of domesticity. She found that only a very few professional women had the money to patronize such feminist entrepreneurs. And she found that those women who needed the services the most — such as single mothers — were the least likely to be able to pay. As a last resort, Ethel Puffer Howes attempted to utilize the new, mass circulation women's magazines and the women's colleges and professional associations to organize housewives across class lines, but she was too late to prevail against the antifeminist backlash of the 1920s.

The first lesson of material feminism is that women of all classes have to unite if they are to defeat the patriarchal assumption, expressed by individual men, that women should provide men with free, or at least very cheap, personal domestic service. The second lesson is that capitalists as a class, as well as individual men, have a strong economic interest in keeping women subordinate.

If material feminists could not create experiments which simultaneously defied patriarchal authority and defeated capitalism, it does not diminish the importance of their struggle. These women had the imagination to conceive of changing the culture, the economy, and the physical environment to support programs for workers'

control of the reproduction of society, a notable theoretical achievement. The resistance they encountered illuminates the interrelatedness of patriarchy and capitalism by revealing that male-dominated private life and corporate-dominated public life are mutually reinforcing. Not only did corporations support male home ownership, believing that "Good Homes Make Contented Workers," but they also needed "Mrs. Consumer" to purchase and maintain mass-produced homes and consumer goods and to rear a new generation of male and female children for this same way of life.

Thus the problems material feminists faced were far more complicated than those confronting male reformers who attempted to organize wage workers into trade unions during the same period. Not only did the material feminists have to deal with poorly paid domestic servants, whom the trade unions largely ignored, but unpaid domestic work performed by housewives in the private home was promoted as a social and religious duty. The extensive Red-baiting of feminists by manufacturers in the 1920s underlines the importance of the housewife, as an unpaid worker, to the structure of the capitalist economy, and the importance of the home, as an unacknowledged workplace, to the other, socialized forms of production under capitalism. Women are not only a reserve army of labor available for paid employment during economic boom periods and wartime. They are constantly performing domestic labor, and without that unpaid labor, the entire paid work force would stop functioning.

Hampered by the difficulties of attacking private domestic life as a political issue, unwilling to justify themselves as more efficient exploiters of female labor than male capitalists, the first material feminists found out how hard it would be to establish women's economic autonomy in the United States. Although they were unable to create housewives' producers cooperatives strong enough to enforce their demands for homelike neighborhoods, they pointed the way to economic and social equality for women.

Material feminists were dramatic propagandists, feminists who used new approaches to architecture and urban design to illustrate new ideals of equality through their proposals for community kitchens, laundries, dining halls, kitchenless houses, and feminist cities. The material feminists' unrealized plans provide glimpses of daily life in a socialist, feminist world we have not yet seen. Beyond their architectual outlines the kitchenless houses and community kitchens transmit important messages about housing, women, and work. If they could be constructed today, they might appear to be creations of the future, as much as experiments from the past, for environmental changes are a necessary condition for ending the exploitation of women's labor in all societies.

In addition to their design proposals, the community organizations developed by material feminists also have a relevance to political practice today. As Eli Zaretsky has stated in his book, *Capitalism, the Family, and Personal Life,* "A socialist movement that anticipates its own role in organizing society must give weight to all forms of socially necessary labour, rather than only to the form (wage labor) that is dominant under capitalism." [16] As women and men within socialist movements everywhere reassess their theoretical perspectives in the late twentieth century, they must reevaluate the mid-nineteenth-century Marxist emphasis on organizing skilled, male, industrial workers. If one agrees with Zaretsky that the proletarian and the housewife are the two characteristic adults of contemporary capitalist society, then material feminism has an immediate relevance as a continuous political tradition addressed to ending women's unpaid domestic labor in industrial society. It offers a wealth of political experience on these issues.

Somewhere in between the isolated suburban tract and the profitable factory, material feminists envisioned workers' cooperatives performing the necessary labor involved in the reproduction of society and creating homelike, nurturing neighborhoods in the process. By attempting to define the social, economic, and spatial structure of cooperative neighborhood organizations, material feminists addressed the most crucial problem of their time, and ours. They created a positive, concrete ideal of feminist homes linked to Frances Willard's ideal of making a homelike world as a way of improving and expanding woman's sphere. This positive ideal of home enabled them to recruit feminist women for whom household work was a basic activity. In contrast, contemporary feminists who have attacked the family home have had little to offer housewives as an alternative ideal of home life, although every woman, feminist or not, has to live somewhere. As a result, many contemporary feminists' attempts to increase women's civil rights and to help women enter previously male areas of work have been cut off from woman's traditional base, the home. By abandoning a vision of feminist homes, feminists have lost ground to right-wing activists such as Phyllis Schlafly, members of the John Birch Society, and members of the Family Defense Leagues, who have been quick to seize their opportunity to capture the protection of home as a conservative, rather than a feminist, issue. There is still a great potential for mobilizing women in both advanced industrial societies and developing nations around the ideal of feminist homes and the homelike world. The home is a workplace, a place to begin to develop the theory and practice of a more egalitarian life. It is not necessary for feminists to endorse the Victorian concept of woman's sphere, but rather to accept woman's sphere as an essential, historical, material base.

Envoi

Today domestic conflicts continue, while ideals of home and neighborhood falter. Housewives are still isolated and unpaid. American corporations steadily promote commercial goods and services as profitable enterprises (14.3). Charlotte Perkins Gilman's fictional businesswoman, Viva Weatherstone, predicted that various commercial forms of domestic work would become, in capitalist society, "one of the biggest businesses on earth, if not *the* biggest," and she was correct.[17]

In Los Angeles, every morning at 8:30 a.m., the Rent-A-Maid Volkswagen bus, carrying six middle-aged black women, driven by a young, mustachioed white male in an open-necked shirt, turns the corner of Sunset Boulevard, heading for the first drop-off house. The women have been riding one hour on the freeway from East Los Angeles. Each will work until 3:00 p.m. for $25.00, scrubbing floors, doing laundry, dusting, cooking, cleaning up an affluent, white, Beverly Hills household.

A few miles away in West Los Angeles, forty people of all ages are eating McDonald's Eye Openers, ninety-nine cent breakfasts of orange juice, scrambled eggs, toast, and coffee, their faces pale in the fluorescent light. Three young single people sit alone at three separate tables, hold cigarettes, and drink coffee. They rest their elbows on the plastic trays, next to the paper plates and plastic ware, having left their expensive, individual bachelor apartments to breakfast on the way to work.

Down the street, Michael Jones, Susan Jones, and Janie Jones, ages eight, six, and five, are watching a commercial for Sugar Pops, in between cartoons and games on a children's TV show. Their parents are preparing for a day in their respective offices,

14.3 Colonel Sanders's Kentucky Fried Chicken, 1978, with advertisement showing Los Angeles outlets, 1979

while the television serves as a baby sitter. On the way to work they will drop off the dirty clothes at a new, inexpensive Chinese laundry. The freezer in the basement is stocked with TV dinners, making it unnecessary to stop at the supermarket on the way home.

Suppose Melusina Peirce, Marie Stevens Howland, Mary Livermore, Ellen Richards, Mary Hinman Abel, Caroline Hunt, Charlotte Perkins Gilman, and Ethel Puffer Howes assembled to evaluate these commercial domestic services. Peirce, I think, would see that the nonunionized women working as maids, fast-food workers, and laundry workers were exploited economically; Howland would notice the silly, brief costumes some women are forced to wear on TV or at work, which exploit them sexually; she would comment on the loneliness of the young single people; she would criticize television as a poor substitute for developmental child care. Richards and Abel would scorn the inadequate nutrition in a diet of fast food and coffee, or Sugar Pops and TV dinners. Mary Livermore and Charlotte Perkins Gilman would notice that nowhere were there any women managers. Howes might inquire why Mrs. Jones worked three-quarter time and learn that there was no after-school child care. She might also find out that Mrs. Jones' part-time job carries no health benefits or pension, and that Mrs. Jones is desperately trying to help her husband pay off a mortgage on a suburban house purchased in 1979 when Los Angeles house prices averaged $84,200.[18]

Perhaps none of them would notice the racism in the Rent-A-Maid system or the Chinese laundry; perhaps none would interrogate Mr. Jones about his domestic contributions. But surely they would be forced to remember their worst fears about industrial capitalism and its potential for affecting women's lives. "The business organizations of men," warned Livermore in 1886, "which have taken so many industrial employments from the home, wait to seize those remaining. . . . " [19]

Her prediction was as accurate as that of Mary Hinman Abel, in 1903, who believed that "we may wake up any morning to find that a mighty food company is ready to furnish anything we may call for — hot, cold, or luke-warm — at prices with which the individual household cannot compete. . . . Individual housekeepers are helpless, but in combination they have a power yet to be realized and used." [20] Perhaps Caroline Hunt would repeat her appeal to middle-class housewives to realize that the products they consumed often represented the broken lives of others, the female factory workers.[21] Mary Hinman Abel might interrupt, with a discussion question from her successful home economics textbook, *Successful Family Life on the Moderate Income:* "Suppose housewives went on a strike and refused to do the housework, what would be the effect on the family incomes? On the total amount of useful products made by the nation, or the national product?" [22] These are still the crucial questions for all those who care about feminist homes, cities, and neighborhoods.

Bibliographical Note

Extended bibliographical footnotes discuss
the secondary literature and manuscript
sources on which this work is based. The
greatest problems for the researcher lie in
the peculiar way in which academic fields,
as they are now defined, have avoided
coming to terms with domestic life and domestic work at all. This note is a brief
comment on shifting fields, rather than on
specific literature.

Analysis of that social and architectural
unit we think of as the household is
difficult without a theoretical framework
that integrates many disciplines. At the
end of the nineteenth century the founders
of the field of home economics attempted
to transcend the housewife's *cri de coeur* and
the traditional domestic economy manual
with the creation of a professional literature synthesizing many disciplines. They
defined home economics (or domestic science) as a comprehensive social and physical science encompassing sociology, economics, nutrition, sanitation, and architecture. Many significant insights were derived from the synthesis of disciplines, and
in the 1880s and 1890s scholars such as Ellen Swallow Richards of MIT developed
ecology and nutrition as applied sciences.
Nevertheless home economics became a
low-status field dominated by women.
Some of its members had encountered severe discrimination in other academic disciplines. By the 1920s, many of them had
accepted the consultancies offered by industrial corporations lobbying for a con-
sumption-oriented definition of the Ameri-

can household and woman's position within it, although some pioneers in the field did hold to unorthodox, feminist views.

Members of other academic disciplines have looked down on the pragmatic, applied field of home economics but none have dealt with household questions with marked success in the past century. Anthropologists have produced fascinating studies of the forms of dwellings and their cultural significance and have rightly insisted that no society can be adequately understood without giving home life a weight equal to public affairs. Yet the skills of anthropologists have often been directed at the domestic customs of remote peoples, although the position of a woman charged with housekeeping in a Mongolian tent or serving a meal to her husband in "the Lord's corner" of a Swiss farmhouse may have more in common with a housewife living in a New Jersey suburb than the scholar may be prepared to admit.

Sociology has not often responded to the challenges which anthropology has rejected. In the early years of sociology, such pioneers as Herbert Spencer and Lester Ward attempted sweeping analyses of the evolution of human society which included discussion of progress for women. Melusina Peirce and Charlotte Perkins Gilman called themselves "sociologists" because they saw themselves as working in this tradition. By the turn of the century, however, many specialists in sociology accepted an ideal of the Christian family and the submissive Christian wife as a "normal" human condition. While these extremely debatable assumptions about the household and woman's role in it often went unchallenged in the field of "family sociology," measurement and analysis of kin networks, childrearing, and neighborhoods in modern industrial society progressed in technical sophistication. A few researchers such as Helen Lopata, Mirra Komarovsky, and Ann Oakely have developed the sociology of housework, especially through studies of working-class housewives, but such research has not yet received the attention it warrants as a field dealing with the lives and work of one half of the population. Feminist urban sociologists such as Gerda Wekerle, Hilary Rose, and Sylvia Fava are helping the sociologists of housework to right the balance.

Economics has an even poorer record on the subject of women than sociology, for both Marxist and neoclassical economics have evolved as theoretical systems without any significant consideration of household work and its economic value. Under Richard Ely at the University of Wisconsin in the 1890s home economists were encouraged to challenge this tradition, but there was little theoretical support in the profession as a whole for their endeavors. As government programs developed in the United States they reflected the economists' bias: housewives have never been eligible for Social Security or unemployment benefits. The gross national product includes no unpaid household labor; therefore it grows when previously nonmarket activities are replaced by the commercial services of fast-food companies, dry cleaners, and child care services. What appears to be economic growth for the country and a rising standard of living is often in fact a transfer of housewives' activity into commercial activity, with a significant decline in quality in many cases.

In recent years a "new home economics" movement has attempted to take this omission into account. At the same time Marxist economists, perhaps reacting to "wages for housework" campaigns, have attempted to reconcile the "socially necessary labor" performed in the household with the emphasis on production in Marxist theory. In both cases a rather narrow literature has developed to shore up obvious gaps in existing theories, rather than attempts to develop new economic theory which deals with all human work and its value. The work of Ann Markusen is a notable exception.

Geographers have concerned themselves with the home in much the same way as applied economists. Mortgage markets are evaluated for their spatial and financial effects but rarely if ever has the private home been evaluated as a place where consumption depends upon a specific spatial organization. As feminist geographers now begin to organize, their focus is here; Marxist geographers such as David Harvey and Richard Walker are already showing the role of urban and suburban spatial systems in supporting monopoly capitalism, but they have not been particularly interested in the implications for women.

Architects, urban planners, and builders who have erected tens of millions of housing units in the past century have been, like their academic colleagues, promoters of woman's "place" in the home. While a substantial critique of the isolated home and a good many visionary plans for collective domestic services were produced in the Progressive Era, the isolated home has received relatively little sustained criticism within these fields since the 1920s. The largest amount of literature on American homes treats style rather than function as the key issue. Building costs and land costs have risen, and energy consumption is now a sincere concern, but condominiums and apartment developments designed to cut costs are not usually planned with any thought for the problems of the family where both parents are employed. In the 1920s, 1930s, and 1940s male architects, planners, and builders employed both home economists and female architects to develop models of family homes that would have broad appeal. Like their colleagues in home economics who worked as consultants for industrial corporations manufacturing home appliances, these professional women often chose to embellish the stereotype of the stay-at-home wife rather than destroy it. Only very recently has a feminist architectural historian, Gwendolyn Wright, begun to analyze the history of single family housing designed to reinforce stereotyped domestic roles for women.

Social historians, including specialists in the history of women, have led all scholars in the serious analysis of family life and household work. Histories of childhood and womanhood have pointed out the historical context of age and gender. Biographies of domestic reformers have illuminated the intricacies of domestic ideology. Historical studies of housework are getting more exact all the time. Economic historians, as well as historians of education and historians of technology, have begun to scrutinize the home and to produce some very broad conclusions about American society: Heidi Hartmann, Stuart Ewen, Barbara Ehrenreich and Deirdre English, Susan Strasser, and Ruth Schwartz Cowan are all making very significant contributions to knowledge about the corporate world and its historical manipulation of the housewife.

While today there is a ferment of scholarly activity concerning the American home and the women, men, and children within it, much research continues to incorporate sexist assumptions and domestic stereotypes which have long hampered scholars' perceptions of women and the home. American scholars still need an objective anthropology, sociology, economics, geography, architecture, and history of women and children before anyone will be able to say what American domestic life has been, or could be, all about.

Notes

Chapter 1

1

I am using Linda Gordon's definition of "feminist" as "sharing in an impulse to increase the power and autonomy of women in their families, communities, and/or society." As she notes, the nineteenth-century terms, "the woman movement," and "advancing" the position of woman, are more exact, but have no convenient adjectives attached. *Woman's Body, Woman's Right: A Social History of Birth Control in America* (Harmondsworth, England: Penguin Books, 1977), xiv.

2

A "grand domestic revolution," Stephen Pearl Andrews, *The Baby World,* 1855, reprinted in *Woodhull and Claflin's Weekly,* 3 (June 8, 1871), 10, and 3 (October 28, 1871), 12. Other phrases were also popular: "grand cooking establishments," Caroline Howard Gilman (writing under the pseudonym Clarissa Packard), *Recollections of a Housekeeper* (New York: Harper, 1834); "eating houses," Jane Sophia Appleton, "Sequel to the Vision of Bangor," in Jane Sophia Appleton and Cornelia Crosby Barrett, eds., *Voices from the Kenduskeag* (Bangor, Maine: D. Bugbee, 1848); "cooperative housekeeping," Melusina Fay Peirce, "Cooperative Housekeeping I," *Atlantic Monthly,* 22 (November 1868), 513–524; "socialization of primitive domestic industries," Feminist Alliance, as reported in "Feminists Debate Plans for a House," *New York Times,* April 22, 1914; "the big socialized kitchen," Anita C. Block, "Woman's Sphere," editorial, *New York Call,* July 20, 1913, 15; "coordination of women's interests," Ethel Puffer Howes, 1925 (name of research institute at Smith College).

3

The general term *to socialize domestic work* will be used throughout the book to describe various proposals with one underlying aim: to make private domestic work social labor. In the popular usage of American psychology, individuals are often said to be "socialized" or made to conform to societal expectations and norms, but I will use "socialize" in its original sense, to refer to the process of reorganizing work to suit the common needs of a social group. Socialized labor does not imply socialism; whether it is a capitalist or so-cialist enterprise depends on the economic rela-tionship of capital and labor.

None of these reformers was interested in communal housekeeping, a term I reserve to de-scribe rural and urban experimental communi-ties where four or more members, unrelated by blood, lived as one large family. They sought in-stead to retain the family, and to preserve pri-vate family living quarters, while at the same time reorganizing the economic and environ-mental basis of "woman's" work to make it so-cial rather than personal labor.

4
Carl N. Degler, in his introduction to the 1966 edition of Gilman's *Women and Economics,* men-tions no political practice (New York: Harper and Row, 1966), vi–xxxv, nor does William L. O'Neill's introduction to Gilman's *The Home: Its Work and Influence* (Urbana: University of Illinois Press, 1972). Degler's "Revolution without Ideol-ogy," *Daedalus* 93 (Spring 1964), 653–670, and his *At Odds: Women and the Family in America from the Revolution to the Present* (New York: Oxford, 1979) wrongly bemoan feminists' "failure" to generate ideology. William L. O'Neill, in *Every-one Was Brave: A History of Feminism in America* (1969; New York: Quadrangle, 1971), called feminist thought on domestic issues "weak and evasive" (p. 358) but knew very little of the writing.

5
"Social feminists" is a term developed by O'Neill, *Everyone Was Brave,* p. x: "I have found it useful to distinguish between those who were chiefly interested in women's rights (whom I call hard core or extreme feminists), and the social feminists who, while believing in women's rights, generally subordinated them to broad social re-forms they thought more urgent." These terms imply that suffragists were extremists, a false po-sition O'Neill then exploits to argue that femi-nists had no clear ideology. J. Stanley Lemons in *The Woman Citizen: Social Feminism in the 1920s* (Urbana: University of Illinois Press, 1973), car-ries on this term but writes from a more objec-tive position, and does not, for example, indulge in O'Neill's obnoxious habit of deciding whether feminists were "normal" or not (p. 142).

The term "domestic feminism" was intro-duced by Daniel Scott Smith in "Family Limita-tion, Sexual Control, and Domestic Feminism in Victorian America," *Clio's Consciousness Raised: New Perspectives on the History of Women,* ed. Mary Hartman and Lois W. Banner (New York: Har-per Colophon Books, 1974), 119–136. Smith pointed to very real gains made by women within the family, especially "sexual control of the husband by the wife" (p. 123) arguing, ". . . domestic feminism viewed woman as a person in the context of relationships with others. By defining the family as a community, this ideology allowed women to engage in some-thing of a critique of male, materialistic, market society and simultaneously proceed to seize power within the family" (p. 132). This "domes-tic feminism" he sharply distinguished from the "public feminism" of Stanton and Gilman (p. 131). Stanton, however, was a leading advocate of "voluntary motherhood" and Gilman of so-cialized domestic work.

6
Frances Willard, quoted in Sheila Rothman, *Woman's Proper Place: A History of Changing Ideals and Practices, 1870 to the Present* (New York: Basic Books, 1978), 67.

7
Ida Husted Harper, *The Life and Work of Susan B. Anthony,* 2 vols. (Indianapolis: Bowen Merrill, 1899), I, 134. See also Mrs. Goodrich Willard's "Bill of Rights of Woman," *The Revolution* 7 (March 16, 1871), 177–178, which demands edu-cation, votes, homes, child custody, and wages for women because of their roles as mothers and wives.

8
Aileen S. Kraditor, *Up from the Pedestal, Selected Writings in the History of American Feminism* (Chi-cago: Quadrangle, 1968), 8.

9
Aileen S. Kraditor, *The Ideas of the Woman Suf-frage Movement, 1890–1920* (1965; Garden City, New York: Doubleday-Anchor, 1971), 5.

10
Degler, "Introduction," xix; Kraditor, *Ideas,* 99.

11

For a discussion of Myrdal's work with Sven Markelius, see Sven Markelius, "Kollektivhuset som bostadsform," *Form Svenska Slöjdföreningens Tidskrift Areang* 31 (1935), 101–128; Lily Braun debated these issues with Clara Zetkin in the Social Democratic party in Germany and was criticized for her heretical thinking about the "one-kitchen house," discussed in her *Frauenarbeit und Hauswirtschaft,* Berlin, 1901. Engels's position appears in *The Origin of the Family, Private Property, and the State* (1884; Moscow: Progress Publishers, 1977), 74; Lenin's in *The Emancipation of Women* (New York: International Publishers, 1975), 69.

For a critical review of some past and current debates on women's work, see Ellen Malos, "Housework and the Politics of Women's Liberation," *Socialist Review* 37 (January–February 1978), 41–71, and M. Jane Slaughter, "Socialism and Feminism," *Marxist Perspectives,* 7 (Fall 1979). Also useful is the section entitled "Just a Housewife" in Gerda Lerner, *The Female Experience: An American Documentary* (Indianapolis: Bobbs-Merrill Co., 1977), 108–147.

12

Friedrich Engels, *The Origin of the Family, Private Property, and the State* (1884; Moscow: Progress Publishers, 1977), 74.

13

C. B. Purdom, *The Garden City* (London: J. M. Dent, 1913), 98.

14

Sam Bass Warner, Jr., *The Urban Wilderness: A History of the American City* (New York: Harper and Row, 1972); *The Private City: Philadelphia in Three Periods of Its Growth* (Philadelphia: University of Pennsylvania Press, 1968); *Streetcar Suburbs: The Process of Growth in Boston, 1870–1900* (New York: Atheneum, 1971). David M. Gordon, "Capitalist Development and the History of American Cities," in William K. Tabb and Larry Sawyers, eds., *Marxism and the Metropolis: New Perspectives in Urban Political Economy* (New York: Oxford University Press, 1978), 25–63.

15

Frederick Law Olmsted, *Public Parks and the Enlargement of Towns,* speech given to the American Social Science Association (Cambridge, Mass., Riverside Press, 1870), 7–9.

16

Susan T. Kleinberg, "Technology and Women's Work: The Lives of Working Class Women in Pittsburgh, 1870–1900," *Labor History,* 17 (Winter 1976), 58–72.

17

August Bebel, author of *Woman Under Socialism,* tr. Daniel De Leon (1883; New York: Schocken, 1971), was, with Engels, the most popular of the theorists in Europe.

18

Siegfried Giedion, *Mechanization Takes Command: A Contribution to Anonymous History* (1948; New York: Norton, 1969), describes the "mechanization of the household" as a process resulting from numerous inventions, all freeing women from drudgery. He mentions that large-scale domestic technology preceded small devices but assumes that women preferred the small-scale devices to be used at home. Other writers, notably Kleinberg, "Technology and Women's Work"; Susan May Strasser, "Never Done: The Ideology and Technology of Household Work, 1850–1930," Ph.D. dissertation, State University of New York, Stony Brook, 1977; and Ruth Schwartz Cowan, "The 'Industrial Revolution' in the Home: Household Technology and Social Change in the 20th Century," *Technology and Culture,* 17 (January 1976), 1–23, discuss the slow diffusion of various inventions. Both Strasser and Cowan have books in progress which should define women's experience of domestic technology much more exactly. See Heidi Hartmann, "Capitalism and Women's Work in the Home, 1800–1930," unpublished Ph.D. dissertation, Department of Economics, New School for Social Research, 1975, for a detailed study of laundry technology, as well as an analysis of the household. There are also two rather brief surveys, William D. Andrews and Deborah C. Andrews, "Technology and the Housewife in Nineteenth Century America," *Women's Studies,* 2 (1974), 309–328, and Anthony N. B. Garvan, "Effects of Technology on Domestic Life, 1830-1880," in *Technology in Western Civilization,* I, ed. Melvin Kranzberg and Carroll Pursell, Jr. (New York: Oxford University Press, 1967), 546–559.

19

Nancy F. Cott, *The Bonds of Womanhood: "Woman's Sphere" in New England, 1780–1835* (New Haven: Yale University Press, 1977), 98. On "woman's sphere" as inseparable from the rest of the society, see also the excellent analyses by Kathryn Kish Sklar, *Catharine Beecher, A Study in American Domesticity* (New Haven: Yale University Press, 1973), and Leonore Davidoff, "The Separation of Home and Work? Landladies and Lodgers in Nineteenth and Twentieth Century England," in Sandra Burman, ed., *Women's Work: Historical, Legal, and Political Perspectives* (London: Croom Helm, 1979); and Leonore Davidoff, "The Rationalization of Housework," in D. Barker and S. Allen, eds., *Dependence and Exploitation in Work and Marriage* (London: Longman, 1976).

20

Quoted in Cott, *The Bonds of Womanhood*, p. 68.

21

Strasser, "Never Done," 72–73. Another excellent discussion of work is Laurel Thatcher Ulrich, " 'A Friendly Neighbor': Social Dimensions of Housework in Northern Colonial New England," paper read at the 1978 Berkshire Conference, Mount Holyoke College.

22

Voltairine de Cleyre, speech to a labor church in Bradford, England, reported in *The Adult: The Journal of Sex* 1 (January 1898), 6; Helen Campbell, *Household Economics: A Course of Lectures in the School of Economics at the University of Wisconsin* (New York and London: G. P. Putnam's Sons, 1896), 59.

23

Gilman, *The Home*, 84.

24

Peirce, "Cooperative Housekeeping II," *Atlantic Monthly* 22 (December 1868), 684.

25

Marie A. Brown, "The Pecuniary Independence of Wives," *The Revolution* 3 (June 10, 1869), 355.

26

Zona Gale, "Shall the Kitchen in Our Home Go?" *Ladies' Home Journal* 36 (March 1919), 35ff; Ada May Krecker, "The Passing of the Family," *Mother Earth* 7 (October 1912), 260–261.

27

David M. Katzman, *Seven Days A Week, Women and Domestic Service in Industrializing America* (New York: Oxford, 1978). On servants see also Theresa M. McBride, *The Domestic Revolution: The Modernization of Household Service in England and France 1820–1920* (New York: Holmes and Meier, 1976), and Susan Strasser, "Mistress and Maid," *Marxist Perspectives*, 4 (Winter 1978), 52–67.

28

One of the most perceptive discussions of domestic labor appears in Rachel Campbell, *The Prodigal Daughter* (Grass Valley, Calif.: published by the author, 1885). This is a pamphlet on prostitution.

29

Gordon, "Capitalist Development," 49–55.

30

Industrial Housing Associates, *Good Homes Make Contented Workers* (Philadelphia: Industrial Housing Associates, 1919); Barbara Ehrenreich and Deirdre English, *For Her Own Good: 150 Years of the Experts' Advice to Women* (Garden City: Doubleday, 1978), 134; Richard Walker, "Suburbanization in Passage," unpublished draft paper, University of California, Berkeley, Department of Geography, 1977; Stuart Ewen, *Captains of Consciousness: Advertising and the Social Roots of the Consumer Culture* (New York: McGraw-Hill, 1976).

31

Two recent books by architectural historians trace the history of single-family dwellings and underscore their symbolic importance: Gwendolyn Wright, *Moralism and the Model Home: Domestic Architecture and Cultural Conflict in Chicago, 1873–1913* (Chicago: University of Chicago Press, 1980), and David Handlin, *The American Home: Architecture and Society 1815–1915* (Boston: Little Brown, 1979). Wright's book deals with the single-family home and its supporters very effectively but she tends to ignore the numerous collective options posed in the same era by such figures as Frances Willard or Henry Hudson Holly. Handlin surveys U.S. housing, but without much knowledge of the substantial literature on women's history, he constructs a male-oriented view of the home as cultural artifact.

He does deal with cooperative housekeeping, although he disconnects it from its communitarian socialist roots and incorrectly states that Melusina Peirce's Cambridge Cooperative Housekeeping Society was the most ambitious experiment ever mounted (p. 297).

32

For an example of Red-baiting, see the 1926 address by the president of the National Association of Manufacturers, John Edgerton, reprinted in Judith Papachristou, *Women Together, A History in Documents of the Women's Movement in the United States* (New York: Knopf, 1976), 201, which echoes the moralism of Rose Terry Cooke, "Is Housekeeping a Failure?" *North American Review* (February 1889), 249.

33

Ruth Schwartz Cowan has reported that a West Coast utility company sold small electric appliances very cheaply to subscribers in order to increase the demand for electricity at midday when lights were not necessary. She has also noted that in the 1920s General Electric's most economical refrigerator was abandoned in favor of one which had a lower initial cost but used more electricity, in order to increase demand for municipal electrical generating equipment sold by the same company. Both examples were discussed in a presentation she gave the MIT Seminar on Technology and Culture, November 1977.

34

On advertising see Ewen, *Captains of Consciousness,* and Ruth Schwartz Cowan, "Two Washes in the Morning and a Bridge Party at Night: The American Housewife Between the Wars," *Women's Studies,* 3 (1976), 147–172.

35

Survey of AFL-CIO Members' Housing 1975 (Washington, D.C.: AFL-CIO, 1975), 16.

36

Betty Friedan, *The Feminine Mystique* (1963; New York: W. W. Norton, 1974), calls the home "a comfortable concentration camp," p. 307; Peter Filene, *Him/Her/Self: Sex Roles in Modern America* (New York: Harcourt Brace Jovanovich, 1974), speaks of the "domestic mystique," p. 194, suggesting that men are victims too.

37

Joann Vanek, "Time Spent In Housework," *Scientific American* (November 1974), 116–120; Ehrenreich and English call this the "manufacture of housework," p. 127. Also see Ann Oakley, *Woman's Work: The Housewife, Past and Present* (New York: Pantheon, 1975), p. 7, for time studies.

38

Batya Weinbaum and Amy Bridges, "The Other Side of the Paycheck," *Capitalist Patriarchy and the Case for Socialist Feminism,* ed. Zillah R. Eisenstein (New York: Monthly Review Press, 1979), 199.

39

Meredith Tax, *Woman and Her Mind: The Story of Daily Life,* quoted in Eli Zaretsky, *Capitalism, The Family and Personal Life* (New York: Harper Colophon Books, 1976), 74.

40

Marilyn French, *The Woman's Room* (New York: Jove Books, 1978). One of her characters proposes a form of cooperative housekeeping as an alternative.

41

Anne S. Kasper, "Women Victimized by Valium," *New Directions for Women* 8 (Winter 1979–1980), 7.

42

Lawrence Goodwyn, *The Populist Movement: A Short History of the Agrarian Revolt in America* (Oxford: Oxford University Press, 1978), xiv–xv.

Chapter 2

1
Robert Owen, *A New View of Society; or, Essays on the Principle of the Formation of the Human Character* (London: Cadell and Davies, 1813); and, by the same author, *The Book of the New Moral World, Containing the Rational System of Society,* parts I–VII (London: E. Wilson, 1836–1845). On Owen's achievements, see John F. C. Harrison, *Quest for the New Moral World: Robert Owen and the Owenites in Britain and America* (New York: Charles Scribner's Sons, 1969); Arthur Bestor, *Backwoods Utopias: The Sectarian Origins and the Owenite Phase of Communitarian Socialism in America, 1663–1829,* 2d ed. (Philadelphia: University of Pennsylvania Press, 1970); and Margaret Steinfels, *Who's Minding the Children? The History and Politics of Day Care in America* (New York: Simon and Schuster, 1973), 35.

2
Sheila Rowbotham, *Women, Resistance and Revolution* (Harmondsworth, England: Penguin Books, 1972), 47.

3
Quoted in Rowbotham, *Women, Resistance, and Revolution,* 49. See also Barbara Taylor, "The Men Are As Bad As Their Masters . . . ," *Feminist Studies,* 5 (Spring 1979), 7–40.

4
Charles Fourier, *Théorie des quatre mouvements* (1808), quoted in Rowbotham, *Women, Resistance and Revolution,* 51; Charles Fourier, *Oeuvres complètes,* I, 131–33 (1846), trans. in Jonathan Beecher and Richard Bienvenu, eds., *The Utopian Vision of Charles Fourier* (Boston: Beacon Press, 1971).

5
Charles Fourier, *Traité d'association domestique-agricole* (1822), quoted in Beecher and Bienvenu, eds., *Utopian Vision.*

6
The Phalanx, I (February 8, 1844), 317–319, reprinted in Nancy F. Cott, *Root of Bitterness: Documents of the Social History of American Women* (New York; E. P. Dutton, 1972), 246–247.

7
Alcander Longley, quoted in *The Co-operator* (London), August 1, 1865, 87.

8
Marx Edgeworth Lazarus, *Love vs. Marriage* (1852), reprinted in Taylor Stoehr, *Free Love in America: A Documentary History* (New York: AMS Press, 1979), 85; letter from the women of Trumbull Phalanx, July 15, 1847, published in *The Harbinger,* 5 (August 7, 1847), reprinted in Cott, *Root of Bitterness,* 244.

9
Mary Antoinette Doolittle, *Autobiography of Mary Antoinette Doolittle* (New Lebanon, N.Y.: 1880). New work on Shaker women by D'Ann Campbell and other scholars should provide many more insights into their lives and roles.

10
John Humphrey Noyes, *History of American Socialisms* (1870; New York: Dover Press, 1966), 23.

11
For an extensive discussion of the ideological and architectural history of the North American Phalanx, see Dolores Hayden, *Seven American Utopias: The Architecture of Communitarian Socialism, 1790–1975* (Cambridge, Mass.: MIT Press, 1976), 148–185.

12
Ibid., 224–259.

13
John Humphrey Noyes, address on "Dedication of the New Community Mansion," *Oneida Circular* (Oneida, N.Y.), February 27, 1862, 9. Also see Hayden, *Seven American Utopias,* 186–223.

14
Barbara S. Yambura, with Eunice Bodine, *A Change and a Parting: My Story of Amana* (Ames, Iowa: Iowa State University Press, 1960), 79.

15
Oneida Circular, February 14, 1870, 380.

16
Charles Nordhoff, *The Communistic Societies of the United States* (1875; New York: Dover 1966), 401.

17
Judith Fryer, "American Eves in American Edens," *American Scholar,* 44 (Winter 1974–1975), 89. Louis J. Kern, "Ideology and Reality: Sexuality and Women's Status in the Oneida Community," *Radical History Review* 20 (Spring-Summer 1979), 180–205, explains the campaign against dolls as part of a campaign against women's "maternal instincts" in the community.

18

Beatrice Brodsky Farnsworth, "Bolshevism, the Woman Question, and Aleksandra Kollontai," *The American Historical Review,* 81 (April 1976), 292.

19

Elizabeth Cady Stanton, *Eighty Years and More: Reminiscences 1815–1897* (New York: Schocken, 1971), 134.

20

Ibid., 147.

21

The Revolution, 2 (December 10, 1868), 362; 4 (July 15, 1869), 42; 4 (July 29, 1869), 57–58; Theodore Stanton and Harriot Stanton Blatch, eds., *Elizabeth Cady Stanton As Revealed in Her Letters, Diary, and Reminiscences* (New York: Harper, 1922), II, 346.

22

D. C. Bloomer, *Life and Writings of Amelia Bloomer* (Boston: Arena Publishing Co., 1895), 273–277.

23

Charles Neilson Gattey, *The Bloomer Girls* (London: Femina, 1967), 160.

24

Jane Sophia Appleton, "Sequel to the Vision of Bangor in the Twentieth Century," in Jane Sophia Appleton and Cornelia Crosby Barrett, eds., *Voices from the Kenduskeag* (Bangor: D. Bugbee, 1848), republished in Arthur Orcutt Lewis, *American Utopias: Selected Short Fiction* (New York: Arno Press, 1971), 243–265.

25

Appleton, "Sequel to the Vision of Bangor," 253–255.

26

Ibid., 256–257.

27

Ibid., 258.

28

Ibid., 255–256.

29

Edward Kent, "A Vision of Bangor in the Twentieth Century," in Lewis, *American Utopias,* 59–73.

Chapter 3

1

Kathryn Kish Sklar, *Catharine Beecher: A Study in American Domesticity* (New Haven: Yale University Press, 1973), 153. See also chapter 1, note 5, for a definition of domestic feminism.

2

Ibid., 153; Catharine E. Beecher and Harriet Beecher Stowe, *The American Woman's Home* (1869; Hartford, Conn.: Stowe-Day Foundation, 1975), 13. Beecher was the most influential advocate of domestic feminism, but many other writers on domestic economy, including Caroline Howard Gilman, Lydia Maria Child, Sarah Josepha Hale, and Marion Harland, followed this line. The contradictions the domestic feminist strategies entailed are endless: the writers themselves, for example, defied their own recommendations that women not venture beyond domestic life. Ultimately the paradox of advocating women's power but limiting it to household affairs was one these authors passed on to the home economists, or domestic scientists, who attempted to make a recognized, paid professional field out of "woman's work" at the end of the nineteenth century.

3

Catharine E. Beecher, "How to Redeem Woman's Profession from Dishonor," *Harper's New Monthly Magazine,* 31 (November 1865), 710. Beecher sometimes gives instructions about the mistress-servant relationship, however, for those who have not taken her advice about eliminating servants.

4

Ibid., 712.

5

Ibid., 716.

6

Catharine E. Beecher, *A Treatise on Domestic Economy, For the Use of Young Ladies at Home and at School,* rev. ed. (New York: Harper, 1846), 172.

7

Beecher and Stowe, *American Woman's Home,* 13.

8

Ibid., 334. This is first proposed in Christopher Crowfield (Harriet Beecher Stowe), *House and Home Papers* (Boston: Fields Osgood and Co., 1865), 223.

9

Siegfried Giedion, *Mechanization Takes Command: A Contribution to Anonymous History* (1948; New York: Norton, 1969), 567–572, mentions these inventions.

10

Susan May Strasser, "Never Done: The Ideology and Technology of Household Work, 1850–1930" (Ph.D. dissertation, State University of New York, Stony Brook, 1977), 138.

11

Harriet Beecher Stowe, "A Model Village," *The Revolution,* 1 (April 2, 1868), 1.

12

First Annual Report of the Woman's Education Association, for year ending January 16, 1873 (Boston: W. L. Deland, 1873); *Woodhull and Claflin's Weekly,* 3 (July 1, 1871).

Chapter 4

1

Melusina Fay Peirce, *Cooperative Housekeeping: How Not to Do It and How to Do It, a Study in Sociology* (Boston: James R. Osgood, 1884), 181.

2

Her scientific work is mentioned in "Charles Sanders Peirce," *Dictionary of American Biography,* and Thomas S. Knight, *Charles Peirce* (New York: Washington Square Press, 1965), 24.

3

Melusina Fay Peirce, "Cooperative Housekeeping," *Atlantic Monthly,* 22 (November 1868), 519. This is the first of a series of five articles that appeared in vols. 22 and 23, November 1868 to March 1869, and were published as *Cooperative Housekeeping: Romance in Domestic Economy* (Edinburgh: John Ross and Company; London: Sampson, Low, and Son and Marston, 1870). On Peirce's contention that women enjoyed greater power in colonial days, see Mary Beth Norton, "The Myth of the Golden Age," in *Women of America, A History,* eds. Carol Ruth Berkin and Mary Beth Norton (Boston: Houghton Mifflin, 1979), 37–46.

4

Peirce, "Cooperative Housekeeping" (November 1868), 519.

5

She was guided by Eugen Richter, *Cooperative Stores* (New York: Leypoldt and Holt, 1867), in her rules for establishing an association.

6

Peirce, "Cooperative Housekeeping" (December 1868), 691.

7

Peirce, *Cooperative Housekeeping,* 87.

8

Ibid., 94–95.

9

Peirce, "Cooperative Housekeeping" (December 1868), 691.

10

Ibid. (March 1869), 293.

11

A note on definitions: in the 1880s the general term, apartment house, included both (*A*) a building consisting entirely of private apartments, as in today's common usage, and (*B*) a building (also called an apartment hotel, family hotel, or residential hotel) consisting of both private apartments and extensive common facilities such as kitchen, laundry, and dining rooms. Type *A* could include apartments of one story (also called French flats), or two stories (duplexes). It usually included kitchens in every private unit, although a "bachelor apartment house" offered units without kitchens. The private apartments in type *B,* an apartment hotel, might be hotel suites or studios (consisting of bed-sitting room, or bedroom and sitting room); semi-housekeeping suites (bedroom, sitting room, dining room); or housekeeping suites (bedroom, sitting room, dining room, and kitchen).

12
Andrew Alpern, *Apartments for the Affluent: A Historical Survey of Buildings in New York* (New York: McGraw-Hill, 1975), 1.

13
St. James Richardson, "The New Homes of New York," *Scribner's Monthly,* 8 (May 1874), 68.

14
Ibid., 69. See also "Notes and Comments," *Carpentry and Building* (December 1881), 233–234, which suggests that Haight experimented in "French Flats" at 256 and 258 West Thirty-Seventh Street as early as 1852.

15
Richardson, "New Homes of New York," 75–76.

16
John Modell and Tamara K. Hareven, "Urbanization and the Malleable Household: An Examination of Boarding and Lodging in American Families," in *Family and Kin in Urban Communities, 1700–1930,* ed. Tamara K. Hareven (New York: New Viewpoints, 1977), 165. Also see Susan May Strasser, "Never Done: The Ideology and Technology of Household Work, 1850–1930" (Ph.D. dissertation, State University of New York, Stony Brook, 1977), 197–217.

17
Melusina Fay Peirce, quoted by Nathan Meeker, in "Co-operation: Model Tenement Houses and Cooperative Housekeeping," *New York Tribune* (semiweekly), August 31, 1869.

18
Hélène Lipstadt, "Housing the Bourgeoisie," *Oppositions,* 8 (Spring 1977), 39.

19
Richardson, "New Homes," 75; Meeker, "Cooperation."

20
Philip S. Foner, *History of the Labor Movement in the United States,* vol. 1, *From Colonial Times to the Founding of the American Federation of Labor* (1947; New York, International Publishers, 1975, 183).

21
Ellen duBois, "The Search for a Constituency: The Working Women's Association," *Feminism and Suffrage: The Emergence of an Independent Women's Movement in America, 1848–1869* (Ithaca: Cornell University Press, 1978), 126–161.

22
Foner, *History of the Labor Movement,* 1, 442, 436.

23
Sylvia Wright Mitarachi, presentation on Melusina Fay Peirce, Seminar on Women and Domestic Life in the United States, MIT, December 1978. She is at work on a biography. See her "Melusina Fay Peirce: The Making of a Feminist," Radcliffe Institute Working Paper, Radcliffe College, 1978.

24
Caroline Howard Gilman (writing under the pseudonym Clarissa Packard), *Recollections of a Housekeeper* (New York: Harper Brothers, 1834), 151–155.

25
America's Working Women, ed. Rosalyn Baxandall, Linda Gordon, and Susan Reverby (New York: Vintage Books, 1976), 15.

26
Record of Peirce's talk entitled "Womanhood Suffrage," November 15, 1869, "Record Book of the Weekly Social Meetings of the New England Women's Club," 1868–1871, Schlesinger Library, Radcliffe College, unpaged.

27
"Cooperative Housekeeping," *The Revolution,* 2 (December 10, 1868), 32; 4 (July 15, 1869), 42; 4 (July 29, 1869), 57–58.

28
Loose page, contained in Cambridge Cooperative Housekeeping Society, "Record of the Proceedings of the CCHS," May 1869 to March 1870. This unpaged manuscript notebook includes printed announcements and clippings. Collection of Sylvia Wright Mitarachi.

29
The Co-operator (London), August 28, 1869, 613;
"The Future Household," *New York Times*, July
23, 1869, reprinted from the *Boston Times*, July
18, 1869.
30
"Record of the Proceedings of CCHS," unpaged. In September 1869, "Cooperative Housekeeping Association" was amended to "Cooperative Housekeeping Society." Mrs. Horace Mann,
"Co-operative Housekeeping," *Hearth and Home*,
1 (October 30, 1869), 716 and (November 20,
1869), 762–763.
31
Cambridge Cooperative Housekeeping Society,
Prospectus, October 5, 1869 (Social Ethics pamphlet collection, Widener Library, Harvard University). This announcement was reported in the
Boston Daily Evening Transcript, October 5, 1869,
2. The nine towns probably included Medford,
Massachusetts, since Peirce had told the New
England Women's Club the preceding March
that a group there was ready to undertake a
kitchen and laundry. See the March 28, 1869,
entry, "Record Book of the Weekly Social Meetings of the New England Women's Club," 1868–
1871, Schlesinger Library, Radcliffe College. In
1870 cooperative steam laundries were launched
by women in Winchester and Springfield, Massachusetts, according to Peirce, *Cooperative Housekeeping*, 95. Whether these were inspired by
Beecher and Stowe or by Peirce is unclear.
32
"Record of the Proceedings of the CCHS," unpaged. They were: President, Mrs. Nathan Shaler; Treasurer, M. F. Peirce; Directors, Mrs.
Horace Mann, Mrs. Henry Warren Paine, Mrs.
Nathaniel P. Willis, Mrs. James Fisk.
33
Ibid. This committee included Gordon McKay,
Nathan S. Shaler, James C. Fisk, James C. Watson, and Theodore A. Dodge.
34
Peirce, *Cooperative Housekeeping*, 108–109.
35
Ibid. This was perhaps his first public acknowledgment of her scientific training, as she wrote
a section of the report, *Report of the Superintendent
of the U.S. Coast Survey Showing Progress for Fiscal*

Year 1870 (Washington, D.C.: U.S. Government
Printing Office), 125ff. Cited in Arthur W.
Burks, ed., *Collected Papers of C. S. Peirce* (Cam-
bridge, Mass: Harvard University Press, 1958).
Scholars studying C. S. Peirce have been quick
to point out when his ideas are expressed in her
work, but are often vague about her contribu-
tions to his work, or their collaboration.
36
For mention of The Club see Edwin H. Cady,
*The Road to Realism: The Early Years of William
Dean Howells (1837–1885)* (Syracuse: Syracuse
University Press, 1956, 145–146; and Van Wyck
Brooks, *Howells: His Life and World* (London:
J. M. Dent and Sons, 1959), 59.
37
Peirce, *Cooperative Housekeeping*, 109.
38
Ibid., 107, 110.
39
Theodore A. Dodge, James C. Watson, and Mrs.
Nathan S. Shaler, *Report of the CCHS* (Selling-off
Report), Cambridge, 1872, Cambridge Public
Library. This report was located by Beth Ganis-
ter, who discussed it in an unpublished paper on
Melusina Fay Peirce in 1976.
40
Women and men in the Union Colony of
Greeley, Colorado, were introduced to her ideas
by Nathan Meeker, a journalist who had written
about them for the *New York Tribune* (semiweekly; August 31, 1869). Early British reviews
of her work include "Co-operative Housekeeping," *Chamber's Journal of Popular Literature, Science
and Art* (4th series), 273 (March 20, 1869),
177–179; and Mary C. Hume-Rothery, "Cooperative Housekeeping," *The Co-operator* 11
(April 29, 1871 and May 13, 1871), 262,
289–290.
41
Mrs. E. M. King, "Co-operative Housekeeping,"
Contemporary Review, 23 (December 1873), 66–91;
Mrs. E. M. King, "Co-operative Housekeeping,"
The Building News (April 24, 1874), 459–460.
42
Roswell Fisher, "The Practical Side of Cooperative Housekeeping," *The Nineteenth Century*, 7
(September 1877), 283–291.

43

Melusina Fay Peirce, "Co-operation," paper read at Fourth Woman's Congress, Philadelphia, October 4, 1876.

44

Peirce, *Cooperative Housekeeping*, 184.

45

Ibid., 187.

46

Ibid., 141–142. Melusina Fay Peirce's views on "Womanhood Suffrage" were expressed fully in a speech given in New York in 1869 and are repeated in the Record Book of the New England Women's Club, meeting of November 15, 1869. She wanted to bring "a pure and elevating feminine influence to bear directly upon society and the world." She suggested that all women over 21 not wait for "manhood" suffrage but immediately gather in towns and cities and exercise "Womanhood" suffrage, by electing women officers and committees to see about women's affairs. She called for women to form standing committees, and the first was to be a domestic committee on household reform, followed by committees on education, health, pauper and criminal protection, aesthetics, fine arts, innocent recreation and festivity, gardening and landscaping, newspapers and magazines. The primacy of domestic reform implies cooperative housekeeping as an economic base, followed by basic areas of concern such as health, education, and welfare, while the emphasis on "innocent recreation and festivity" recalls the Fourierist "Festal Series," or group responsible for celebrations and parades found in most Fourierist utopian communities.

47

S. E. B., East Orange, N.J., "Cooperative Housekeeping," *The Woman's Journal* (March 29, 1884), 102.

48

"Cooperative Housekeeping," *New York Times,* January 28, 1884, 3, col. 1.

49

"A Domestic Revolution," *New York Daily Tribune,* February 3, 1884, 8.

50

Melusina Fay Peirce, "What's Wrong with the World?" in *New York, A Symphonic Study* (New York: Neale Publishing Co., 1918), 13–16.

51

Helen Campbell, *Household Economics* (New York: G. P. Putnam's Sons, 1896), 248; Lucy Salmon, *Domestic Service* (1890; New York, Macmillan, 1897), 186–193; Mary Hinman Abel, "Recent Phases of Cooperation Among Women," *The House Beautiful,* 13 (April 1903), 364; Arthur W. Calhoun, *A Social History of the American Family* (1919; New York: Barnes and Noble, 1945), vol. 3, 179–198.

52

February 18, 1868, "Record Book of the Weekly Social Meetings of the New England Women's Club," 1868–1871, Schlesinger Library, Radcliffe College.

53

Ednah D. Cheney's presentation on public facilities for women's work was conducted February 8, 1869, when the work of Madame Pinoff of Breslau, Germany, was discussed; March 22, 1869, was devoted to cooperative kitchens; May 31, 1869, to cooperative laundries. Mary Peabody Mann's committee on cooperative kitchens reported on one association in Königsberg that gave prizes to faithful servants and another in Hamburg that trained skilled domestic workers, including Froebel nursery teachers. They recommended the cooperative kitchen, which, they believed, would generate a school for cooks but warned that it must not be allowed to "degenerate into a mere restaurant and secure neither economy nor healthful cooking." March 22, 1869, "Record Book of the Weekly Social Meetings of the New England Women's Club," 1868–1871.

54

Peirce, "Cooperative Housekeeping" (March 1869), 297. In that same year Mary Peabody Mann presented the society as if its main purpose were improving domestic service (in articles cited in note 30), a view probably acceptable to Harriet Beecher Stowe, editor of *Hearth and Home,* which published Mann's remarks.

Chapter 5

1
Marie Stevens Howland, *The Familistère* (original title, *Papa's Own Girl,* 1874; Philadelphia: Porcupine Press, 1975), 67. This line is spoken by Dr. Forest, one of the two feminist men in the novel.

2
The information on Marie Stevens Howland's life is drawn chiefly from her correspondence and other papers, in the possession of Ray Reynolds, and from Ray Reynolds, *Cat's Paw Utopia* (El Cajon, California: published by the author, 1972); Robert Fogarty, introduction to Howland, *The Familistère,* unpaged; Edward Howland, "Marie Howland," *Social Solutions,* 2 (May 28, 1886), 1–4; "Marie Howland Passes On," *Fairhope Courier,* September 23, 1921; Marie Howland, "Biographical Sketch of Edward Howland," *Credit Foncier of Sinaloa,* February 1, 1891.

3
Thomas Dublin, "Women, Work, and the Family: Female Operatives in the Lowell Mills, 1830–1860," *Feminist Studies,* 3 (Fall 1975), 31–33. On the architecture, see John Coolidge, *Mill and Mansion: A Study of Architecture and Society in Lowell, Massachusetts, 1820–1865* (New York: Columbia University Press, 1942).

4
Lucy Larcom, *A New England Girlhood,* quoted in Rosalyn Baxandall, Linda Gordon, and Susan Reverby, eds., *America's Working Women: A Documentary History, 1600 to the Present* (New York: Vintage Books, 1976), 44.

5
Massachusetts House of Representatives, hearings on industrial conditions, 1845, quoted in Baxandall, Gordon, and Reverby, eds., *America's Working Women,* 49.

6
Madeleine Stern, *The Pantarch: A Biography of Stephen Pearl Andrews* (Austin, Tex.: University of Texas Press, 1968), 88.

7
Ibid., 87.

8
Ibid., 88–89.

9
Hal D. Sears, *The Sex Radicals: Free Love in High Victorian America* (Lawrence, Kans.: Regents Press of Kansas, 1977), 26.

10
Ibid., 6.

11
Ibid., 4.

12
Ibid., 22.

13
Ibid., 174.

14
Marie Stevens Howland, letter to Edmund Clarence Stedman, Fairhope, Alabama, April 21, 1907, Stedman Papers, Columbia University Library.

15
F. L. Mott, *History of American Magazines* (Cambridge, Mass.: Harvard University Press, 1938), II, 207–208, also see L. L. Bernard and Jessie Bernard, *Origins of American Sociology: The Social Science Movement in the United States* (New York: Crowell, 1943), 60. The Bernards discuss the "Albert Kimsey Owen group" and early social science. An account of The Club is Taylor Stoehr, *Free Love in America: A Documentary History* (New York: AMS Press, 1979), 319–331.

16
Edward F. Underhill, "The Unitary Household, Letter from Mr. Underhill in Reply to the Article in the *Times,*" *New York Times,* September 26, 1860, 2.

17
"Practical Socialism in New York," *New York Times,* June 22, 1858, 5.

18
Ibid.

19
Stern, *The Pantarch,* 96. According to Underhill, the turnover was remarkably high, for more than three hundred persons lived in the Unitary Home at one time or another between 1858 and 1860.

20
"Free Love: Expose of the Affairs of the Late 'Unitary Household,'" *New York Times,* September 21, 1860, 5. Also see: "The Unitary Household and the Free Love System," *New York Times,* September 26, 1860, 4.

21
Margaret Steinfels, *Who's Minding the Children?
The History and Politics of Day Care in America*
(New York: Simon and Schuster, 1973), 36.
22
Edward Howland, "The Social Palace at Guise,"
Harper's New Monthly Magazine, 44 (April 1872),
701; Jean-Baptiste-André Godin, *Social Solutions,*
trans. Marie Howland (New York: John W.
Lovell Co., 1873).
23
Edward Howland, *Republic of Industry or First
Guise Association of America: A Concise Plan for the
Reconstruction of Society* (Vineland, N.J., 1876). Re-
print of *Harper's* article, with additional contributions by Thomas Austin and Sada Baily.
24
Marie Howland, *The Familistère,* 510.
25
Ibid., 515.
26
Ibid., 519.
27
Ibid., 512–513.
28
Edward Howland, "Marie Howland," 3–4.
29
Marie Howland, *The Familistère,* 358–359. The
speaker is Count Frauenstein.
30
Fogarty states that the Boston Public Library
and others banned Howland's novel. Arthur E.
Bestor, Jr. once mentioned to me that thirty-one
years earlier a Boston bookseller had cut the
pages on free love from a translation of Fourier
and sold the cut pages as a pornographic pamphlet.
31
Ida Husted Harper, *The Life and Work of Susan B.
Anthony,* I (Indianapolis: Bowen Merrill, 1899),
390.
32
Victoria Woodhull, "Sixteenth Amendment, Independence vs. Dependence: Which?," *Woodhull
and Claflin's Weekly,* 1 (June 25, 1870), 5; *Tried as
by Fire, or The True and the False, Socially* (New
York: Woodhull and Claflin, 1874), 43.

33
Stephen Pearl Andrews, "The Weekly Bulletin
of the Pantarchy," *Woodhull and Claflin's Weekly,*
3 (June 8, 1871), 10; 3 (October 28, 1871), 12.
34
Philip S. Foner, *History of the Labor Movement in
the United States,* Vol. 1, *From Colonial Times to the
Founding of the American Federation of Labor* (1947;
New York: International Publishers, 1975), 416.
35
Ibid., 415–416. For background on the International, see also G. D. H. Cole, *A History of Socialist Thought,* II (London: Macmillan, 1954),
201–202, and Mari Jo Buhle, forthcoming book
on socialist women. Buhle analyzes Section 12
from a feminist point of view.
36
Albert K. Owen, *Integral Co-operation: Its Practical
Application* (New York: John W. Lovell Co.,
1885), 112–113. Fogarty believes that Marie
Stevens Howland was the author of much of this
tract.
37
Paul Buhle, "The Knights of Labor in Rhode Island," *Radical History Review,* 17 (April 1977), 59,
cites *People,* December 5, 1885, and April 23,
1887.
38
Marie Howland to Albert Kimsey Owen, Hammonton, N.J., August 13, 1875.
39
Marie Howland to Albert Kimsey Owen, Hammonton, N.J., October 28, 1887, and April 17,
1880.
40
Owen, *Integral Co-operation,* 120–121.
41
C. Matlack Price, "A Pioneer in Apartment
House Architecture: Memoir on Philip G.
Hubert's Work," *Architectural Record,* 36 (July
1914), 74–76; Emilie McCreery, "The French
Architect of the Allegheny City Hall," *Western
Pennsylvania Historical Magazine,* 14 (Spring 1931),
237–241.
42
"Co-operative Apartment Houses," *American Architect and Building News,* 9 (February 19, 1881),
88–89 (reprinted from the *New York Times*).

43
Owen, *Integral Co-operation,* 120–121.
44
John W. Lovell, *A Co-operative City and the Credit Foncier of Sinaloa* (New York: Credit Foncier Co., 1886), 8.
45
Ibid., 7.
46
Reynolds, *Cat's Paw Utopia,* 58, 63.
47
Ibid., 81.
48
Mrs. Laurie B. Allen, letter to Ray Reynolds, Fairhope, Ala., August 20, 1964.
49
Marie Howland to Edmund Clarence Stedman, April 21, 1907.

Chapter 6

1
Mary A. Livermore, "Co-operative Housekeeping," *The Chautauquan,* 6 (April 1886), 398. An abbreviated version, "Cooperative Experiments," appeared in *The Nationalist,* 1 (1889), 198–203. Yet another version appeared in *The Boston Cooking School Magazine,* 2 (June-July 1897), 12–14.
2
Robert E. Riegel, "Mary Ashton Rice Livermore," in Edward and Janet James, eds., *Notable American Women, 1607–1950* (Cambridge, Mass.: Harvard University Press, 1971), vol. 2, 410–413; Mary Livermore, *The Story of My Life,* Hartford, Conn.: A. D. Worthington), 1897.
3
Alice Peloubet Norton, *Cooked Food Supply Experiments in America* (Northampton, Massachusetts: Institute for the Coordination of Women's Interests, 1927), 23. See also Livermore's own account of this experiment, "The Story of a Co-Operative Laundry," *Boston Cooking School Magazine,* 1 (June 1896), 5–7; and "Cooperative Housekeeping," *Woman's Journal,* 2 (November 20, 1880).
4
Quoted in Riegel, "Livermore," 412.
5
Ibid.
6
Judith Papachristou, *Women Together* (New York: Knopf), 1976, 66–67.
7
Ida Husted Harper, *The Life and Work of Susan B. Anthony* (Indianapolis: Bowen Merrill Company, 1899), vol. 1, 324–325.
8
"Homes for Working Women," *Woman's Column,* 9 (January 11, 1896), 3; "A Town Built by a Woman," *Woman's Column,* 12 (September 23, 1899), 4.
9
"Modern Housekeeping," *Woman's Journal,* 1 (July 9, 1870), 1.
10
"Men as Housekeepers," *Woman's Journal,* 5 (October 3, 1874); "Mr. Howard's Housekeeping," *Woman's Journal,* 18 (October 1, 1887); James

Buckham and Napoleon S. Hoagland, "New Co-operative Housekeeping," *Woman's Journal,* 32 (October 26, 1901); Helen Campbell, "Seven Co-operators," *Woman's Journal,* 32 (November 30, 1901); Mary A. Allen, M.D., "Shall the Boys Help Mother?" *Woman's Column,* 5 (March 5, 1892). See also an earlier example, Mrs. H. E. G. Arey, "Housework for Boys," *The Home: A Monthly for the Wife, the Mother, the Sister, and the Daughter,* 3 (May 1857), 229–230.

11
"Farmers and Housekeepers," *Woman's Column,* 1 (May 26, 1888), 2–3. In the same volume, "The Wife's Wages for Husbands," 1 (July 14, 1888).

12
Alice Stone Blackwell, *Lucy Stone: Pioneer of Woman's Rights* (Boston: Little, Brown, 1930), 239–240.

13
Lucy Stone, "Cooperative Kitchens," *The Woman's Journal,* 24 (April 22, 1893), 114.

14
Riegel, "Livermore," 412.

15
Karen Blair, "Origins of the General Federation of Women's Clubs: Domestic Feminism and the Woman's Literary Club in Late Nineteenth Century America," unpublished paper, Third Berkshire conference, June 1976, 14.

16
Livermore, "Co-operative Housekeeping," 398.

17
Julia A. Sprague, "New England Women's Club," *Woman's Journal,* 11 (June 26, 1880), 206. Sprague was a member of a communal house-hold that included Karl Heinzen, a German immigrant and radical journalist; and the well known feminists Dr. Marie Zakrzewska and Mary Louise Booth. Heinzen's *The Rights of Women and the Sexual Relations* (1852; Chicago: Charles H. Kerr Company, 1891), advocated the economic independence of women through state employment in domestic and welfare activities, 149–153.

18
Charles H. Codman, "Co-operation," *Woman's Journal,* 11 (October 9, 1880).

19
Livermore, "Co-operative Housekeeping," 397.

20
Ibid.

21
Ibid., 398.

22
Ibid.

23
Ibid.

24
Ellen Weiss, "The Wesleyan Grove Camp-ground," *Architecture Plus,* 1 (1973), 44–49; Caroline R. Siebens, *Camp Meeting* (Old Yarmouth, Mass.: published by the author, 1963).

25
Charlotte Perkins Gilman, "From Chautauqua," *The Woman's Column,* 16–17 (September 3, 1904), 2. She wanted to install a model laundry, a food laboratory, and a "baby garden," in keeping with the spirit of "association" there which she felt was appropriate to a "city of the future."

26
Livermore, "Co-operative Housekeeping," 399.

27
Ibid., 396, 399.

28
The Kitchen Garden, 1 (October 20, 1883), 1. See also Robert J. Fridlington, "Emily Huntington," *Notable American Women,* vol. 2, 239–240.

29
The Kitchen Garden, 1 (October 20, 1883), 3.

30
Peirce's Cambridge Cooperative Housekeeping Society had included Mrs. Alexander Agassiz, who was Pauline Agassiz Shaw's sister-in-law, and Mary Felton, her first cousin. Peirce's Woman's Education Association, founded in 1872, had involved her sister-in-law and her step-mother, Elizabeth Cary Agassiz. Peirce had attended the School for Young Ladies, run by Shaw's father and step mother, in the early 1860s. Geoffrey Blodgett, "Pauline Agassiz Shaw," *Notable American Women,* vol. 3, 279–280.

31
Phyllis Keller, "Mary Porter Tileston Hemenway," *Notable American Women,* vol. 2, 179–181.

32
Keturah E. Baldwin, *The AHEA Saga: A Brief History of the Origin and Development of the American Home Economics Association and a Glimpse at the Grass Roots from Which It Grew* (Washington, D.C.: American Home Economics Association, 1949).
33
The Kitchen Garden, 1 (October 20, 1883), 3.
34
Livermore, "Co-operative Housekeeping," 399.
35
Ibid.
36
Woman's Journal (October 13, 1888), cited in Mary Jo Buhle, unpublished manuscript on socialist women.
37
Riegel, "Livermore," 413.

Chapter 7

1
Arthur E. Morgan, *Edward Bellamy* (New York: Columbia University Press, 1944), 247–252.
2
Edward Bellamy, *Looking Backward 2000–1887* (1888; Cambridge, Massachusetts: Harvard University Press, 1967), 168–169.
3
Ibid., 193.
4
Sylvia E. Bowman, *The Year 2000: A Critical Biography of Edward Bellamy* (New York: Bookman, 1958), and *Edward Bellamy Abroad: An American Prophet's Influence* (New York: Twayne, 1962).
5
Marie Howland, *The Familistère* (1874; Philadelphia: Porcupine Press, 1975), 62.
6
Mary E. Bradley Lane, "Mizora: A Prophecy," serialized in *Cincinnati Commercial,* 1880–1881. Also see Howard P. Segal, "Technological Utopianism and American Culture, 1830–1940," Ph.D. thesis, Princeton University, 1975.
7
Anna Bowman Dodd, *The Republic of the Future, or Socialism A Reality* (New York: Cassell, 1887), 40. Carroll Pursell supplied this reference.
8
Ibid., 40.
9
Ibid., 31.
10
William Dean Howells, *A Traveler From Altruria, A Romance* (New York: Harper, 1894).
11
Eugen Richter, *Pictures of the Socialistic Future,* trans. Henry Wright (1893; London: Swan Sonneschein, 1907), 42.
12
Bradford Peck, *The World a Department Store: A Story of Life under A Co-operative System,* illustrated by Harry C. Wilkinson (Lewiston, Maine: published by the author, 1900). Similar works, without elaborate illustrations, include W. H. Bishop, *The Garden of Eden, U.S.A.* (Chicago: C. H. Kerr, 1895), which describes the establishment of Eden City in the South and includes long accounts of public kitchens, and Titus K.

Smith, *Altruria* (New York: Altruria Publishing, 1895). For a catalog of utopian fiction, see Kenneth M. Roemer, *The Obsolete Necessity: America in Utopian Writings, 1888–1900* (Kent, Ohio: Kent State University Press, 1976).

13
Wallace Evan Davies, "A Collectivist Experiment Down East: Bradford Peck and the Cooperative Association of America," *New England Quarterly,* 20 (December 1947), 473.

14
The details of this experiment in practical cooperation are discussed in Francine Cary, "Bradford Peck and the Utopian Endeavor," *American Quarterly,* 29 (Fall 1977), 370–384.

15
King C. Gillette, *The Human Drift,* introduction by Kenneth Roemer (1894; Delmar, New York, Scholars' Facsimiles and Reprints, 1976). Also see Russell Adams, *King Gillette: The Man and His Wonderful Shaving Device* (Boston: Little, Brown, 1978).

16
Hal D. Sears, *The Sex Radicals: Free Love in High Victorian America* (Lawrence, Kans.: Regents Press of Kansas, 1977), 231.

17
Ibid., 243.

18
Roger Grant, "Henry Olerich and Utopia: The Iowa Years," *Annals of Iowa,* 43 (Summer 1976), 354.

19
Henry Olerich, *A Cityless and Countryless World* (Holstein, Iowa: Gilmore and Olerich, 1893), 51, 54–56.

20
Ibid., 87.

21
Ibid., 117.

22
Ibid., 94.

23
Ibid., 95.

24
Henry Olerich, *Modern Paradise, An Outline or Story of How Some of the Cultured People Will Probably Live, Work, and Organize in the Near Future* (Omaha, Neb.: Olerich Publishing Company, 1915); and Henry Olerich, *The Story of the World a Thousand Years Hence: A Portrayal of Ideal Life* (Omaha, Neb.: Olerich Publishing Company, 1923).

25
Olerich, *Cityless and Countryless World,* 64. Olerich may have been influenced by Edwin C. Walker's *Practical Cooperation,* published in Valley Falls, Kansas, in 1884, which advocates a "cooperative township" to free rural residents from the boredom of the countryside. Walker was a free lover and for a time partner with Moses Harman in *The Lucifer.* Olerich may also have read Kropotkin on the importance of electricity for decentralization. Olerich was an eccentric as well as a visionary: he and his wife exhibited their adopted daughter, Viola, as a child prodigy, according to Grant, "Henry Olerich and Utopia," 359–361.

26
Edward Bellamy, "A Vital Domestic Problem: Household Service Reform," *Good Housekeeping,* 10 (December 21, 1889), 74–77; Edward Bellamy, "Women in the Year 2000," *Ladies' Home Journal,* 7 (February 1891), 3.

27
Bellamy, "Vital Domestic Problem," 76.

28
Fannie E. Fuller, "Practical Co-operation," *Good Housekeeping* 11 (July 19, 1890), 125–142; Mary Livermore, "Cooperative Experiments," *The Nationalist,* 1 (1889), 198–203; and unsigned articles, "Domestic Cooperation Experiments" (Evanston, Ill., and San Francisco), *The New Nation* (May 9, 1891), 235; "Cooperative Cooking" (Junction City, Kans., and Utica, N.Y.), *The Woman's Column,* 5 (April 30, 1892), 3.

29
"Home Correspondence," *Good Housekeeping,* 10 (March 29, 1890), 262.

30
Edward Atkinson, L.L.D., "The Art of Cooking," *Popular Science Monthly,* 36 (November 1889), 18–19. In *Equality,* the sequel to *Looking Backward,* Bellamy went on at greater length about scientific cooking and scientific cleaning, the latter consisting of hosing down dwellings constructed with hard surfaces and furnished with disposable paper furniture (discussed in Bowman, *The Year 2000,* 290–291).

Chapter 8

1

Mary Hinman Abel, "Cooperative Housekeeping," *House Beautiful,* 13 (April 1903), 363. From a nine-part series, "Recent Phases of Cooperation Among Women," *House Beautiful,* 13–14 (March 1903–November 1903.)

2

For a definition of "social feminist," see chapter 1, note 5.

3

Robert Hunter, *Tenement Conditions in Chicago: Report by the Investigating Committee of the City Homes Association* (1901; New York, Mss. Information Corp., 1972). See also Susan J. Kleinberg, "Technology and Women's Work: The Lives and Working Class Women in Pittsburgh, 1870–1900," *Labor History,* 17 (Winter 1976), 58–72, for an excellent discussion of what tenement conditions meant in terms of women's physical work.

4

Hunter, *Tenement Conditions,* p. 100.

5

Elizabeth Bisland, "Co-Operative Housekeeping in Tenements," *Cosmopolitan,* 8 (November 1889), 35, 42; unpublished research by Susan Levine on women in the Knights of Labor.

6

Ellen Swallow Richards, Mary Hinman Abel, et al., *Plain Words About Food: The Rumford Kitchen Leaflets* (1893; Boston, Home Science Publishing Company, 1899). I am grateful to Helen Slotkin of MIT for bringing this work to my attention.

7

For a brief account of Shaw's activities, see Allan F. Davis, *Spearheads for Reform: The Social Settlements and the Progressive Movement, 1890–1914* (New York: Oxford University Press, 1967).

8

Robert Clarke, *Ellen Swallow: The Woman Who Founded Ecology* (Chicago: Follett Publishing Company, 1973); her lower-middle-class origins are stressed by Carol Lopate, unpublished paper on Richards, read at the 1978 Berkshire Conference. Richards, while still an undergraduate at MIT, had run an experimental course in chemistry at the Girls' High School in Boston, financed by the Woman's Education Association beginning in February 1873. Melusina Peirce founded the WEA and chaired its committee on the Intellectual Education of Women, the previous year, so one can assume she knew Richards and perhaps even had a hand in her project, although Peirce left the WEA in 1873. Her hopes that women go through "a course of study in some degree equivalent to that of Harvard College" were so large a scheme the WEA was unwilling to back it, according to the *First Annual Report of the Woman's Education Association,* January 16, 1873 (Boston: W. L. Deland, 1873), 9.

9

Clarke, *Ellen Swallow,* 145.

10

"New Science," *Boston Daily Globe,* December 1, 1892, 1.

11

Ellen S. Richards, *Euthenics: The Science of Controllable Environment,* 2d ed. (Boston: Whitcomb and Barrows, 1912), 51–52.

12

Ellen S. Richards, "Scientific Cooking Studies in the New England Kitchen," *Forum,* 15 (May 1893), 356.

13

Edward Atkinson, "The Art of Cooking," *Popular Science Monthly,* 36 (November 1889), 18–19.

14

Jane Addams, *Twenty Years at Hull-House* (1910; New York: New American Library, 1960), 102.

15

Caroline Hunt, *The Life of Ellen S. Richards* (Boston: Whitcomb and Barrows, 1912), 220. Olneyville was where the Knights of Labor had previously established a day nursery for employed women's children.

16

Richards, *Plain Words About Food,* 12.

17

Hunt, *Life of Richards,* 224–225.

18

Ibid., 225

19

Anzia Yezierska's novel, *Bread Givers* (1925; New York: Persea Books, 1975) includes several poignant scenes about a woman worker who cannot get enough to eat at home or in cheap restaurants.

20

Captain M. P. Wolff, *Food for the Million: A Plan For Starting Public Kitchens* (London: Sampson, Low, Marston, Searle, and Rivington), 1884.

21

See Davis, *Spearheads for Reform* for a fuller account of social settlement work; for a fuller discussion of home economics, see Isabel Bevier and Susannah Usher, *The Home Economics Movement* (Boston: Whitcomb and Barrows, 1906); Keturah E. Baldwin, *The AHEA Saga: A Brief History of the Origin and Development of the American Home Economics Association and a Glimpse at the Grass Roots from Which It Grew* (Washington, D.C.: American Home Economics Association, 1949); Barbara Ehrenreich and Deirdre English, "The Manufacture of Housework," *Socialist Revolution,* 26 (October-December 1975), 5–40; Emma Seifrit Weigley, "It Might Have Been Euthenics: The Lake Placid Conferences and the Home Economics Movement," *American Quarterly,* 26 (March 1974), 79–96. Ehrenreich and English are very critical and quote Helen Campbell out of context to make her look ridiculous, but they are far better in their assessment of advertisers' manipulation of home economics consultants than Weigley, who offers no criticism of Lake Placid's founders.

22

Gerda Lerner, "Placing Women in History: Definitions and Challenges," *Feminist Studies,* 3 (Fall 1975), 6.

23

Fiske Kimball, "The Social Center, Part II, Philanthropic Enterprises," *Architectural Record,* 45 (June 1919), 526–543. See also Allen B. Pond, "The Settlement House III," *The Brickbuilder,* 2 (1902); Guy Szuberla, "Three Chicago Settlements: Their Architectural Form and Social Meaning," *Journal of the Illinois State Historical Society,* 14 (1977), 114–129. I am grateful to Helen L. Horowitz for a chance to read her unpublished draft, "Hull-House as a Woman's Space," which discusses architectural style in light of the settlement workers' needs.

24

Robert A. Woods and Albert J. Kennedy, eds., *Handbook of Settlements* (New York: Russell Sage Foundation, N.Y. Charities Publication Committee, 1911).

25

Addams, *Twenty Years,* 127.

26

Ibid., 101.

27

Ibid., 102; Richards, "Scientific Cooking," 358, reports gross sales in Boston of $20,000 per year.

28

Mary Kenney, unpublished autobiography, excerpted in Allen F. Davis and Mary Lynn McCree, eds., *Eighty Years at Hull-House* (Chicago: Quadrangle Books, 1965), 34.

29

Addams, *Twenty Years,* 105.

30

Kenney, quoted in Davis and McCree, *Eighty Years,* 35.

31

Addams, *Twenty Years,* 106.

32

Addams counts fifty members (ibid., 106). Kenney, quoted in Davis and McCree, eds., *Eighty Years,* says only that they occupied the entire building within one year (36). Milton B. Marks, "How the Jane Club Keeps House," *Good Housekeeping,* 32 (Fall 1900), 480–483, notes that, after letting the group become too large, members decided that thirty was the ideal number, and thirty lived in the new building designed by Pond and Pond (481).

33

Esther Packard, *A Study of Living Conditions of Self-Supporting Women in New York City* (New York: YWCA, 1915), quoted in Rosalyn Baxandall, Linda Gordon, and Susan Reverby, *America's Working Women: A Documentary History, 1600 to the Present* (New York: Vintage Books, 1976), 149.

34

Packard, *A Study of Living Conditions,* photograph opp. 79.

35

"A Gigantic Failure," *Faith and Works* 3 (June 1878), 146. Mari Jo Buhle provided this reference. At Stewart's Hotel, the carpets, china, silver, and mirrors were discussed by journalists when the hotel opened, as perhaps being too luxurious for the expected clientele, "ladies who write for the press, draw designs, superintend departments, carry on modest stores, are cashiers, milliners, etc." *The Daily Graphic,* New York, April 3, 1878, 231.

36
"Convention of Working Girls' Clubs," *The Woman's Journal,* 25 (June 9, 1894), 184.

37
Of course, one writer admitted, voluntary cooperation was not the source of the hundred or so women's boarding homes in existence in 1898, but he argued that if they succeeded, it was the cooperative support of the residents which sustained them, rather than the efforts of the philanthropic women who had started them. Robert Stein, "Girls' Cooperative Boarding Clubs," *Arena,* 19 (March 1898), 403. This article contains a catalog of 110 homes in 68 cities in the United States and Canada.

38
Mary Alice Matthews, "Cooperative Living," bachelor's thesis, School of Library Science, University of Illinois, Urbana, 1903, 30–31. See also Eliza Chester, *The Unmarried Woman* (New York: Dodd, Mead and Co., 1892), chapter on cooperation among working women. Naomi Goodman supplied this material by Chester.

39
J. P. Warbasse, "Cooperative Housing," *Cooperation,* 5 (January 1919), 4.

40
Matthews, "Cooperative Living," 24.

41
Stein, "Girls' Cooperative Boarding Clubs," 414–415; Matthews, "Cooperative Living," 22; "Hotel for Single Women," *The Woman's Column,* 6 (March 25, 1893), 1.

42
David M. Katzman, *Seven Days a Week: Women and Domestic Service in Industrializing America* (New York: Oxford University Press, 1978), 73, 112; Susan M. Strasser, "Mistress and Maid, Employer and Employee: Domestic Service Reform in the United States, 1897–1920," *Marxist Perspectives,* 1 (Winter 1978), 52–67.

43
George J. Stigler, *Domestic Servants in the United States, 1900–1940,* National Bureau of Economic Research, Occasional Paper 24, April 1946, New York. Martha Lampkin found this useful study for me.

44
Ibid., 2. In 1880 black washerwomen in Atlanta, Georgia, formed an association. Three thousand went on strike in 1881, but white landlords and police broke the strike. In 1886 the Knights of Labor included perhaps 50,000 women members, or 8 to 9 percent of the total membership. Twelve of the ninety-one women's assemblies were housekeepers; five, laundresses; and fifteen black women's assemblies included housekeepers, chambermaids, laundresses, and farmers together. The Knights lost power in the 1890s, and this integration of thousands of housekeepers and servants into a larger trade union was never again achieved. Smaller unions were attempted at the turn of the century. In April 1897 Mary Hartropp organized the American Servant Girls Association in Kansas City, Missouri, and claimed a national membership of 5,000. In 1900 Mother Jones attempted to form a union of domestic servants in Scranton, Pennsylvania. In July 1901 the Workingwomen of America included three hundred servants in Chicago. None of these organizations lasted. Slightly more successful was Jane Street, founder of Denver's Domestic Workers' Industrial Union, IWW Local No. 113, who organized about eighty domestic servants in 1916 in the face of opposition from male IWW members who refused to charter her union, and caused her more grief than all of the bourgeois women and domestic employment agencies of Denver combined. She inspired similar servants' unions in Tulsa, Duluth, Chicago, Cleveland, and Seattle, but these disappeared when the federal government used the Espionage Act during World War I to dismantle the IWW. See Philip S. Foner, *Women and the American Labor Movement, From Colonial Times to the Eve of World War I* (New York: Free Press, 1979), 188, 241–243, 283, 407–411; Jane Street, "Denver's Rebel Housemaids," *Solidarity* (April 1, 1916); and Daniel T. Hobby, ed., "We Have Got Results: A Document on the Organization

of Domestics in the Progressive Era," *Labor History* 17 (Winter 1976), 103–108. Susan Levine is at work on a study of women in the Knights of Labor.

45
Florence Kelley, later to become active at Hull-House on labor issues, took part in a lively debate on "Cooperation in Domestic Service," *Woman's Journal* (August 29, 1885), 274–275. Writing from Heidelberg, Germany, she noted that the Workingmen's Party of Germany was attempting a thorough analysis of the economics of domestic service, showing that the percentage of workers in service declined as the numbers of commercial substitutes for domestic products increased. She quoted a proposal, first made by Mrs. E. M. King in England in 1873, in a review of Peirce's book, that cooperative residences for servants be established and that servants work eight-hour shifts. She admired also the cooperative laundries established for workers in Sir Titus Salt's model corporate town, Saltaire.

46
The Woman's Column, 6 (September 16, 1893). For a summary of Addams's presentation, see May Wright Sewall, ed., *The World's Congress of Representative Women* (Chicago: Rand McNally, 1894), 625–627; Jane Addams, "The Servant Problem," *Good Housekeeping,* 37 (September 1903); also see Jane Addams, "Household Adjustment," *Democracy and Social Ethics* (New York: Macmillan, 1902), for her first proposal of residential clubs for servants.

47
Mary Hinman Abel, "Labor Problems in the Household," *Lake Placid Conference on Home Economics, Proceedings, 1903,* 29–37. See also *Lake Placid Conference on Home Economics, Proceedings, 1907,* 37, and Woman's Education Association, Committee on Domestic Economy, "Report of the Household Aid Company, 1903–1905," by Ellen S. Richards, Schlesinger Library, Radcliffe; and a broadside giving services and prices, *Household Aid Company,* Massachusetts Historical Society.

48
Lake Placid Proceedings, 1907, 29–43; Abel, "Adjustment of the Household," 380–384. The ultimate *noblesse oblige:* in 1910 the Countess of Aberdeen opened a similar home for servants at Letchworth Garden City in England so that servants could go out by the day to nearby middle-class households, but not have to live in. Pamela Horn, *The Rise and Fall of the Victorian Servant* (New York: St. Martin's Press, 1975), 156.

49
Matthews, "Cooperative Living," 22, 27.

50
Woods and Kennedy, *Handbook of Settlements,* 60.

51
Addams, *Twenty Years,* 309.

52
Ibid., 75.

53
Kimball, "The Social Center, Part II," 533; at the Gad's Hill Settlement in Chicago, also designed by Allen Pond, the architect of Hull-House, rooms for men and women were located on the same floor, at opposite ends of the corridor, and reached by separate stairways, an architectural solution reminiscent of the Shakers' celibate communities.

54
Addams, *Twenty Years,* 309.

55
Davis and McCree, eds., *Eighty Years,* 27.

56
Ibid., 57.

57
Kathryn Kish Sklar, unpublished paper on Florence Kelley, 1979.

58
Kimball, "The Social Center, Part II," 543.

59
Caroline L. Hunt, *Home Problems from a New Standpoint* (Boston: Whitcomb and Barrows, 1908), 145.

60
Caroline L. Hunt, "The Housekeeper and Those Who Make What She Buys," *Life and Labor,* 1 (March 1911), 77.

61
Willard, quoted in Aileen Kraditor, *The Ideas of the Woman Suffrage Movement, 1890–1920* (1965; Garden City, New York: Doubleday Anchor, 1971), 63.

62
Addams, quoted in Kraditor, *Ideas of the Woman Suffrage Movement,* 54.

63

Caroline Hunt, "Woman's Public Work for the Home: An Ethical Substitute for Cooperative Housekeeping," *Journal of Home Economics,* 1 (June 1909), 219–224.

64

Ella H. Neville, "The Essentials of Cooperation: Public Interest in Problems of Right Living," *Lake Placid Proceedings,* 1907, 130–134.

65

Mary Hinman Abel, "Cooperative Housekeeping," 365.

66

Mary Hinman Abel, "Labor Problems in the Household," 34.

67

Jane Addams, "The Servant Problem," *Good Housekeeping,* 37 (September 1903). Addams was quoting a study supervised by Richards and executed by Gertrude Bigelow, *Comparison of the Cost of Home-Made and Prepared Food,* from data collected by Boston Branch, Association of Collegiate Alumnae, School of Housekeeping (Boston: Wright and Potter, 1901), reprinted from *Massachusetts Labor Bulletin,* 19 (August 1901). See also Hunt, *Life of Richards,* 207.

68

See especially Bertha Bass, "Co-operative Housekeeping," *New England Kitchen Magazine,* 2 (January 1895), 159–163.

69

Lake Placid Proceedings, 1907, 133; *Lake Placid Proceedings,* 1903, 39–40.

70

Journal of Home Economics, 12 (May 1920), 235.

71

Hunt, *Home Problems,* 141–144.

72

For instance, Mary Hinman Abel, *Successful Family Life on the Moderate Income* (Philadelphia: J. B. Lippincott, 1921).

73

Abel, "Labor Problems in the Household," 29.

74

Ellen S. Richards, *The Cost of Shelter* (New York: John Wiley and Sons, 1905); the Hull-House project derived from Mabel Hyde Kittredge's Practical Housekeeping Centers in New York, beginning in 1901.

Chapter 9

1

Charlotte Perkins Gilman, *The Home: Its Work and Influence* (1903; Urbana: University of Illinois Press, 1972), 277.

2

"Gilman's argument represented the full elaboration of the feminist impulse": William Chafe, *The American Woman: Her Changing Social, Economic, and Political Role* (New York: Oxford University Press, 1975), 9; Peter Filene, in *Him/Her/Self: Sex Roles in Modern America* (New York: Harcourt Brace Jovanovich, 1974), calls it a "socialist" premise, and a "radical" proposal, but "not unprecedented," and cites Peirce's experiment, 63–65.

3

Charlotte Perkins Gilman, *The Living of Charlotte Perkins Gilman, An Autobiography* (1935; New York: Harper Colophon Books, 1975), 6. Also see Mary A. Hill, *Charlotte Perkins Gilman: The Making of a Radical Feminist, 1860–1896* (Philadelphia: Temple University Press, 1980), and Carol Ruth Berkin, "Private Woman, Public Woman: The Contradictions of Charlotte Perkins Gilman," in *Women of America, A History,* eds. Carol Ruth Berkin and Mary Beth Norton (Boston: Houghton Mifflin, 1979), 150–176.

4

Gilman, *Living,* 12.

5

Ibid., 113, 122.

6

Ibid., 129–130. His daughter was a protégée of Ellen Richards and painted her portrait; his secretary was an advocate of cooperative housekeeping for working women in 1893.

7

Ibid., 187.

8

Lester Frank Ward, *Dynamic Sociology* I (New York: Appleton, 1883), 656–657.

9

Gilman, *Living,* 263.

10

Ibid., 142. Unlike Hull-House, the "Little Hell" Settlement did not fit the model of efficient domesticity that Campbell, Gilman, and some of their colleagues in settlement work and domestic space longed for. There were five residents and a maid, and Gilman recalled that Campbell, as the head, "cooked special treats for us when the settlement maid was worse than usual." On one occasion Gilman brought the group some of Campbell's gingerbread with the proclamation, "Made by our Ma!–Not marred by our Maid!"

11
Helen Campbell, *Household Economics: A Course of Lectures in the School of Economics of the University of Wisconsin* (New York and London: G. P. Putnam's Sons, 1896), 244.

12
Ibid., 59.

13
Ibid., 243.

14
Ibid., 272–273.

15
Ibid., 269, gives Stuckert's address as Chicago, in 1896, although she had represented Colorado in 1893 at the fair.

16
Ibid., 270.

17
Ibid., 275–276.

18
Gilman, *Living,* 198.

19
Ibid., 131. Her publications were often used by women's groups within the Socialist Party, however, and she was a frequent speaker at Socialist Party events. See Bruce Dancis, "Socialism and Women," *Socialist Revolution,* 27 (January–March 1976), 91.

20
Gilman, *Living,* 26.

21
Charlotte Perkins Gilman, *Women and Economics: A Study of the Economic Relation Between Men and Women as a Factor in Social Evolution* (1898, New York: Harper Torchbooks, 1966), 75.

22
Ibid., 182.

23
Ibid., 246.

24
Ibid., 242, 243–244, 314.

25
J. Pickering Putnam, *Architecture Under Nationalism* (Boston: Nationalist Educational Association, 1890), 13.

26
J. Pickering Putnam, "The Apartment House," *American Architect and Building News,* 27 (January 4, 1890), 5.

27
Putnam, *Architecture Under Nationalism,* 13.

28
"Over the Draughting Board, Opinions Official and Unofficial," *Architectural Record,* 13 (January 1903), 89–91.

29
Ibid., 90.

30
Ibid., 91.

31
Gilman, *The Home,* 121; Charlotte Perkins Gilman, "The Passing of the Home in Great American Cities," *The Cosmopolitan,* 38 (December 1904), 137–147.

32
Gilman, *The Home,* 30–31, 339, and *Women and Economics,* 246–247. She laughed at middle-class men who in 1897 were attempting to do laundry cooperatively at Prestonia Mann's Summer Brook Farm: *Living,* 230.

33
Charlotte Perkins Gilman, "Why Cooperative Housekeeping Fails," *Harper's Bazar,* 41 (July 1907), 629. Another, earlier exponent of the "good business" view is Helen Ekin Starrett, "The Housekeeping of the Future," *Forum* 8 (September 1889), 108–115.

34
Charlotte Perkins Gilman, "What Diantha Did," part 11 of a serial novel in 14 parts, *The Forerunner,* 1 (September 1910), 9.

35
Gilman, "Diantha," part 14 (December 1910), 9–11.

36
Quoted in Ann J. Lane, "Introduction," to Charlotte Perkins Gilman, *Herland* (1915; New York: Pantheon Books, 1979), xii. Lane is at work on a biography of Gilman.

37
Gilman, *Living,* 182.

38

June Sochen, *The New Woman: Feminism in Greenwich Village, 1910–1920* (New York: Quadrangle, 1972), 3–25. Born in New York in 1878, Rodman attended Teachers College at Columbia University, and became an English teacher in New York public schools. She was a socialist and a believer in free love who enjoyed a lively circle of feminist and radical friends in Greenwich Village, including Crystal Eastman, Ida Rauh, Floyd Dell, and Max Eastman. She led five hundred school teachers in the Teachers Association in support of the striking seamstresses and shirtwaist makers in New York. In Paterson, New Jersey, Rodman also led a demonstration in support of free speech for Elizabeth Gurley Flynn, the militant I.W.W. organizer who called Rodman, "a truly remarkable woman" who was never afraid of Red-baiting. Elizabeth Gurley Flynn, *The Rebel Girl: An Autobiography, My First Life (1906–26),* (1955; New York: International Publishers, 1973), 117, 172.

39

Charlotte Perkins Gilman, "The Passing of Matrimony," *Harper's Bazar,* 40 (June 1906), 496.

40

Heidelberg and his partner Harry A. Jacobs designed an orphanage about this time, but I can find no other information on his practice. See Clara de L. Berg, "A New Home Ideal for the Orphan," *Craftsman,* 27 (January 1915), 441–444. The National Birth Control League directors are listed in *The Masses* (April 1917), 35.

41

"Feminists Design a New Type Home," *New York Times,* April 5, 1914. Mary M. Huth of the University of Rochester Library kindly provided this reference in the *New York Times,* and the following ones.

42

George MacAdam, "Feminist Apartment Hous to Solve Baby Problem," *New York Times,* Section 5, January 24, 1915, 9.

43

"Feminists Design . . . ," April 5, 1914.

44

"Feminists Debate Plans for a House," *New York Times,* April 22, 1914.

45

Ibid.

46

Laura Fay-Smith, "That Feminist Paradise Palace," *New York Times,* April 25, 1915, V, 21.

47

"A Difficult Problem Made Harder," editorial, *New York Times,* April 23, 1914, 12. Also see "Feminists' Model Home," *New York Times,* May 13, 1914, 22; "Feminists Plan a Home," *New York Times,* April 16, 1914, 3.

48

"Futurist Baby Raising," editorial, *New York Evening Post,* June 17, 1914. Of course this was why Engels objected to all philanthropic housing reform programs in *The Housing Question.*

49

May Wood Simons, "Co-operation and Housewives," *The Masses,* woman's number 1 (December 1911); K. W. Baker, " 'Raising' Babies," *The Masses,* 6 (February 1916).

50

Katzman, *Seven Days A Week,* 284, 292.

51

Filene, *Him/Her/Self,* 27. In 1915 only 39 percent of all female alumnae from eight major women's colleges and Cornell were married.

52

Quoted in Dancis, "Socialism and Women," 94. A forthcoming book on socialist women by Mari Jo Buhle should make their roles clearer. Meanwhile see Buhle's *Women and the Socialist Party, 1901–1914* (Somerville, Mass: New England Free Press, 1970).

53

May Walden Kerr, *Socialism and the Home* (Chicago: Charles H. Kerr and Company, 1901), is a rather conventional critique of capitalist homes. But she does advocate cooperative housing and housekeeping a few years later in "Socialist Cooperative," *Chicago Daily Socialist* (October 30, 1907), 34. Lida Parce Robinson, " 'Work' and Housework," *The Socialist Woman* 2 (August 1908) 5, argues for housework on business principles, following Gilman.

54

Gilman, *Women and Economics,* 313.

55

Ibid., 340.

Chapter 10

1
E. Blair Wall, "A Cooperative Kitchen That Works," *World's Work*, 20 (September 1910), 13405.

2
Ibid., 13406.

3
Ibid., 13407.

4
Ibid. See also Blanche McNerney, "A Cooperative Kitchen," *Journal of Home Economics*, 3 (December 1911), 464–466.

5
Iva Lowther Peters, *Agencies for the Sale of Cooked Foods without Profit* (Woman's Committee, U.S. Council of National Defense; Washington, D.C.: U.S. Government Printing Office, 1919), 46–47.

6
Myrtle Perrigo Fox and Ethel Lendrum, "Starting a Community Kitchen: Just How It Can Be Done with Little Outlay," *Ladies' Home Journal*, 36 (June 1919).

7
Lucy Stone, "Cooperative Kitchens," *The Woman's Journal*, 24 (April 22, 1893), 114.

8
Mary Alice Matthews, "Cooperative Living," bachelor's thesis, State Library School, University of Illinois, 1903; Alice Peloubet Norton, *Cooked Food Supply Experiments in America* (Institute for the Co-ordination of Women's Interests; Smith College, Northampton, Mass., 1927); Mary Hinman Abel's correspondence is mentioned in Peters's preface.

9
"Cooperative Cooking," editorial, *The Independent*, 54 (March 6, 1902), 590–591.

10
Harriet Taylor Upton, "Anyone Can Do It: The Simple and Sensible Plan of a Successful Cooperative Eating Club That Has Prospered for Twenty Years," *Woman's Home Companion*, 50 (October 1923), 34.

11
Upton, "Anyone Can Do It," 34.

12
Matthews, "Cooperative Living," 79–80.

13
Ibid., 82.

14
Ibid., 88.

15
Wall, "Cooperative Kitchen," 13406.

16
Upton, "Anyone Can Do It," 34. Emily Newell Blair, a Missouri suffragist and Upton's counterpart as Vice-Chairman of the Democratic Party, may well have been associated with the Cooperative Kitchen in Carthage, Missouri, described by "E. Blair Wall." Since McNerney credits this article to "Mrs. Blair" I suspect that Wall is a pseudonym. Carthage was Blair's home town. But again the suffrage histories offer no information.

17
Matthews, "Cooperative Living," 88.

18
Ibid., 89; *American Kitchen Magazine*, 17 (1902), 238–239; Sarah T. Rorer, "Cooperation in Housekeeping," *Ladies' Home Journal*, 12 (January 1895), 14.

19
Leland Stanford, "Co-operation for Women," *The Woman's Journal*, 18 (October 8, 1887). On other dining clubs, see Eliza Putnam Heaton, "A Cooperative Colony," *Woman's Journal* 19 (January 28, 1888); "Cooperative Cooking," *The Woman's Column* 5 (April 30, 1892); "Cooperative Housekeeping," *The Woman's Column*, 16 (August 8, 1903).

20
Lucy Stone, "A Cooperative Kitchen," *Woman's Journal*, 24 (March 18, 1893), 84.

21
"Domestic Cooperation Experiments" (from the New York *Sun*), *The New Nation* (April 25, 1891), 198. Also see Matthews, "Cooperative Living," 74–75; "The Servant Girl Problem," *New York Times* (December 23, 1890); Mrs. Arthur Stanley, "Cooperation in Housekeeping," *Good Housekeeping*, 12 (March 1891), 145–146.

22
"Domestic Cooperation Experiments," 198.

23
Ibid.

24
Ibid.
25
Mary Hinman Abel, "Co-operative Housekeeping," *House Beautiful,* 13 (April 1903), 364. One
of a series of nine articles, "Recent Phases of Cooperation among Women," *House Beautiful* 13–14
(March 1903 to November 1903). She reports
that the food arrived lukewarm in Evanston,
and that the steward was dishonest, although
the "promoters were unusually intelligent and
capable women." Also see Christine Terhune
Herrick, "Cooperative Housekeeping in America," *Munsey's Magazine* 31 (1904), 185–188.
26
Frances Wait Leiter, "The Central Kitchen,"
Woman's Home Companion, 32 (February 1905),
12–13.
27
"Cooperative Housekeeping At Last," *Good
Housekeeping,* 32 (1901), 490–492. On the same
experiment in New Haven, see "Cooperative
Housekeeping," *Woman's Journal,* 32 (August 10,
1901), 250–251; Matthews, 62ff. On other
cooked food services, see Henrietta I. Goodrich,
"A Possible Alleviation of Present Difficulties in
Domestic Service," *Bulletin of the Domestic Reform
League,* 1 (January 1907), 2–5; "Ready-to-Serve
Dinners for Hostesses," *New York Times,* January
19, 1919, III, 3; "Complete Cooked Meals
Brought to Your Door," *New York Times,* July
28, 1918, VI, 9; Alice E. Baker, "The Roland
Park Community Kitchen," *Journal of Home Eco-
nomics* 13 (January 1921), 35–38.
28
Annesley Kenealy, "Travelling Kitchens and
Co-Operative Housekeeping," *Lady's Realm,* 11
(February 1902), 513–520.
29
Leiter, "The Central Kitchen," 13.
30
Charlotte Perkins Gilman, "What Diantha
Did," part XI, *The Forerunner,* 1 (September
1910), 13–15. (Entire novel runs from November
1909 to December 1910, vol. 1, nos. 1–14.) See
also Gilman's "Hot Food Served At Home," *The
Forerunner* 6 (April 1915), 111, and Charlotte Tal-
ley, "A Cooperative Kitchen . . . ," *Journal of
Home Economics,* 7 (August 1915), 373–375.

31
Gilman, "Diantha," 15–16.
32
Fox and Lendrum, "Starting a Community
Kitchen."
33
Peters, *Agencies for the Sale of Cooked Foods,* 51–55;
"Community Kitchens," *Woman Citizen,* 4
(August 23, 1919), 284–285, 291.
34
Peters, *Agencies for the Sale of Cooked Foods,* 54.
35
Ibid., 22.
36
Ibid., 7.
37
Zona Gale, "Shall the Kitchen in Our Home
Go?," *Ladies' Home Journal,* 36 (March 1919),
35ff. See also "One Kitchen Fire for 200 Peo-
ple," *Ladies' Home Journal,* 35 (September 1918),
97.
38
Mary Hinman Abel, "For the Homemaker:
Public Kitchens," *Journal of Home Economics,* 12
(June 1920), 266–267.

Chapter 11

1

Lewis C. Mumford, "Community Cooking," *Forum*, 52 (July 1914), 98. He believed that "community cooking is not necessarily limited to any particular economic class (as the apartment hotel is); in fact, the community cooking idea should more especially attract the lower wing of the middle class, and finally, possibly the very lowest in the economic scale." In 1978 Mumford explained to me that this article was prompted by a crisis in his family during which he had to do all the cooking himself.

2

Ebenezer Howard cites Howland and Owen's work on cooperation in *Garden Cities of To-Morrow* (1902; Cambridge, Mass.: MIT Press, 1970), 115; on Howard's relationship to Bellamy, see Peter Marshall, "A British Sensation," in Sylvia G. Bowman, ed., *Edward Bellamy Abroad: An American Prophet's Influence* (New York: Twayne Publishers, 1962), 87. The best account of Howard's work is included in Robert Fishman, *Urban Utopias of the Twentieth Century* (New York: Basic Books, 1977).

3

Ebenezer Howard, "A New Way of Housekeeping," *The Daily Mail* (London), March 27, 1913, 4.

4

H. G. Wells, *A Modern Utopia* (London: Chapman and Hall, 1905), 217.

5

Ebenezer Howard, "A New Outlet for Woman's Energy," *Garden Cities and Town Planning Magazine*, 3 (June 1913), 152–159. See also *Homesgarth: A Scheme of Co-operative Housekeeping and a Solution of the Problem of Domestic Service* (Letchworth, England: Garden City Press, n.d.); Ebenezer Howard, "Letchworth Cooperative Houses," *The Garden City*, 2 (October 1907), 436–438; Barry Parker and Raymond Unwin, *The Art of Building a Home: A Collection of Lectures and Illustrations*, 2d. ed. (London: Longmans, Green & Company, 1901), 91–108; "Copartnership Homes for the Aged at Hampstead Garden Suburb," *Garden Cities and Town Planning*, 4 (November 1909), 248–249; M. H. Baillie Scott, "Cooperative Houses," in *Houses and Gardens* (London: George Newnes, Ltd., 1906), 116–118.

6

W. L. George, *Women and Tomorrow* (New York: D. Appleton, 1913), 89.

7

The fad for kitchenless houses can be gauged by some of the fan mail Howard received. George Bernard Shaw's sister, Lucy Carr Shaw, wrote excitedly to Howard, saying she had great problems with housekeeping and servants. She enthused about his plans: "One of your)64 houses presents itself to me as a paradise after the turmoil of private housekeeping. Are there any cooperative establishments likely to be built nearer London, as Letchworth is rather far away for an inveterate theatre-goer?" Allan Chappelow, ed., *Shaw the Villager and Human Being: A Biographical Symposium* (New York: Macmillan Company, 1962), 184–185.

Cooperative housekeeping was deleted from the history of the Garden Cities movement in subsequent editions of C. B. Purdom's books. In his history of the movement, published in 1913, Purdom waxes enthusiastic: ". . . the unscientific drudgery of housekeeping and of maintaining the out-of-date house is becoming more and more apparent and intolerable. . . . The ideals of Victorian society about home, the family, and women are as dead as all the other ideals of that time" (p. 98). He quotes another author approvingly: "It is not too much to say that there are hundreds of women who are being overworked into premature old age and bad health by needless, futile housework." An entire chapter is devoted to "Cooperative Housekeeping in Garden City," a description of the Homesgarth project, Howard's first, and the one where Howard lived with his wife. In the 1925 edition, Purdom had four successful projects to contend with but allotted them only two and a half pages. In the 1949 edition, he reduced this to three paragraphs, his only comment, "Interesting." C. B. Purdom, *The Garden City* (London: J. M. Dent, 1913); C. B. Purdom, *The Building of Satellite Towns* (London: J. M. Dent, 1925 and 1949).

8
Fishman, *Urban Utopias,* 197; Peter Serenyi, "Le Corbusier, Fourier, and the Monastery of Ema," *Art Bulletin,* 49 (December 1967), 277–286.
9
David Gebhard and Robert Winter, *A Guide to Architecture in Los Angeles and Southern California* (Santa Barbara: Peregrine Press, 1977), 344.
10
Una Nixson Hopkins, "A Picturesque Court of 30 Bungalows: A Community Idea for Women," *Ladies' Home Journal,* 30 (April 1913), 19.
11
Such arrangements were also proposed by Henrietta Rodman's friend Crystal Eastman; see *Crystal Eastman on Women and Revolution,* ed. Blanche W. Cook (New York: Oxford University Press, 1978).
12
Rob Wagner, "A Unique Melange of Red and Black," *Western Comrade,* 1 (October 1913), 235–236.
13
Charles Alma Byers, "The Bungalow Court Idea Shown in Practical Cooperation," *The Craftsman,* 27 (December 1914), 317–319. Even that tireless promoter of single-family homes, Gustav Stickley, editor of *The Craftsman,* came out in favor of community kitchens in "The Modern Home and the Domestic Problem," *The Craftsman* 11 (January 1907), 452–457:
The idea of home is as sacred and beautiful as ever, but the reality is too often exactly the opposite of what it was meant to be. Instead of a refuge from the cares of the world, it is made a burden that taxes to the last limit of endurance the energy and resources of the man who maintains it, and the woman who presides over it finds herself old before her time with the nerve-racking strain and worry of housekeeping and entertaining. . . . A thoroughly good cook, running a large well-organized kitchen with facilities for supplying twenty or a hundred families, and filling each individual order for cooked food . . . would give much better and more economical service. . . . The old order of things is nearly at an end, for each year it is becoming more impossible to keep our houses running on the old cumbersome basis.
14
Alice Constance Austin, "Building a Socialist City," and "The Socialist City" (series of seven articles), *Western Comrade,* 4–5 (October and November 1916; January, February, March, April, and June 1917), and *The Next Step: How to Plan for Beauty, Comfort, and Peace with Great Savings Effected by the Reduction of Waste* (Los Angeles: Institute Press, 1935). A detailed account of the Llano del Rio community is included in Dolores Hayden, *Seven American Utopias: The Architecture of Communitarian Socialism, 1790–1975* (Cambridge, Mass.: MIT Press, 1976).
15
Austin, *The Next Step,* 63.
16
Austin, "Building a Socialist City" (October 1916), 17.
17
Austin, "The Socialist City" (June 1917), 14.
18
Ibid.
19
Mary Alice Matthews, "Cooperative Living," bachelor's thesis, State Library School, University of Illinois, 1903.
20
On Lamb, see Hazel Hammond Albertson, "News of Industrial Cooperation," *The Arena,* 41 (March 1909), 379.
21
Edgar Chambless, *Roadtown* (New York: Roadtown Press, 1910), 20.
22
Charlotte Perkins Gilman, review of *Roadtown, The Forerunner,* 2 (February 1911), 57–58; "But Here Is a House You Have Not Seen," *Ladies' Home Journal* 36 (February 1919), 121.
23
Howard, *Garden Cities,* 51–54; Austin, "Building a Socialist City" (October 1916), 17.
24
David Gebhard, *Schindler* (New York: Viking, 1972), 47. It is curious to note a possible connection to Alice Constance Austin: a "J. Harriman" requested that Schindler prepare plans for a colony for him in 1925. If this was Job Harriman, former head of Llano del Rio, there may have been a link between Austin's introduction of kitchenless houses and Schindler's espousal of cooperative housekeeping.

25
R. M. Schindler, "A Cooperative Dwelling," *T-Square* (February 1932), 20–21.
26
Gebhard, *Schindler,* 47. On the personal relationships within the house, see Esther McCoy, *Vienna to Los Angeles: Two Journeys* (Santa Monica, California: Arts and Architecture Press, 1979). The Chases left within one year; architect Richard Neutra and his wife eventually replaced them.
27
Charles H. Whitaker, "Will the Kitchen Be Outside the Home?" *Ladies' Home Journal,* 36 (January 1919), 66.
28
Milo Hastings, "A Solution of the Housing Problem in the United States," *Supplement to the Journal of the American Instutute of Architects,* 7 (May 1919), 261.
29
Robert Anderson Pope, "A Solution of the Housing Problem in the United States," *Supplement to the Journal of the American Institute of Architects,* 7 (May 1919), 314.
30
Clarence Stein, *Toward New Towns for America* (1957; Cambridge, Mass.: MIT Press, 1971).
31
J. P. Warbasse, "A Finnish Homebuilding Association," *Cooperation,* 5 (March 1919), 33. This journal is extremely useful for tracing the progress of cooperative housing; the editor's interests ranged from the projects of King C. Gillette to Soviet workers' restaurants. The Finnish cooperative societies also sponsored many cooperative boardinghouses in the east and midwest, usually for men only.
32
Warbasse, "A Finnish Homebuilding Association," 34.
33
"Cooperative Housing DeLuxe," *Cooperation,* 12 (December 1926), 221–223; "Cooperative Home Builders in New York," *Cooperation,* 12 (February 1926), 22–24; Calvin Trillin, "U.S. Journal, The Bronx, The Coops," *New Yorker,* 53 (August 1, 1977), 49–54; Mark Crosley, "Two Worker-Sponsored Housing Cooperatives — Collective Space in New York City, 1924–1931," un-

published paper, 1978, which includes interviews conducted by the author and Richard Polton with Herman Jessor.
34
Anita Wallman Schwartz and Peter Rosenblum, "The Utopia We Knew," in *The Coops: The United Workers Cooperative Colony 50th Anniversary, 1927–1977* (New York: Semi-Centennial Coop Reunion, 1977), 20.
35
Ibid., 9.
36
Ibid., 10.
37
"Amalgamated Cooperative Apartments," *Cooperation,* 14 (February 1928), 22–25; "Amalgamated Dwellings," *Cooperation,* 17 (February 1931), 22; Edith Elmer Wood, *New Directions in American Housing* (New York: Macmillan, 1931), 180–183.
38
"Cooperative Housing Pulls Through," *Consumers' Cooperation* (September 1936), 140.
39
"More Cooperative Housing," *Cooperation,* 14 (February 1928), 34–35.
40
C. Long, "Consumers' Cooperative Services," *Cooperation,* 16 (March 1930), 42–44; Leslie Woodcock, "Mary Ellicott Arnold: Creative Urban Worker," *Great American Cooperators* (American Institute of Cooperation, 1967), 39–41.
41
Anatole Kopp, *Town and Revolution: Soviet Architecture and City Planning, 1917–1935* (New York: Braziller, 1970).
42
Fred Dunn, "When Is a Cooperative House Not a Cooperative?" *Co-operation,* 11 (June 1925), 117.
43
Hudson View Gardens Graphic, rental brochure, 1924, 12, 18. Edith Elmer Wood Papers, Avery Library, Columbia University.
44
Hudson View Gardens Graphic, 8–9.
45
Charlotte Perkins Gilman, "Why Cooperative Housekeeping Fails," *Harper's Bazar,* 41 (July 1907).

46

Phyllis Halpern, "Ruth Adams '04: Architect Rediscovered," *Vassar Quarterly,* 74 (Fall 1977), 17.

47

The Yelping Hill Association's Archives, vol. 13, September 8, 1922. These are housed in the community barn in West Cornwall, Connecticut, and include long accounts of the construction and organization of the community.

48

Yelping Hill Association Archives, vol. 1, "The Beginnings of Yelping Hill."

49

Interview with Pauline Schindler, 1977.

50

Purdom, *The Garden City,* 98.

Chapter 12

1

Ethel Puffer Howes, "Accepting the Universe," *Atlantic Monthly,* 129 (April 1922), 444–463, and "Continuity for Women," *Atlantic Monthly,* 130 (December 1922), 731–739.

2

Josiah Royce, Chair, "Report of the Committee on Honors and Higher Degrees of the Division of Philosophy in Harvard University," typescript, Smith College Archives. Biographical information is based on "Ethel Puffer Howes," obituary, *Smith College Quarterly* (February 1951), 93, and Benjamin Howes, letter to his daughters, Birmingham, Michigan, May 3, 1966, Smith College Archives. Professor George Palmer praises her work in a letter to Ethel Puffer Howes, Paris, June 25, 1905, Smith College Archives.

3

"Woman in Harvard Faculty," unidentified newspaper clipping, before 1908, Smith College Archives. Ellen Swallow Richards's name was removed from the MIT catalog for similar reasons in 1871, according to Robert Clarke, *Ellen Swallow: The Woman Who Founded Ecology* (Chicago: Follett Publishing Company, 1973), 46.

4

Ethel Puffer Howes, letter to her mother, c. 1910, quoted in Peter Filene, *Him/Her/Self: Sex Roles in Modern America* (New York: Harcourt Brace Jovanovich, 1974), 62.

5

Ethel Puffer Howes, "The Meaning of Progress in the Woman Movement," *The Annals of the American Academy of Political and Social Science,* 144 (May 1929), 2–3.

6

Howes, "Continuity for Women," 735.

7

Ibid., 733.

8

Ibid., 739.

9

Ibid., 731.

10

Ethel Puffer Howes, "The Revolt of Mother," *Woman's Home Companion,* 50 (April 1923), 30–31;

"Day Off For Mother," *Woman's Home Companion,* 50 (May 1923), 30–31; "Getting Together," *Woman's Home Companion,* 50 (June 1923), 32; "True and Substantial Happiness: A Talk about Cooperation for the Home, Past, Present, and Future," *Woman's Home Companion,* 50 (September 1923), 32ff. See also Ethel Puffer Howes and Myra Reed Richardson, *How to Start a Cooperative Kitchen, How to Start a Cooperative Laundry,* and *How to Start a Cooperative Nursery,* booklets published by *Woman's Home Companion,* 1923.

11
Howes, "True and Substantial Happiness," 32.

12
Ibid.

13
Howes, "Revolt," 30.

14
Howes, "True and Substantial Happiness," 32.

15
Ethel Puffer Howes, *The Progress of the Institute for the Co-Ordination of Women's Interests* (report at Alumnae conference, ICWI, Smith College, Northampton, Mass., October 12, 1928), 8.

16
Howes, *Progress,* 8.

17
Alice Peloubet Norton, *Cooked Food Supply Experiments in America* (Northampton, Massachusetts: ICWI, 1927). See also Ethel Puffer Howes and Doris M. Sanborn, *The Dinner Kitchen Cook Book,* including report for 1928–1929 of the Smith College Community Kitchen (Northampton, Mass.: ICWI, 1929), and Mary Tolford Wilson, "Alice Peloubet Norton," *Notable American Women,* ed. Janet and Edward James (Cambridge, Mass.: Harvard University Press, 1971), vol. 2, 637–638.

18
Howes, *Progress,* 11.

19
Roy Lubove, "Edith Elmer Wood," *Notable American Women,* vol. 3, 644–645.

20
Ethel Puffer Howes and Dorothea Beach, *The Cooperative Nursery School — What It Can Do for Parents* (Northampton, Mass.: ICWI, 1928).

21
Howes and Richardson, *How to Start a Cooperative Nursery,* 6. Also see Institute for the Coordination of Women's Interests, *The Nursery School as a Social Experiment* (Northampton, Mass.: ICWI, 1928).

22
Ethel Puffer Howes and Esther H. Stocks, "Co-Operating Mothers," *Woman Citizen* 12 (February 1927); Ethel Puffer Howes and Esther H. Stocks, "The Home: A Project," *Child Study,* 7 (December 1929).

23
Esther H. Stocks, *A "Home Assistant's" Experiment* (Northampton, Mass.: ICWI, 1928).

24
Henry A. Frost and William R. Sears, *Women in Architecture and Landscape Architecture* (Northampton, Mass.: ICWI, 1928); Alma Luise Olson, *Free-Lance Writing as an Occupation for Women* (Northampton, Mass.: ICWI, 1927). The Frost-Sears booklet took a somewhat patronizing tone concerning women's abilities, emphasizing the suitability of small, domestic building and landscaping projects to women's talents, but this may have been due to the authors' commission to stress part-time work.

Arthur Calhoun, noted social historian of the American family, was enlisted as the author of a study of cooperative services in the United States. (Calhoun's monumental, three-volume history of the American family had appeared between 1917 and 1919.) Ruth Haefner was commissioned to analyze the history of the Amana Community and its tradition of community kitchens and kitchenless apartments. Neither of these works ever appeared in print.

25
Ethel Puffer Howes, "The Woman's Orientation Course — What Shall Be Its Basic Concept?," *Journal of the American Association of University Women,* 20 (June 1927), 106–109.

26
Howes, "The Meaning of Progress," 7.

27
Mary Ryan, *Womanhood in America from Colonial Times to the Present* (New York: New Viewpoints, 1975), 260.

28
Stuart Ewen, *Captains of Consciousness: Advertising and the Social Roots of the Consumer Culture* (New York: McGraw-Hill, 1976), 161. His analyses of the "patriarch as wage slave," and the "new woman" as consumer are insightful.
29
Mary Ormsbee Whitton, "The New Housekeeping Based on Friendly Cooperation," *Woman's Home Companion,* 54 (June 1927), 62.
30
"Housewives, Incorporated," *Woman's Home Companion,* 55 (June 1928), 1.
31
Ethel Puffer Howes, letters to Edith Elmer Wood concerning publication of the book, May 4, 1927, May 28, 1927, June 1, 1927, June 2, 1927, in the Edith Elmer Wood papers, Avery Library, Columbia University School of Architecture, box 57. For background on Wood, see Eugenie Ladner Birch, "Edith Elmer Wood and the Genesis of Liberal Housing Thought, 1910–1942," Ph.D. dissertation, Urban Planning, Columbia University, 1976. (She does not mention the missing book manuscript.)
32
Household Management and Kitchens, Reports of the Committees on Household Management, Kitchens, and Other Work Centers, The President's Conference on Home Building and Home Ownership (Washington, D.C.: U.S. Government Printing Office, 1932), 52–60.
33
Ryan, *Womanhood in America,* 259.
34
Howes, "Continuity for Women," 738.
35
Howes, "Meaning of Progress," 2–3.
36
Filene, *Him/Her/Self,* 146.
37
Lawrence K. Frank, letter to President Thomas C. Mendenhall, Smith College, Belmont, Massachusetts, May 7, 1963, Smith College Archives. This is the only written explanation of why the institute ended. The author who was instrumental in arranging the Rockefeller grant to ICWI, states that faculty resistance was the problem.

38
Eli Chinoy, paper on ICWI, December 15, 1969, reported in minutes of "The Club," Smith College Archives.

Chapter 13

1
J. Stanley Lemons, *The Woman Citizen: Social Feminism in the 1920's* (Urbana, Ill.: University of Illinois Press, 1973), 209–227. Documents quoted here are reprinted in Judith Papachristou, *Women Together: A History in Documents of the Woman's Movement in the United States* (New York: Knopf, 1976), 196–200.

2
Papachristou, *Women Together,* 198–200.

3
Ibid., 201.

4
Ibid., 200.

5
On Kollontai, see Richard Stites, *The Woman's Liberation Movement in Russia* (Princeton, N.J.: Princeton University Press, 1977). On housing in the U.S.S.R., see N. A. Miliutin, *Sotsgorod: The Problem of Building Socialist Cities,* trans. Arthur Sprague (Cambridge, Mass.: MIT Press, 1974).

6
V. I. Lenin, "The Tasks of the Working Woman's Movement in the Soviet Republic," *The Emancipation of Women* (New York: International Publishers, 1975), 69. Although Engels and Lenin favored the socialization of domestic work, they wrote about industrial production as "real" work compared to nurturing.

7
Ibid., 69.

8
Ibid., 69–70.

9
Industrial Housing Associates, *Good Homes Make Contented Workers* (Philadelphia: Industrial Housing Associates, 1919).

10
Barbara Ehrenreich and Deirdre English, "The Manufacture of Housework," *Socialist Revolution,* 26 (October–December 1975), 16.

11
Christine Frederick, *Household Engineering: Scientific Management in the Home* (Chicago: American School of Home Economics, 1920).

12
Christine Frederick, *Selling Mrs. Consumer* (New York: The Business Bourse, 1929), 43–54. Her career is assessed in Stuart Ewen, *Captains of Consciousness: Advertising and the Social Roots of the Consumer Culture* (New York: McGraw-Hill, 1976), and Susan M. Strasser, "The Business of Housekeeping," *Insurgent Sociologist,* 8 (Fall 1978), 153–156.

13
Frederick, *Mrs. Consumer,* 245–255.

14
Ibid., 388–394.

15
Ibid., 3–5.

16
Housing Programs and Objectives, volume 11 of the final report of the President's Conference on Home Building and Home Ownership (Washington, D.C.: U.S. Government Printing Office, 1932), xv. Planning committee members are listed, pp. iii–iv.

17
"Woman's Oldest Job," *Woman Citizen,* 7 (February 10, 1923), 13, 26.

18
Hannah Mitchell, "The Eight Hour Day at Home," and "How Shall We Dignify Housework?" *Woman Citizen,* 7 (February 24, 1923), 12–13, 15.

19
Marjorie M. Brown, "Help Wanted — Why," *Woman Citizen,* 8 (July 14, 1923), 16–17.

20
Alice Cone Perry, "Domestic Labor — Privileged," *Woman Citizen,* 8 (June 2, 1923), 23.

21
Isabel Kimball Whiting, "Business Ideals at Home," *Woman Citizen,* 7 (March 10, 1923), 12ff.; Ruth Sawyer, "Teamwork on Woman's Oldest Job," *Woman Citizen,* 7 (March 24, 1923), 11–12; Lila V. H. Bien, "The Housework Problem Minus Help," *Woman Citizen,* 7 (May 5, 1923), 12–13.

22
"Reinforcements on the Housework Problem," *Woman Citizen,* 8 (December 1, 1923), 15.

23

Hilda D. Merriam, "A Community Answer," *Woman Citizen,* 7 (May 19, 1923), 16; Mary Alden Hopkins, "Fifty-Fifty Wives," *Woman Citizen,* 7 (April 7, 1923), 12–13. Hopkins took part in a cooperative dining club with Rheta Childe Dorr, Katherine Anthony, Madge Jenison, and Elizabeth Watkins, when they all lived in a City and Suburban Homes Company model tenement on East Thirty-First Street in New York, according to Dorr, *A Woman of Fifty* (New York: Funk and Wagnalls, 1924), 213–214.

24

M. S. Dawson, "Housekeeping — A Man's Job," *Woman Citizen,* 9 (March 21, 1925), 14–15.

25

Marie Clotilde Redfern, "Helpers Only," *Woman Citizen,* 8 (September 22, 1923), 28.

Chapter 14

1

Patricia Mainardi, "The Politics of Housework," in *Sisterhood Is Powerful: An Anthology of Writings from the Women's Liberation Movement,* ed. Robin Morgan (New York: Vintage, 1970), 447–454. Also see Jane O'Reilly, "The Housewife's Moment of Truth," *Ms.,* preview issue (Spring 1972), 54–59.

2

Susan Edminston, "How to Write Your Own Marriage Contract," *Ms.,* preview issue (Spring 1972), 66–72.

3

Married women's participation in the labor force, figures from Peter Filene, *Him/Her/Self: Sex Roles in Modern America* (New York: Harcourt Brace Jovanovich, 1975), 241.

4

Shirley Conran, *Superwoman* (London: Sidgwick and Jackson, 1975); Deborah Haber, "A Good Nan is Hard to Find," *New York Magazine* (March 20, 1978), 72–76.

5

Louise Kapp Howe, *Pink Collar Workers: Inside the World of Women's Work* (New York: Avon, 1977), Chart M.

6

Mary Witt and Patricia K. Naherny, *Women's Work — Up From 878; Report on the DOT Research Project,* Women's Education Resources, University of Wisconsin Extension, 1975, quoted in Howe, *Pink Collar Workers,* 236–239. These jobs are now being reclassified.

7

Lisa Leghorn and Betsy Warrior, *What's a Wife Worth?* (Somerville, Mass.: New England Free Press, 1974); the literature on wages for housework is extensive and groups in favor of the idea are active in England, Italy, Canada, and the U.S. See *Power of Women,* a journal from London, and *Wages for Housework Notebooks,* published in Canada and the U.S. For a perceptive review of past and current debates on this subject, see Ellen Malos, "Housework and the Politics of Women's Liberation," *Socialist Review* 37 (January–February 1978), 41–71.

8

U.S. Department of Labor, "Twenty Facts on Women Workers," August 1979; Dolores Hayden, "What Would a Non-Sexist City Be Like?" *Signs: A Journal of Women in Culture and Society,* supplement to volume 5, *Women in the American Cities* (Spring 1980).

9

Eli Zaretsky, *Capitalism, The Family, and Personal Life* (New York: Harper Colophon Books, 1976), 30.

10

Ella Reeve Bloor, *We Are Many: An Autobiography* (New York: International Publishers, 1940), 80–81, describes her advocacy of cooperative family organizations.

11

Ida Husted Harper, *The Life and Work of Susan B. Anthony,* 2 vols. (Indianapolis: Bowen Merrill, 1899), I, 142.

12

Lillie D. White, "Housekeeping," *The Lucifer,* 1893, quoted in Hal Sears, *The Sex Radicals: Free Love in High Victorian America* (Lawrence, Kans.: Regents Press of Kansas, 1977), 246.

13

"Cooperation in the Household," editorial, *New England Kitchen Magazine* 2 (January 1895), 205.

14

Robert Ellis Thompson, *The History of the Dwelling-House and Its Future* (Philadelphia: J. B. Lippincott Company, 1914), 129–135.

15

Melusina Fay Peirce, "Cooperative Housekeeping II," *Atlantic Monthly,* 22 (December 1868), 684.

16

Zaretsky, *Capitalism, The Family and Personal Life,* 25. Zaretsky's views are rather different from those of Christopher Lasch, who argues that the socialization of reproduction has already occurred, since advertising agencies, mass media, schools, health and welfare services have taken over many of the functions of the home. In *Haven in a Heartless World: The Family Besieged* (New York: Basic Books, 1977), and in *The Culture of Narcissism: American Life in an Age of Diminishing Expectations* (New York: Warner Books, 1979), 267–317, Lasch, who mistakes Ellen Rich-ards for a founder of the field of social work, berates social workers and psychiatrists more often than corporations. He ignores women's continuing responsibility for unpaid household work, a serious error which gives an antifeminist tone to his work.

17

Charlotte Perkins Gilman, "What Diantha Did," part 14, *The Forerunner,* 1 (December 1910), 9–11.

18

William V. Thomas, "Back to City Trend Displaces Minorities, Poor," *Los Angeles Times,* V, March 4, 1979, V, 21. New houses averaged $95,400.

19

Mary Livermore, "Cooperative Housekeeping," *The Chautauquan,* 6 (April 1886), 398.

20

Mary Hinman Abel, "Recent Phases of Cooperation Among Women," part 4, *House Beautiful,* 13 (June 1903), 57.

21

Caroline Hunt, *Home Problems from a New Standpoint* (Boston: Whitcomb and Barrows, 1908), 145.

22

Mary Hinman Abel, *Successful Family Life on the Moderate Income* (Philadelphia: J. B. Lippincott, 1921), 24.

Appendix: Cooked Food Delivery Services and Community Dining Clubs

Table A.1 lists details of the operations of twenty cooked food delivery services, and Table A.2 lists details for thirteen community dining clubs. These lists are not exhaustive, but are provided as a guide to further research. The lists exclude experiments in communal living and cooperative boarding clubs (both often described as cooperative housekeeping). They exclude communities which functioned only in the summer. I have also omitted all experiments which reached the planning stage but whose actual operation I was unable to verify, such as Springfield, Illinois (1890); Portage, Nealsville, and Madison, Wisconsin (before 1903); and Milwaukee, Wisconsin (1913–1914).

Table A.1
Cooked Food Delivery Services, Founded 1869–1921

Location	Name and Address of Service	Dates Active	Organizer or Leading Member	Size	Organization	Technology
1. Cambridge, Mass.	Cambridge Cooperative Housekeeping Society, Bow Street	1869–1871 (bakery store and laundry only)	Melusina Fay Peirce, Mary P. Mann	40 families	Consumers' coop	?
2. New York, N.Y.	?	Started Sept. 1884, still active in 1889	?	?	Commercial	Horses and wagons; double-walled, copper-lined boxes; steam tanks; refrigerators
3. Boston, Mass.	Boston Food Supply Company	1887–1888?	?	?	Commercial	?
4. Evanston, Ill.	Evanston Cooperative Housekeeping Association	Dec. 1890– Jan. 1891	?	40 or 45 families, over 200 people	Town-wide consumers' coop; board of managers and steward (Harry L. Grau)	Horses and wagons with "Norwegian kitchens"
5. Philadelphia, Pa.	Neighborhood of Powelton Avenue and 33rd Street	Active for 6 months in 1893	?	9 families, 52 people	Near neighbors' consumers' coop	?
6. Palo Alto, Calif.	?	Active for 2 years in mid 1890s	?	8 families, 40 people	Near neighbors' consumers' coop; women took turns planning menus and buying food	?
7. New Haven, Conn.	Twentieth Century Food Company, 78–80 Court Street	June 1900– Sept. 1901	Samuel H. Street (cereal manufacturer)	100 families	Commercial, large menu, much choice	Horses and wagons, heat retainers

Number and Wages of Employees	Cost per Person (3 meals/day unless otherwise noted)	Additional Services	Why Discontinued	Citations[a]
Laundress	(Never actually delivered meals)	Began with bakery, laundry, store	Lack of custom from members	Peirce, 1884 (chapter 4); Abel, 1903
?	$12.00/week ($18.00/week for family of two)	?	?	Livermore, 1886 (chapter 6); Livermore, 1889 (chapter 6)
?	?	?	?	Livermore, 1889 (chapter 6)
?	$4.00/week	Laundry	Incompetent steward; food retailers' boycott; servants' strike; food not hot (?)	*New York Times,* 1890; Stanley, 1891; *New Nation,* 1891; Abel, 1903; Matthews, 1903; Herrick, 1904
Home economist ($30/month, room, board); cook ($40/month); assistant cook ($20/month); delivery boy; scullery maid	$3.00/week	No	Poor management	Stone, March 1893; April 1893; Rorer, 1895
Cook (Chinese); delivery boy (student); maid; nurses	$.15/meal (children half price)	House cleaning, child care	?	Matthews, 1903; Rorer, 1895
All men (in photo, 1901)	Single dinner, $.50–$1.00	No	Capital too small, poor management	*Woman's Journal,* 1901; *Good Housekeeping,* 1901; Matthews, 1903

[a] Full citations are in the notes to Chapter 10 unless another chapter is noted.

Table A.1 (continued)

Location	Name and Address of Service	Dates Active	Organizer or Leading Member	Size	Organization	Technology
8. Mansfield, Ohio	Hawthorne Hill, outskirts of Mansfield	Started Dec. 1901, still active Feb. 1905	Bertha L. Grimes	5 to 40 families in 6 mile radius; 175 meals maximum	Commercial	Horses and wagons, heat retainers
9. Pittsburgh, Pa.	20th Century Food Supply Company	1902–1906	Bertha L. Grimes, Emma P. Ewing, Maude P. Kirk, Jennie B. Prentiss	?	Commercial	Heat retainers
10. Boston, Mass.	Laboratory Kitchen and Food Supply Co., 50 Temple Place	April 1903–?	Bertha Stevenson, Frances Elliot, Domestic Reform League of Women's Educational and Industrial Union	City and suburban delivery	Commercial, nonprofit, educational	Heat retainers
11. Montclair, N.J.	Montclair Cooperative Kitchen, 1 Mountain View Place	April 1915– 1919	Emerson D. Harris, Matilda Schleier	5 to 20 families	Consumers' coop, 2 mile radius	Automobiles, heat retainers
12. Haverford and Wynnewood, Pa.	Main Line Community Kitchen	1917(?)– 1920(?)	Adelaide Cahill	150 families	Consumers' coop	Automobiles
13. Burlington, Vt.	?	1917(?)– 1920(?)	?	?	Vegetarian	?
14. New York City and Princeton, N.J.	American Cooked Food Service	Feb. 1918– Feb. 1920	Jessie H. Bancroft	250 members, 75–100 dinners/day	Consumers' coop, 20 mile radius	Automobiles
15. Evanston, Ill.	Evanston Community Kitchen	1918–1951	Mrs. James A. Odell, Nellie F. Kingsley (Mrs. H. H.), Mrs. Rufus Dawes, Community Kitchen Committee of Evanston Woman's Club	20–25 families, citywide	Consumers' coop, then commercial	Automobiles

Number and Wages of Employees	Cost per Person (3 meals/day unless otherwise noted)	Additional Services	Why Discontinued	Citations[a]
?	$2.75/person, 2 meals/day for family of 4	Catering	?	Matthews, 1903; Leiter, 1905
?	?	?	?	Matthews, 1903; city directories, Pittsburgh, 1902–1906; company brochure, Western Pennsylvania Historical Society
?	Dinners only, $4/week	Bakery, lunchroom	?	*Bulletin* of Domestic Reform League, 1903; Lake Placid Conference on Home Economics, *Proceedings,* 1903 (chapter 8)
Black delivery men (in photo, 1918)	Single dinner, $.50	Coop store, boarding club	World War I	*Ladies' Home Journal,* 1918; Gilman, 1915; Talley, 1915
?	Lunch and dinner only	No	Private cooks available again after World War I	Norton, 1927
?	?	?	Wartime only	Norton, 1927
15 staff in NYC	Lunch, $.35; dinner, $.50–$1.00	Cleaning, marketing	Business declined after war	*New York Times,* 1918, 1919; Norton, 1927
?	Single dinner $.85 (1927)	Cooked food shop	?	Norton, 1927; *Journal of Home Economics,* 1921

[a] Full citations are in the notes to Chapter 10 unless another chapter is noted.

Table A.1 (continued)

Location	Name and Address of Service	Dates Active	Organizer or Leading Member	Size	Organization	Technology
16. ?	?	1918(?)	Myrtle Perrigo Fox, Ethel Lendrum	22 people	Commercial	Old cereal boxes; local children to make deliveries on foot
17. Brookline, Mass.	Brookline Community Service	Started 1918, still active 1927	?	50–100 meals/ day	Commercial, 20 mile radius	Automobiles
18. East Orange, N.J.	East Orange Community Kitchen	Started 1918, still active 1927	(Kitchen in proprietor's house)	30 families	Commercial	Automobiles
19. Roland Park, Md.	Roland Park Community Kitchen Upland Apartments	Started Jan. 1920, still active Jan. 1921	Alice E. Baker	?	Consumers' coop	Automobile
20. Flushing, N.Y.	Flushing Community Kitchen	Started 1921, still active 1927	?	50–100 meals/day	Commercial	Automobile

Number and Wages of Employees	Cost per Person (3 meals/day unless otherwise noted)	Additional Services	Why Discontinued	Citations[a]
None	Single dinner $.25	No	?	*Ladies' Home Journal,* 1919
?	Single lunch $.75–$1.00; single dinner $1.00–$1.25	Catering, school lunches	?	Norton, 1927
?	Single dinner $.75, delivery $.25	No	?	Norton, 1927
?	?	?	?	*Journal of Home Economics,* 1921
Proprietor (cook), 2 helpers, chauffeur	Single dinner $1.00, delivery $.20	Restaurant planned, 1927	?	Norton, 1927

[a] Full citations are in the notes to Chapter 10 unless another chapter is noted.

Table A.2
Cooperative Dining Clubs, Founded 1885–1907

Location	Name and Address	Dates Active	Organizer or Leading Member	Size	Organization	Male Involvement
1. Evansville, Wis.	Purchased house	1885–1888	Mrs. Robert M. Richmond	20 families	Consumers' coop; superintendent, steward, treasurer	?
2. Ann Arbor, Mich.	?	1886–1889	?	?	Consumers' coop	?
3. "Acadia," N.J.	Built dining hall	Summer 1887–?	?	12–15 families	Consumers' coop; chiefly not but not exclusively summer residents; paid steward, manager who were also members	?
4. Jacksonville, Ill.	Westminster Club, 235 Westminster Street; rented house	1889–1891	Mrs. Sarah M. Fairbank	5 families	Consumers' coop; residents within one block of club	?
5. Utica, N.Y.	71 Plant Street	1890–1893	Emma Mason Thomas (Mrs. Robert T.)	22–60 people	Consumers' coop	As managers
6. Decatur, Ill.	The Roby (former boardinghouse)	1890–?	Fannie Fuller, Elizabeth Guyton	54 people	Consumers' coop; superintendent, president, secretary, treasurer	?
7. Kansas City, Mo.	?	1891–?	Mrs. W. J. Kupper	50 people	Consumers' coop, board of directors, officers	?
8. Junction City, Kansas	Bellamy Club	Jan. 4, 1891– still active in 1895	Mrs. Milton Edward Clark	44 people	Consumers' coop, officers and executive committee	Likely

Employees and Salaries	Cost per Person (3 meals/day)	Additional Services	Reason Stated for Ending Experiment	Citations[a]
Housekeeper, servants	$2.50/week (5% dividend paid on stock)		Hard to find good housekeeper	Livermore, 1886 (chapter 6); Matthews, 1903
?	?	?	?	Livermore, 1886 (chapter 6)
2 laundresses and others	$4.00/week	Laundry		Heaton, 1888
Matron and 3 daughters, $3.00/week/apiece	Under $3.00/week	No	One family withdrew; housekeeper resigned; outsiders attempted to patronize	Matthews, 1903
Boardinghouse manager, cook, 5 waitresses	$3.00–$3.50/week	No	"Did not pay"	Stanley, 1891; *New Nation*, 1891; *Woman's Column*, 1892; Matthews, 1903
Housekeeper, 2 cooks, 3 waitresses	$2.75–$3.50/week	Members could board	?	Fuller, 1890 (chapter 7); Matthews, 1903
?	$2.50/week	?	?	Stanley, 1891; Matthews, 1903
Cook ($20.00/month); 3 waitresses ($20.00/month); 2 assistants ($20.00/month)	$2.50/week with loan of table; $3.00/week without; $1.25/week children	No	Changes in neighborhood	Matthews, 1903; *Woman's Column*, 1892

[a] Full citations are in the notes to chapter 10 unless another chapter is noted.

Table A.2 (continued)

Location	Name and Address	Dates Active	Organizer or Leading Member	Size	Organization	Male Involvement
9. Longwood, Ill.	Longwood Home Association, 2021 Kenwood Avenue, Longwood	Oct. 1900–Oct. 1902	Mrs. Helen C. Adams	12 families, 50 people	Consumers' coop; 3 block radius, female members rotate housekeeping in 2-week turns	Male buyer of food, men cultivated coop vegetable garden
10. Sioux City, Iowa	?	Jan. 1902–July 1902	?	5 families, 20 people	Consumers' coop; women did catering, men buying	Yes, as buyers
11. Ontario, Ca.	Cooperative Family Club; rented house	1903–?	?	12 families, 43 people	Consumers' coop; women rotated catering	?
12. Warren, Ohio	Mahoning Club; house owned by members	Started 1903, still active 1923	?	22 people	Consumers' coop, neighbors; men and women shared catering, a week at a time	Yes
13. Carthage, Mo.	Cooperative Kitchen; rented house	1907–1911	E. Blair Wall	60 people	Consumers' coop	Yes

Employees and Salaries	Cost per Person (3 meals/day)	Additional Services	Reason Stated for Ending Experiment	Citations[a]
Chef ($45.00/month); 3 waitresses ($3.00 week)	$3.00/week; $1.50/week children	No	Not enough congenial families	Matthews, 1903; Herrick, 1904
Cook ($20.00/month and board); Dishwasher/waiter (board)	$2.50/week	No	?	Matthews, 1903
4 employees (total wages $150.00/month)	$.11/meal	No	?	*Woman's Column*, 1903
Cook, dishwasher, 2 waitresses	$3.25/week (1903); $7.00/week (1923)	No	Did continue after death of leader, date and reason for discontinuation unknown	Upton, 1923
Manager ($35.00/month plus room and board); 2 cooks ($7.50/week); 2 waitresses ($5.00/week); 1 dishwasher	$3.50/week/adult; $1.75/week/child	2 boarders, reading room, dances	High cost of food	Wall, 1910; McNerney, 1911; Peters, 1919

[a] Full citations are in the notes to chapter 10 unless another chapter is noted.

Index